Learning Resources for THE ANALYSIS OF MUSICAL FORM

Exclusively from Prentice Hall

To enhance the learning experience, Prentice Hall and James Mathes have prepared the following additional resources to accompany this book.

finale PrintMusic® *Software and Notated Examples Disc Package*

MakeMusic!® Finale PrintMusic® notation software and an accompanying Finale® Example Disc that includes many of the examples in this book is available. The files are open for you to work with so that you can

- Listen to the examples through MIDI playback;
- Work on homework and other assignments;
- Print out the exercises.

When purchased with the book, this package is available at a special price, offering considerable savings over the MakeMusic!® Finale PrintMusic® software alone.

Audio CD

Also available is an audio CD that features professional recordings of select music examples and aural exercises in Chapters 1–5. A CD icon adjacent to the corresponding examples and exercises identifies excerpts included on the CD. The audio CD may also be packaged with the book for additional savings.

Online Listening at 

Students or professors who would like to listen to the full recordings of many of the examples in this book may purchase, through Prentice Hall, a special six-month subscription to *classical.com* at a significant discount from the usual price. A playlist of the examples in this book is available on the *classical.com* Web site. The subscription also allows unlimited listening to over 75,000 classical recordings, plus up to thirty free downloads to any audio player. More information may be found at *www.prenhall.com/music*.

The Analysis of Musical Form

JAMES MATHES

Florida State University

Upper Saddle River, New Jersey 07458

Library of Congress Cataloging-in-Publication Data

Mathes, James

The analysis of musical form / James Mathes.
p. cm.
Includes bibliographical references (p.) and index.
ISBN-13: 978-0-13-061863-4 (alk. paper)
1. Musical analysis—Textbooks. 2. Musical form. I. Title.

MT6.M349A63 2007
781.8—dc22

2006025912

This book is dedicated to my parents

Jeanne and Robert Mathes

President, Humanities/Social Sciences: Yolanda de Rooy
Editor-in-Chief: Sarah Touborg
Executive Editor: Richard Carlin
Director of Marketing: Brandy Dawson
Assistant Marketing Manager: Andrea Messineo
Director of Production and Manufacturing: Barbara Kittle
Senior Managing Editor: Lisa Iarkowski
Production Liaison: Joe Scordato
Editorial Assistant: Marlene Gassler
Manufacturing Manager: Nick Sklitsis
Manufacturing Buyer: Ben Smith
Art Director: Jayne Conte
Cover Image: William Blake, "The Ancient of Days" 1794. Metal relief etching. Hand-colored. 9 1/8" x 6 5/8" (23.3 x 16.9 cm). Peter Willi/Library of Congress, Washington, DC./ Superstock, Inc.
Manager, Cover Visual Research & Permissions: Karen Sanatar
Composition/Full-Service Management: Stratford Publishing Services/Edith Bicknell
Printer/Binder: Bind-Rite Graphics
Cover Printer: Phoenix Color

Credits and acknowledgments borrowed from other sources and reproduced, with permission, in this textbook appear on the appropriate page within text.

Pearson Education LTD.
Pearson Education Singapore, Pte. Ltd
Pearson Education, Canada, Ltd
Pearson Education-Japan
Pearson Education Australia PTY, Limited
Pearson Education North Asia Ltd
Pearson Educacion de Mexico, S.A. de C.V.
Pearson Education Malaysia, Pte. Ltd

10 9 8 7 6 5 4 3 2 1
ISBN-10 0-13-061863-2
ISBN-13 978-0-13-061863-4

TABLE OF CONTENTS

AUDIO CD TRACK LIST

1. Chopin, Prelude No. 1 in C major, Op. 28
2. Handel, *Messiah,* "The Lord Gave the Word"
3. Weill, "My Ship" from *Lady in the Dark*
4. Tchaikovsky, Symphony No. 4 in F minor, III
5. Bach, *Well-Tempered Clavier,* Book I, Prelude in E major
6. Beethoven, Piano Sonata in A major, Op. 2, No. 2, III
7. Bach, Brandenburg Concerto No. 2 in F major, I
8. Haydn, Symphony No. 104 in D major, III
9. Schubert, Symphony No. 8 in B minor, I
10. Liszt, *Vallée d'Obermann*
11. Vivaldi, *Four Seasons,* "Spring," I
12. Haydn, Symphony No. 93 in D major, IV
13. Mozart, Symphony No. 40 in G minor, IV
14. Brahms, Piano Quintet in F Minor, Op. 34, III
15. Tchaikovsky, *Nutcracker Suite,* Overture
16. Bach, Brandenburg Concerto No. 3 in G major, I
17. Mozart, *Così fan tutte,* No. 9, "Di scrivermi ogni giorno"
18. Verdi, *La Traviata,* Prelude
19. Chopin, Fantasie in F minor, Op. 49
20. Handel, *Messiah,* "Sinfony"
21. Schumann, *Fantasiestücke,* Op.12, No. 2, "Aufschwung"
22. Handel, *Messiah,* "For Unto Us a Child Is Born"
23. Handel, *Water Music,* III
24. Mozart, Symphony No. 40 in G minor, I
25. Mozart, Piano Concerto No. 17 in G major, K. 453, III
26. Beethoven, Symphony No. 5 in C minor, III
27. Schubert, Symphony No. 8 in B minor, I
28. Chopin, Prelude No. 3 in G major, Op. 28
29. Mahler, Symphony No. 4 in G major, I
30. Faure, *Requiem,* "In Paradisium"
31. Wagner, *Die Meistersinger,* Overture
32. Bach, Concerto for Two Violins in D minor, I
33. Verdi, *La Traviata,* Prelude
34. Beethoven, Piano Sonata in C major, Op. 53, I
35. Tchaikovsky, *Nutcracker Suite,* Overture
36. Handel, *Messiah,* "Rejoice, Rejoice"
37. Beethoven, Symphony No. 3 in E♭ major, IV
38. Beethoven, Symphony No. 3 in E♭ major, I
39. Chopin, Ballade No. 2 in G minor, Op. 23
40. Schubert, Symphony No. 8 in B minor, I
41. Bach, Orchestra Suite No. 2 in B minor, "Badinerie"
42. Beethoven, String Quartet Op. 131 in C♯ minor, IV
43. Beethoven, Symphony No. 3 in E♭ major, I

PREFACE

This text presents a study of the analysis of musical form that emphasizes consideration of music as design and process. A basic premise of the text is that musical forms are influenced by both style and genre. By considering musical form in light of these elements and by emphasizing the aural awareness of formal processes, it is hoped that a musical and flexible approach to analyzing form will be presented.

The text focuses on the study of Western classical music of the eighteenth and nineteenth centuries—the Baroque through late Romantic periods—but includes examples from popular and twentieth-century art music. A discussion of innovative approaches to formal processes in twentieth-century music is also presented in a separate chapter. While no new theories of musical forms are developed, ideas drawn from recent scholarship in musicology and theory are incorporated in the text. Many studies of musical form and style have contributed to ideas presented in this text; those by Donald Tovey, Wallace Berry, Douglas Green, Edward Cone, Leonard Meyer, Charles Rosen, Leonard Ratner, William Rothstein, Janet Schmalfeldt, Peter Spencer, Peter Temko, and William Caplin have been particularly influential. Any adaptations and modifications of their various ideas are solely those of the author.

The standard categories of musical form engage much of the central portion of the book, but the discussions attempt to enrich the scope of the subject in several ways. First, traditional aspects are examined with regard to their use in various historical styles and genres. This approach confronts the sometimes-arbitrary separation of form, style and genre encountered in some studies, emphasizing instead the interrelationship of these aspects and their influence on musical designs. The text is not intended as a historical survey nor as a systematic or thorough examination of the substantial number of genres and specific styles one may encounter in Western music. The historical emphasis is intended to lead to a consideration of how composers drew upon, modified, or disregarded the forms of earlier music, influenced by prevailing or personal aesthetics. Similarly, consideration of some important genres of Western music is incorporated to suggest some ways the analysis of form may take into account the genre of a composition. Second, the concepts of form as design and form as process, and the distinction between formal design and formal structure serve to clarify the diverse ways basic types of musical form may be realized. This distinction provides one basis for addressing questions that are important to understanding a piece of music: given a musical idea or event, what happens next and why? Third, an emphasis on aural experience and contextual listening is incorporated in the text, with ancillary exercises to supplement the discussions. This emphasis reflects the author's belief that the analysis of music should augment listening skills and aural comprehension as well as cultivate critical, interpretive thinking. CD recordings of select examples and exercises accompany the text and are an integral part of it. Finally, analytic notes are presented periodically to examine the issues of criteria and interpretation that are involved in musical analysis.

This text is intended for undergraduate music majors who have completed at least one, though preferably two years of the study of harmony and voice leading. It is essentially designed as a text for classes on musical form and basic analytic techniques; it might also serve as supplemental reading in music history or literature courses. The text is divided into two large sections. In Part I, after an introductory discussion on the nature of musical form, some basic analytic tools and concepts that can be applied to a wide range of styles and genres are presented. Discussions of tonal design, thematic processes and phrase structure, phrase rhythm, formal functions, and musical texture are addressed in separate chapters. Basic elements and formal principles of Baroque, Classical, and Romantic music are discussed with reference to examples presented in each chapter. The text makes no attempt to focus on any specialized analytic methodology. Rather, basic tools useful to the analysis of form are emphasized. It is the author's belief that these tools may inform, as well as be informed by, specific analytic methodologies an instructor may wish to incorporate with the text.

Part II examines the traditional forms of Western music, generally organized from the smaller forms found in a wide range of styles, to the larger forms of classical music. Contrapuntal forms and ritornello forms of the Baroque period, which tend to emphasize form as process rather than as recurring design, are included in separate chapters. The emphasis in Part II is on large-scale design, though details of formal structure are addressed in select works. Included in this section is a chapter on vocal forms and genres. Operatic and choral forms are examined briefly, though given the challenges of analyzing opera and the scope of the topic, the discussion is primarily limited to solo vocal forms. While examples of traditional forms in twentieth-century music are cited throughout Part II, a concluding chapter addresses innovative approaches to musical form in twentieth-century music. Here, as in previous sections, a comprehensive discussion of genre and style is beyond the scope of the text. Rather, the intent of this section is to consider how marked changes in musical style relate to new ways of generating formal structures.

Generally the text is organized from consideration of lower levels of design and structure to larger levels Within parts, each successive chapter is intended to build on the previous chapter, although some portions may be omitted or reordered. For example, the chapter on tonal design has an extensive discussion on cadences and key relations, which may not be necessary for more experienced students. It may serve as a review but also reinforces the importance of tonality to formal design in tonal music. Similarly, the somewhat speculative discussion of musical form in Chapter 1 might be read selectively. Chapters 3–5, however, present ideas and concepts that are particularly important for the analysis of formal design and structure. In Part II, chapters on binary form and sonata form might be studied successively; ternary and rondo forms may be coupled in a similar manner. The last three chapters may be studied selectively, reordered, or omitted to fit the needs and interests of a particular class. Throughout the text, the analytic techniques from Part I should be applied to reinforce and develop analytic skills and to examine in greater detail the formal structures of select works at the instructor's discretion.

The text draws on examples of musical repertoire that are widely recognized or well-regarded, with an emphasis on ensemble literature that should be of interest to all students. Familiar repertoire is used when possible to help students draw on their aural experience and their intuitions about music. A number of works are referenced as examples throughout the text to facilitate analysis of large-scale movements or works and to familiarize students with acknowledged masterpieces of the literature.

The aural comprehension of elements of musical form is emphasized in two ways. First, the accompanying CD assists readers in completing aural exercises and examples intended to be completed without the aid of a score in Chapters 1–5. Second, recordings of musical examples and works for analytic exercises may accessed at designated Web sites. (See Notes at the end of this Preface.) All of the exercises are intended to not only reinforce basic analytic skills or formal concepts, but also to lead the reader to consider unique and interesting characteristics of the music. They also stress the connection between the aural and visual study of music. It is this connection and the understanding of the formal structure and style of a composition that, in the opinion of the author, should be a primary goal of any musical analysis.

NOTES

- Works cited in the Burkhart Anthology are indicated with an * (asterisk).
- Works cited from the Kostka/Greybill Anthology are indicated with + (plus sign).
- In the musical examples, reference to major keys use a capital letter alone; minor keys are specified, as in B minor.
- In many musical examples dynamics and articulations have been omitted to facilitate reproduction.
- When referring to movements in a multi-movement work, upper case roman numerals are used alone: Beethoven, *Symphony No. 5*, III refers to *movement* III of that work.
- While scores are provided for select exercises, it is assumed that the reader will obtain or have access to scores for the other exercises and works cited for further study.
- Recordings of works cited for score analysis and further study may be obtained through the playlist at Classical.com.

ABOUT THE AUTHOR

James Mathes is Associate Professor of Music Theory and Coordinator of Music Theory and Composition at the Florida State University College of Music. After studies at the University of Pittsburgh he earned a B.S. in Music Education from the University of Maryland and an M.M. and Ph.D. in Music Theory from Florida State University. He has published articles and presented papers based on his research and interests in musical form, the analysis of twentieth-century wind ensemble literature, music theory pedagogy, and the relationship between analysis and performance. He has also worked professionally as an accompanist and saxophonist, and is an experienced conductor, having worked with community choruses, senior youth orchestras, and church music programs. At FSU he teaches courses on the analysis and performance of masterworks, Classical form and style, and tonal harmony and counterpoint.

ACKNOWLEDGMENTS

Many people contributed to the development and completion of this book. I would like to express my sincere thanks to them.

To those who reviewed earlier versions of the manuscript for this book for their helpful critiques and ideas: Joyce Dorr (University of North Carolina Asheville, retired), Matt Whitfield (Gardener-Webb University), Jeff Gillespie (Butler University), Robert Fleisher (Northern Illinois University), Ralph Turek (University of Akron), Dr. Gene Trantham (Bowling Green State University), Thom Ritter George (Idaho State University), and Claire Boge (Miami University).

To the many people at Pearson Prentice Hall involved in the production of this text: Sarah Touborg, Editor-in-Chief for the Arts, Philosophy and Religion, who gave this project attention whenever it was needed, Richard Carlin, Executive Editor of Music, who took this project over and hit the ground running to expedite its completion, Lisa Iarkowski, Senior Managing Editor, for making the tough decisions, and Joe Scordato, for his skill at keeping things on track.

To the team at Stratford Publishing Services: Edith Bicknell, Project Manager, for her patience and care in the production of the text and music, and her excellent staff: copy editor Evangeline Dollemore, proofreader Shelley Belgard, and music engravers Peg Martin and Chris Hatcher, and to the many other staff members of Pearson Prentice Hall and Stratford Publishing Services who contributed to the success of this project.

To my long-standing colleagues at the Florida State University College of Music, Peter Spencer and Jane Clendinning, for many valuable pedagogical discussions over the years.

To my colleagues Peter Spencer, Michael Buchler, Evan Jones, and Matt Shaftel who read through various portions of the text and gave many valuable suggestions.

To Sheila Guo, Kathy Biddick, Emmy Valet, Sean Johnston, Rachel Lim, Olivia Swedberg, and Richard Zarou, graduate students who provided great assistance in the development of notated examples and exercises, and the editing of various portions of the text.

To Margaret Pendleton for her expertise in obtaining permissions, and her excellent staff at Beethoven & Company for their assistance in obtaining scores.

To Lonnie Hevia of the Florida State University College of Music Library for his help in gaining access to scores.

To Sean Malone for his meticulous production of the accompanying audio CD.

To many family members and friends, too numerous to mention, who gave encouragement throughout the process of writing this book.

To Margaret and Jon for their love and support.

PART I

Formal Design and Structure:

Analytic Concepts and Tools

1 The Nature of Musical Form

Form: the shape or structure of something . . .
(1) structural pattern of a musical composition (2) a specific type (as fugue, rondo, sonata) of such pattern[1]

"All music is nothing more than a succession of impulses that converge towards a definite point of repose."[2]

Igor Stravinsky

"Form [is the] balance between tension and relaxation."[3]

Ernst Toch

Introduction

What is musical form? As the quotes above suggest, there are different answers to this question, in part because music occurs in different guises. Most people would agree that music is an aural and temporal phenomenon: it is organized sound that occurs in time. The evocative statements by Stravinsky and Toch reflect the fact that the experience of music is both aural and physical, that it is something we hear and feel as we listen to or play music. Music also occurs in the form of notated scores that one can study and learn to perform. Further, music is something that we may internalize, that is, imagine in our mind's ear.

Each of these representations of music will lead us to different perspectives on musical form. Music in the tradition of Western classical and popular music is normally notated in a musical score. Apart from establishing a text for all musicians to perform the work, a score provides a basis for visual perception of musical designs. It represents the music outside of its temporal context, which allows us to study the content of a composition as if frozen in time. Using a score helps us to understand musical design and compositional techniques that may be elusive from an aural standpoint. We can isolate and analyze various aspects of the music, compare passages separated in time, and contemplate details as well as long passages.

While a score makes possible and encourages a synoptic view of the music, a purely aural representation—a performance—encourages and even demands an awareness of musical ideas as they unfold in time. That is, as we listen and particularly when we perform, we experience the music as it occurs from moment to moment. In this mode, we may be more attentive to gestures, shapes, motion, and sonic qualities rather than to codified aspects of the formal design. Presented aurally or visually, our perception of musical form will vary according to which elements we are attentive to, as well as the length and complexity of the music.

---

[1] By permission. From Webster's *Third New International*® Dictionary, Unabridged. © 1993 by Merriam-Webster, Inc. (www.merriam-webster.com), 892.

[2] Reprinted by permission of the publisher from *Poetics of Music in the Form of Six Lessons* by Igor Stravinsky, translated by Arthur Knodel and Ingolf Dahl, p. 35, Cambridge, Mass.: Harvard University Press, Copyright © 1942, 1947,1970,1975 by the President and Fellows of Harvard College.

[3] By permission. From *The Shaping Forces of Music* by Ernst Toch. © 1977 by Dover Publications, 157.

This chapter introduces some basis conceptions of musical form as understood in Western music, informed by the various modes of musical representation briefly outlined above. The basis for traditional classification of musical form is first presented along with some principles that underlie these formal classifications. The concepts of formal design, formal structure and formal processes, which are important to the analysis of musical form, are then introduced. Additional discussion will briefly consider the influence of style and genre on musical forms. Finally, consideration of musical form as a mode of perception addresses how the study of musical form can enhance our skills as active listeners.

Categories of Musical Form

FORMAL DESIGN

Although the term *form* takes on various meanings in reference to music, most often it is used to refer to the large-scale design of a composition. The various types of musical form represent large-scale designs that occur in many different styles and genres. One traditional basis for classifying types of musical designs is by the number and relationship of sections that occur in a composition. *Sections* may be understood and recognized as self-contained passages of music marked off by various degrees of closure and defined by thematic material, tonality, rhythm, and/or texture. Of the numerous designs one might imagine, many different compositions can be divided into two or three sections. By convention, these designs have been represented by letter schemes such as A A′, A B, or A B A. These designations represent formal principles of similarity and contrast that are fundamental to the organization of musical form. Sing through the familiar folk song given in Example 1. You will note that this simple song contains three short sections; the middle section contrasts with the two identical outer sections. This song therefore is a small three-part form: A B A. The principle of restating a musical idea after presenting a contrasting idea is a prevalent feature of musical form.

Sectional formal design can be straightforward, especially in simple music such as folk tunes. Two- or three-part forms may be expanded by presenting more elaboration or *development* of ideas or by adding more contrasting sections. In more complex and lengthy music, the perception of sections can vary according to the criteria used and the style of the music. In other works, such as instrumental preludes, a single musical idea is continuously elaborated. No contrasting sections are perceived and often such works may be understood as a one-part form. Listen to the Chopin Prelude in C major. While we may be able to break this short prelude into smaller segments, the continuous rhythms and brevity convey a single section for the complete piece. Other genres, such as fugues, which rely on contrapuntal textures throughout, are often based on alternating statements and elaborations of initial themes without clearly separate or distinctly contrasting sections. Such works are considered *through-composed* rather than sectional.

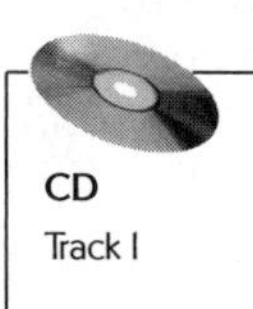

CD
Track I

Although several compositions may all be identified as having the same type of form, each may be different with regard to how the content of its sections is generated and the relative durations of the sections. Further, in many compositions the form or overall design is novel, and eludes standard classification. Such compositions will still have a discernible formal design because most music can be chunked into segments of varying length, which will group into discernible formal designs.[4] Whether it is unique or employing a standard category of musical form, any composition will have a formal design.

[4] "Chunking" here refers to the process of grouping information into recognizable bits of information. See *Aural Skills Acquisition* by Gary S. Karpinski (Oxford: Oxford University Press, 2000): 73 ff.

To reiterate, formal design in a comprehensive sense takes into account not only the large-scale design but also the specific organization of a composition from its smallest segment to its largest sections. A fundamental aspect of traditional formal design in music is that it is *hierarchic*. In this context, hierarchic means that smaller segments group into larger and larger segments. In music, motives of short melodic ideas of 1–2 measures group into a phrase; one or more phrases group into sections, and one or more sections form a complete composition. The length of a particular segment will define formal levels in a design. The higher the level, the longer the segment of music being considered.

Short segments that are combined to make larger segments or groups form a *grouping structure*.[5] A grouping structure will reveal how small segments group into longer segments. One basic way to define a group in music is by the time span it occupies, which can be done most simply by counting measures.

Example 1 *Segmentation and grouping of Twinkle, Twinkle Little Star.*

A relatively straightforward example of a grouping structure is given in Example 1. We have already noted that the form of this piece is an A B A design. Further consideration of the grouping structure reveals that this familiar tune may be grouped in segments of two measures each. The two-measure segments are articulated or marked by the repeated rhythmic pattern, while the melodic patterns distinguish the segments from one another. The brackets in Example 1 indicate the grouping of the segments. The designation of melodic/motivic content by letter names is one basic way to identify similarities or differences among segments. In this example, the scheme of ab b′ b′ ab shows the melodic or thematic patterning of the tune and the two-measure grouping. At the next level, a four-measure grouping indicates a three-part design of A B A. Such designations give a basic view of the arrangement and organization of thematic content.

Each of the four-measure segments described concludes with a relative sense of repose or *closure*, although the closure of the middle section is weaker than the other two. The progression and movement toward points of closure is basic to segmenting music and thus to the articulation of musical form. Establishing precise criteria for determining closure and its relative strength can be challenging given the number of factors and the perceptual judgments that may be involved. Closure may be affected by changes in harmony, rhythm, melodic motion, thematic material, texture and timbre, separately and in myriad combinations.

While all of these elements may contribute to our perception of closure and formal boundaries, the formal design is most readily discerned by considering three elements: tonality, themes, and textures. These composite elements all serve to segment music into phrases and sections and thus provide the primary basis for interpreting the formal design of a piece. Each of these aspects will be examined in detail in subsequent chapters.

The symmetrical and straightforward grouping structure of this short tune with the clear coordination of thematic and tonal elements is by no means representative of all music. The various elements of an individual composition may not coordinate to convey a single, unambiguous grouping structure. Formal boundaries often are subject to different interpretation in more complex music. As will be discussed, establishing consistent

[5] Grouping structure is defined as "a hierarchical segmentation of the composition into motives, phrases and sections," in Lerdahl and Jackendoff, A Generative Theory, 8.

criteria to decide how a piece is segmented into hierarchic groups is a fundamental task of any well-crafted formal analysis. These interpretations may be reflected not only in an analysis of a formal design but in the performance of the music as well.

Another aspect of formal design is that of *proportional durations*, which takes into account the length of the various phrases and sections of a form in relation to one another. These durations may be identified in terms of measure numbers at various levels of the formal design, as in Example 1: the tune is twelve measures long, and is in three, four-measure groups of 2+2 each. They also may be measured in terms of real time, for example, the first section lasts for five minutes while the next section is forty-five seconds. From a listener's viewpoint, proportional durations may not be readily apparent—we tend not to count measures or use a stopwatch when we hear music. Moreover, the formal classifications of large-scale design offer no indication of formal proportions: two compositions in the same form may be vastly different with regard to their length and formal proportions. Nonetheless, it may be argued that durations of events are a palpable part of the listening experience. We may intuit that a passage or section of music is relatively short or long, for example, and the durations of passages influence the expressive effect or the sense of tension or stability. For the composer, a feeling for proportional durations, though often intuitive, is a critical element of the composition, providing a sense of balance and proportion to the design.

FORMAL STRUCTURE

Formal design and the classification of the large-scale forms of music are concerned with the number and grouping of the musical ideas, and the arrangement of a composition into phrases, and sections. This perspective tends to emphasize a synoptic or comprehensive view of musical form, usually facilitated through the use of a notated score. Conversely, the temporal or "real time" perspective experienced in performance or listening focuses our attention on what we hear from moment to moment as the music unfolds in time. From this perspective, form is concerned with how musical ideas are generated, developed, and connected, with how the elements of the music—the melodic lines, the rhythms and harmonies, and the textures—shape these ideas and convey various qualities of motion. This view of musical form leads to consideration of the formal structure, the processes and functions that shape musical design.

The term *structure* when used with reference to music refers to the underlying progressions and patterns of the various elements that shape the music. Thus one may speak of tonal structure, rhythmic structure, melodic structure, and so on. For the purpose of this study, the term *formal structure* is used to refer to the underlying formal processes and functional relations among segments at various levels of the design. Two concepts are particularly important in understanding musical structure in general. First, it is generative, which means it results from processes and compositional techniques that create and shape the music. Second, it is *hierarchic* in that it distinguishes some elements and events as structural and some as embellishing, distinctions that can be assessed at various levels or time spans. The role of the various musical elements in shaping the structure will vary; in tonal music the term *structure* is normally understood to be a reference to the tonal structure. Tonal structure refers to a hierarchy of linear motions, harmonic progressions, and cadential goals that underlie the formal design and connect events separated in time.

FORMAL PROCESSES

Processes involving tonality, themes, and textures also are essential to the formal structure. The processes may be briefly explained and summarized as follows:

Tonal processes include harmonic and linear progressions, the process of modulation, and the confirmation of keys through cadences, which are fundamental to the articulation and shape of the formal structure and design. Awareness of aspects such as when and how modulations take place, or of fluctuations in harmonic rhythm makes us attentive to processes that shape the tonal motion of a composition.

Thematic processes can be defined in terms of how themes (melodic ideas) generate phrases and sections of a design. Given a melodic idea, a composer may use various thematic processes such as repetition, sequence, fragmentation, extension, or introduction of a contrasting idea.

Textural processes such as variation in the number and range of lines, or changes in the types of texture are also prominent features of music that shape and articulate phrases and sections.[6]

These various musical processes are compositional techniques that serve in the invention and arrangement of musical ideas. Where processes are initiated and completed, and which elements are considered, are important criteria for determining how we segment a composition and where its formal boundaries are.

In tonal music, analysis of tonal processes will inform the analysis of formal structure and design. In Example 1, we may observe some basic processes and functions that generate this simple A B A design. The process of *repetition* of the rhythmic idea of measure 1 can be observed throughout. The *varied repetition* of the melodic shape is important in grouping the segments. Measures 3–4 serve as a response to the ascending line of measures 1–2; measures 5–8 present identical varied repetitions of measure 2 but a step higher. Measures 9–12 are a *restatement* of measures 1–4. The pattern of linear and harmonic motion is critical to determining segmentation and grouping of these repetitions. The A section closes on the tonic scale degree and harmony each time, while the middle B section emphasizes dominant harmony with an arrival on scale degree 2. The restatement of the A section resolves the B section with a return to tonic. Consequently we group segments a and b together, and apart from segment b′ rather than grouping segments b and b′ together. Measures 3–4 function as a contrasting continuation, which in turn serves to delineate the larger formal design of A B A. This observation reflects the hierarchy of elements referred to previously.

FORMAL FUNCTION

Formal function refers to the role of segments of music at various levels of the structure. At small levels, for example, formal functions such as initiation, contrast, continuation, or closure may be used to explain the internal structure of phrases. At larger levels, some sections of music may be distinguished as transitional in function, while other passages may function to present complete thematic ideas. Consideration of formal processes, defined by the activity of the various elements, helps explain why or how we hear a passage functioning in a certain way. A cadential function, for example, is characterized by certain linear and harmonic progressions that signal the closing segments of phrases or sections. In this regard, formal processes and formal functions are closely related concepts that help us consider why ideas are shaped and arranged as they are, and what the expressive or structural intents of compositional choices may be. These aspects of form will be discussed in greater detail in the next several chapters.

Musical processes also may be considered in terms of the basic shapes that we hear or feel in the music. Musical shapes result from processes such as ascending and descending motion, or changes in rhythmic motion or dynamics. Intangible, often kinesthetic, qualities of the music that we experience as we play or actively listen may also characterize musical processes. These include opposing qualities such as tension/resolution, stability/instability,

[6] Note that texture here is understood not simply in terms of general categories such as homophony or polyphony, but in the broadest sense of all elements that affect the sound of the music. This point will be addressed more fully in Chapter 5.

continuity/discontinuity, the arrival and dissolution of climaxes, and patterns of accentuation and movement. Listen to the Chopin Prelude in C major. Intuitively we might describe and outline its form as follows:

- A short idea repeats and ascends, only to return for a brief moment of repose.
- The melody starts again, ascends higher, briefly turns back then ascends even higher.
- The music reaches a climax that turns back to a point of repose though the melody continues.
- The melodic idea resolves and the final chords repeat; the ending is confirmed by a gently rolled tonic harmony.

The form as a basic shape might be outlined as shown in Figure 1, which shows the contour of the piece in a very simple manner. We previously noted that the prelude as a whole is a continuous one-part form. We have now observed smaller segments in its design and described some of the elements that shape the formal structure.

As this description and diagram illustrates, musical form may be understood in terms of directed motion toward goals and climaxes, and in terms of gestures and shapes. It is to this intuitive perspective on musical form that both Stravinsky and Toch refer, in different ways, in the statements quoted at the start of the chapter. As with formal proportions, these aspects of form are less tangible than some of the elements of design and structure previously discussed. Nonetheless, these qualities are basic to our experience of music and inform much of what we intuit about musical design. In particular, contrasts between stability and instability, and between tension and its resolution, especially in tonal music, shape our perceptions of musical form as we listen or perform.

Figure 1.1 *Basic Shape of Chopin, Prelude No. 1 in C major, Op. 28.*

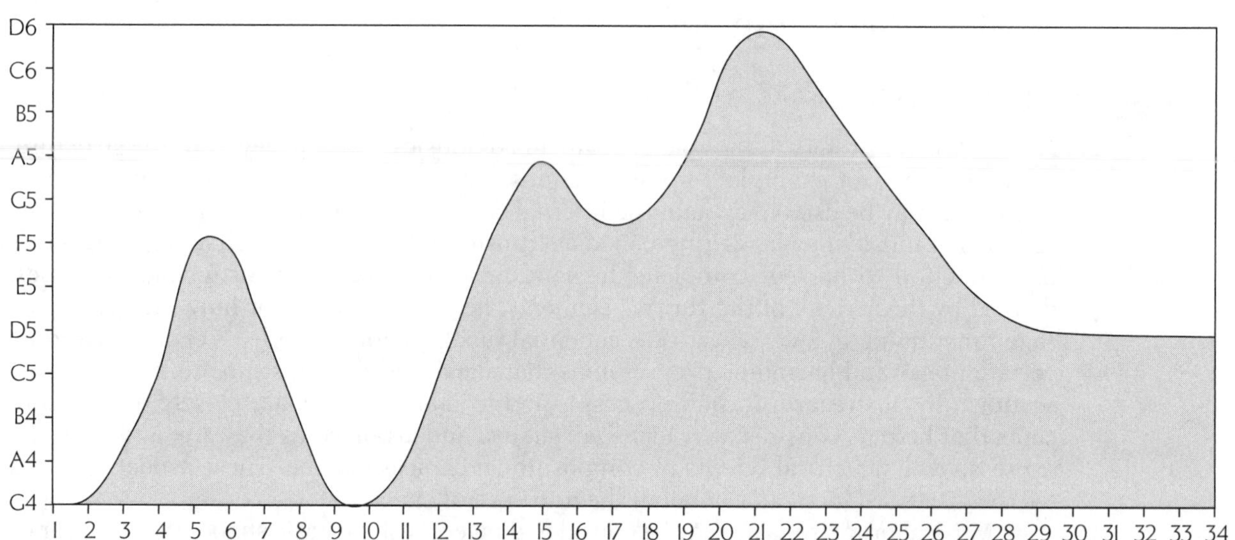

Form, Style, and Genre

The concepts presented up to this point reflect different perspectives on musical form that apply to a wide range of musical styles and genres. As with musical form, musical *style* can refer to a number of different things. Style may refer to the basic vocabulary and language of the music (tonal vs. atonal), to a particular historical period (Baroque vs. Classical), to a particular region (Italian vs. French), to the medium (vocal vs. instrumental), to a specific composer (Beethoven vs. Chopin) or to the genre (oratorio vs. opera). The study of musical style, as this partial list suggests, is a broad topic that could fill volumes. For the purposes of this text, we will focus on the influence of historical styles and genres of Western music on musical form.

With regard to historical style, it is useful to observe how the prevailing aesthetic and style of the period is reflected in the types of forms used and how they are structured. This perspective can help explain differences in the use of similar forms in different styles as well as provide insight to the formal principles of different periods. In addition, certain genres are often associated with particular forms. For example, a dance movement, such as a *gigue* or a *sarabande*, would be expected to be in some type of two-part form; the particular design and structure of the piece will reflect the style of the era, of the composer, and of that particular composition. Other genres, such as a *concerto*, adapt various types of forms and styles in ways directly related to the genre.

Another element of style that relates to form is the type and arrangement of expressive topics or gestures that can be heard as the music unfolds. The flow of musical ideas is sometimes interpreted as a narrative of topics or gestures associated with a particular style or genre, or with a particular expressive effect. For example a funeral march, pastoral effects, and virtuosic passage work, are associated with specific rhythmic/melodic figures or gestures that shape the musical ideas and may influence the formal design. Recognition of particular rhythms, textures, and harmonies associated with a particular style or expressive convention gives an awareness of the dramatic flow of ideas or the character of the music. Conversely, formal processes and function may be agents for the dramatic or expressive intent of music. Such interpretations are often subjective and not applicable to all music, but in many types of compositions, particularly vocal music, program music,[7] and the dramatic forms of the classic and romantic periods, they can inform our understanding of the arrangement and development of musical ideas.[8]

The Perception of Musical Form

As this introductory discussion suggests, our perceptions of musical forms are informed in part by the way in which we experience the music and what elements we are attentive to in the music. Studies have shown that listeners of a wide range of backgrounds and abilities tend not to process music with regard to large-scale form or design unless called upon to do so.[9] This observation leads us to question the necessity and value of knowing formal design and of labeling formal aspects. It seems reasonable, as has been argued, to assume that music can be enjoyed and understood in basic ways without recourse to formal analysis and study of the score. This assertion may also apply to performing a work as well; an accurate rendition of the notated parts informed by good musical intuitions often serves musicians just fine. In all music, however, and especially in music of any considerable length, complexity, or sophistication, awareness of form in one or more of its dimensions

[7] Program music usually refers to instrumental music that is intended to express or represent nonmusical ideas, whether a story, a character, an image, or an idea. Vivaldi's *The Four Seasons* and Tchaikovsky's *Romeo and Juliet* are examples.

[8] See Ratner, Classic Music, 3–28 for a historical classification and discussion of expressive "topics" and styles. The more problematic idea of music as rhetoric is discussed in Bonds, Wordless Rhetoric.

[9] Smith, Alan, "Feasibility of tracking musical form as a cognitive listening objective," *Journal of Research in Music Education* 21 (1973): 200–213; see also, Cook, "Musical Form."

can be valuable in gaining a greater understanding of the work and deepening our experience as performers and listeners. Other studies have shown that actively engaged listeners tend to be involved in anticipating what will happen next in the music.[10]

Awareness of basic formal processes in the music such as repetition, sequence, cadential progressions, or points of imitation, enhances this activity and leads us to hear music in larger segments and in terms of directed motion towards goals. Such hearing sharpens our focus as listeners, which enhances our understanding of what we hear. Perhaps the most valuable result of analytic listening and thinking is that we enhance our memory of a work and our ability to internalize it. As the American composer Roger Sessions has observed, to know and understand a piece of music is to be able to "reproduce it in our mind's imagination."[11]

Summary

Musical form may be defined and understood in various ways. Formal design refers to the grouping of musical ideas and their arrangement into phrases and sections. The analysis of formal design entails consideration of tonal, thematic, and textural elements to determine the segmentation and grouping structure. Formal designs are continuous or sectional in varying degrees, and are based on principles of similarity and contrast. General types of musical forms have been identified based on common formal designs that are found in many works. The identification of the type of formal design evident in a composition is useful in that it provides one basis for understanding the unique formal aspects in relation to a basic model. Many compositions will have no standard formal design, but all music will exhibit some type of formal design. Durational proportions of the sections of a design are a distinguishing feature of individual compositions.

Formal structure results from the specific ways in which the content of a composition is generated. The analysis of formal structure focuses on the processes that shape the music and on the formal functions of segments. The relationship between structure and design is a complex subject that theorists continually debate.[12] Generally, design is considered the outward manifestation of the formal structure. While both of these aspects of form may be well coordinated, they may produce different views of how the music is segmented and organized.

In the best of music, the formal structure is a result of the musical ideas themselves. That is, the invention and elaboration of the musical ideas generates the specific formal structure. A composer may use a common or preconceived large-scale design, but the specific formal structures are an outgrowth of the content. This is why most theorists believe that form and content are interconnected rather than separate aspects of music. Finally, in this study the focus on formal design and formal structure will lead us to questions of "what" and "when" events occur. Without a clear picture of these aspects, it is difficult to adequately consider the important, though admittedly subjective questions, of "why" or "to what effect" the music is organized or to explain compositional choices. As with any analysis, the goal is to synthesize all of our observations and judgments into a greater understanding of a composition as a whole, which in turn informs our listening and performing experience.

[10] See Karpinski, *Aural Skills*, 68–69.

[11] Sessions, Roger. *The Musical Experience*, 23.

[12] The distinction between design and structure is sometimes referred to in terms of "outer form" and "inner form." See Rothstein, *Phrase Rhythm*, 104. See also David Beach, "Schubert's Experiments with Sonata Form."

SUGGESTED READINGS

In addition to the works cited in notes for this chapter, the following readings are recommended for class discussions:

1. For a lively debate that addresses the perception of musical form see Repp, Bruno H., et al. "Music in the Moment: a Discussion." *Music Perception* 16.4 (Summer 1998): 463–494.
2. Leonard Meyer presents an informative discussion of the hierarchical nature of musical form and the elements of music in *Exploring Music*, 81–104.

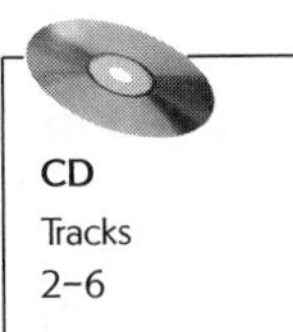

CD
Tracks
2–6

AURAL EXERCISES

Listen to recordings of the works listed below without a score. Listen to each piece several times. Consider whether each piece as a whole tends to be sectional or continuous, and the extent to which it relies more on similarity or contrast. As you listen to each composition, take note of how many different thematic ideas you hear and the number of sections. Is there a distinct moment of climax, several climactic moments, or an absence of distinct climax? Make a diagram of the formal design using letter designations, descriptions of textural or expressive elements, or graphic symbols of your own invention that represent shapes you hear in the music. Consider the extent to which the answers to these questions vary according to which elements of the music you are most attentive to.

Handel, *Messiah*, "The Lord Gave the Word"
Weill, "My Ship" from *Lady in the Dark*
Tchaikovsky, Symphony No. 4, III
Bach, *The Well-Tempered Clavier,* Book I, Prelude in E
Beethoven, Piano Sonata Op. 2, No. 2, III (Scherzo)

2 Tonal Design

Introduction

In the preceding chapter the concepts of formal design and formal structure were introduced in order to distinguish between the overall form of a composition—its formal classification or layout into sections—and the formal functions, processes, and proportions that shape the design. Both perspectives require that we "chunk" or segment music into meaningful units and group them in some hierarchic manner, whatever the form.

Three basic aspects of musical form—tonality, themes, and textures—were introduced. Though all three of these aspects can function to define and group segments, the extent to which they are coordinated or work independently will vary widely. Thematic patterning and changes in rhythmic texture and density are important cues for discerning phrases and sections. It is the tonal motion of the music, the progression of harmonic and linear activity, however, that is most important in articulating formal structure and design. In the following discussion, the focus will be on tonal motion and design with an emphasis on the role of tonality in articulating phrases, and on the concepts of cadence, modulation, and key relations. A rather extensive survey of cadences is presented because recognizing cadential harmonies is fundamental to the analysis of musical form. Thematic and textural processes and functions will be addressed further in subsequent chapters.

Phrase, Cadence, and Key

One fundamental aspect of form is the idea that music is organized into phrases. One of the most basic components of phrase structure is the melodic and harmonic progression toward cadence. Cadences mark the ends of phrases by conveying a sense of completion and resolution. Thus they are a primary basis for segmenting and grouping tonal music in any form.[1] In tonal music, the order, type, and relative weight or degree of emphasis of the cadences and modulations are an important determinant of form. We will call this profile the *tonal design*. Analysis of tonal design entails identifying the pattern of cadences and any modulations that take place, and assessing their hierarchy and weight. Put simply, we may ask which cadences and keys are most important, and what relations or patterns are evident among them. Because the notion of cadence is directly tied to that of phrase, the definition of a musical phrase must be considered and clarified before further discussion of cadences.

The term *phrase* as it applies to music has at least two different meanings. Performers often use the term as a verb to refer to the manner in which they shape or "phrase" the music through control of dynamics, articulation, accentuation, balance, and tempo. From this perspective, a "phrase" may refer to any segment of music that is perceived as a

[1] In post-tonal music, other elements of music, especially texture, timbre, and rhythm become equally or often more important than harmonic and linear elements in the articulation of musical form. This issue will be addressed in a later chapter.

complete or self-contained unit, and must be projected as such in a performance. Such segments may be as short as a melodic idea of 2–3 notes, or as long as several measures of music. When used with reference to musical form, the term *phrase* refers to a passage of music that is marked by completion of directed motion toward a cadence. The emphasis on directed motion and cadential arrival implies that a phrase has a distinct beginning, middle and end.

In both of these interpretations, what performers and attentive listeners perceive is motion toward varying degrees and moments of *closure*, which may be defined as resolution or completeness. A sense of closure is what leads us to perceive segments of music and to group these segments as units. As we will see, because closure is a relative concept, what constitutes a phrase can be subject to diverse interpretations in many instances. By formally defining a phrase in terms of directed motion toward cadential closure, we can distinguish between a complete phrase and segments within a phrase. Since this distinction hinges on a precise definition of cadences, we will examine types of cadences in tonal music before turning to the concepts of modulation and key relations.

Cadences and Segmentation

The term "cadence," from the Latin *cado* meaning "to fall down," refers to the completion of a harmonic and melodic progression in tonal music that serves to articulate or mark the end of a phrase. The idea of falling is reflected by the sense of resolution that is heard in the cadential motion of the melody and bass line. From the study of harmony and voice leading we know that specific harmonic progressions and linear motions characterize various types of cadences. *Authentic cadences* resolve a dominant chord or leading-tone chord to a root position tonic triad; *half cadences* resolve to a root position dominant triad; *deceptive cadences* employ a resolution of V to vi or to some chord other than tonic; *plagal cadences* employ a resolution of IV (or some other non-dominant chord) to a root position tonic triad. A summary of common voice-leading patterns in various cadences is given in Example 2.1 Note that each of the cadence formulas is marked by arrival on a root position triad, which provides the stability requisite for a sense of resolution and cadential closure. The exception is the use of a I6 chord that may be used to avoid or weaken a sense of harmonic closure, creating an imperfect authentic cadence.

Example 2.1 *Summary of voice-leading patterns in tonal cadences in C major.*

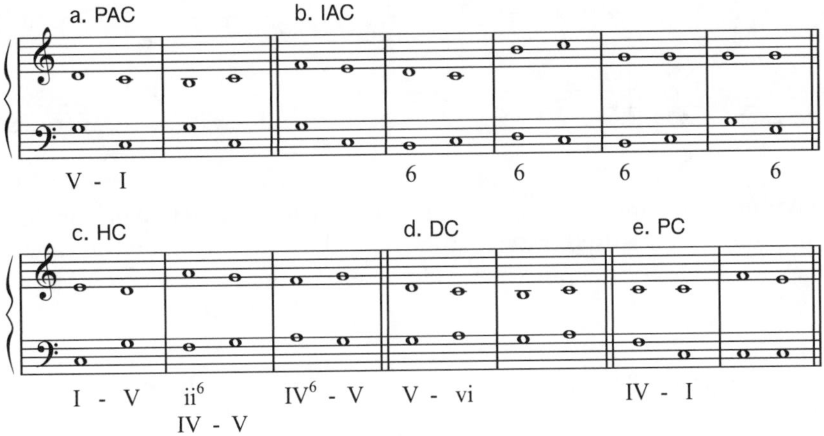

A brief analysis of the first two phrases of the well-known minuet shown in Example 2.2 will serve as an introduction to phrase segmentation and will clarify the importance of cadential harmonies in articulating phrases. The first eight measures of the minuet break into two, four-measure segments, the first of which can be further chunked into two-measure segments. The two-measure segments are articulated by the melodic repetitions and changes from eighth to quarter notes. Measures 5–8 might be grouped in two-measure segments, though the repeated rhythms based on the musical idea introduced in measure 1 give a sense of continuous motion through measure 8. Thus, measures 5–8 are best interpreted as one continuous four-measure unit. This grouping of [2+2] +4] is indicated in the example by brackets while numbers indicate the beginnings and endings of phrases. The two-measure and four-measure segments in this phrase are easily recognized and would be projected in any competent performance. These segments are not, however, complete phrases as defined above, since there is no cadential arrival until measure 8. The term *subphrase* refers to a short segment of music, usually 2–4 measures in length, that is part of a larger, complete phrase.[2] Though measure 4 seems to complete a melodic motion toward cadence, the harmonic motion does not entail a cadential bass line of root position chords; both the implied dominant chord (m. 3 beat 3) and the tonic (m. 4) are in inversion. Further, measure 5 is a continuation of the melodic motion from measures 1–4. Measure 8 does reach a clear half cadence, stressed by the strong metric placement and arrival of the dominant chord, as well as by the prolonged duration of the melody. Similarly, measures 9–16 comprise a single phrase, with a strong bass line emphasizing a perfect authentic cadence. While further discussion of phrase structure will be considered in the next chapter, the point here is the importance of cadential harmonies in articulating complete phrases.

Example 2.2 Christian Petzold (attributed), *Minuet from the Notebook for Anna Magdalena Bach,* mm. 1–16.

When analyzing cadences, one can distinguish between the final chord of the cadence and the cadential progression.[3] The chord upon which the cadence is completed, the harmonic goal of the phrase, is referred to as the *point of cadence*. It is this chord and

[2] See Rothstein, *Phrase Rhythm*, 30–32 for further discussion of subphrase characteristics. Other terms one encounters include phrase segment and phrase member.

[3] The distinctions here are drawn in part from William Caplin's discussion of cadence in *Classical Form*, 43–44.

the chord preceding it that distinguishes the various types of cadences as described above. The *cadential progression* refers to the series of harmonies leading to and including the point of cadence. The progression may be a simple V-I motion using root position chords at the end of a phrase, or a complete cadential progression of primary, functional harmonies covering one or more measures of the phrase.

Several factors besides harmonic and linear progressions can contribute to establishing the point of cadence. Some of the most prevalent techniques, which may occur in various combinations, include:

- A change in the rhythmic motion, which normally entails a sense of deceleration or acceleration by changing linear rhythms and/or harmonic rhythm.
- A change to a longer note value melodically at the point of cadence. Rests or fermatas following arrival at the cadence are not uncommon.
- Repetition or introduction of thematic material to initiate the next phrase.
- Placement of the cadential chord on a metrically strong beat.
- Prolongation of the point of cadence through repetitions or melodic elaborations around the dominant.
- A change in textural density and a coalescence of voices in similar rhythms.

As this list suggests, rhythmic factors are critical to the perception of cadences. Other ways to emphasize cadences include the use of a cadential six-four chord, trills, anticipations, and/or suspensions.

Formally, the most important cadence is the *authentic cadence*. A *perfect authentic cadence* (PAC) with cadential progressions of three or more chords, consisting of predominant, dominant, and tonic harmonies, gives the strongest sense of closure. Example 2.3 shows some of the most common cadential bass lines and the implied harmonic progressions that are used in authentic cadences. Play through or sing the bass line of each example. Note that these progressions and bass lines may incorporate chromatic, pre-dominant harmonies using $\sharp\hat{4}$ or $\flat\hat{6}$, including borrowed chords, secondary dominant chords, Neapolitan sixth chords, and augmented sixth chords.

Example 2.3 *Voice-leading patterns for authentic cadential progressions.*

Although a seemingly endless variety of cadences using different rhythms and textures may be found in the repertoire, the bass lines and harmonies shown in Examples 2.3 and 2.4 are pervasive. Example 2.4 illustrates some authentic cadential progressions from eighteenth and nineteenth-century classical music. Examples 2.4a, b, and d illustrate PACs that all employ root position dominant and tonic triads. The dotted rhythms and hemiola in Example 2.4a are devices commonly used to give emphasis to a cadence. Example 2.4c from Handel's *Messiah* makes use of a vii°6–I cadence that results from contrary, stepwise motion to the tonic scale degree in octaves. Here the leading-tone harmony is used in place of the dominant harmony. This cadence is an outgrowth of pre-tonal (modal) music that stresses such voice leading at points of cadence. Though cadential tonic chords must be in root position, penultimate dominant chords of an authentic cadence may be in inversions. However, the most formally significant authentic cadences normally use root position dominant chords.

The cadence illustrated in Example 2.4e is an *imperfect authentic cadence (IAC)*, which results when the 3rd or 5th of the tonic triad is used in the soprano voice at the point of cadence. Occasionally the tonic chord is used in first inversion at a point of cadence, which may be interpreted as an IAC. Note also Brahms's use of suspensions to delay the resolution, which then occurs on a metrically weak beat. These techniques attenuate the degree of closure, while serving to emphasize the eventual resolutions. Listen to the examples several times with particular attention to the outer voices.

Cadential progressions may be reiterated or prolonged for a more decisive sense of closure. The resultant emphasis on cadential arrival is a hallmark of the classical style of Haydn, Mozart and Beethoven. An entire phrase may consist of an extended cadential progression; such a cadential phrase is often found at the end of a large section of a work or movement. The close of the first section of Mozart's Symphony No. 41, first movement (Example 2.4f) uses a cadence formula associated with the Mannheim composers of the eighteenth-century.

The *half cadence* (HC) makes use of progressions similar to the PAC but with a marked arrival on the dominant chord that separates it from the subsequent chord to which it resolves. The HC is clearly less stable than an authentic cadence, thus creating a strong expectation of continuation. All of the progressions shown in Example 2.4 may occur in half cadences if the tonic resolution is interrupted or delayed. The rhythmic and textural factors cited previously contribute to establishing the dominant chord as the point of cadence. The change to a longer note, prolongation of the cadential dominant chord, and repetition of thematic material to initiate the next phrase are particularly effective in marking half cadences. These changes cause an interruption in motion on the dominant chord followed by a *re-beginning*.

Example 2.4 *Authentic Cadences.*

a. Bach, *English Suite in G minor,* Prelude, mm. 29–33.

b. Mozart. *Così fan tutte,* No. 17, mm. 21–24.

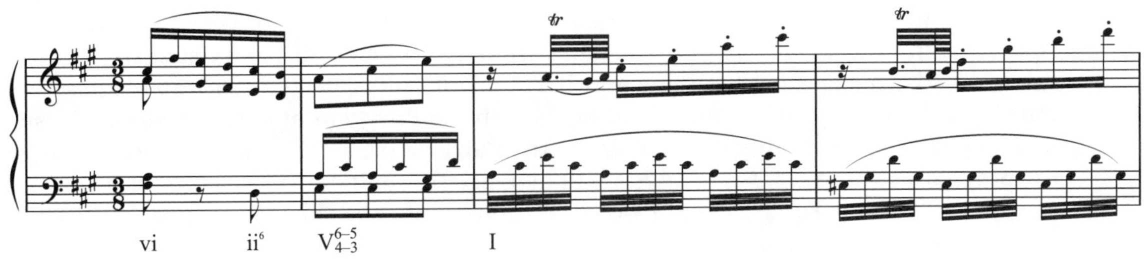

c. Handel, *Messiah,* "*Hallelujah.*"

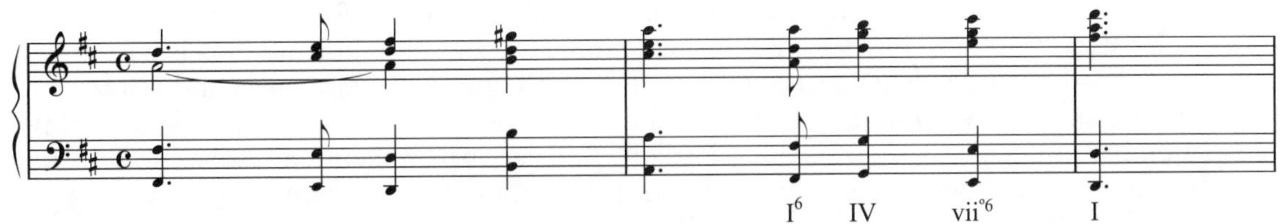

d. Schubert, *Erlkönig,* final cadence.

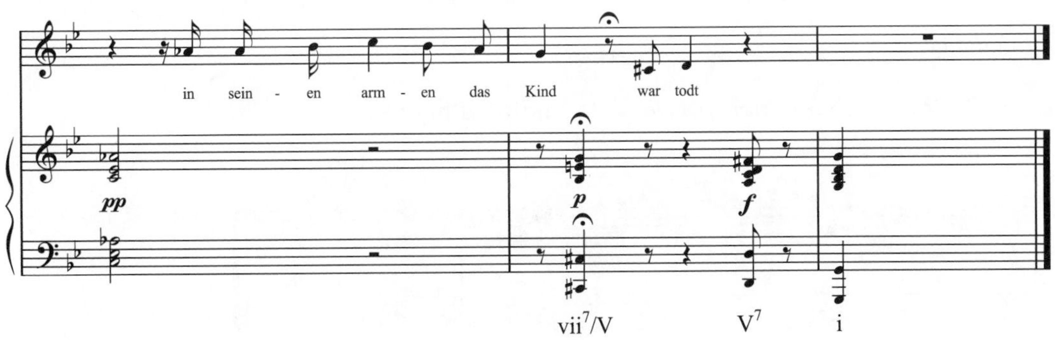

e. Brahms, *Intermezzo in A,* Op. 118, No. 2, mm. 7–8.

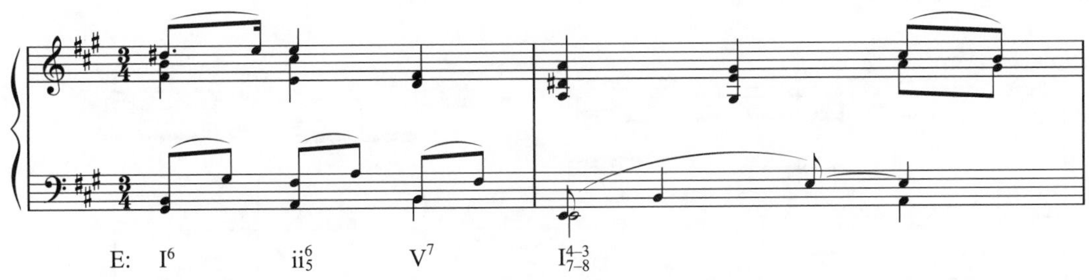

f. Mozart, *Symphony No. 41,* IV, mm. 145–150.

Some frequently encountered types of half cadence progressions are illustrated in Example 2.5. Example 2.5a illustrates a descending, stepwise approach to a V chord using ♭$\hat{6}$–$\hat{5}$ motion in the bass. This bass line typically is harmonized with iv6–V progression, though other predominant sonorities such as ii°4/3, or an augmented sixth chord can be used. This specific bass line and harmonization is referred to as a *Phrygian half cadence*. A byproduct of the voice leading used in the Phrygian mode in pre-tonal music, it is encountered frequently in the music of the Baroque period. Example 2.5b shows how the progression ii6–V6/4–5/3 creates a half cadence through metric accentuation and linear descent to a 6/4 sonority that resolves to dominant. The subsequent rest helps separate this resolution to V from the next phrase.

Half cadences normally arrive on the root position, dominant triad rather than the V7 to give stability to the point of cadence. In Example 2.5c, the placement of the cadential chord on a metrically accented (strong) beat and the sustained emphasis give arrival on a V7 the effect of a half cadence. Often the dominant chord is preceded by a V/V or vii°7/V. This progression does not normally indicate a modulation and thus is best understood as a *tonicized half cadence* (THC), though the degree of emphasis and reiterations of the secondary dominant may give the impression of an authentic cadence on the dominant. Because the dominant chord of a half cadence most often resolves to the tonic harmony at the beginning of the next phrase, in some instances one might perceive the tonic triad as the point of cadence. Whether the cadential arrival should be felt as an authentic cadence or a half cadence may be subject to interpretation and influenced by the performance.[4]

Example 2.5 *Half Cadences.*

a. Bach, *Brandenburg Concerto No. 4,* II, ending. Phrygian HC.

b. Mozart, *Così fan tutte,* No. 17, mm. 6–11.

[4] Another view, espoused by Schenkerian analysts, is that the HC dominant is an interruption and is not resolved by the subsequent tonic. Rather, the next phrase "starts over" and the HC dominant reaches its resolution at the PAC that ends the subsequent phrase. Others make the case that the HC dominant resolution is satisfied in a two-fold manner: weakly when the next phrase begins on tonic, and more strongly when the next phrase ends on tonic (following the dominant's return).

c. Brahms, *Intermezzo,* Op. 119, No. 2, mm. 32–35. Tonicized HC.

A *deceptive cadence* results when an authentic cadential progression resolves the dominant chord to a chord other than the expected tonic triad. A listener is "deceived" by having expectation of the resolution to a tonic triad thwarted. The most common resolution of the dominant harmony in a deceptive cadence is to a submediant harmony (vi or VI) as in Example 2.6a. This deceptive resolution is often followed by a continuation of the phrase, which will subsequently reach the goal of tonic resolution. Thus a deceptive cadence may be understood as an avoidance of an implied authentic cadence that is realized by a phrase extension. Such is the case in Example 2.6b, where the V7–vi progression occurs at an expected point of cadence. Though a V-vi progression is typical of deceptive cadences, other deceptive resolutions are not uncommon. In some instances, the deceptive resolution may be to a tonic chord that is altered to become a V7/IV as in Example 2.6c. In this case, the altered tonic serves as a point of cadence that initiates the next phrase, but its bass line motion is deceptive and unstable. A deceptive cadence may also resolve to a vi or ♭VI chord which is then assumed as a new tonic. This technique serves to initiate a new phrase with a direct shift in key, as in Example 2.6d.

A cadence similar to the deceptive cadence is an *evaded cadence*, associated in particular with the classical period. An evaded cadence occurs when an authentic cadential progression is interrupted. Evaded and deceptive cadences have important consequences for extending phrase structure, which will be discussed in a later chapter.

Example 2.6 *Deceptive Cadences.*

a. Mozart, *Così fan tutte,* No. 9, Farewell Quintet, mm. 17–19.

b. Bach, *The Well-Tempered Clavier*, Book I, Prelude in E, conclusion.

c. Bach, *Brandenburg Concerto No. 5*, I, mm. 124–126.

d. Chopin, *Impromptu No. 2 in F♯*, mm. 35–39.

The *plagal cadence* is used less frequently than the aforementioned cadences, and most often serves as an extension after an authentic cadence has been reached. Frequently it marks the end of a section or movement, and traditionally has been associated with sacred music in the form of the so-called "Amen cadence," a IV–I progression. Perhaps the most famous example of the plagal cadence is the end of the "Hallelujah" chorus from *Messiah* by Handel (Example 2.7a). Used frequently in Baroque music, plagal cadences are noticeably absent from the classical style; they return to use in the nineteenth century. Example 2.7b shows a plagal cadence that concludes a movement from a Brahms clarinet sonata. Note the use of the $\flat\hat{7}$ which inflects the tonic triad as a secondary dominant of IV, and the added G that colors the subdominant harmony, as well as the tonic pedal underlying the cadence. These harmonic devices are often used in closing plagal cadences.

Though plagal cadences are normally defined as IV–I progressions, any subdominant related harmony that resolves to a cadential tonic may have the effect of a plagal cadence. Such progressions might include vi or ♭VI, or ♭II. This more inclusive definition includes chromatic progressions often found in nineteenth-century music such as those in Examples 2.7b and c. Example 2.7d is similar to a plagal cadence in its exclusion of a leading tone but uses a borrowed chord (♭VII) to create what can be termed a *modal cadence*. Each of these progressions is indicative of the highly individualistic styles of romantic composers and the increased emphasis on subdominant related harmonies in nineteenth-century music.

Example 2.7 *Plagal Cadences.*

a. Handel, *Messiah*, "Hallelujah," final cadence.

b. Brahms, *Sonata for Clarinet and Piano,* Op. 120, No. 1, final cadence.

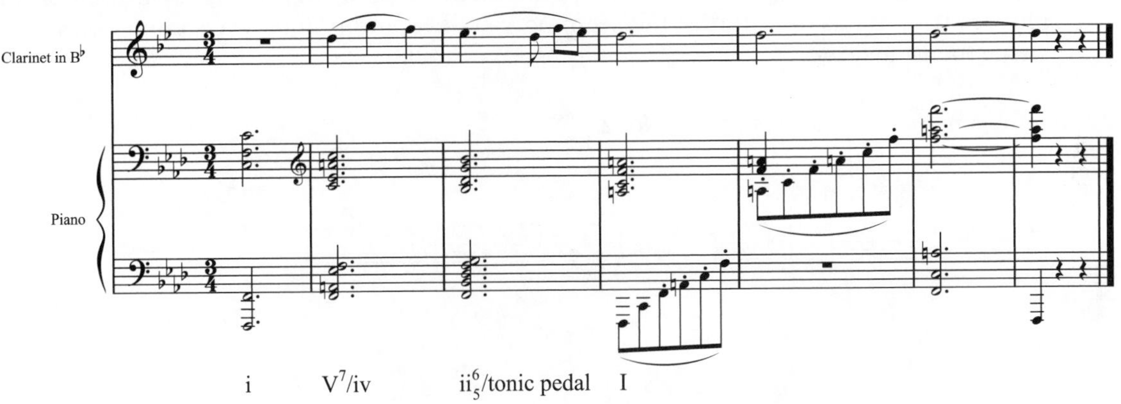

c. Wolf, *In dem Schatten*, final cadence.

d. Schumann, *Humoreske,* Op. 20, final cadence.

Some cadences are unusual in that they defy simple classification. One such cadence is the resolution of a vii$^{\circ}{}^{4}_{3}$ (a diminished seventh chord) to a root-position tonic triad but with a $\hat{4}$–$\hat{1}$ scale degree motion in the bass. The final measures of Example 2.6a illustrate this cadence, which combines a leading-tone harmony with a plagal bass-line motion. Examples may be found in music by Bach as well as later nineteenth-century composers. Many nineteenth-century works make use of unique cadences such as the striking conclusion of Liszt's Piano Sonata in B minor, in which an F major chord resolves to a B major tonic triad.

The foregoing discussion emphasizes the importance of cadential progressions—melodic, harmonic, and rhythmic—in articulating phrase structure. In as much as a sense of closure and completion of a musical idea can be marked by a wide array of techniques, the distinction between subphrases and phrases is subject to interpretation. The opening of the Beethoven String Quartet, Op. 59, II, (Example 2.8a) conveys a sense of initiation-continuation-closure that suggests a complete phrase, even in the absence of any melodic and harmonic progression. Similarly, some melodic motions often give a strong sense of closure and completion while the harmonic motion avoids cadential closure. These points emphasize the need to maintain a flexible approach to the analysis of phrase structure as one studies the seemingly endless and unique ways composers may shape their music.

Example 2.8 Beethoven, *String Quartet,* Op. 59, No. 2.

Tonal Design and Key Relations

In all tonal music, the pattern and degree of emphasis given to various keys and harmonies in a composition is a vital element of its tonal design. The arrangement and hierarchy of cadences, defined by motion away from and back to the tonic or home key, is basic to the unique shape of an individual piece of music. This is particularly important for understanding extended or complex compositions in which modulation to and from various keys as well as a diverse array of points of cadential closure may be found. While the concept of key relations has been explained in a number of ways and debated by theorists, what follows are some commonly accepted ways of classifying key relations.

Figure 2.1 *Key relations as shown on a diagram of the circle of fifths.*

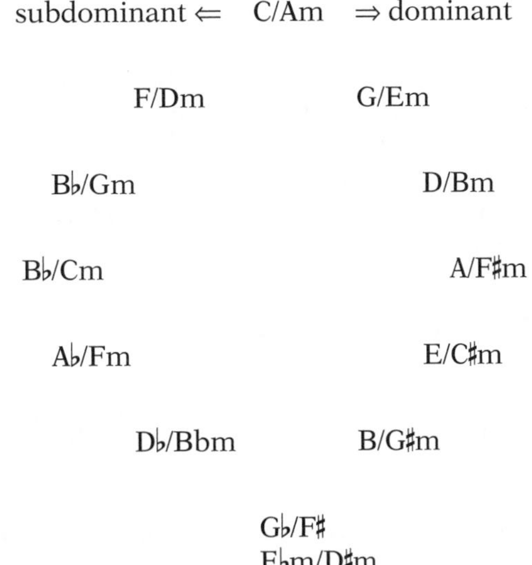

The relations between the keys of a movement can be determined by consideration of the circle of fifths (see Figure 2.1) and the scale upon which the tonic is built. In a given tonic key, the relative major or minor, and the keys adjacent to the tonic in the circle are closely related. Thus, if the tonic is C major, the keys of A minor, G major, E minor, F major, and D minor are closely related. If the tonic is C minor, then the keys of E♭ major, G minor, B♭ major, F minor, and A♭ major are closely related keys. In a given key, then, the major or minor triads formed on the various diatonic scale degrees can serve as a tonic triad. In a minor mode, key relations are considered in relation to the natural minor scale. *Put most simply: tonic, dominant, subdominant, and their relative keys are all closely related.*

The further one goes from the tonic in either direction of the circle, the more distant the key relations. Thus the key a tritone away from the original tonic (for example, C to F♯ major) is the most distant key. Keys moving in a clockwise direction on the circle are sometimes characterized as dominant related keys or "sharp side" while those moving counterclockwise are sometimes characterized as subdominant related keys, or "flat side" keys.[5]

While the notion of close and distant keys is a common gauge of key relations, the relations between parallel major and minor keys are another important consideration. By drawing on chords from the combined scales of relative major and minor keys, referred to as *modal mixture*, key relations may be expanded. Most often modal mixture occurs in major keys by borrowing the modal scale degrees 3, 6, or 7 from the parallel minor mode. This is referred to as *primary mixture*. Such alterations may entail a shift from major to minor mode by altering the third of the chord. This alteration occurs on the tonic, subdominant, or dominant keys. (Note that an alteration of the tonic triad results in a change in *mode* but not in tonic). Thus in C major, one might alter the C major (I), F major (IV) and G major (V) chords to become minor. The use of ♭III, ♭VI, or ♭VII as borrowed chords or key areas is different in that it results from an altered root or fifth of the chord.

[5] For discussions of key relations see Arnold Schoenberg, *Structural Functions of Harmony*, revised edition, Chapters 3 and 4; Donald Tovey, *The Forms of Music*, 57–66; and Charles Rosen, *Classical Style*, 23–29.

Another type of modal mixture results from altering diatonic triads using chromatic pitches not found in the minor mode. Thus in C major, a move to A major would entail use of a C♯ rather than the expected C♮. In this case, called *secondary mixture*, the new tonic triad is not a borrowed chord but an altered diatonic chord. More remote keys may be reached by combining primary and secondary mixture, in what is termed *double mixture*. In *double mixture* a modulation is made to a triad borrowed from the minor mode, which is then altered. For example, a modulation to B♭ minor from C major may be understood as a move to ♭VII—a chord borrowed from C minor—which is then altered to a minor triad by use of the chromatic pitch D♭. The most common types of harmonic/key relations based on modal mixture are summarized below.[6]

Figure 2.2 *Modal mixture and key relations based on C major as tonic.*

a. Primary Mixture: use of borrowed scale degrees from minor mode in major keys

I, IV, V ➔ i, iv, v   C minor, F minor, G minor

iii, vi, vii° ➔ ♭III, ♭VI, ♭VII   E♭ major, A♭ major, B♭ major

b. Secondary Mixture: diatonic triads changed to major

ii, iii, vi ➔ II♯, III♯, VI♯   D major, E major, A major

c. Double Mixture: borrowed chord is changed to minor

♭III, ♭VI, ♭VII ➔ ♭iii, ♭vi, ♭vii   E♭ minor A♭ minor, B♭ minor,

Within the array of 11 major and minor keys to which a composition may modulate, certain choices are prevalent in tonal music. Modulation to the dominant (V) of a major key, or to the dominant minor (v) or relative major (III) in a minor key, is characteristic of a great deal of tonal music including eighteenth-and nineteenth-century art music, folk music and popular music. This reflects the importance of tonic-dominant and relative key relations in the tonal system. Modulation to dominant creates the strongest need to resolve back to tonic, a tendency that different styles of music have treated in different ways. The "polarity" or tension between tonic and dominant, as has often been noted, is a foundation of tonality. Relative major and minor keys have the same groups of pitches, which allows for smooth motion from one key to another, creating a contrast in mode. Whatever the pattern of modulations, the departure from and return to the tonic harmony or key is a fundamental aspect of musical form in tonal music.

Within any style of music one may observe a wide range of modulations in extended compositions; however, the use of certain types of key relations and modulations can be associated with the general tendencies of historical styles. Baroque music typically modulates to closely related keys, with more remote modulations used sparingly and most often in the programmatic contexts of vocal music. While the move to the dominant and relative keys is common in Baroque music, movements often take a "tour" of closely related keys using modulation by sequence or common chord, or, occasionally, shifts from relative minor to relative major keys. The sequence of keys in a Baroque work is not standardized and often the various modulations are given equal emphasis. In the Classical period, a wider range of modulations may be found, but moves to the dominant or

---

[6] The terminology on mixture is drawn, in part, from Aldwell and Schacter, *Harmony and Voice Leading*, 3rd ed. 390–403, 561ff.

relative major are emphasized in the formal design, a critical element of the style. In addition, shifts from major to minor mode are exploited for dramatic emphasis.

In the nineteenth century, though moves to dominant and relative keys were still standard, moves to more remote keys became common. Certain tendencies of Romantic music may be cited. The first is the increasing use of keys a third apart using secondary and double mixture. These chromatic third relations, referred to as *chromatic mediants*, most often appeared as modulations from I-III♯ or VI♯ or ♭VI (from C major to E major, or C major to A major or A♭ major, for example). Sometimes a symmetrical pattern of modulations through thirds is used, resulting in a series of remotely related keys. Another Romantic tendency is the emphasis on subdominant keys rather than dominant-related keys. Further, the use of relative or parallel keys as competing tonics is evident in works such as Chopin's F minor Fantasie, which begins in F minor only to end in A♭ major. Generally speaking, the nineteenth century progressively exploited more remote and complex key relations until the idea of a clear and unambiguous tonality was threatened. In programmatic music, notably art song and opera, key relations may be based on specific characterizations or conventions as well as a tonal plan that gives coherence to a work.

TYPES OF MODULATIONS

The relations between keys can be a factor in the types of modulation that take place. Modulation to closely related keys is most easily effected by common chord modulation; more distant keys may require chromatic or enharmonic pivot chords, or the use of modal mixture. Sometimes direct modulations are used, in which a phrase or section simply begins in a new key. Sequence is another common way of effecting modulation in a wide range of styles.

Of equal if not greater importance to the tonal motion is the varied weight and emphasis given to modulations within a composition. Some modulations are merely passing through one key to another, while others are marked by emphatic cadences followed by presentation of thematic material. In other words, one can distinguish between structurally significant modulations and passing modulations that are part of a larger progression. The term *tonicization* is used to describe passing modulations in which a reiterated secondary chord or secondary progression implies a new key, but either a weak cadence or no cadence occurs. Generally, structural keys within a tonal design are defined by marked cadential closure. Key changes may be confirmed by the introduction or restatement of thematic material following a cadence.

Another factor to consider is the length of time in which the music remains in a particular key and its effect on the motion of the piece. Though a key may not be confirmed by cadential closure, it may be given emphasis by prolonged use. Conversely, keys may briefly sound as a temporary tonic marked by a cadence, only to aburptly turn toward another key, creating a sense of instability and tension. Whether modulations are heard as real (structural) modulations or as tonicizations is often subject to different interpretations. Making interpretations based on careful consideration of the musical context and effect is part of the analyst's and performer's task.

THE PERCEPTION OF MODULATIONS AND KEY RELATIONS

Although awareness of specific keys to which a composition modulates can be elusive from a perceptual viewpoint, active listening and practice can heighten awareness that a modulation has taken place and of the manner of modulation. Listen to the excerpts listed in the Aural Examples on the following page without the aid of a score. The excerpt from the Brandenburg Concerto No. 2, first movement contains a strong PAC in A minor followed by a direct shift back to F major. Here A minor may be understood as a substitute for its relative key C major, which is the dominant in F major. In the first half of the minuet from Symphony No.101 by Haydn, the repeated phrase following a half cadence contains a modulation to the dominant. This modulation is emphasized by repetition of melodic patterns that stress the leading tone to the dominant, G♯, followed by reiteration of cadential phrases that are highlighted by dynamics and syncopation. Conversely, a passage from the Schubert Symphony No. 8, movement I, contains a dramatic and abrupt modulation to G major after a decisive cadence in B minor. Finally, the piano piece by Liszt makes several modulations in its opening phrases by use of double mixture. The precise sequence of keys may be elusive, but the coloristic effect of such modulations is markedly different from the preceding examples.

CD
Tracks
7–10

AURAL EXAMPLES: MODULATIONS

a. Bach: Brandenburg Concerto No. 2, I, direct modulation from A minor to F major.
b. Haydn: Symphony No. 104, Minuetto, modulation to dominant key.
c. Schubert: Symphony No. 8, modulation from B minor to G major.
d. Liszt: Vallee d'Obermann, modulating period.

As these aural examples illustrate, the type of modulation and the choice of keys are important features of the music that can vary widely as to effect and salience. Though we may not be aware of specific keys, changes in the keys and the manner of modulation used alter the sound and the expressive effect of the music as well as its tonal design. These factors are important in our perceptions and analysis. Harmonic analysis through study of a score will clarify the specific key relations and modulations in a composition.

A problem that is both analytic and perceptual is whether we gauge key relations in terms of the original tonic, or in immediate context. For example, we may hear a move to B♭ major in a composition in C major as a modulation to ♭VII, a key drawn from the parallel minor mode. However, if B♭ major is preceded by a modulation to F major, the B♭ major may be understood as the subdominant (IV) of F. While this may be an issue of taxonomy, there is arguably a perceptual difference. Different ways of analyzing and hearing modulations are possible. In addition, the possibilities in shaping and varying specific tonal motion are so great that in many works, particularly masterworks, the relation of formal structure and tonality is unique. The study of musical form in tonal music is, in part, a study of how composers explore the possibilities of tonal motion in relation to the themes and textures they invent.

The Analysis of Tonal Design

For the purposes of analyzing the tonal design of a work, the most important structural keys in the design should be understood in relation to tonic. Examination of a few contrasting compositions will give an idea of how to determine tonal design. In short, relatively simple songs such as folk tunes and hymns, the tonal design is apparent by the clearly delineated phrases and cadences, often marked with fermatas. The hymn "Eternal Father" shown in Example 2.9 illustrates this point. The first phrase modulates to the dominant, which may be heard as a perfect cadence in A or a tonicized half cadence in D major.[7] The second phrase has a stronger modulation to E minor marked by the use of the cadential 6/4 progression; the third phrase returns to tonic to close the hymn.

The varied harmonic activity and goals of each phrase gives the hymn a continuous tonal motion, which counteracts the repetitious motivic rhythms. The tonal design based on the cadences may be diagrammed as shown in Figure 2.3. In this hymn, no other

[7] While either interpretation might be argued, the notion of a tonicized HC more accurately reflects the brevity of the time in G major, and the fact that the music turns back toward tonic to begin the next phrase.

Figure 2.3 *Diagram of tonal design of Example 2.10.*

Measures:	1	4	8	12
Keys:	I	V	iii	I
Cadences:		THC	PAC	PAC

passing modulations are evident though sequences with secondary dominant chords are used.

In forms that utilize repeats or double bars, the large-scale tonal design will be outlined by the cadences and keys at the ends of the parts or sections. Again, modulations to dominant and relative keys predominate. Two basic types of tonal design can be identified that distinguish formal designs based on the closing cadence of sections. Forms in which the first section begins and ends in the same key on an AC are said to be *tonally closed* or *sectional;* forms in which the first section ends in a key other than tonic, or that conclude with half cadences, are said to be *tonally open* or *continuous*. The first half of the Minuet in G, given in Example 2.2, ends with a PAC in the tonic key and is thus tonally closed. The second half makes a strong close on the dominant in its first 8 measures followed by a return to tonic and a PAC. The tonal design of the entire minuet is thus tonally closed: I-I: ‖:-I-V-I. If the first half of the minuet had modulated or closed with a HC on dominant (I-V: ‖:V-I), the tonal design would be tonally open or continuous. These two categories of tonal motion are general but useful in distinguishing otherwise similar forms.

Example 2.9 Hymn, "Eternal Father."

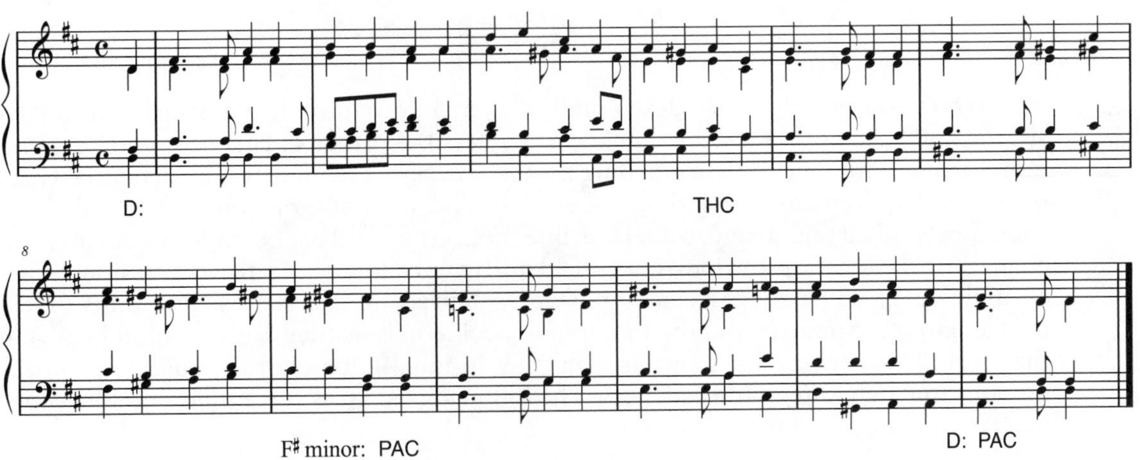

In compositions with more diverse harmonic activity and textures, judgments may vary as to the relative weight of cadences and the tonal motion. The distinctions between passing and structural keys in these cases are sometimes ambiguous, and identifying important cadences and keys may involve a detailed consideration of the tonal motion. Consider the Two-Part Invention in D minor by Bach (Example 2.10), a relatively short but instructive example. In this imitative, continuous composition, no repeat signs or obvious breaks in rhythmic motion immediately clarify the cadences. Attention to sequential activity, harmonic motion, and motivic repetition gives cues to the tonal design of the composition. After the opening statements in D minor, a modulation to the relative major, F, is effected by a sequence and confirmed by extensions, a dominant pedal and a PAC in measures 17–18. Note the use of an octave leap, a dotted rhythm, and an anticipation to emphasize the cadence. Subsequently the emphasis on G♯ and the pedal tone E in measures 26–38 are strong indications of the key of A minor (the dominant minor), confirmed by a similar cadence in measures 37–38. Note the cadential bass line and changes in rhythmic texture in measure 37, which mark the cadence. Measures 38–40 briefly tonicize G minor—observe the use of E♭-F♯-Bb—though G minor is used to effect a return to F major, in measures 40–42. Measure 42 seems to be an arrival in F major, but the motives subsequently incorporate B and C♯ to effect a modulation back to D minor. This modulation is confirmed by the return of the opening motive in the tonic key in measure 44. The deceptive cadence four measures from the end leads to the decisive close on D minor.

The tonal design of this invention may be diagrammed as shown in Figure 2.4. Measure numbers indicate where keys are first established; passing modulations or tonicizations are given in parentheses. The brief emphasis on G minor in measures 23–24, and 38–40 must be understood as tonicizations that are part of the broader tonal motion toward cadential goals. Further analysis of thematic and textural processes as well as tonal motions would be necessary to illuminate the formal structure of the composition. The tonal design as sketched below gives a basis for doing so and summarizes the tonal motions of the composition.

Figure 2.4 *Tonal Design of Example 2.11.*

Measures:	1	10–18	18–38	38–42	42	49	52
Keys:	i	III	III-v	(iv-III)	i		
Cadences:		PAC	PAC			DC	PAC

While awareness of tonal design naturally emanates from detailed harmonic analysis, the ability to peruse a score quickly and assess the principal cadences and keys of a movement is a valuable skill in grasping the tonal design. Familiarity with cadential types is the first requirement in scanning a score. The cadential progressions illustrated above should be studied and memorized. Bass line motions as well as thematic statements and changes in texture are obvious cues in identifying cadences. As the discussion of the examples given above suggests, an important skill in scanning a score is the ability to recognize harmonic activity and the function of accidentals as they are seen (and heard) in the score. Underlying this ability is a fluency in identifying chords, scales, and linear motions that define keys and cadences. The following list gives some tools and tonal cues to learn and use when scanning a score.

1. Scan the bass line looking particularly for cadential bass lines coordinated with changes in rhythm or texture, as well as melodic closure.
2. Scan a score for scalar patterns and accidentals. Distinguish between embellishing chromatic pitches and chromatic pitches that persist or lead to cadences. The following accidentals are strong indicators of scale degree/ harmonic functions:
   a. A sharp or natural sign may be indicative of a leading tone.
   b. A flat sign may be indicative of $\flat\hat{6}$-$\hat{5}$ motion or a $\hat{4}$-$\hat{3}$ motion in a new key.
   c. Consecutive accidentals may be indicative of $\sharp\hat{6}$-$\sharp\hat{7}$ motion in a minor key.

Example 2.10 Bach, *Two-Part Invention in D minor.*

3. **3.** Identify the leading tone of each scale degree and the associated V and vii° chords. Of particular importance is the use of $\sharp\hat{4}$ and $\sharp\hat{2}$ of tonic as indicators of motion to V and V/V respectively, and of $\flat\hat{7}$ as an indication of a V7/IV. In C major for example $\sharp\hat{4}$—F♯—is $\sharp\hat{7}$ in the key of G, the dominant. B♭ is $\flat\hat{7}$ in C but will serve as $\hat{4}$ in F, the subdominant.
4. **4.** Take note of sustained or reiterated pitches, which are normally pedal points that are strong indicators of tonality.

In scanning a score for accidentals, it is necessary to distinguish between chromatic pitches that are embellishments, or part of a chromatic harmony within a key, from those that are used to effect a modulation. Some accidentals that create secondary harmonies are reversed or restored within the phrase, as in Example 2.9, where G♯ is restored to G♮ in measures 5, 10, and 12. Thus the broader harmonic context of C major prevails. In Example 2.10 the persistent use of B♮, G♯, and F♯, and the pedal E are clear visual and aural cues of the move to A minor. Note the scalar patterns based on A melodic minor. While some complex textures will require closer harmonic analysis to clarify tonal motions, sensitivity to the obvious visual cues and attentive listening for cadential patterns can be developed through practice.

Summary

The composite interaction of tonal motion with thematic and textural processes provides a basic framework for formal design. Of these aspects, tonal motion, defined as the harmonic, linear and rhythmic progression toward points of closure or stability, is the most important in delineating cadences and phrases. The pattern of cadences and modulations in a composition and the heirarchy of keys and cadential weight give the tonal design of the composition. Forms may be continuous (tonally open), or they may be sectional (tonally closed). These categories can distinguish various types of tonal design. Though there are many recurring large-scale tonal designs, the specific tonal motions and the interactions with thematic and textural elements is often unique to a given movement. In more extended or complex works, a great variety of modulations and degrees of cadential closure are possible. Basic questions to ask regarding the tonal design include 1) where are the most strongly emphasized cadences; and 2) what factors contribute to the presence and relative weight of the cadences?

SUGGESTED READING

See Schmalfeldt, "Cadential Processes," for an extensive discussion of cadences with a focus on evaded cadences. See Brinkman and Marvin, "The Effect of Modulation" for an interesting discussion of an experimental study on form and closure in tonal music.

Exercises

A. In-class Activities: Play or sing the following familiar tunes and determine the types of cadences at the end of each phrase.

- America the Beautiful ($\frac{4}{4}$)
- Swing Low Sweet Chariot, Opening refrain
- I Got Rhythm ($\frac{2}{4}$) measures 1–8
- Ode to Joy ($\frac{4}{4}$) 8 measures (2 cadences)

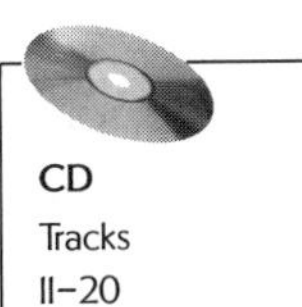
CD
Tracks
11–20

B. Aural Analysis: Listen again to the examples of various cadences given above. Then listen to each of the following short excerpts without the aid of a score and identify by type the cadences that conclude each excerpt : IAC, PAC, HC, PC, or DC. Determine the last two pitches of the bass line in each cadence by letter name.

1. Vivaldi: *The Four Seasons,* Op. 8, No. 1 "Spring" in E major
2. Haydn: Symphony No. 93 in D major, IV
3. Mozart: Symphony No. 40 in G minor, IV
4. Brahms: Piano Quintet in F Minor, Trio in C major, III
5. Tchaikovsky: *Nutcracker Suite,* March, B♭ major
6. Bach: *Brandenburg Concerto No. 3* in G major, I
7. Mozart: *Così fan tutte*, No. 9 in F major
8. Verdi: Overture to *La Traviata*, E major
9. Chopin: *Fantasie*, A♭ major
10. Handel: *Messiah*, Sinfony, E minor

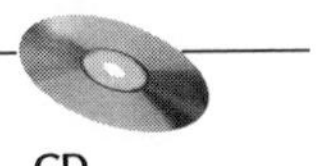
CD
Tracks
5 and 6

C. Analysis of Tonal Design, Exercise 1: Listen several times to the works by Bach and Beethoven shown on the next two pages. Then do the following for each excerpt without using the recordings:

1. Scan the scores for accidentals, scalar passages, and for cadential bass lines. *On the scores,* in the measures indicated, identify the type of cadence, the key by letter name, and provide a roman numeral and figured bass for each cadential progression.
2. Label pedal points and consider which elements of the music mark the cadential arrivals. Are other keys tonicized or treated as passing modulations? Which cadences have the greatest weight and why?

Bach, *The Well-Tempered Clavier,* Book 1, Prelude in E.

Identify cadences in measures 8, 12–13, 14–15, 22, and 23–24. Consider which one of the interior cadences is given the most emphasis or weight. Identify aspects of the music that support your conclusions.

Beethoven, *Piano Sonata,* Op. 2, No. 2 in A major, III: Scherzo.

Identify cadences in measures 4, 8, 12, and 19. Where do cadences occur after measure 19? Is measure 30 a point of cadence? Which key is most remote in relation to tonic? How might the key be related to the other keys to which the music modulates? Which modulation is given the most emphasis in the second half? How is the final cadence metrically disruptive and forceful?

D. The following questions are intended as a guide to the analysis of tonal design in the works cited. Keys should be identified by letter name and mode, for example, A minor. In each composition, consider the relations of the various keys to the original tonic and which keys or cadences are given the most weight or emphasis. Make a diagram showing the tonal design of each composition.

1. *Handel, Aria "Where'er You Walk" from *Semele.*

a. The movement is in the key of ________________.

b. The first modulation of the movement is to the key of ________________. This key is the ________________ of the key of the movement. This modulation takes place in measure ________________.

c. The cadence in measure 7 is a(n) ________________ cadence in the key of ________________.

d. The cadence in measure 19 is a ________________ cadence in the key of ________________.

e. After measure 19, the next key to which the music modulates is ________________. The relation of this key to the key of the movement is ________________. The type of modulation to this key is a ____________.

f. In measure 26 there is a perfect authentic cadence in the key of ______________. The modulation to this key took place in measure __________. The pivot chord for this modulation is a ____________ chord, which functions as ____________ in the new key. (chord symbol) (roman numeral)

2. *Mendelssohn, *Songs Without Words* Op. 62, No.1.

a. The movement is in the key of ______________.

b. The first cadence of the movement in measure 4 is a __________ cadence.

c. The first modulation of the movement is to the key of ____________. The relation of this key to the key of the movement is ____________. The modulation to this key takes place in measure ______________. The chromatic pitch that leads to this new key is ______________.

d. The modulation to the key in the previous question is reinforced by a cadential extension in measure 8–9. In measure 8, on beats 3–4, a chromatic chord referred to as a(n) ____________ leads to a cadential 6/4 in measure 9.

e. In measure 17 the theme in measure 1 returns, but now in the key of ____________. The chord on beats 3–4 of measure 16 is a ____________ chord, a type of chromatic harmony referred to as a ____________.

f. In measure 22, the opening theme returns in the key of ____________. The chord in the first half of measure 22 is a ____________ (chord symbol), which is a ______________ (roman numeral and figured bass).

g. In measure 29–30 there is a ______________ cadence, embellished by a ______________ (roman numeral) on the first beat of measure 30.

E. Additional Exercises. Besides working with the familiar tunes suggested, you may work on score scanning and key/cadence identification in selected compositions of a more elaborate nature, though virtually any piece of tonal music can be used for practice. Baroque works are useful since they will often modulate through several keys. The following works are recommended for practice in scanning scores for modulations and cadences. Here and throughout the text, works in the Burkhart Anthology are indicated with * and those in the Kostka/Graybill Anthology with +.

Bach: *The Well-Tempered Clavier,* Book 1—A♭ major Prelude, G minor Prelude* and Fugue+, and G major Prelude
Bach: *The Well-Tempered Clavier,* Book 2—C minor Prelude+ and G major Prelude
Bach: *Two-Part Inventions** and *French Suite No. 5,* Gavotte
+Corelli: Concerto Grosso, Op. 6, No. 8, IV
Vivaldi: *Gloria,* I
+Haydn: *Creation,* No. 25, "In Native Worth"
*Mozart: Sonata K. 333, I, development section
Beethoven: Op. 2, No. 1, Minuetto
*+Schubert: "Erlkönig"
*Schumann: "Widmung," mm. 1–30
*Brahms: *Intermezzo in C major*
+Wolf: "In dem Schatten"

3 Thematic Design and Phrase Structure

Introduction

In the preceding chapter a definition of a musical phrase was introduced based on the idea of directed motion toward cadential closure. A paradigm of statement/continuation/cadence served as a basis for distinguishing complete musical phrases from subphrases (phrase segments) that may be contained within a phrase. In this chapter we will examine thematic models of phrase structure to further clarify the nature of a musical phrase. The discussion will give an overview of thematic design and process as an aspect of form, and then address how themes are generated and organized. The various models and processes discussed will also be considered in light of some distinctions between Baroque, Classical, and Romantic music.

Thematic Design

A *theme* in music generally refers to the principal melodic lines. Thematic content is such a salient feature of music that many theories of form, particularly those of the nineteenth century, view thematic patterning as the primary basis of musical form. The discussion in the preceding chapter reflects the view that thematic design is best understood in light of the tonal design of a piece of music. The tonal motion toward cadences, however, is supported by the presentation and completion of melodic ideas. Thus, the interaction of thematic and tonal processes is a basic aspect of musical form.

While the manipulation of themes and their constituent motives can be extremely elaborate in some genres and styles, basic thematic processes may be identified that guide our perception of formal design. Given presentation of an initial melodic phrase, subsequent ideas may entail:

- an exact repetition
- a varied repetition or elaboration
- a contrasting idea
- a restatement of an initial theme following contrasting ideas.

Consider the well-known tune in Example 3.1. It contains four distinct phrases marked by clear beginnings and continuations to cadences. The pattern of statement, repetition, presentation of a contrasting idea, and restatement of the initial melodic idea, illustrated here, is evident in a great number of short songs and hymns. By convention, thematic ideas are labeled with alphabetical designations; thus the four phrases of this song comprise a thematic design that would be labeled A A B A.[1] The song is an example of the formal principle of *statement/contrast/restatement*. In this case, statement(s) and restatement of an initial phrase or phrases frame a contrasting middle phrase. This formal

[1] This common design is referred to as a "quatrain" since it contains four phrases, discussed further below.

principle is basic to works of many styles and proportions. Note the HC at the end of phrase B and the return to the tonic harmony at the point of restatement, both of which are critical to emphasizing the thematic return.

By contrast, in Example 3.2 we observe a pattern of a four-measure statement followed by a four-measure contrasting melodic idea. Tonally the first phrase closes on a HC in the submediant, which creates expectation of a continuation and return to the tonic. The PAC in tonic fulfills this expectation and closes this simple hymn. In this case the form may be labeled A B since the two phrases contain different melodic and harmonic patterns. This hymn illustrates the formal principal of *statement/contrast*. The consistent texture and rhythms as well as the continuous tonal motion give coherence to this short hymn and join the phrases into a single unit.

Example 3.1 *Drink to Me Only.*

Example 3.2 *Hymn, "St. Flavian"* from *Day's Psalter 1562.*

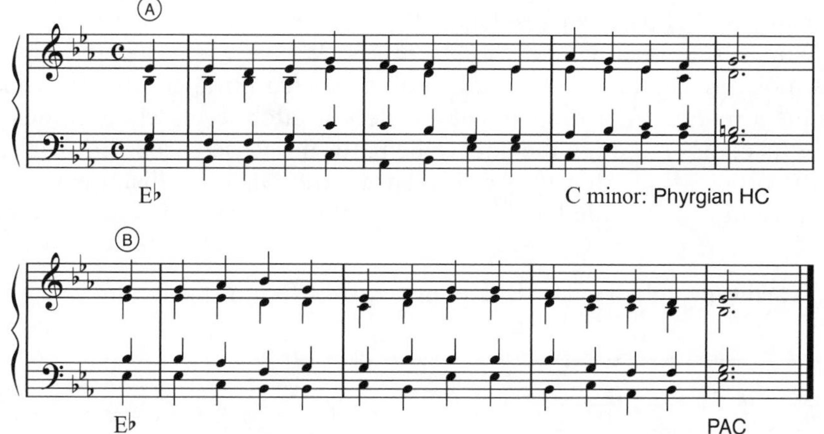

The hymn "Eternal Father" (see Example 2.10) illustrates the formal principle of *statement/elaboration*. Each of the phrases utilizes similar rhythms and some recurring intervallic patterns such that its thematic design may be labeled A^1 A^2 A^3. Conversely, the contrasting melodic patterns and tonal motions of each phrase suggest an A B C design. Our perception and labeling of a formal design thus may vary according to which elements of a composition we consider or privilege in our analysis.

In comparison to the clear phrase divisions of the preceding examples, the Two-Part Invention in D minor by Bach, discussed in Chapter 2, has a great number of repetitions and elaborations of the motives presented in the first two measures. Clearly separated phrases and thematic contrasts are not evident. This fact reflects a Baroque practice of composing imitative works using the initial motives throughout. The monothematic design and continuous rhythmic motion results in an example of a *through-composed* form; the basic thematic process is that of continuous elaboration of a musical idea. Nonetheless, restatements of the opening two measures at points of cadence are strong indicators of phrase articulation and give cues for determining formal design.

In each of the examples discussed, thematic and tonal design are coordinated and complement one another in articulating phrase structure. The harmonic progressions and cadences result in distinct tonal designs in each work. These works illustrate thematic designs and processes that can be found in compositions of small and large proportions, and may also apply to the generating of phrase structure to which we now turn our attention.

Motives and Themes

A musical *motive*, a short melodic idea characterized by rhythm, contour, and interval succession, is often identified as the basic building block of musical phrases. Such is the case in many styles of music, though not all, as will be discussed. The length of a motive may vary from a few notes to 1 or 2 measures of music. A motive is recognized on the basis of repetition, and rhythm often is the most salient feature of a motive. The Overture from *Messiah* by Handel, for example (Example 3.13), uses a motivic dotted rhythm extensively while the contour and pitch patterns are varied. Other themes may exhibit one or more recurring pitch patterns that serve as motives. Example 3.14 from Cantata No. 4 by Bach shows two distinct motives in its opening measures: a neighbor-note figure and a scalar figure, labeled *x* and *y* respectively.

The opening theme of the second movement of Tchaikovsky's Symphony No. 4 illustrates additional techniques of motivic variation. Measures 1–2 present a melodic idea comprised of two motives, labeled *x* and *y*. Note how contour and metric placement are distinguishing features of these motives. Motive *x* is a descending, upbeat pattern, while motive *y* is an ascending/descending pattern initiated on a downbeat. Measure 3 contains a repetition of motive *x* at a different pitch level, while in measure 4 motive *y* retains its contour, though the intervallic pattern is varied according to the harmonic and melodic progression. Measures 6–7 illustrate motivic embellishment, as the descending interval of motive *y* is filled in with passing tones creating a similarity to motive *x*.

Example 3.3 Motivic variation, Tchaikovsky, Symphony No. 4, II, mm. 1–21.

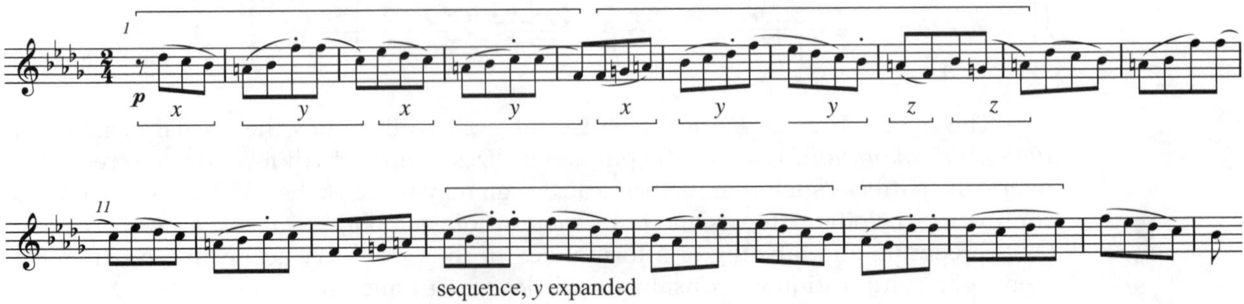

Upon repetition of the entire melody in measures 14–19, this two-measure idea is used in *sequence*, a repetition of a motive or melodic idea at different pitch levels. This sequential repetition contains a *melodic* or *mirror inversion*, a reversal in contour of the first two pitches of motive *y*. Sequence, embellishment, inversion and fragmentation are common techniques of motivic variation. Strict diminution and augmentation of a motive, in which note values are uniformly reduced or expanded, and retrograde, in which the pitch patterns are given in reverse order, are also encountered. These techniques will be addressed in subsequent chapters.

While many themes will have unique and distinct motivic ideas, conventional patterns or figures such as scales, arpeggios, and repeated notes may serve as motives. However, the term *figure* generally is used to refer to conventional patterns that are repeated throughout a passage or composition but are not considered motivic. Most often figures are accompaniment patterns such as those found in Example 3.8. Conversely, motives are not only repeated but are also subjected to variation or development as described above. Thus repetition *and* development are defining characteristics of a motive.

Motivic patterns are manifested quite clearly in the examples cited thus far. Often, however, motivic pitch patterns are "hidden" within the music, in which case the motives may be understood as underlying linear motions that are elaborated by the actual melodic lines. In Example 3.4, the variation by Bach is based on a motivic bass-line pattern that is embellished by *diminution* or melodic/rhythmic elaborations of the original bass given below the excerpt and shown by the circled pitches.[2] Measure 2 of Example 3.5 can be understood as an elaboration of the motion from D–B, a continuation of the descending third motion of measure 1. The actual rhythms and pitches of this measure thus can be understood as diminutions of the descending third motive. While these examples are relatively straightforward, the analysis of concealed motives and hidden repetitions can be quite complex as one seeks to identify underlying linear patterns at various levels of structure. The analysis of underlying pitch motives gives insight into the unity and coherence of a composition and may amplify or clarify an analysis of formal structure.

Example 3.4 Bach, *Goldberg Variations,* Var. 1, beginning.

a. Variation 1. in 1 Clar.

b. Contrabass.

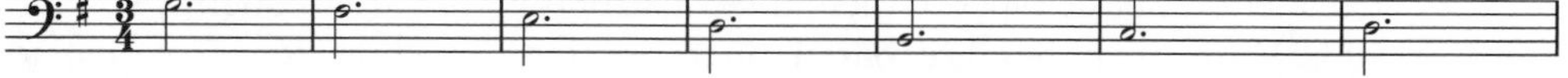

[2] As noted above, diminution may also refer to uniform reduction of note values to compress a motive such that its length is shortened. The opposite alteration, augmentation, expands the length of the motive. In neither case are pitches added. These techniques are addressed further in Chapters 11 and 12.

Motivic analysis in its most basic form usually entails identification of motives, their recurrences, and the ways in which they are varied. Such descriptive analysis can be helpful in delineating sections and phrases of a composition, and can be a means of observing basic compositional techniques. The mere labeling of motives does not, however, address the more important questions of phrase functions and the formal context in which the motives are being used. Moreover, not all themes are generated by motivic repetitions and elaborations of one or two short motives. The opening eight measures of the Mozart Piano Concerto No. 23 (Example 3.5) illustrate this point. Within this theme, all the measures, apart from the repetition in measure 6, contain distinct rhythmic ideas, held together by strong linear and harmonic progressions. Here, as in many eighteenth and nineteenth-century themes, short melodic ideas of a few measures are joined to create phrases. These melodic ideas may contain distinct motives that can be subject to elaboration later in the movement, but the phrases are not generated solely by motivic repetitions. In the analysis of musical form, then, the analysis of motives may inform our understanding of segmentation, grouping, and phrase functions. In order to understand these formal elements, basic processes and models for generating phrases must be considered.

Example 3.5 Mozart, Piano Concerto in A major, K. 488, I, mm. 1–8.

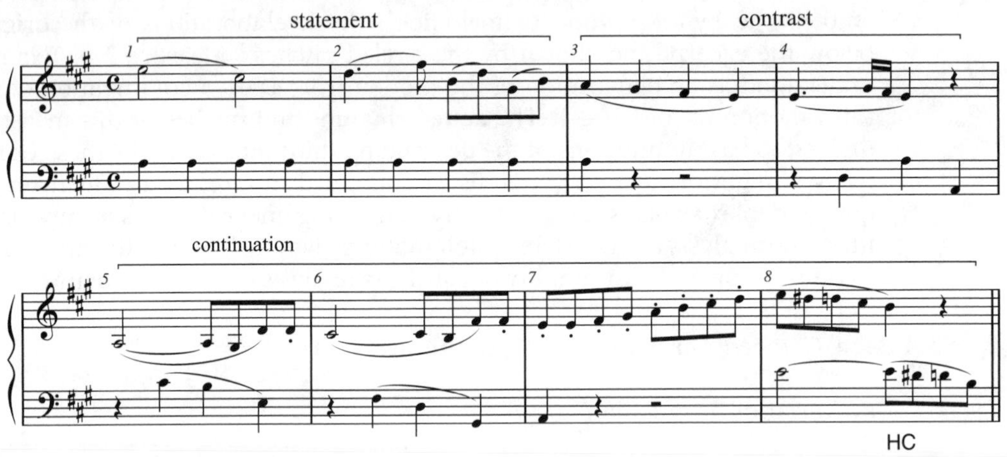

Thematic Models of Phrase Structure

The structure of a phrase is a composite of its length (indicated in measures), the grouping structure of its segments, and the functions of the various segments. Phrases can be as short as one measure or as long as 32 measures or more, though such extremes are rare. There is no standard length to a musical phrase, though arguably the most common phrase structures are 4 or 8 measures long. Certainly phrases of irregular (asymmetrical) lengths of 3, 5, or 7 measures are found, but phrase lengths of even numbers, usually multiples of 2 or 4, permeate a great deal of dance and folk music as well as Classical/Romantic music of the eighteenth and nineteenth century. Moreover, many irregular or asymmetrical phrases, as will be demonstrated, can be explained as contractions or expansions of duple units. While phrases may be structured in a great number of specific ways, the following discussion of phrase structure will focus on basic types of thematic construction that are frequently encountered.

Many melodies are based on repetitions of short ideas of one to two measures. Example 3.6 illustrates this process in some familiar tunes. Each of these phrases is based on varied repetition of two-measure melodic patterns that group into phrases. Example 3.6a might be analyzed as a pair of four-measure phrases, but measures 5–8 of the melody have a sense of continuing rather than beginning or initiating the melodic and harmonic motion again. The underlying harmonic progressions group the four-measure units into a larger

Example 3.6 *Phrases built on repetition of two-measure rhythmic patterns.*

a. *For He's a Jolly Good Fellow.*

b. *My Country 'Tis of Thee.*

phrase with strong cadential arrival in measure 8. Note that "My Country" is based on duple groupings but is a six-measure phrase, which is not as common as four or eight-measure phrase structures. The symmetry and repetitions of rhythmic motives are characteristic of many popular folk tunes.

Analytic Note: The numbers placed within measures in these and subsequent examples are used to denote the length of phrases; actual measure numbers will be placed above the music. The brackets show the grouping of the phrase segments or *subphrases*. Recall that a subphrase is a short segment of music, usually of two to four measures in length, that is part of a larger, complete phrase.

Another process frequently used to generate phrases is that of sequential repetition. A sequence, as noted previously, results from a systematic repetition of a musical idea at different pitch levels.[3] Typically, sequences contain three statements of an idea—the initial one and two repetitions, as illustrated in Example 3.7. Here, following a statement and repetition of a tonic triad in measures 1–2, a harmonic sequence of descending fifths is heard in conjunction with a melodic sequence in stepwise motion. Following the sequence, a cadential progression brings the theme to a tonicized half cadence. Often, as in this example, the cadential progression is marked by a distinct cadential melodic idea. The use of sequence as a formal-thematic process normally entails repeated melodic and harmonic patterns as in Example 3.7 (see also Example 3.3). Sequences serve as the basic process for generating many nineteenth-century themes and are an important process in Baroque phrase structures.

Example 3.7 Dvorak, Symphony No. 8, IV, principal theme.

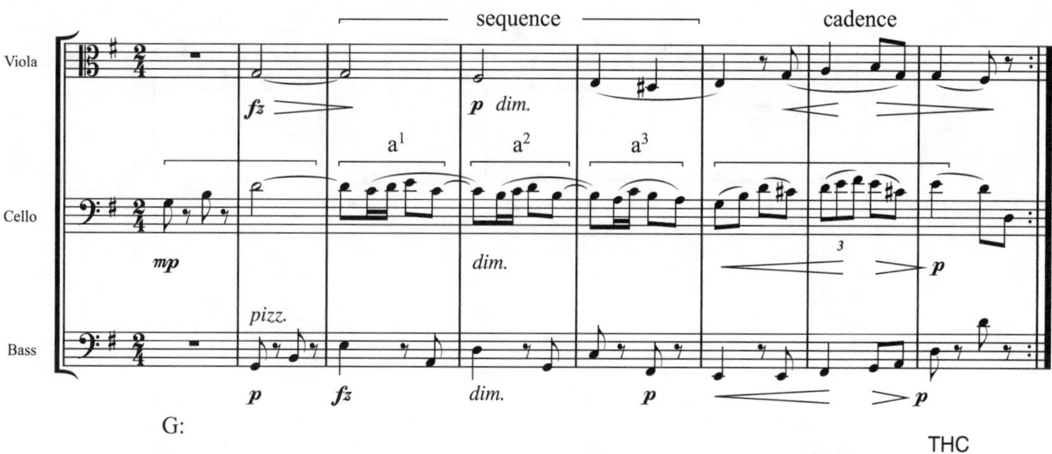

[3] Summaries of different types of sequences may be found in most harmony and counterpoint texts. See, for example, Aldwell and Schachter, *Harmony and Voice Leading, 3rd edition*, 246 ff.

SENTENCE STRUCTURES

A common model of phrase structure is the *sentence*.[4] A sentence is a phrase comprised of a statement, a repetition, and a continuation that leads to a cadence. The three parts of a sentence are normally in proportions of 1:1:2 or multiples thereof. These proportions are also a defining characteristic of a sentence.

Example 3.8 gives a number of phrases that illustrate sentence structures. Though in different meters and styles, each of these themes has a similar grouping structure based on the proportions of 2:2:4. The statement/repetition comprises the first half of a sentence. In each theme we hear an initial melodic idea of two measures followed by a repetition of the idea. The repetition may be 1) an *exact repetition*, as in the Verdi excerpt, or a *varied repetition* as in the Beethoven; 2) a *response-repetition*, as in the Chopin excerpt, in which a transposed repetition or varied repetition of the first two-measure idea occurs *with a change in harmony;* and 3) *sequential repetition*. The harmonic structure may vary in the first half of a sentence, though I/V or I-V/V-I progressions normally shape the tonal motion. Example 3.8a also illustrates the use of a *melodic complement,* in which inverting the melodic line varies the repetition—in this case a descending varied repetition follows an initial ascending statement. Contour and rhythm are the most salient features retained in melodic complements, which may be found in many thematic types.[5] Note in the Chopin Mazurka (Example 3.8b) how a two-measure repetition in measures 1–4 is grouped as one four-measure unit by the continuous harmonic motion over the tonic pedal, though the melody contains a *melodic sequence* that delineates two-measure segments.

Example 3.8 *Sentence Structures: Statement/Repetition—Continuation/Cadence.*

a. Beethoven, Contredanse.

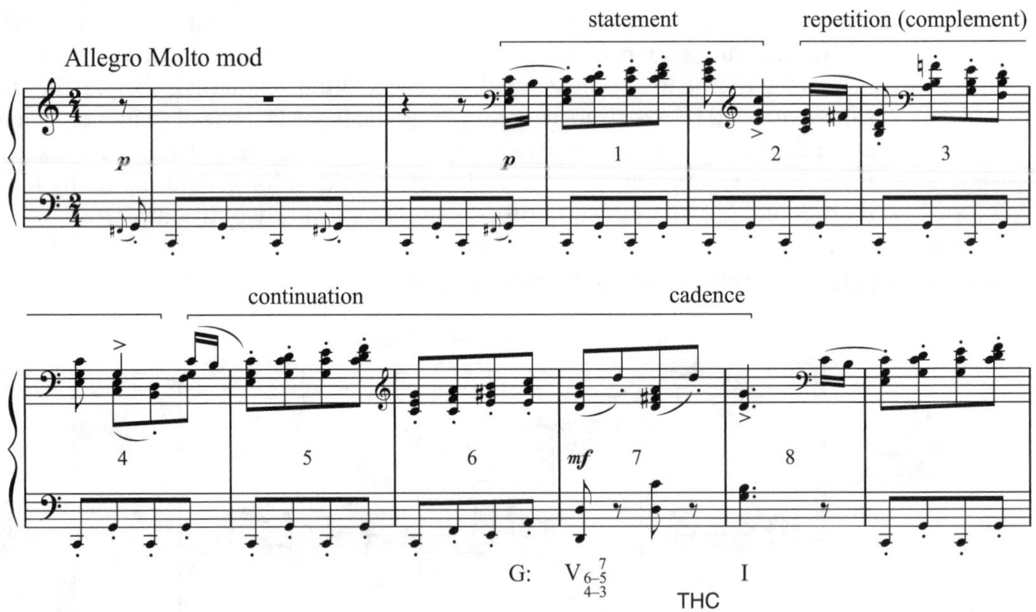

[4] The composer Arnold Schoenberg, who was interested in how motivic processes shaped complete themes, developed the concept of a sentence. See *Fundamentals of Musical Composition*, 20–63, for a discussion of sentence and period construction as viewed by Schoenberg. Musical phrases and periods are sometimes compared to sentences in language, a more general use of the term than employed here.

[5] See Meyer, *Style and Music*, 246 ff., for a discussion of complementary melodic construction.

b. Chopin, Mazurka, Op. 67, No. 3, C major.

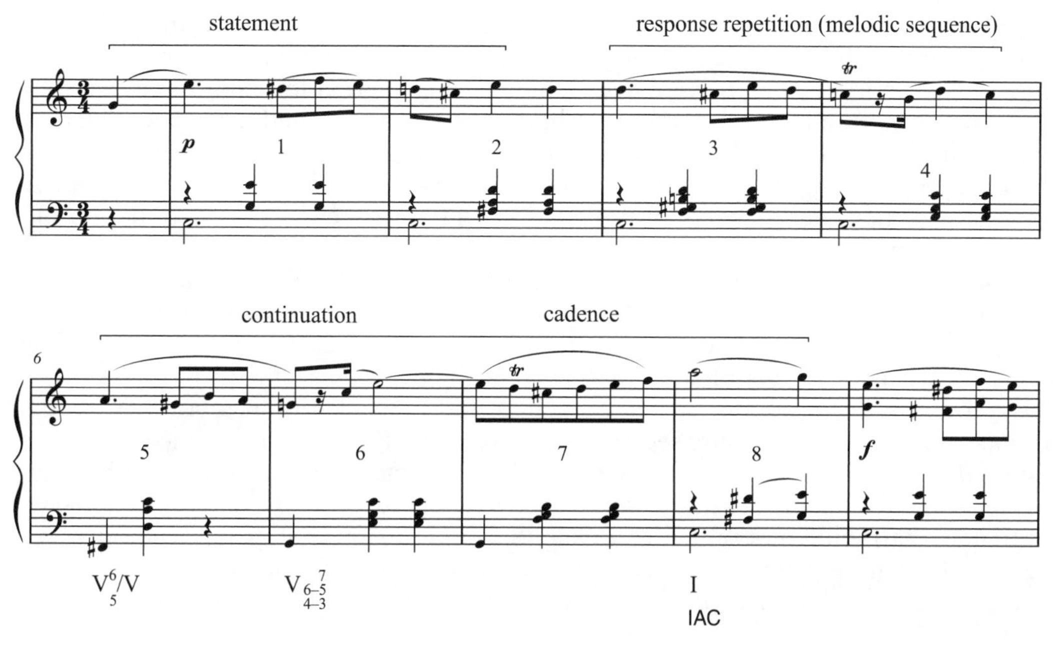

c. Verdi, *Aida,* "Celeste Aida," mm. 1–8.

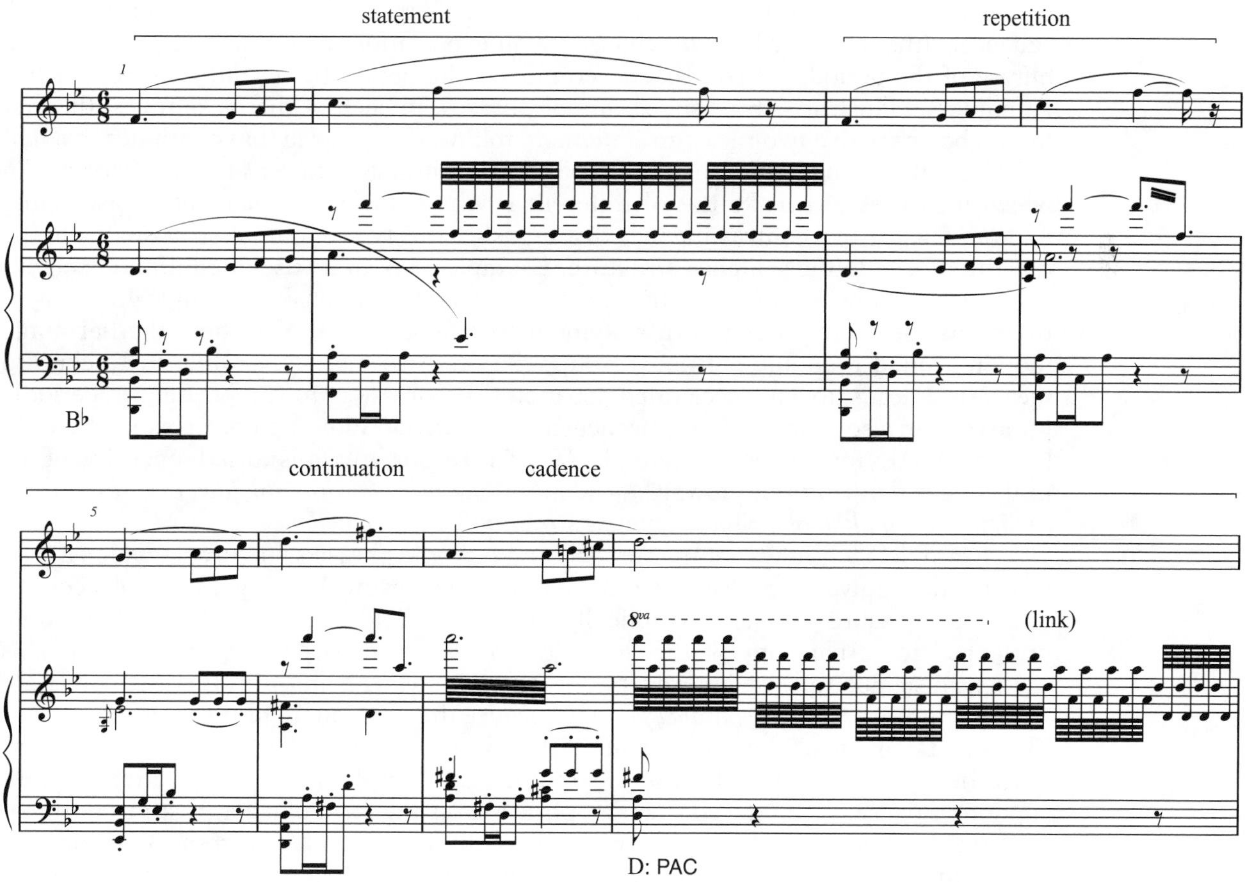

statement

repetition

1

B♭

continuation cadence

5

8va

(link)

D: PAC

Following a statement/repetition, the second half of a sentence is a *continuation* rather than an initiation or beginning. A continuation phrase is shaped by one or more of the following processes: a) *fragmentation*, whereby the length of phrase segments is shortened by using motivic fragments from the initial idea, presented in varied repetitions or sequence; b) an increase in harmonic tension by using chordal inversions and non-tonic or chromatic harmonies; c) an increase in harmonic rhythm, sometimes sequential; d) an increase in the rhythmic activity by use of shorter durations; and e) introduction of a cadential progression. Any or all of these processes may be used to convey a sense of continuation function, but a cadential progression will always close the continuation of a complete theme.

Bach's Minuet in G, measures 1–8, from the *Notebook for Anna Magdalena Bach* (Example 2.2), is an excellent example of an eight-measure sentence that uses all of these processes. These processes give the continuation a sense of acceleration as smaller fragments group into a segment longer than each of the first two segments of the sentence. This produces the grouping structure and proportions described above. Note that Example 3.8c uses two-measure segments in its continuation, but the absence of the brief rest (and breath) in measure 6 and the modulation suggest that measures 4–8 be heard and performed as a four-measure continuation to cadence. Similarly, Example 3.8b has a continuous harmonic motion using a cadential progression that groups measures 5–8 together. Though sentences, like any phrase, may be expanded to larger proportions, the processes and functions described above will be evident.

PERIODS

Another approach to phrase construction is to state a melodic idea and continue with an idea that completes a progression toward cadence. Such phrases often occur in pairs to create what is termed a *period*. The first phrase of a period, the *antecedent*, leads to a weak cadence, either a HC or IAC, which creates an expectation of continuation. The second phrase of the period, the *consequent*, completes the period by reaching a stronger AC. Example 3.9 illustrates three such pairs of phrases. In each of these examples, the first phrase begins with a two-measure statement, followed by an idea that continues to a half cadence. The second half of the phrase often is a contrasting idea as in Example 3.9a, in which measures 3–4 make use of different rhythms and a complementary ascending motion. The use of a contrasting idea distinguishes this type of phrase structure from the repetition used in the sentence structure. Example 3.9b, in its use of continuous eighth notes, has a strong feeling of continuity from measures 2–4, masking a duple grouping of the phrase segments based on a statement/contrast-cadence. Note how the harmonic motion around the tonic harmony groups the first two measures, while the pickup to measure 3 leads to an accelerated harmonic progression toward cadence. Periodic phrases may also make use of four-measure *statement/response* patterns as in the well-known "Ode To Joy" shown in Example 3.9c. The response entails varied repetition of the initial ideas that continues toward a cadence. *Whether a contrasting idea or a response is used, the second half of a periodic phrase structure leads to a cadence.*

Example 3.9d shows another model for a periodic phrase structure, in which a contrasting idea is given in measure 2 and continues in measure 3, giving a sense of a continuous four-measure phrase. Rhythmically the phrase divides into 1 + 2 + 1, though the prolonged tonic harmony of the first three measures masks this segmentation. This example also illustrates an antecedent phrase that ends with an IAC rather than an HC.

Examples 3.9a–d are *parallel periods* because the consequent phrase initially sounds like a restatement of the antecedent. The restatement after the weak cadence of the antecedent phrase has the effect of "beginning again" or of "starting over" after an interruption or pause. When the consequent phrase takes the form of a contrasting continuation, rather than a restatement, the result is a *contrasting period*. Example 3.2 above is a good example of an eight-measure, contrasting period. In Example 3.9e the consequent phrase contains processes associated with continuation: a contrasting melodic idea begins over a harmonically unstable 4/2 chord. In this particular contrasting period, the consequent initially closes with an IAC, which allows for a repeat of the consequent to reach a more conclusive PAC. The result is an asymmetrical period of three phrases. Finally, modulating periods, defined as those in which the consequent phrase closes on a PAC or HC in a new key, are not uncommon. As Example 3.9a shows, in major keys the modulation often takes the form of a move to the dominant, or to the relative major in minor keys.[6]

Analytic Note: *Symmetry*, when used with reference to musical phrases, is distinguished in different ways. It may apply to a single phrase or a group of phrases. A phrase is symmetrical if its subphrases (phrase segments) are of equal length or multiples, or its length is an even number. A phrase group or period is symmetrical if it contains an even number of phrases of the same length. Conversely, a phrase is asymmetrical if it is has an odd number of measures; a period or phrase group is asymmetrical if it has an odd number of phrases, *or* if the phrases are of unequal length. Other distinctions are possible.

Example 3.9 *Periodic Phrase Structures.*

a. Haydn, Symphony No. 104, II, mm. 1–8.

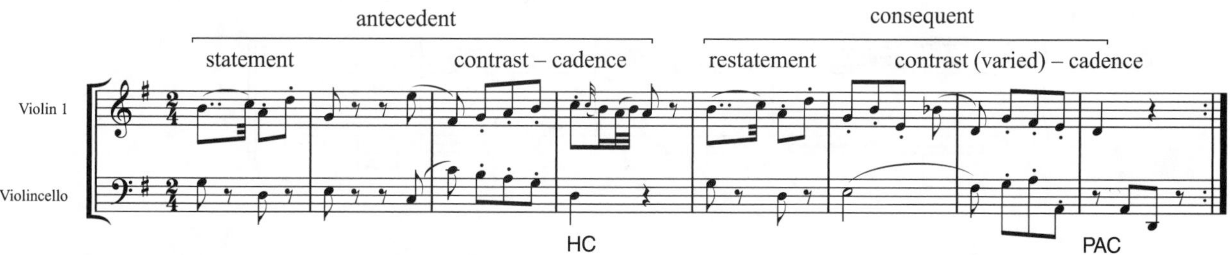

b. Tchaikovsky, Nutcracker Suite, Overture, mm. 1–8.

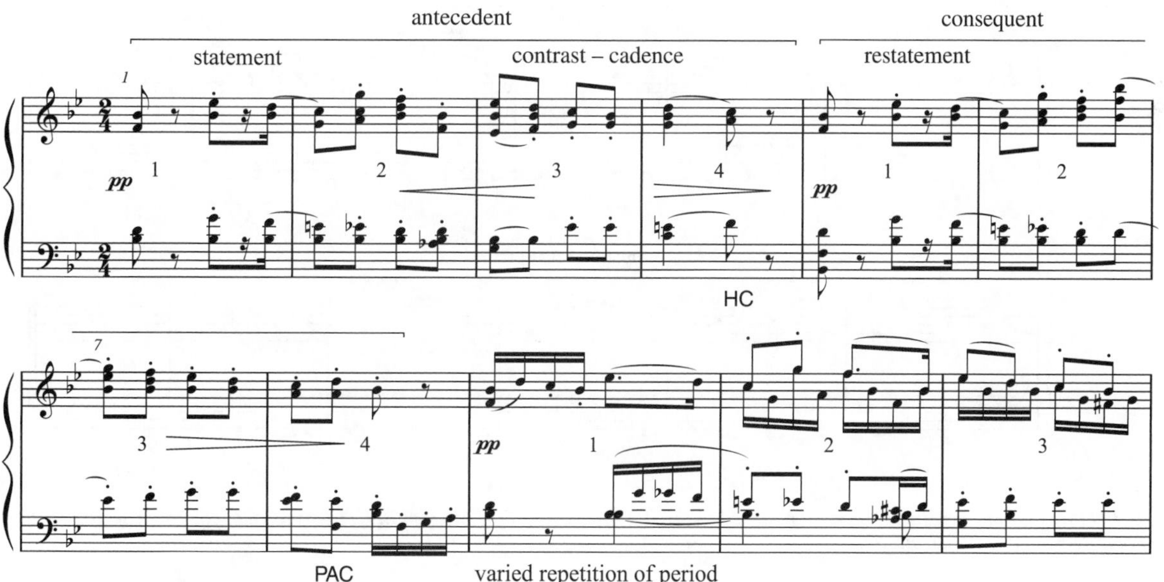

[6] Arguably Example 3.9 closes with a THC, though the strong cadential progression gives the effect of a modulation.

c. Beethoven, *Ode to Joy,* mm. 1–8

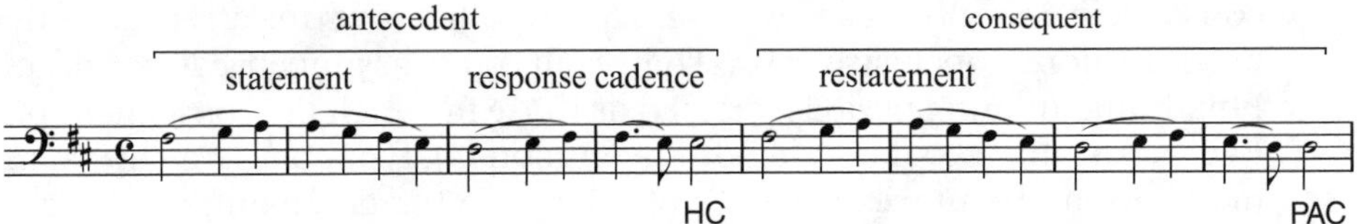

d. Schumann, "Knecht Ruprecht," Op. 68, No. 12, mm. 1–8.

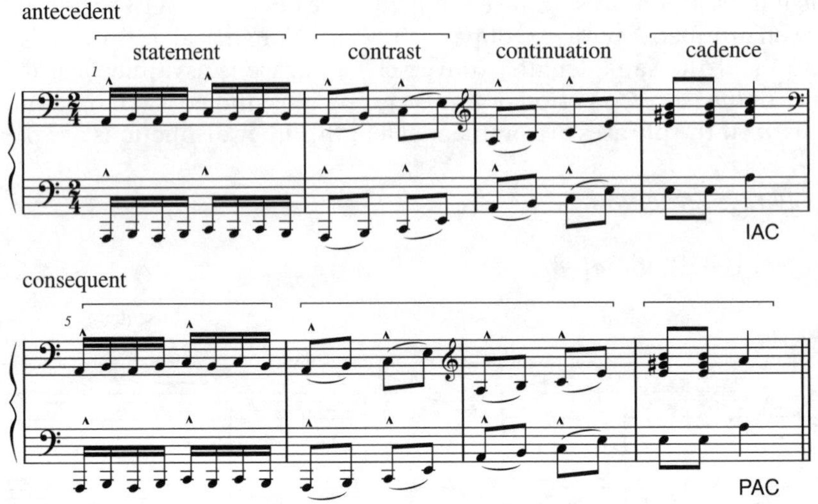

e. Weissenborn, *Method for Bassoon,* Practical Exercises, No. 5, contrasting Period.

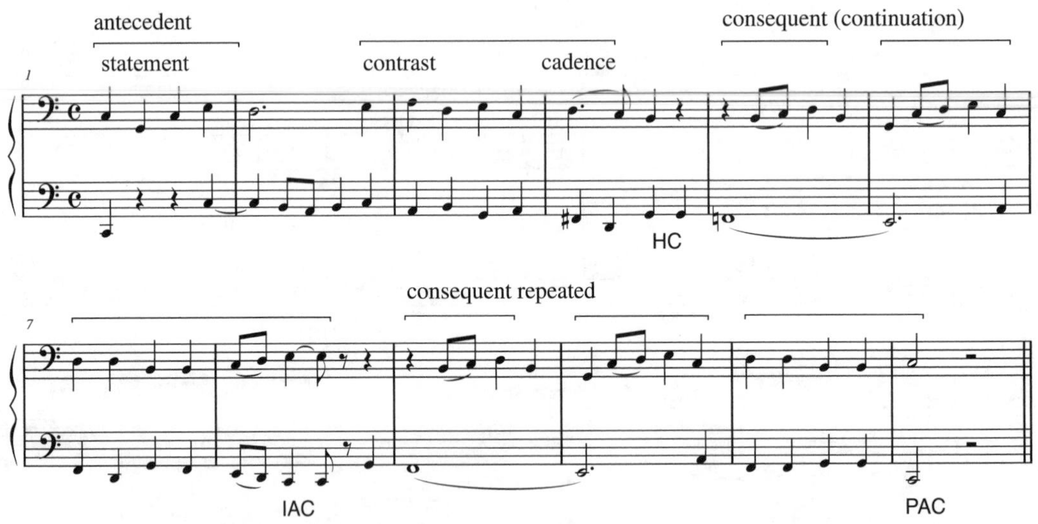

A sentence and a complete period may be understood as contrasting models for constructing a theme. The sentence is often identified thematically as an a a b pattern (statement/repetition/continuation) while the period is characterized as an a b, a b′ pattern (statement/response or contrast; restatement/varied response) comprised of two phrases.

The two phrase types are not necessarily opposing models, however, and in practice their characteristics are often combined. The contrasting period, for example, makes use of a continuation function in the consequent phrase, a function associated with a sentence structure. Similarly, a sentence is one way of constructing a phrase and as such may be used in the phrases of a period. The parallel period shown in Example 3.10a contains a small sentence structure in each of its phrases, evident in the 1+1+2 proportions, the use of fragmentation and the increased harmonic rhythm in its continuation.

Example 3.10b shows a sixteen-measure period in which two phrases may be perceived in the antecedent and in the consequent phrase for a total of four phrases. Such phrase combinations are referred to as *double periods*. In this example, the antecedent and the consequent contain two four-measure phrases that are small sentence structures as well. Note the importance of the PAC of measure 16 in contrast to the IAC of measure 8, and the parallel thematic material of measures 1 and 9 in conveying a sense of a large, parallel period.

Example 3.10 *Periods using sentence structures.*

a. Mozart, Piano Sonata in A major, K. 331, I, mm. 1–8.

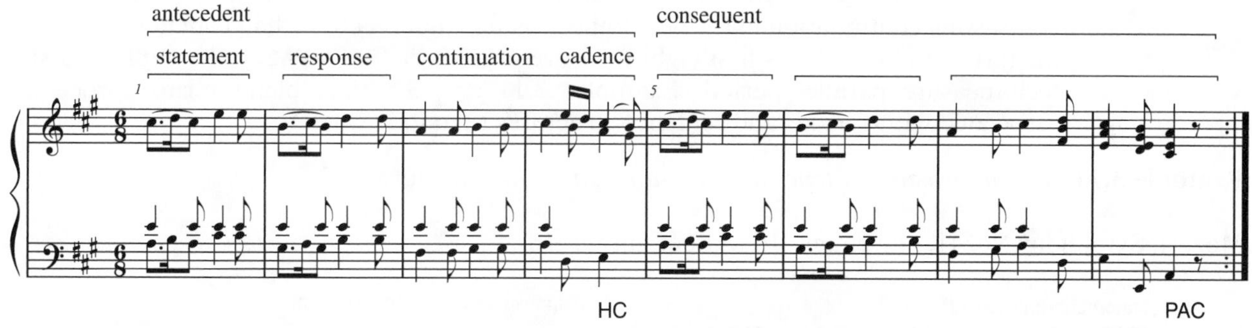

b. Schubert, Impromptu No. 2 from Four Impromptus, Op. 42, mm. 1–16.

More common than sixteen-measure double periods are phrase combinations of 16 measures that comprise sentence structures or periods, or a combination of both. The eight-measure sentence structure that opens the Chopin Mazurka shown in Example 3.8b is followed by a restatement of the phrase that concludes with a PAC. The two eight-measure sentence structures complete a sixteen-measure parallel period. Similarly, Example 3.8c is an eight-measure sentence that forms the first half of a parallel period.

By contrast, Example 3.11 illustrates a sixteen-measure sentence that modulates to the dominant. Here the first eight measures may be understood as a four-measure statement and a four-measure response repetition, and the second eight measures as a continuation, forming a sixteen-measure sentence with 4:4:8 proportions. *Using two ideas in the first four-measure statement and in the subsequent response expands the sentence structure.* Consequently, it is entirely plausible to hear the first eight measures as a parallel period, with the statement/response repetition forming an antecedent/consequent relationship. Moreover, the eight-measure continuation of Example 3.11 is also a sentence structure embedded within the larger sixteen-measure sentence. As this example illustrates, the halves of a sentence structure may have sufficient harmonic activity to be understood as complete phrases.[7] See also, for example, measures 1–4 of Example 3.8.

An additional example, the opening theme of the Mozart Piano Concerto in A major (Example 3.5) begins with a statement/contrast in its first four measures, followed by a contrasting continuation in the next four measures that reaches a half cadence. A restatement (not shown) of this first eight-measure phrase reaches a PAC and completes a sixteen-measure parallel period. Examples 3.11 and 3.5 thus blend formal processes associated with periods and sentence structures in unique ways.[8]

Example 3.11 *Sixteen-measure sentence incorporating an eight-measure period.*

Mozart, Symphony No. 41, movement III, Minuet, mm. 1–16.

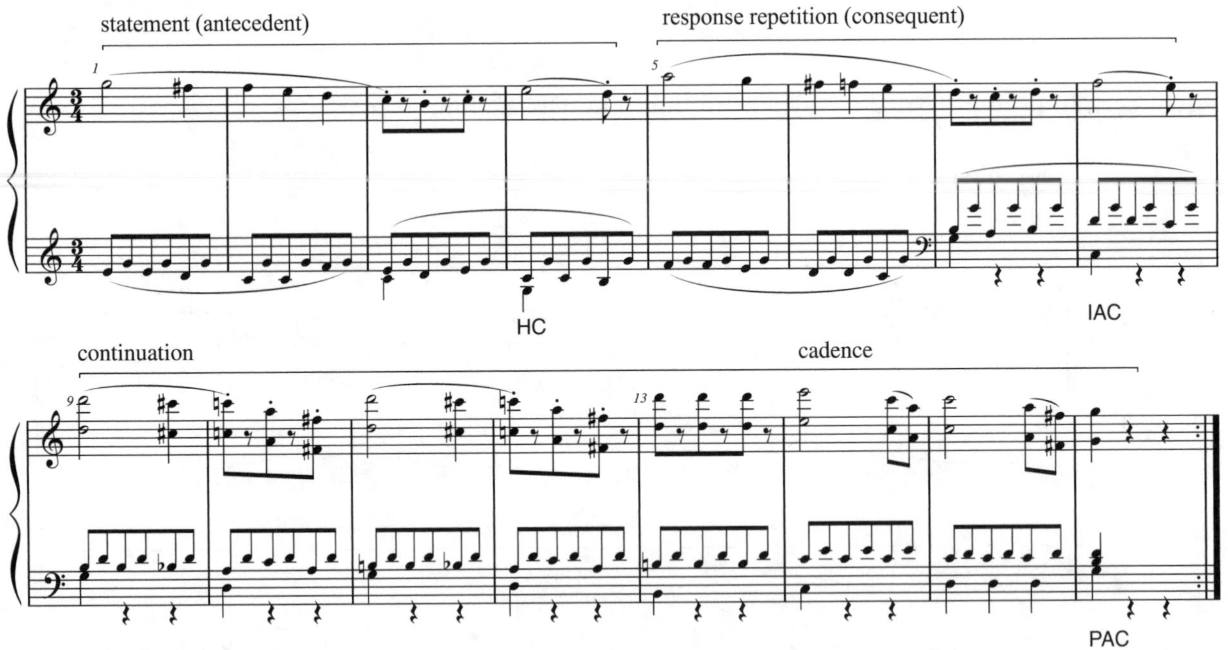

[7] Caplin refers to the use of two-bar, contrasting ideas in the first half of a sentence as a "compound basic idea," in Caplin, *Classical Form*, 61. In his view, contrary to the interpretation above, a compound basic idea lacks sufficient harmonic activity to constitute an antecedent phrase. For examples similar to 3.11 see Mozart, Piano Concerto in G, K. 453, I, mm. 1–16, and Beethoven, Piano Concertos Nos. 1–3, opening theme.

[8] One might hear the first 8 measures of Example 3.5 as two phrases, therefore this might be considered a double period. The first four measures conclude with IV-I progression however, which may be understood as a larger motion to the dominant at the half cadence in measure 8.

Analytic Note: The preceding example, as well as others cited below, raises the question of what constitutes a phrase and when completion of a thematic idea is indicative of a cadence. Does a phrase always close with a cadence? How long does a phrase have to be? As was discussed in Chapter 2, any discrete segment of music from a motive to large section of music might be considered a phrase in the sense of having a distinct shape, and a clear beginning and ending. The view espoused here is that if we are to distinguish these large and small classes of musical events, we must not use the term phrase at different levels. Thus the distinctions between subphrases and phrases have been introduced based on the traditional notion of cadential arrival as a hallmark of phrase completion. As is often observed, interesting or complex music may contain ambiguities that allow multiple interpretations. The emphasis in analyzing phrase structure should be on processes and functions, and on the grouping of segments.

PHRASE REPETITION

Phrases also may be grouped together on the basis of simple repetition. Examples 3.12a and b show pairs of phrases in which the second phrase is merely a repetition of the first, with identical cadences at the end of each phrase. Such repetitions, whether ending on half or authentic cadences, create an expectation of continuation and/or contrast. In the Vivaldi example, the irregular length of the phrases and "echo effect" are typical of much Baroque music, and the repetitions of simple diatonic motives in homophonic textures are Italianate characteristics. In the excerpt from the Beethoven String Quartet, Op. 131, the varied repetition of both the antecedent (shown) and the consequent phrases result in the expansion of a sixteen-measure period into a thirty-two measure, two-part form. Similarly, an entire period may be repeated and varied upon repetition. A repeated period, or one with repeated phrases in each half, should not be confused with the double period described above, in which the antecedent and consequent are each composed of two different phrases.

FORTSPINNUNG MODELS/PHRASE GROUPS

The sentence and periodic phrase structures described in the previous paragraph may be found in Baroque music, though they are more often found in late eighteenth-century and nineteenth-century music. This reflects the influence of popular dances and songs on

Example 3.12 *Repeated Phrases.*

a. Vivaldi, Concerto, Op. 8, No. 1 in E major, "La Primavera" ("Spring"), mm. 1–6.

(This excerpt continues on p. 50.)

(Example 3.12a, continued.)

b. Beethoven, String Quartet, Op. 131, IV, mm. 1–16.

antecedent

1

p

HC

repetition of antecedent

9

HC

classical and romantic music, in which clearly articulated phrases and subphrases are characteristic. Conversely, much Baroque music is characterized by continuous rhythmic motion and the use of related motivic patterns in generating melodic lines. These commonly noted "motor rhythmic" and "monothematic" aspects of Baroque style reflect an aesthetic in which continuity of motion and expressive effect is valued or sought. As a result, Baroque phrases often use a theme type described as *fortspinnung*[9] or "spinning out." Though this

---

[9] This term is attributed to the German musicologist Wilhelm Fischer. See Rothstein, *Phrase Rhythm*, 127.

term is often associated with the use of sequence, it also implies more general processes of statement and varied repetitions of motives. In this type of fortspinnung, short phrases often run one into the next until a decisive cadence is reached. A good example of this process is the opening of the overture from *Messiah* by Handel (Example 3.13).

In this example, the continued use of the dotted rhythm, characteristic of the French overture, gives the impression of overlapping or continuous short phrases that drive to a decisive cadence in measure 12. Given the repetitious motivic rhythm, the harmonic and linear motion and the changes in duration in the bass line or melody are most important in delineating the phrase structure. Root position triads, melodic descents, and $\hat{5}$–$\hat{1}$ bass line motions in measures 4 and 6 give brief impressions of cadential arrival, particularly in measure 6 where the half note duration and descent in the melody to F♯ emphasize a tonicization of D major. The rhythmic motion in the inner voices counters the change to a melodic half note in measure 8 that marks an arrival on dominant. A strong sense of drive to cadence is conveyed in measures 9–10 by the trill and rhythms in contrary lines, but the IAC and continuation of the dotted rhythm, as in measure 8, propels the music forward. The strongest and clearest sense of cadential arrival, however, occurs in measures 11–12, marked by 1) the reiterated bass note C in measure 11 that resolves to the dominant; 2) the anticipation of the resolution to V; and 3) a sustained dominant chord in the upper voices in measure 12. This Phrygian half cadence is connected to the next measure by the rhythmic motion after the point of cadence.

The distinction between phrase and subphrase, and the grouping boundaries of Example 3.13 are less obvious than in many of the examples given above. Each point of arrival cited may be heard as a continuation or an overlap that groups with the next segment. Thus measures 1–6 could be grouped together and analyzed as a 3+3 grouping with overlap at measure 4; measures 1–10 may be grouped together on the basis of tonal motion away from and back to tonic with measures 10–12 serving as an extension. In performance, such passages require thoughtful consideration of dynamics and pacing, which affect our perception of small and large units. However one may group these segments, they may be understood as small phrases that group together into a complete unit of 12 measures. A series of phrases that group together on the basis of continuation and/or motivic connections without the cadential relations of a period are referred to as a *phrase group*. In a phrase group, as illustrated in Example 3.13, cadences may vary as to strength and weight; a final conclusive cadence marks the ending of the group.

Example 3.13 Handel, *Messiah,* Sinfony, mm. 1–12.

Some phrases in baroque music will entail a fortspinnung based literally on one or more sequences that lead to a cadence. A good example of this is found in the instrumental introduction of an aria from Bach's Cantata No. 4, shown in Example 3.14. Here, a statement and two sequential repetitions generate measures 1–3 in a sequence of ascending thirds—I-III-V—leading to a PAC in measures 4–5.

Example 3.14

a. Bach, Cantata No. 4, III, mm. 1–5.

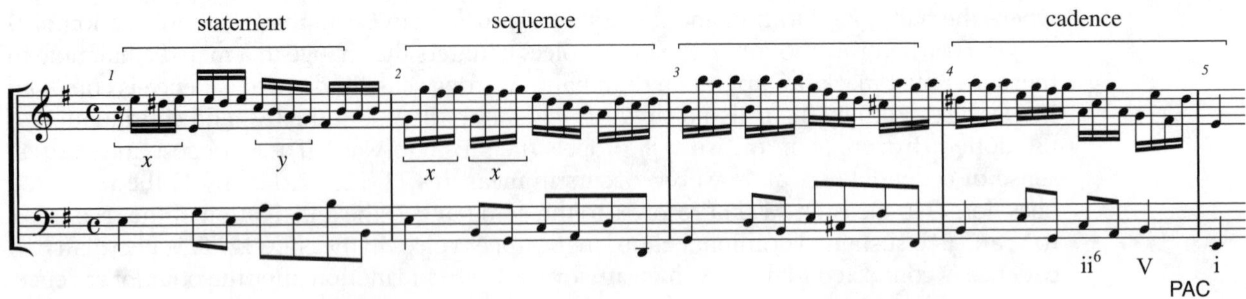

b. Bach, Sonata No. 3 for Violin, BWV 1005, Largo.

There are also Baroque melodies, usually in slow movements, that "spinout" phrases with continuous elaborations of ideas that have no obvious motivic connections. Excellent examples of this type are found in slow movements such as the Largo from Bach's Sonata No. 3 for Violin.[10]

Another fortspinnung model of phrase structure makes use of sequence as a basis for continuation following initial statements of motives. In this model, outlined in Figure 1, the initial statements and repetitions establish the key, normally through emphasis on tonic and dominant harmonies. Sequences then function as a continuation that departs from tonic harmony before leading to cadential closure. Because this type of phrase structure is prevalent in *ritornellos* (in recurring themes that begin movements), it is instructive to identify it as *ritornello phrase structure*.[11] Ritornellos function to introduce thematic material in

Figure 3.1 *Ritornello model of phrase structure.*[12]

Process:	Statement/Repetition or Response	Sequence(s)	Cadence
Function:	**a)** Initiate **b)** Establish key	Continue Elaborate	Close PAC in tonic

[10] Robert Gauldin refers to these types of melodies as "auto generative" in *A Practical Approach to 18th-Century Counterpoint*, 27.

[11] Though the use of a ritornello is usually associated with concerto forms, historically its origins lie in Baroque vocal music in which a ritornello (Italian for "refrain") of instrumental music marked off the sections of a movement and the vocal entrances. Examples are addressed in Chapter 13.

[12] Fischer labels these processes as *Vordersatz—Fortspinnung—Epilog*. See Lawrence Dreyfus, "J.S. Bach's Concerto Ritornellos and the Question of Invention," in *Musical Quarterly* 71(1985), 327–358.

a movement and to confirm the initial tonic and keys to which the music modulates in the course of a movement. They are also used to close movements, thus ritornellos serve to frame sections of a movement or work.

This ritornello model described above may be understood as a sentence structure. Sequential repetition of short motives, and overlapping of subphrases of unequal lengths are distinguishing features. In practice, the processes outlined above may be combined, omitted, expanded and compressed in a flexible manner. The length of the opening statements and sequences will vary, as will the placement of cadences within a ritornello. *Consequently asymmetrical phrases are equally if not more prominent than the four to eight measure phrase structures associated with sentences and periods*. Sometimes a ritornello is based merely on sequential repetitions followed by cadence as in Example 3.14, while occasionally ritornellos may omit sequences. Typically, though, a ritornello phrase structure in its full form contains all of the processes outlined below. Ritornello forms will be discussed further in Chapters 9 and 13.

The beginning of "For Unto Us a Child is Born," No. 12 from Handel's *Messiah*, Example 3.15a illustrates a clear example of a ritornello phrase structure. Note that measures 1–2 present a statement/imitation rather than statement/repetition. *Imitation* results when a repetition occurs in a different voice on a different pitch, a common process in Baroque phrase structures. The opening of the Two-part Invention in D minor by Bach offers another example of imitation used as part of an expanded ritornello. (see Exercise 2.11, Chapter 2) The first six measures give three statements of the scalar motive based on a I-V(vii) harmonic motion, a phrase structure based on an imitative texture. The next eight measures comprise two sequences that effect a modulation to the relative key of F major, followed by an extension and cadential progression in measures 15–18.

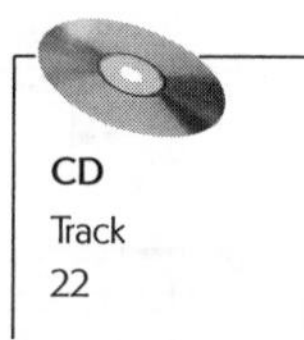

CD
Track
22

The opening ritornello of Bach's Brandenburg Concerto No. 5 shows a more flexible placement of sequences and cadences. Following the opening two-measure statements, a descending harmonic sequence in measures 3–4 leads to a cadential progression in measure 5. A deceptive cadence in the midpoint of measure 5 allows Bach to reiterate the sequence in varied form and lead to an evaded cadence in the midpoint of measure 7. Here a new figure leads to the strong cadential progression in measures 8–9, emphasized by the octave bass-line motion and dotted rhythms. This example illustrates the flexibility of the ritornello model, particularly in the hands of Bach. Such flexibility is typically exploited in recurrences of ritornellos, in which subphrases may be omitted and presented in varied form. The processes and functions of the ritornello models illustrated in these examples represent formal principles that are characteristic of much baroque music.

Example 3.15 *Ritornello models of phrase structure.*

a. Handel, *Messiah,* "For Unto Us a Child is Born," mm. 1–7.

(This excerpt continues on p. 54.)

(Example 3.15a, continued.)

b. Bach, Brandenburg Concerto No. 5, I, mm. 1–9.

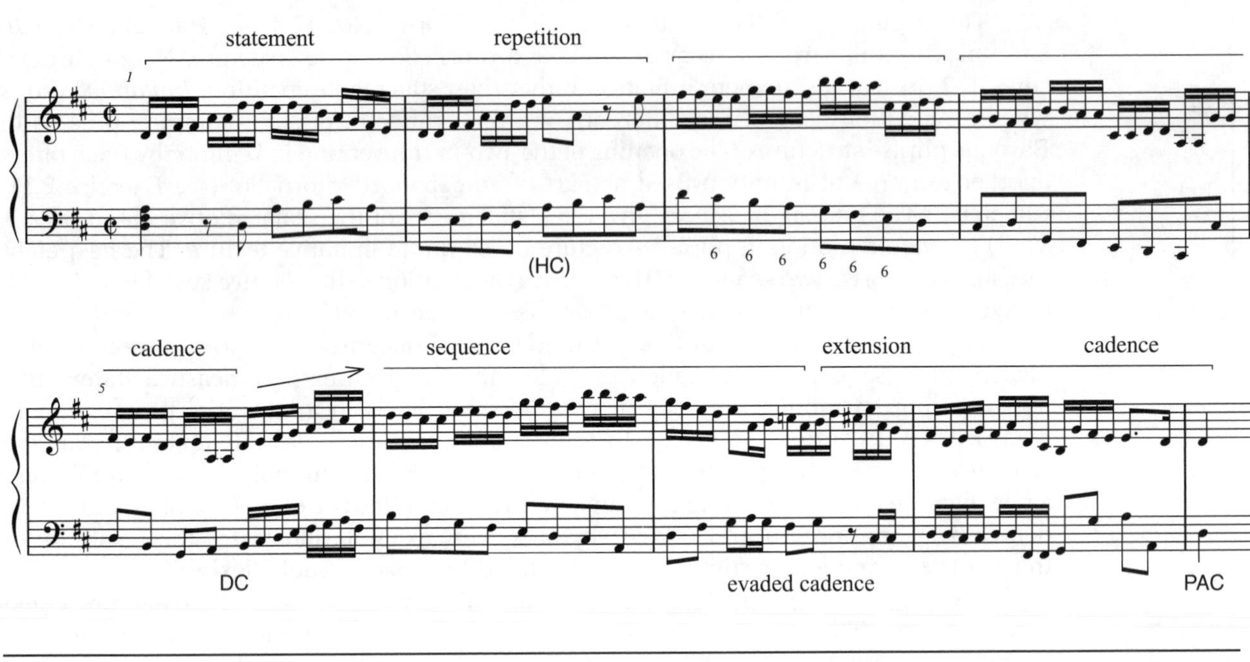

Summary

A theme is a self-contained musical idea of one or more phrases. The thematic processes of statement/contrast/restatement and statement/elaboration are basic principles of formal design. By convention, themes are labeled with alphabetical designations. Themes may be understood in terms of processes that generate phrases and define internal functions. Phrases can be initiated by 1) statement/repetition or imitation; 2) statement/response repetition; 3) statement/contrast; or 4) statement/sequential repetition. Phrases are completed by continuation toward cadence. Continuation is characterized by departure from tonic harmonies, a quicker harmonic rhythm, use of sequence or fragmentation of previous ideas, and a sense of motion toward cadence. Various combinations of these processes characterize frequently encountered models of phrase structure including sentences, periods, and fortspinnung types.

A sentence structure is comprised of three segments: statement/repetition/continuation. Sentences normally exhibit a segmentation of 2+2+4 or comparable proportions in smaller (1+1+2) or larger (4+4+8) phrases. The sentence is often heard as a single phrase particularly in small sentences of 1+1+2. In eight-bar and especially sixteen-bar sentences, each half may be understood as a complete phrase if sufficient harmonic activity is heard. A period normally is comprised of two phrases referred to as antecedent and consequent phrases. The consequent will have a more conclusive cadence than the antecedent phrase and may contain thematic ideas that are parallel or contrasting to the antecedent. Sentences are one way of constructing a phrase and as such may be used in the phrases of a period. Periods and sentences may modulate and be repeated. Double periods consist of two different phrases in the antecedent and in the consequent. They are not common.

Repeated phrases entail repetition or varied repetition of a phrase with both cadences being identical. Phrase groups are sections of music in which a series of phrases group together on the basis of motivic or thematic content and tonal motion. A decisive AC normally marks the end of the group. They are typical of much Baroque music based on varied repetition and elaboration of opening motives. Regarding the distinctions between sentence, period and ritornello models of phrase structure, the summary shown in Figure 3.2 may be helpful.

Figure 3.2 *Diagram of thematic models of phrase structure.*

Three-part phrase: Sentence

a		**a**		**b**
statement		repetition (may be varied) or response repetition		continuation-cadence
1	+	1	+	2
2	+	2	+	4
4	+	4	+	8

Two-part phrase:

a		**a′ or b**
statement		response-cadence or contrast-cadence
2	+	2
4	+	4

Period:	*Antecedent phrase* ab or aa′ or aab HC or IAC	*Consequent phrase* restatement/varied: parallel period; or contrast continuation: contrasting period AC	
Ritornello:	Statement/Repetition or Response or Imitation	Sequence(s)	Cadence

Conclusions

The discussion of thematic processes and models of phrase structure presented here is by no means exhaustive. Many hybrid types may be found as composers are endlessly creative in shaping their material in new ways, utilizing the processes and functions in a variety of combinations. Composers of the late nineteenth century and the twentieth century explored new ways of generating phrases, to be discussed in later chapters. Nonetheless, the processes described can be applied to a wide range of music, and provide conceptual tools to analyze and interpret phrase structure. The analysis of phrases should focus on the way specific processes are used to shape the musical ideas and phrase structures, rather than mere labeling of functions. The identification and segmentation of phrases is often subject to different interpretations, especially in more complex music. In many instances, what constitutes a phrase is subject to diverse interpretations, as in the sixteen-measure sentence cited in Example 3.11 or the slow introduction of the Overture from *Messiah*.

When we study, perform and listen to music, we must be open to ambiguities and diverse interpretations, while striving for consistency in our approach to analysis. It is precisely the possibility of multiple viewpoints that enriches our study of music.

SUGGESTED READING

In addition to the studies by Schoenberg, Meyer, and Dreyfus cited in the footnotes, the following readings are recommended:

Rudolf Reti's *Thematic Process* is a well-known, though often criticized account of themes and motives as elements of formal unity. For a more recent discussion of phrase and motive see William Rothstein, *Phrase Rhythm*, 16–32. Charles Rosen gives a discussion of motives and their functions in classical forms in *Sonata Forms*, 2nd ed., 170–201. For a thoughtful view on the limitations of motivic analysis see Leonard Meyer, "A Pride of Prejudices." For an introduction to motive and levels of structure see John Rothgeb, "Thematic Content, A Schenkerian View" and Charles Burkhart, "Schenker's Motivic Parallelisms." Finally, Jonathan Dunsby provides an historical overview of thematic and motivic analysis in Christiansen, *The Cambridge History of Music Theory*.

Review and Exercises

1. **Terms:** In a concise sentence or two, define the following terms.

motive	repetition	response	continuation	sequence
complement	sentence	antecedent	consequent	fortspinnung ritornello
phrase group	repeated phrase	parallel period		contrasting period

2. **In-Class Activities:** Play or sing the first phrase of the following tunes, which are presumed to be familiar. Do so without reference to a score. Determine their phrase structure and the types of processes used to generate the phrases. Are any theme types used? Enumerate the grouping structure and phrase type based on processes, functions and cadences. The first one is done for you:

   a. Swing Low, Sweet Chariot: 4/4 meter parallel period, non-modulating.

Antecedent		Consequent	
2 +	2 HC	2	+2 PAC
Statement	contrast cadence	Restatement	Response

   b. America the Beautiful: $\frac{4}{4}$ mm. 1–16 (complete)
   c. Long Long Ago: $\frac{4}{4}$ mm. 1–16 (complete)
   d. Working on the Railroad: $\frac{4}{4}$ mm. 1–8
   e. Happy Birthday: $\frac{3}{4}$ complete
   f. I Got Rhythm: $\frac{2}{2}$ (cut time) first phrase

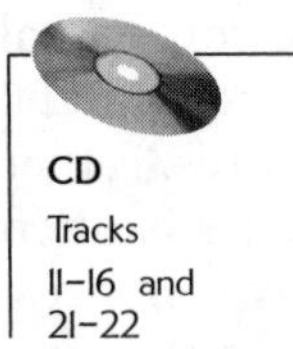

CD
Tracks
11–16 and
21–22

3. **Aural Analysis:** Listen to each of the following excerpts several times without the aid of a score. Identify processes you hear in each excerpt and match the excerpt with the descriptions of phrase structure given below. Note that No. 2 is a hybrid model of phrase structure.

   1. Vivaldi, *The Four Seasons*, "Spring" E major
   2. Haydn, Symphony 93 in D major, Movement IV
   3. Mozart, Symphony No. 40, Movement IV

4. Brahms, Piano Quintet, III, Trio C major
5. Tchaikovsky, *Nutcracker* Suite, B♭ major
6. Bach, Brandenburg Concerto No. 3, I
7. Schumann, *Fantasiestücke*, No. 2 "Aufshwang"
8. Handel, *Messiah*, "For Unto Us a Child Is Born"

   a. Sentence structure, THC concludes phrase
   b. Repeated phrases, each ending with HC
   c. Repeated parallel period with statement/contrast continuation in each phrase
   d. Ritornello with imitation and ascending sequence
   e. Parallel period with statement/contrast and repetition in each phrase
   f. Ritornello structure with a DC, a repeated melodic sequence, and a cadential extension
   g. Repeated period with varied repetition
   h. Sentence structure that modulates from minor to relative major key

4. **Score Analysis:**

   a. Reconsider the Beethoven Scherzo from the Op. 2 No. 2, Piano Sonata given for analysis in the exercises from Chapter 2. What kind of phrase structure is found in the first eight measures? Where is this theme restated after the repeat sign in measure 8? How are these restatements similar or different from the first eight measures? Which restatement is given the strongest emphasis? Explain your answer. Give a letter scheme that illustrates the thematic design of this work. Similarly, consider the phrase structures in the theme from Beethoven's Op. 131 String Quartet (Example 3.12).
   b. Make a diagram of the phrase structure in the following excerpt. Your diagram should include length of phrase segments, processes that are evident, and cadences. You may wish to copy the excerpt and present your analysis as annotations on the score.

Exercise 3.4b Amy Beach, *Scottish Legend* for piano, mm. 1–8.

(This excerpt continues on p. 58.)

(Example 3.4b, continued.)

5. **Additional works for analysis.** Study the following passages and determine the types of phrase structures each illustrates.

   Bach, Cantata 140, No. 6, mm. 1–8
   Bach, Air from the D major Orchestral Suite
   Haydn, Symphony No. 104, Movement III, mm. 1–16
   Mozart, Symphony 39, Movement IV, mm. 1–16 elided to 17
   Beethoven Symphony No. 5, Movement I, mm. 4–20
   Beethoven, *Diabelli* Variations, Theme, mm. 1–16
   Chopin, Waltz Op. 64, No. 2 in C♯ minor, mm. 1–32

Burkhart Anthology

Bach, Prelude in C major
Haydn, Symphony No. 101, III
Mozart, Clarinet Concerto in A major, K. 622, I, mm. 1–16
Beethoven, Sonata Op. 7, II, mm. 1–8
Beethoven, Sonata Op. 10, No. 1, II, mm. 1–8
Beethoven, Sonata Op. 13, II, mm. 1–8
Petzold (attributed), March and Minuet from *Notebook for Anna Magdalena Bach* first sections
Schubert, Impromptu in A♭, mm. 1–16
Schubert, *"Erlkönig,"* mm. 58–65
Chopin, Prelude in E major, entire
Brahms, Intermezzo in A major, mm. 1–32

Kostka/Graybill Anthology

Bach, French Suite No. 5, Gavotte, mm. 1–8, 9–16
Mozart, Piano Sonata in A minor, K. 319, I, mm. 1–8
Haydn, Symphony No. 100, mm. 24–39
Beethoven, Bagatelle, Op. 119, No. 1, mm. 17–24
Schubert, "Auf dem Flusse," mm. 5–12
Schubert, Moment Musicaux, Op. 94, No. 6, mm. 1–16, 78–85

4 Phrase Rhythm and Phrase Structure

Introduction

The discussions of musical phrases thus far have focused on phrase segmentation and grouping structure, and on some basic models of thematic phrase structure. In this chapter, we expand our understanding of musical phrases by considering phrase rhythm and form. This chapter will serve as an introduction to some basic concepts that are instructive in the analysis of phrase structure.

Broadly speaking, *phrase rhythm* refers to the sense of motion within phrases and from one phrase to the next. It results from the length and grouping structure of a phrase, the function of the various segments of a phrase, and the pattern and placement of metric accents in the phrase. These elements collectively create a hierarchy of accentuations that is a fundamental aspect of phrase rhythm. Duration or length, which is counted by the number of measures, and grouping structure have been discussed with reference to thematic models of phrase structure. In this chapter we will address three additional aspects of phrase structure that affect the grouping structure and accentuation of measures: phrase connections, expansions, and contractions. The discussion of these aspects will lead us to consider the organization of phrases in terms of accent and large-scale meter, or hypermeter. An understanding of phrase rhythm provides additional tools with which to analyze more complex and subtle phrase structures.

Phrase Separation and Connection

An important aspect of the continuity of phrases and the sense of motion in music is how and when phrases are separated or connected. Rests often separate phrases, as in the opening of the last movement of Mozart's Symphony No. 40 (Chapter 3 Exercises, CD Track 13). In other cases, phrases may not be rhythmically separated, but a breath or separation is implied. In the close of the first phrase of the Mazurka by Chopin, shown in Example 4.1, the cadential arrival in measure 8 is marked by an appoggiatura in the melody and chromatic embellishments (neighbor tones) in the accompaniment. These non-chord tones serve to delay the full resolution to the tonic triad until the third beat. Beat 3 is thus an afterbeat rather than an upbeat or "pickup" to the next phrase. There is, however, an implied break or breath between the two phrases, resulting from the arrival on tonic and its placement at the end of a four-measure unit typical of dance music. This break is supported by the slurs as well as the resolution described. As this example illustrates, *afterbeats* are rhythmic continuations at a point of cadence that elaborate and group with the cadential harmony.

New phrases also may begin after the point of cadential arrival with an upbeat or anacrusis to the first full measure of the phrase. The term *upbeat* refers to pitches on weak beats that group with a subsequent strong beat; an upbeat that begins a new phrase is referred to as an *anacrusis*.[1] Following a point of cadence, an anacrusis will group with

[1] The term "anacrusis" was originally used to refer to an unstressed syllable that begins a line of verse.

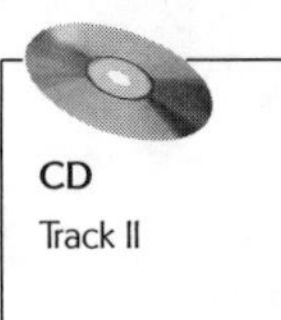

the next phrase, leading to the first downbeat of the phrase. This situation, a common occurrence, is heard in the opening of *The Four Seasons* by Vivaldi (Example 3.12a). In this example, the phrase begins with an upbeat, which establishes the grouping structure indicated. In measure 3, the eighth notes that outline the dominant triad on beats 3 and 4 are afterbeats, while the final eighth note, E4, is an anacrusis to measure 4. An anacrusis following a cadence is normally marked as such by a change of harmony, as illustrated in this example. The cadential arrival and change in harmony imply a slight break or breath before the anacrusis. In each of these examples there is a separation between phrases.

Example 4.1 Chopin, Mazurka, Op. 67, No. 3, mm. 7–8.

Frequently, phrases are connected to one another to give a stronger sense of continuity of motion. The reason and effect of such choices will naturally vary according to the style of the music and the context of the phrases. Phrases usually are connected in one of four basic ways: 1) elision; 2) melodic or bass-line links; 3) continuation of accompaniment; and 4) overlapping of lines. *Elision* occurs when the ending of one phrase is the beginning of the next phrase, and is a strong way to affect continuity of motion as one phrase leads directly to another. This type of connection normally will coincide with a strong beat, usually the downbeat. The Two-part Invention in D minor by Bach shows a clear instance of this in measure 18. (See Example 2.11, mm. 17–18) The point of cadence in F major is also the beginning of a restatement of the principal theme or subject, creating an elision of the two phrases. Other instances may be observed in Example 3.15 ("For Unto Us . . . " CD Track 22), where the first phrase elides with the second phrase in measure 7, and in Example 4.2, in which two phrases elide in measure 9.

It is tempting to consider that two elided phrases share a measure in common. However, the point of cadence on the downbeat is the only part of the elided measure that belongs to the first phrase. Conversely, the entire elided measure is understood and felt as part of the new phrase. In Example 4.2 then, measure 9 is the point of elision, but the first phrase is not nine measures long; rather, the first (eight-measure) phrase is elided to measure 9. This perspective provides a more accurate counting of phrase length. In general, phrase length should be indicated by the number of complete measures.

Analytic Note: Some editions have the slur broken between measures 8 and 9 in Example 4.2. This interpretation suggests that there is a slight break between measures 8 and 9, which would affect the performance. If considered an elided phrase, the first phrase is understood as eight measures (plus an upbeat), which then elides with the next phrase. The two phrases would then be connected in a performance.

A *phrase link*, as the term suggests, is a connection between the end of one phrase and the beginning of another. A link may be labeled according to which component of the texture is involved. *Melodic links* are continuations of a melodic line after a point of cadence, and occur within the cadential measure. They may be understood as extended upbeats or afterbeats, which connect the end of one phrase with the beginning of the next

Example 4.2 Chopin, Waltz, Op. 69, No. 2, (Posthumous) mm. 1–16.

phrase. The link will often occur as other voices drop out, as in Example 4.2. The right hand eighth notes in measure 16, an embellishment of the cadential tonic triad, continue as a link to the next phrase while the lower part is interrupted. The opening phrase of Verdi's "Celeste Aida," Example 4.10b ends with a shimmering, descending figure on D-A-D in the high strings that delicately leads back to the key of B♭ to begin the next phrase. Links may also take place in the bass line, as in the excerpt by Tchaikovsky shown in Example 3.9b. The point of cadence is on beat two of measure 8; as the upper voice rests the bass line continues as a link to the repetition of the period. Both types of links can occur simultaneously as in measure 12 (the first ending) from the Sinfony from *Messiah*. (See Example 3.13, and Example 3.5, m. 8.)

Related to bass-line links is an accompaniment figure that continues across two phrases, thus linking them together. The opening phrase of the Minuet from Symphony No. 41 by Mozart (see Example 3.11) is a good example of this technique. Note how the four-measure melodic phrases are separated by rests, but are supported by an accompaniment figure in the violin II that sounds continuous eighth notes across the two phrases and into the next continuation. See also Example 4.3, in which the orchestral accompaniment continues throughout the vocal entrances.

An important point to consider from a perceptual viewpoint is whether a phrase link is heard as part of the preceding phrase, or as an expanded upbeat and lead-in to the next phrase. Arguably, the link is most often perceived as a lead-in to the next phrase, particularly from a rhythmic viewpoint since the rhythmic motion to the next phrase is frequently continuous, as in Examples 4.2 and 4.10b. In these examples, however, both of the links are elaborations of the cadential harmony and thus group with the *preceding* phrase. Clearly performers can affect this perception and often must make decisions as to how such links are to be grouped with the surrounding phrases. Links may best be understood as exactly what the term implies: a connection between two events that belongs to both and neither. Unlike afterbeats or upbeats, links do not clearly group with one phrase or the other. Moreover, links can be elaborated to expand phrases.

Phrase overlaps are less frequent than elisions and phrase links, and occur most often in rhythmically diverse textures. Overlap is common in contrapuntal textures and is especially prevalent in imitative vocal textures as shown in Example 4.3. In this famous chorus from the oratorio *Elijah*, the various vocal lines each enter at different times and subsequently cadence at different points, effecting an overlapping of vocal phrases. Note again how the continuous accompaniment connects or binds the overlapping phrases.

Phrase Expansions

The idea that phrases can be expanded is based on the perception that some parts of a given phrase are additions to more basic or essential segments of the phrase. We have addressed this point in the foregoing discussion of phrase connections, which can be understood as elaborations within a basic phrase. A phrase expansion refers to the addition of one or more measures to a basic phrase. Expansions can occur at the beginning, at the end, or within a phrase, and are labeled as introductions, extensions, or interpolations, respectively. *Phrase expansions are understood as such if they can be omitted from the music without disrupting the sense of a complete musical phrase.* As the examples below will address, this is often a matter of interpretation.

Example 4.3 *Phrase Overlap.* Mendelssohn, *Elijah,* "He Watching Over Israel," mm. 19–22.

An analogy with language may help clarify this point. Consider the following sentence, which contains a subject, verb, and object: "I walked the dog." The basic meaning of this sentence may be elaborated in various ways, for example: "I walked the frisky dog," or "I walked the frisky dog early in the morning," or after I ate, "I walked the frisky dog early in the morning." The original meaning of the sentence is not altered by these additions, which expand upon the fact and change the flow and length of the sentence. Phrase expansions similarly alter the flow and length of a phrase.

Phrase introductions take three common forms: 1) accompaniment figures that initiate a phrase and lead to the entrance of the phrase melody; 2) motivic anticipations; and 3) elongated upbeats. *Accompaniment lead-ins*, which begin a phrase before the melody enters, are frequently used to begin compositions or sections of a work. Their function is to establish the key and rhythmic motion of the music prior to the entrance of a melody. This function is particularly important in vocal music, providing singers with tonal cues, and is a favorite device of late eighteenth and early nineteenth-century composers. Example 4.4 gives three instances. The Mozart example begins with restless accompaniment figures, while the Schubert and Verdi examples illustrate use of the stock downbeat-afterbeat or "oom-pah" figures heard in many nineteenth-century dances. Although the accompaniments sound as initial downbeats of the phrases, these figures could be omitted without affecting the phrase

CD
Track 24

structure of the melody, which will normally begin with another downbeat emphasis. The measure numbers in parentheses in the examples reflect that these accompaniment lead-ins function as additions to the basic melodic phrase.

An accompaniment lead-in may be perceived as a link as well as part of the new phrase. Unlike a link, an accompaniment lead-in may occur at an elision of phrases and will be perceived as a downbeat that initiates and is part of the new phrase. The Schubert and Verdi excerpts in Example 4.4 illustrate this phenomenon. In the Schubert, measure 41 elides to the downbeat of measure 42, a PAC that begins the next phrase with a new accompaniment. In the Verdi, the music reaches a half cadence, followed by a new accompaniment figure on the subsequent downbeat.

Phrase introductions may also take the form of a *motivic anticipation*, as in the famous opening of Beethoven's Symphony No. 5, Example 4.5. In this case, the dramatic fermatas create the impression of a separate introductory gesture that is not a part of the phrase melody. In Example 4.5b, the first few measures function as an accompaniment

Example 4.4 *Accompaniment as introduction to phrase.*

a. Mozart, Symphony No. 40, I, mm. 1–5.

b. Schubert, Symphony No. 8, I, mm. 38–44.

c. Verdi, *La Traviata,* Prelude, mm. 15–19.

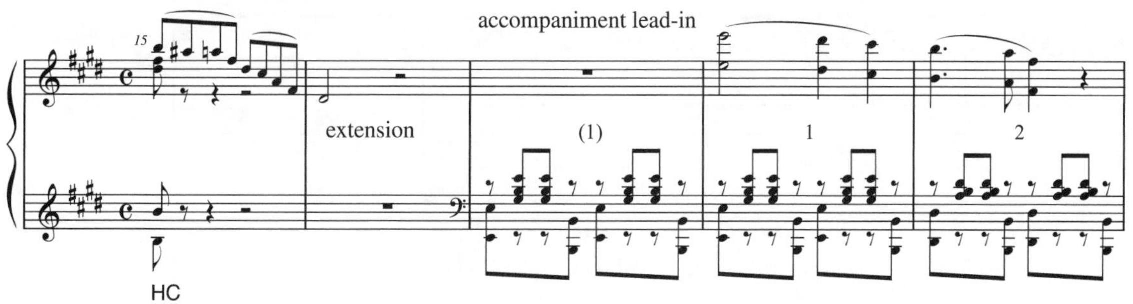

lead-in as well as a motivic anticipation: the upper voice anticipates the initial ascending motive of the violin melody.

Example 4.5 *Motivic Anticipation as Phrase Introduction.*

a. Beethoven, Symphony No. 5, I, opening.

b. Franck, Violin Sonata, I, opening.

Some introductory gestures may take the form of an extended anacrusis or *elongated upbeat*.[2] In most elongated upbeats, the emphasis on dominant harmony and the continuous rhythmic motion are defining characteristics. The opening of the "Minute" Waltz by Chopin, Example 4.6a is one well-known instance, in which an upbeat is elongated by repeating a motivic figure and prolonging the implied dominant harmony. Here the elongated upbeat also entails a motivic anticipation. Elongated upbeats may be perceived as extended links when heard within a composition. In the Chopin Waltz, when the opening gesture returns later in the composition, it gives the sense of an expanded link to the return of the opening theme. The beginning of the Allegro of the first movement of the Haydn Symphony No. 101, Example 4.6b, also has an elongated upbeat, but it is used to different effect. Here the opening measure leads to a strong downbeat on measure 2 of the theme. Upon repetition of the phrase, the opening measure retains its feeling of an elongated upbeat, but may also be perceived as a link, a connection that occurs between phrases.

Example 4.6 *Melodic lead-in as elongated upbeats to phrases.*

a. Chopin, Waltz, Op. 64, No. 1, opening.

[2] See Rothstein, 43, for further examples and discussion of elongated upbeats and other phrase expansions.

b. Haydn, Symphony No. 101, I, Allegro, mm. 23–33.

Analytic Note: The notion of phrase expansions being additions to a basic phrase raises interesting questions regarding phrase length and accent. In both of the excerpts in Example 4.6, the lead-in measures could be reduced to single note pickups and incorporated within a four-measure or eight-measure phrase. The first four measures of the Chopin Waltz thus may be best understood as an expanded anacrusis to the first downbeat of the phrase in measure 5. The Haydn theme would appear to be a five-measure theme, but the extended anacrusis (elongated upbeat) has the effect of adding or expanding a regular four-measure phrase. A sense of this is made clearest by conducting the phrase with each measure equal to one beat of a four-measure pattern. That is, the first measure is conducted as an upbeat and is felt as an extra beat or measure when it recurs. It is the second measure of the theme that is felt as the first downbeat, which is apparent when we conduct the high-level pulse.

The organization of phrases in terms of large-scale metric patterns, with the measure or larger units as a pulse, is referred to as high-level meter or *hypermeter*.[3] Not all music has a sense of hypermeter and the interpretation of metric accents and phrase expansions can vary widely. A feeling of hypermeter is typical of symmetrical phrases found in the periods and sentence models discussed in the previous chapter. Symmetrical phrases tend to convey regularity in large-scale motion and a larger pulse that is requisite for establishing a metric hierarchy of accents. Hypermeter is not readily discerned or as common in music in which irregular phrase lengths and fortspinnung-type phrase structures prevail; thus hypermetric levels of pulse do not often characterize Baroque music.

A basic question when analyzing phrase rhythm is how large of a pulse[4] we can realistically feel in a given composition. Clearly tempo and specific meter are important factors in attempting to answer this question. Dances in quick tempos and triple meter, for example, are more readily felt in terms of a larger pulse that reflects high-level meter than slow movements in duple meter. Another question is which measure is the hypermetric downbeat of the phrase and how expansions are to be counted. While the first measure of a phrase may be assumed to be a hypermetric downbeat, lead-ins and other expansions may alter that assumption. For example, if an accompaniment enters early it is heard as a downbeat to initiate the phrase, but the subsequent melody may be felt as a new

---

[3] This term was coined by Edward Cone in *Musical Form and Musical Performance* (New York: Norton, 1969). See also Rothstein, 8–14.

[4] The term "pulse" here is used to refer to any level of the beat that may be perceived or projected in the music. The term "beat" normally refers to the notated level of pulse indicated by a meter signature in traditional music.

downbeat that begins the phrase again. (See Figure 4.1c.) In the system employed here and throughout, phrase expansions are numbered as separate measures in parentheses or as elongations of other measures. Arrows pointing toward their downbeat goal indicate elongated upbeats.

Figure 4.1 illustrates hypermetric phrase organization that shows the hierarchy of metric accents in four-measure phrases as well as some models that incorporate phrase introductions. In Figure 4.1 the number of dots under each downbeat[5] and the letter designations (strong or weak) correspond to the metric weight at the beginning of each measure of the phrase. Corresponding musical examples are also cited.

The examples cited in Figure 4.1 all illustrate four-beat or *quadruple* hypermeter. This pattern and duple hypermeter are perhaps most common, but three-beat or triple hypermeter is certainly possible. A famous example of triple hypermeter is found in the Scherzo of Beethoven's Symphony No. 9 (Example 4.7). Beethoven makes this hypermeter clear by his designation *ritme de tre battute (in the rhythm of three bars)* in the score. (See also Example 3.12.)

Example 4.7 Beethoven, Symphony No. 9, II, mm. 177–185.

Metric accents do not necessarily correspond to accents that are heard or played, but rather to the hierarchy of points of arrival within phrase units. In other words, we must distinguish metric accents from rhythmic accents and other accents resulting from a performer's action. For our purposes, we will assume the measure to be the primary level of hypermeter. The possibility of higher levels of metric organization and the metric reinterpretation of measures must be considered on an individual basis, with the specific attributes of a given passage taken into account.

Phrase Extensions

Extensions are additions of one or more measures at the end of a phrase, which also group with that phrase. Phrase extensions are most readily perceived when cadential progressions, in part or in whole, are repeated or prolonged. This may take the form of repetitions of the V-I cadential progression as in Example 4.8a, or a repetition of the cadential tonic as in Example 4.8b. In the latter example by Verdi, the cadential tonic triad is extended for seven measures. Note, however, that the last measure has a fermata and is easily felt as a

[5] This method of designation is drawn in part from Lerdahl and Jackendoff (1983).

Figure 4.1 *Hypermetric Schemes.*

a. **S** **w** **s** **w**

1 2 3 4

|--------------|--------------|--------------|--------------| see Example 4.2 and Example 3.10a

. . . .

. .

.

b. **S** **w** **s** **w**

ext. anacrusis 1 2 3 4

|------------------→ |--------------|--------------|--------------|--------------| see Example 4.6b

. . . .

. .

.

c. **S** **S** **w** **s** **w**

(1) accomp. 1 2 3 4

lead in

|-------------------- |--------------|--------------|--------------|--------------| see Example 4.4a

. . . . .

. . .

. .

two-measure unit. (Conduct the last 7 measures as two large $\frac{4}{4}$ measures, to feel this phenomena.)

The Prelude from *La Traviata* by Verdi, Example 4.4c (CD Track 33), also shows how elongating the cadential point of arrival, in this case a dominant harmony, may extend a phrase. Measure 16 could be omitted without disrupting the motion from one phrase to the next; the extension gives a feeling of breadth and drama to this juncture. Another common type of cadential extension is what may be termed an *echo*, in which the final measures of a phrase are repeated by another instrument or voice in the texture

(Example 4.8c). A phrase extension also results when an expected authentic cadence is supplanted by a deceptive resolution, which then requires an extension to reach a conclusive authentic cadence. See Example 2.6 for a clear instance of this type of extension.

Example 4.8 *Phrase Extensions.*

a. Haydn, Symphony No. 104, III, mm. 42–51.

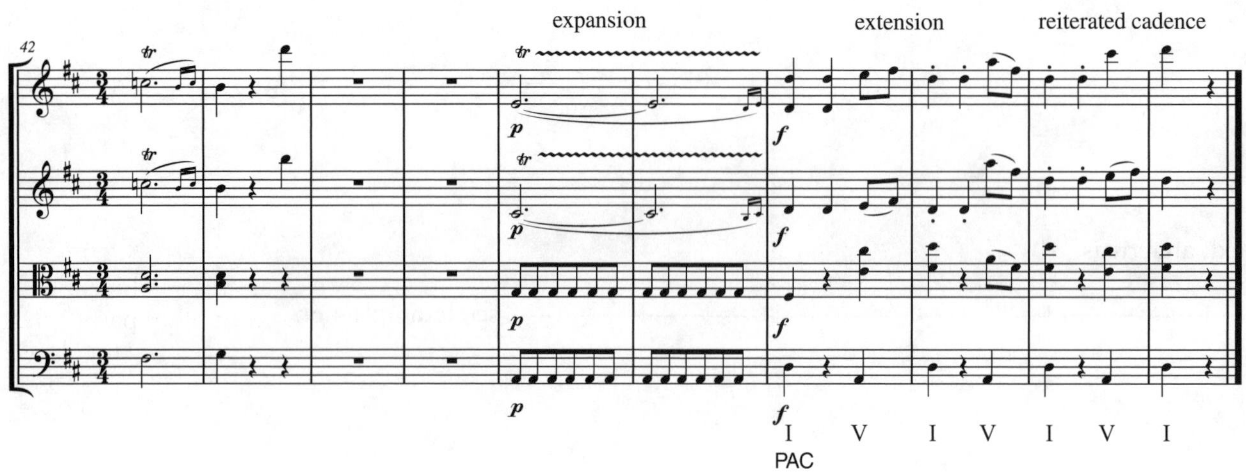

b. Verdi, *La Traviata,* end of Act I.

c. Schubert, "Muth" from *Die Winterreise*.

Internal Expansions. In contrast to phrase introductions and extensions, which occur prior to or at the end of the phrase melody, *internal expansions* occur within a phrase. They often take the form of *interpolations* (a word meaning "to insert between other parts") that occur upon repetition of a phrase. In such instances, the initial statement of the phrase establishes a model, making the expansion clear in the repetition. In Example 4.9a, measures 7–9 are elaborations of the preceding two measures while measure 11 extends the cadential dominant of measure 10. Here the interpolated measures, numbered in parentheses, are motivic elaborations not present in the initial model phrase.

Other internal expansions may be phrase segments that are part of the model phrase in its initial presentation, but which nonetheless may be perceived as expansions of an underlying simpler phrase. Such implicit interpolations normally produce asymmetrical phrases of irregular lengths. They usually result from motivic repetitions or harmonic elaborations which, were they omitted, would leave a simpler but nonetheless complete phrase. In Example 4.9b, measures 60–61 are simply repetitions of the preceding measure that might be omitted. Haydn's internal expansion of the phrase plays with our sense of motion and creates an expectation of change in a witty and humorous manner, enriching the phrase and making the subsequent modulation more dramatic. Notice that the elongated upbeat and motivic anticipations of the theme contribute to these effects as well. In Example 4.8a, an excerpt from the same movement, the dominant harmony of measures 46 and 47 is an expansion of the cadential progression toward tonic. Again, measure 47 could be omitted without altering the basic phrase structure, confirming its role as an expansion of a single harmony within the phrase.

Example 4.9 *Internal expansions of phrases.*

a. Beethoven, String Quartet, Op. 18, No. 5, III, mm. 1–12.

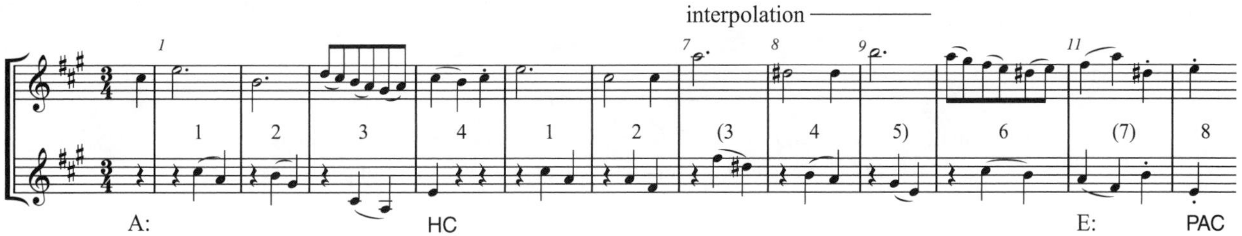

b. Haydn, Symphony No. 104, III, Trio, beginning.

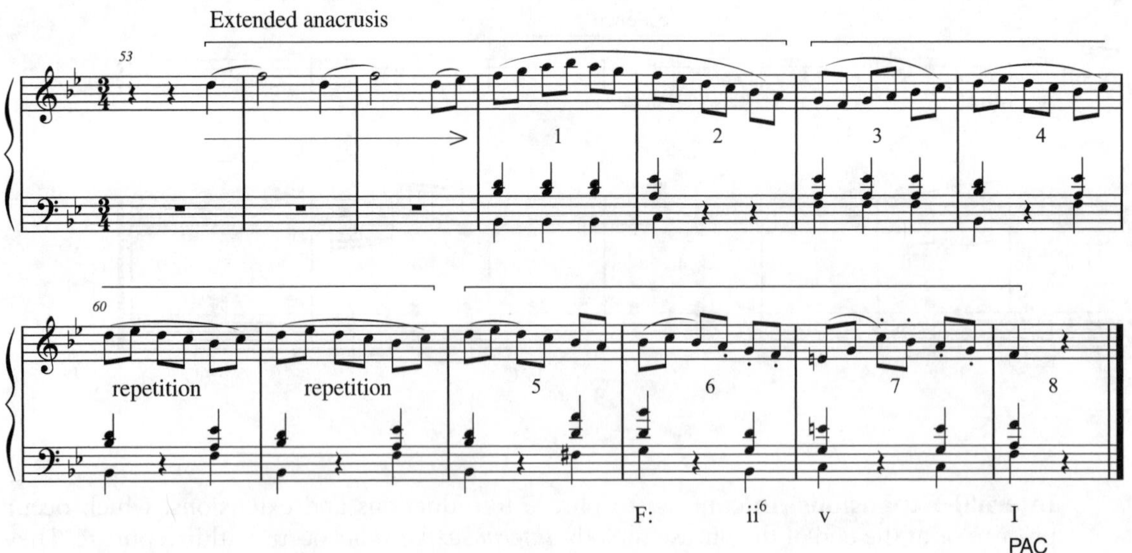

An *evaded cadence* is another technique used to expand a phrase. This technique results when an authentic cadential progression does not reach the root position, tonic harmony, but is interrupted by reiteration of the cadential progressions and usually its thematic content. The repetition and interruption of the cadential progression may occur one or more times, eventually reaching the point of cadence. Often times this will have the effect of a "one more time" repetition, as in Example 4.8b. Note how the second evaded cadence leads to an expansion from 2 to 4 measures of the reiterated cadential progression. This internal expansion dramatically emphasizes the eventual resolution to the cadential tonic.[6]

The perception of expansions can be very subtle and subject to different interpretations. The theme by Dvorak shown in Example 4.10a contains an internal expansion in measure 6, which is an elongation, harmonically, of measure 5 of the phrase. If measure 6 was omitted, the phrase would still be logically constructed. The internal expansion necessitates an extension to give the phrase a symmetrical length of ten measures. Example 4.10b shows a five-measure phrase, the opening of the theme from the Brahms' *Variations on a Theme by Haydn.* One might simply take this phrase to be five measures long with a 3+2 grouping. Measure 3 concludes a $\hat{3}$-$\hat{2}$-$\hat{1}$ melodic descent that may imply an authentic cadence. The harmony in measure 3, however, creates a need for continuation with its V-vi motion that attenuates the melodic closure. Further, measure 3 could be omitted while retaining, in measures 4 and 5, a sense of logical continuation of measures 1 and 2. Thus measure 3 can be understood as an internal expansion, which gives the phrase a breadth and elegance that the four-measure phrase would lack. Though such expansions may be found in many styles of music, nineteenth-century composers, who sought to give their melodies breadth and elasticity, especially favored this technique.[7]

---

[6] See Schmalfeldt "Cadential Processes" for an extensive discussion of this concept.

[7] See Meyer, *Style and Music*, 259 ff., for a discussion of melodic "stretching."

Example 4.10 *Internal phrase expansions as part of the basic phrase.*

a. Dvorak, Symphony No. 8, Op. 88, III, mm. 1–11.

b. Brahms, *Variations on a Theme by Haydn,* Op. 56, mm. 1–5.

As the Brahms example suggests, not all asymmetrical phrases are the result of obvious expansions. They may be the result of a specific melodic/harmonic shape. Whether the phrase is simply asymmetrical or contains an expansion is open to debate. Exercises at the end of the chapter will invite further thought on such interpretations.

Phrase Contractions

Phrases may be constructed to reflect a *contraction* of a basic phrase, which, like interpolation, normally is apparent in relation to an initial presentation of the phrase. Consider the parallel period in Example 4.11a, the principal theme from Haydn's Symphony No. 104, first movement. The *antecedent* is eight measures long with a rest before the consequent phrase. The eighth measure of the *consequent* (m. 32) is in fact the first measure of the next phrase: a metric reinterpretation occurs since the expected eighth measure is replaced by a hypermetric downbeat in the next phrase. In effect, the eighth measure of the consequent, which could have been a measure of tonic harmony, is omitted. This results in a seven-measure consequent phrase that elides in measure 32. To get a rhythmic sense of this phenomenon, conduct the phrase in $\frac{4}{4}$ where the whole note (1 measure) = one beat. Note how the change in dynamics and density also marks the downbeat of measure 32. A different sense of contraction occurs in the period that opens the aria "Celeste Aida." Review the eight-measure antecedent shown in Example 3.8c. The consequent, Example 4.11b, begins as a parallel restatement, but after the initial two-measure statement, a continuation follows: the two-measure repetition heard in the antecedent has been omitted. The result is a contraction, a phenomenon conveyed not only by the omitted measures but also by the increased harmonic rhythm of the parallel major-minor seventh chords (mm. 10–11) that accelerates the motion toward the cadence.

Example 4.11 *Phrase contractions.*

a. Haydn, Symphony 104, I, principal theme, mm. 17–34

b. Verdi, *Aida,* "Celeste Aida," mm. 8–14.

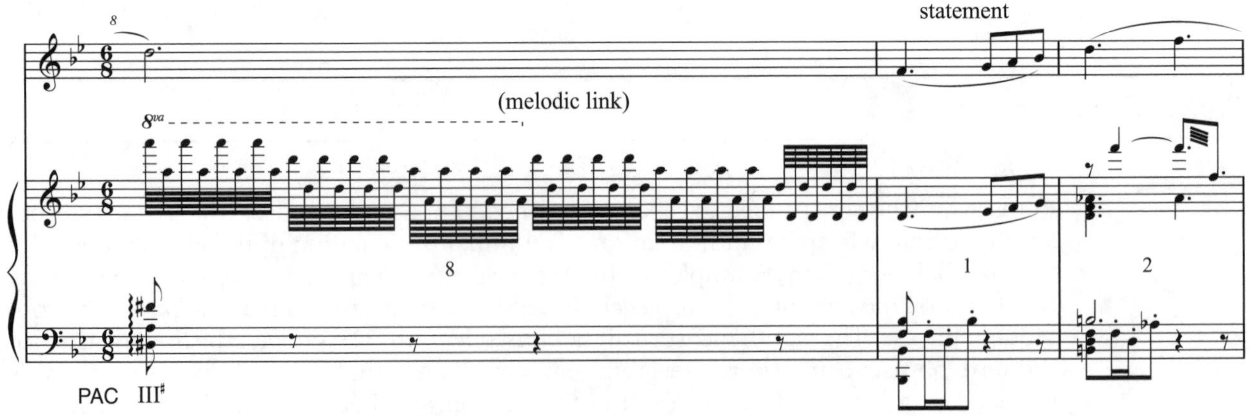

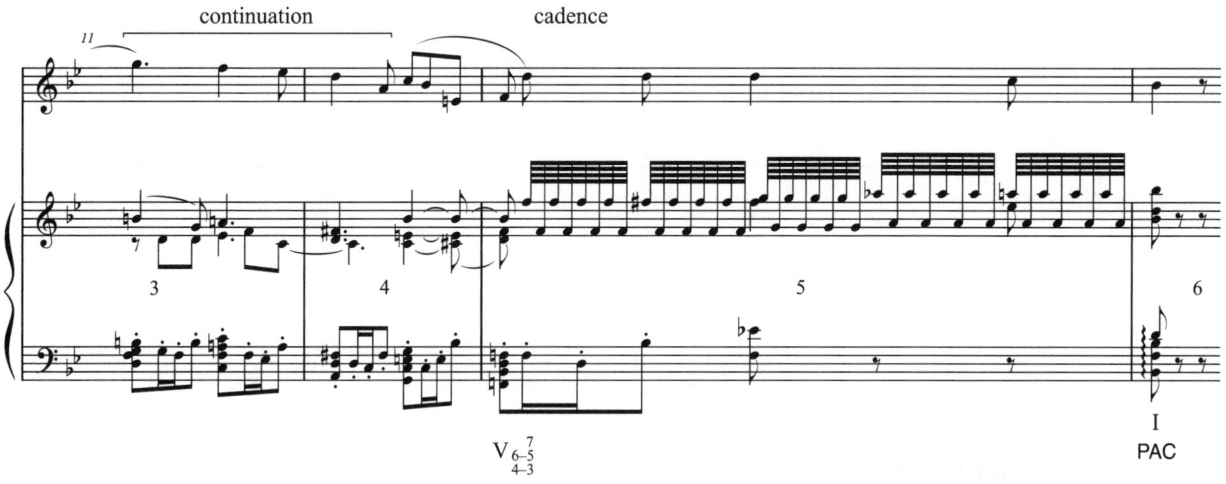

Summary

Phrase rhythm is a complex phenomenon that results from several factors. The length and grouping structure of a phrase, phrase connections, expansions and contractions, and the hierarchy of metric accents all shape the phrase rhythm of music. Phrase connections, if present, usually take the form of elisions or links. An elision takes place when a point of cadence occurs on a downbeat that also begins the next phrase. Continuation of melodic lines, bass lines, and continuous accompaniment figures may all serve as links. Phrase overlap normally occurs in contrapuntal textures as different lines enter and cadence at different points.

Phrase length may be varied by expansion or contraction of a phrase upon repetition or in its initial presentation. Expansions may occur internally or as introductions or extensions. Introductions may take the form of an accompaniment lead-in, a motivic anticipation, or an extended anacrusis. Extensions most often are reiterations of the cadential harmony or the cadential progression, which may take the form of an "echo." Deceptive cadences frequently occur in conjunction with extensions. Internal expansions are most apparent when a model phrase is repeated. They may take the form of interpolations of new material, motivic elaborations, elongations of a given harmony, evaded cadences, or simple repetitions of ideas within the phrase. Many asymmetrical phrases may be explained by the presence of expansions.

A sense of high-level meter or *hypermeter* is present in some music. A hypermetric interpretation of a phrase distinguishes some measures as downbeats and others as upbeats, resulting in a hierarchy of accents among downbeats of each measure in the phrase. Thus a four-measure phrase may be understood as a four-beat hypermeter. Higher levels of hypermeter may be perceptible. Hypermeter is evident most often in themes that have symmetrical phrase structure. The beginning of a phrase is usually the hypermetric downbeat of the phrase, though phrase expansions can alter this perception.

The analysis of phrase rhythm raises complex and interesting analytic issues that have been debated widely by theorists. As Robert Morgan has observed, "matters of phrase division, metrical accentuation, and grouping are of a necessity subjective in character, at least to a significant degree. . . . Interesting and complex music always reveals ambiguities with regard to grouping and metrical accentuation."[8] Thus, the analysis of phrase rhythm is often subject to more than one reasonable interpretation. The concepts presented above serve as an introduction to such analysis and provide some basic tools to inform one's interpretations.

---

[8] Robert Morgan, "Review of *Phrase Rhythm in Tonal Music* by William Rothstein," *Nineteenth-Century Music* Vol. 16, 78–81.

SUGGESTED READING

Edward Cone, *Musical Form and Musical Performance;* Schachter, Carl, "Rhythm and Linear Analysis: A Preliminary Study," and William Rothstein, *Phrase Rhythm in Tonal Music.*

Review and Exercises

1. **Terms:** In a concise sentence or two, define the following terms:

anacrusis	afterbeat	accompaniment lead-in	elongated upbeat
interpolation	evaded cadence	phrase extension	hypermeter
elision	phrase link	phrase overlap	motivic anticipation

2. **In-Class Activities and Discussion.**

   a. Reconsider Examples 4.2, 4.6b, and 4.9. Are sentence structures or periodic phrase structures evident in any of these examples? Conduct examples 4.2 and 4.9a at various levels of pulse. Can any of the examples be felt or conducted with a pulse of two measures? How do the expanded phrases affect our sense of hypermeter?

   b. Reconsider Example 4.8a by Beethoven. How might the second phrase be recomposed to create a 4, 5, 6, or 7 measure phrase? Which measures would be omitted, which altered? Consider why a second expansion (measure 7) was added.

   c. Reconsider the Beethoven Sonata for Piano, Op. 2, No. 2, Scherzo, given in the exercises for Chapter 2. Identify phrase connections and expansions in the movement.

   d. Reconsider Example 4.4a. What other measures might be considered the first hypermetric downbeat? How would this change the numbering of the phrase?

3. **Aural Analysis:** Listen to each of the following excerpts several times until you can reproduce them in your mind. Listen for the phrase expansion(s) in each excerpt and describe the techniques used to create the expansion. Try to determine different levels of the meter by conducting large-scale metric patterns. The tempos and meters are given to assist in making your determinations. Which examples have a discernible pulse at the level of the measure? Which examples do not exhibit hypermetric levels?

CD
Tracks
23–30

   1. Handel, *Water Music*, Overture, $\frac{3}{4}$ Allegro
   2. Mozart, Symphony No. 40, I, $\frac{2}{2}$
   3. Mozart, Piano Concerto No. 17, III, $\frac{2}{2}$ Allegretto
   4. Beethoven, Symphony No. 5, III, $\frac{3}{4}$ Allegro
   5. Schubert, Symphony No. 8, I, $\frac{3}{4}$ Allegro Moderato
   6. Chopin, Prelude No. 3 in G major, $\frac{4}{4}$ Vivace
   7. Mahler, Symphony No. 4, I, beginning
   8. Faure, *Requiem*, "In Paradisium," $\frac{3}{4}$ Andante Moderato

4. **Score Analysis:**

   a. Analyze the 12 measures shown. Consider measures 1–4 as one phrase. What type of phrase expansion takes place in the varied repetition of this phrase in measures 5–11? Consider which measures in the second phrase could be omitted. A harmonic analysis of the passage will be instructive in this regard. How is this second phrase connected to the next phrase, which begins in measure 12? What types of phrase structures are used?

b. The first phrase is stated in measures 1–8. What type of phrase structure is used? Measures 9–29 are an expansion of the first phrase. How are the two phrases connected? Determine the grouping structure of the second phrase. Identify three different types of phrase expansions in this phrase. Consider whether measures 1–8 may comprise two phrases.

c. This theme contains a phrase expansion in the consequent phrase. Identify the expansion and determine how it affects the metric organization of the phrase.

Exercise 4a. Haydn, String Quartet Op. 76, No. 3, IV, mm. 1–12.

(This excerpt continues on p. 76.)

(Exercise 4a, continued.)

Exercise 4b. Liszt, *Consolation No. 2,* Section I, mm. 1–29.

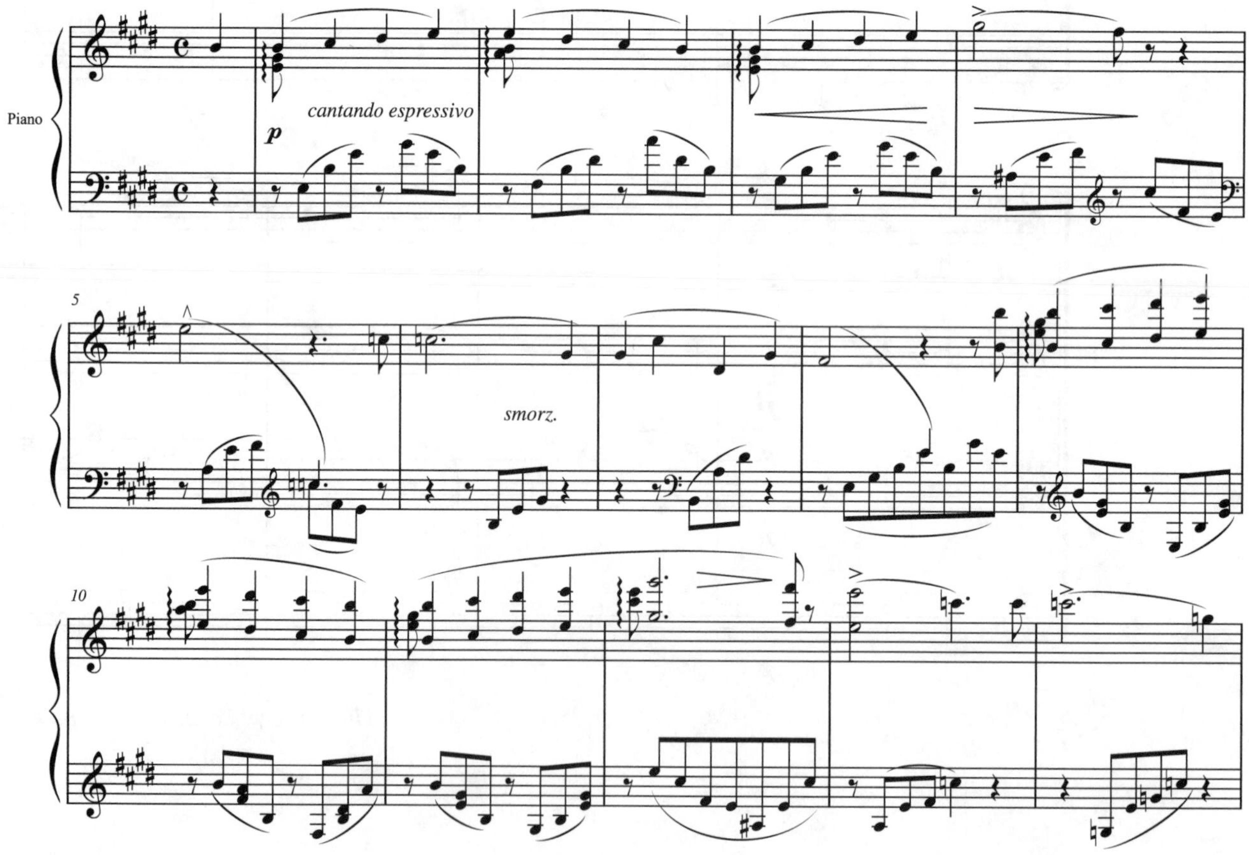

Piano

cantando espressivo

p

5

smorz.

10

Exercise 4c. Mozart, Clarinet Quintet K. 581, Trio II, mm. 1–12.

(This excerpt continues on p. 78.)

(Exercise 4c, continued.)

Exercise 4d. *Additional works for analysis of phrase connections and expansions:*

Burkhart Anthology

March from the *Notebook for Anna Magdalena Bach*
Haydn, Symphony No. 101, III, mm. 1–28
Beethoven, Piano Sonata in F minor, Op. 2, No. 1, III, Minuet, mm. 1–14
Beethoven, Piano Sonata in C minor, Op. 13, III, mm. 1–17
Chopin, Prelude in C major
Schumann, "War Song"
Gershwin, "I Got Rhythm," mm. 25–34

Kostka/Graybill Anthology

Mozart, *The Magic Flute,* No. 7, mm. 10–16
Schubert, Mass No. 2, in G major, mm.16–28
Mendelssohn, "Songs Without Words" Op. 19, mm. 3–15
Grieg, "An der Wiege," Op. 68, No. 5, mm. 17–27

5 Formal Functions and Musical Texture

Introduction

The previous discussions of a musical phrase introduced thematic processes such as statement, repetition, response, contrast, continuation, and fragmentation to illustrate how phrases are generated. The concept of phrase expansion was introduced to clarify additional functions of segments within a phrase, those of introduction, internal expansion, and extension. The discussions focused on how these various functions and processes shaped the internal structure of phrases and affected their grouping structure. In this chapter we will expand our understanding of formal functions by examining how phrases and sections may be differentiated according to their role in the form. Drawing and expanding upon the internal phrase functions identified in the discussion of phrase expansions, basic formal functions and the processes that characterize them will be introduced.

Another factor related to musical form is textural change. The discussions of cadences and phrase connections in previous chapters, and of formal functions in this chapter, refer to the importance of musical texture in shaping and delineating musical form. A review of the aspects of texture and an overview of textural processes will amplify this important point and complete our survey of formal elements.

I. Formal Functions

Six basic formal functions can be identified, which separately and in combination characterize the role which phrases and sections may play in a musical form. These functions are: 1) expository; 2) transitional; 3) developmental; 4) introductory; 5) closing; and 6) parenthetical. A particular function may be characteristic of a phrase segment, a complete phrase, or an entire section. While a phrase or section may have a single, readily identified function, more than one function may be apparent. In fact, one attribute of complex and subtle musical forms is the diversity of ways in which formal functions may be combined or transformed as musical ideas are elaborated or restated. The presence or absence of different types of formal functions can be a distinguishing feature of various musical styles and genres as well. In order to introduce and define these functions, we will focus on them individually with examples that highlight a particular one. It is important to understand, however, that a given passage of music can project more than one function. In subsequent chapters the delineation and interaction of these functions will be addressed as they apply to specific formal designs and structures.

EXPOSITORY FUNCTION

The function of a phrase or section is influenced by the manner in which it is constructed, its content, and its placement within the formal design. *Expository phrases* are those in which distinct thematic material is presented or restated, usually as complete phrase structures. They are characterized by most if not all of the following attributes: 1) the presence of beginning, middle and ending segments that project a complete, self-contained unit; 2) symmetrical grouping structures with or without expansions; 3) a strong sense of rhythmic and tonal stability at beginnings or endings or both; and 4) distinct melodic ideas with a clear sense of closure. These characteristics need not all occur, and expository phrases may incorporate other functions, particularly developmental function, when phrases are expanded or motives are elaborated. The models of thematic phrase structure and phrase combinations presented in Chapter 3, for example, display expository function but also elaborate or develop ideas. Further, themes may be presented at any point in a movement; thus expository function may occur when a new theme is presented as part of a closing section or in the midst of a developmental section. In any case, perhaps the most distinguishing characteristic of solely expository phrases is the presence of distinct thematic ideas with strong closure at the phrase endings.

TRANSITIONAL FUNCTION

In contrast to expository phrases, *transitional phrases* function as connections between expository statements of thematic material, or between different tonal areas and sections. Phrases that exhibit transitional function are characterized by instability or increased tension that creates the expectation of resolution and stability. Such phrases may involve modulations, quicker harmonic rhythms, sequences, expansions of dominant harmony, or more active rhythmic textures, each of which may contribute to a sense of instability. Example 5.1a shows a transitional phrase that connects the end of a trio to the repeat of a minuet, modulating from B♭ major back to the tonic key of D major. The motivic repetitions, the turn to the augmented sixth chord (measure 98) that resolves to the HC, the dynamic recession, and the fermata at its close all contribute to the transitional nature of the phrase. The use of the dominant pedal heard in this phrase, or of prolonged dominant chords is common in transitional phrases. Increased rhythmic activity and marked changes in texture—registral shifts, changes to full textures or single lines—also characterize many transitions. In Example 5.1b, the change to a continuous sixteenth-note rhythm and octave texture in measure 113, along with the systematic ascent of the sequential repetitions, signal a transitional phrase leading to a restatement of the opening theme of the movement. Unlike Example 5.1a by Haydn, this transitional function results from a phrase expansion, extending the figure first interjected in measure 111. In different ways, however, each of these examples illustrates the tension and expectation of resolution, which is characteristic of transitions.

Transitional phrases often have a sense of incompleteness for several reasons. First, such phrases tend to end on half cadences or to be elided to the next phrase. Consequently, they are heard as phrases that require resolution leading to points of stability. Second, when transitions begin with harmonic instability, notably by use of pre-dominant or dominant-function harmonies, they lack a sense of a stable beginning (initiation) heard in many expository phrases. Third, a transition often will entail fragmentation rather than complete statements of themes. Finally, because transitional phrases occur between points of closure and initiation, we tend not to group them with the previous or subsequent phrases. Rather, they stand as a link between thematic statements. Examples 5.1a and b illustrate this point. Nonetheless, transitional function may also be evident in the tonal instability of modulating periods or phrase groups that project expository function.

The types of thematic material used in transitions will vary. Transitions may use previously heard themes, often fragmented and used in new textures in a developmental manner. This observation exemplifies the sometimes close relationship between developmental and transitional function. Conversely, transitions frequently contain *neutral material* or *figuration*.[1] This term refers to figures such as scales and arpeggios that lack a distinct or

---

[1] The term "neutral material" is used by Rothstein, p. 117. Caplin use the terms "characteristic" and "conventional" to make a similar distinction between distinct themes and common figures, p. 37.

Example 5.1 *Transitional Phrases.*

a. Haydn, Symphony No. 104, III, mm. 95–104.

unique melodic identity associated with motives and themes. To be sure, neutral figuration can be treated motivically, a hallmark of many classical compositions, but its use in transitions help to emphasize rhythmic and harmonic elements that lead to thematic material or textures as in Example 5.1b.

Developmental function as previously noted, is closely related to transitional function. Developmental phrases of music frequently have the same characteristics of instability and tension associated with transitions, but they almost always entail manipulation of previously heard themes and motives. Like transitions, developmental phrases make use of modulations, harmonic instability, sequences, and fragmentation or expansions of themes, often in new textures. The textures tend to be more active and complex, often having many different lines in contrapuntal relations. In many forms, notably sonata forms, developmental sections have distinct roles in the design, which will be discussed in later chapters. Expository phrases, particularly restatements, may vary or expand motivic ideas, and thus take on developmental character.

(Example 5.1, continued.)

b. Tchaikovsky, Symphony No. 4, IV, mm. 110–119.

INTRODUCTORY FUNCTION

As the term implies, *introductory function* occurs in passages that initiate a phrase, section, or movement. It is often evident in a phrase segment or phrase in which the texture or musical ideas are in some way incomplete, creating the expectation of an expository entrance. A unison or octave texture can serve as an introduction, not unlike an announcement or signal that a fuller, more complete texture is forthcoming, as in Example 5.2a. The fragmented phrase structure, emphasized by the rests and the fermata after arrival on the dominant harmony, contributes to the introductory function. In solo vocal works such as popular songs, arias, or lieder, an introductory phrase may be stated in the accompaniment as in Example 5.2b. In this example, as in the previous one, the phrase sounds incomplete because it begins like a continuation, using predominant harmonies. In fact, this introduction is the conclusion of the last phrase of the song. The use of sub-phrases or incomplete phrase structures such as these is often characteristic of introductory phrases, especially in vocal music where segments of the concluding phrase may be used as an introduction.

A theme that begins a work may be expository but take on the qualities of an introduction. Example 5.2c shows the opening measures of Symphony No. 8 by Schubert. This theme is a complete eight-measure phrase with a clear melodic shape, but it has an introductory function by virtue of its octave texture and arrival on a sustained dominant pitch. The low register and soft dynamics also give the phrase an introductory quality, a sense of expectation that a fuller texture and new theme may be forthcoming.

In concertos, which involve soloists, a complete introductory phrase that also gives expository presentation of thematic material may precede the entrance of the soloists. This might take the form of a ritornello as in Example 3.15a and b, or an extended section of music as in Classical concertos. Baroque music tends not to have incomplete phrases or accompaniment lead-ins as introductions since that could create contrasts in rhythmic motion, an effect that runs counter to Baroque aesthetics. Rather, as in the examples cited, full ritornellos will often be used at the beginning and the end of a concerto movement,

Example 5.2 *Introductory Function.*

a. Verdi, *La Traviata*, No. 2, "Dell' invito," mm. 1–4.

b. *Take Me Out to the Ballgame.*

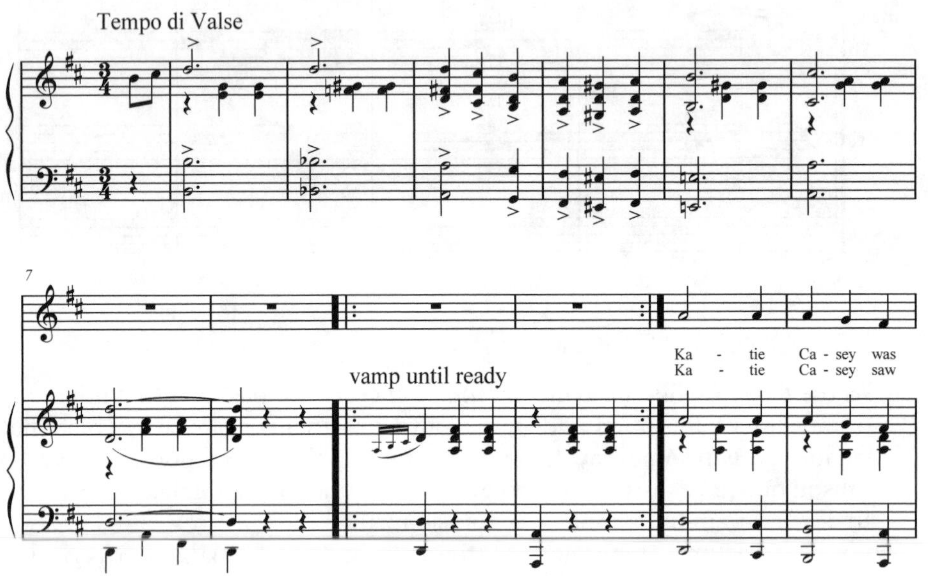

c. Schubert, Symphony No. 8, I, mm. 1–9.

chorus or aria, functioning to frame the movement as a whole. Thus we may refer to *framing function* when similar or identical material is used in introductory and closing phrases. Overtures and symphonies, on the other hand, will often have extended slow introductions of several phrases to begin a work, making a dramatic point of the beginning of the ensuing faster sections. See, for example, the beginning of the Sinfony from *Messiah* by Handel given in Example 3.14. We may then refer to an introductory section of the movement. Recitatives—declamatory phrases that precede the beginning of an aria—may function in a related manner as self-contained sections.

CLOSING FUNCTION

Closing function, as the term implies, occurs in phrases that bring a section or movement to a final cadence. Closing function may be conveyed by cadential progressions, pedal points, reiteration of thematic material, and rhythmic acceleration or deceleration in various combinations. Example 5.3a shows a clear example of a closing phrase. Following a PAC in measure 50, the phrase in measures 51–54 contains a cadential progression marked by ascending melodic motion over a tonic pedal, all of which convey a sense of finality appropriate to the end of the composition. The brief emphasis on subdominant harmony by use of the ♭7 (D natural in this case) in the context of V7/IV is a common tonal motion in closing phrases. Similarly, the closing phrase illustrated in Example 5.3b follows a decisive PAC in measure 129. Here, however, the melodic and harmonic patterns beginning in measure 130 are repetitions of a plagal cadential progression, that lead to an elongated final cadence in a broader tempo. A closing phrase based on an elaborate repeated cadential pattern can be seen in Example 2.4f, the "Mannheim" cadence that closes the first large section of Mozart's Symphony No. 41, first movement.

The excerpts cited in Example 5.3 may be understood as separate, cadential phrases rather than merely extensions of the previous phrase. The term *coda* (Italian for "tail") is used to refer to a closing phrase or phrases that follow a strong point of closure that could have concluded a section, normally a marked PAC. A coda serves to emphasize the conclusion of a composition. Closing function also may result from extensions of phrases. This relation between phrase expansions and closing phrases is addressed further in the Analytic Notes later in this chapter.

Though reiterated cadential progressions are perhaps the most common indicator of closing function in tonal music, the context of a phrase as the last part of a work or movement is often sufficient to convey a closing function. Consider Example 5.3c, the closing phrase in "Muth" from *Winterreise* by Schubert. This short, four-measure sentence is a complete phrase that is identical to the opening introductory phrase, also played by the piano. In this case, as in Baroque ritornellos, complete thematic phrases are being used to frame a movement, functioning as introductory and closing material. *The functions are dictated by their formal placement in the composition.*

Example 5.3 *Closing Function.*

a. Bach, *The Well-Tempered Clavier,* Book II, Prelude in E, mm. 51–54, closing phrase.

b. Handel, *Messiah*, "And the Glory," closing phrase.

c. Schubert, "Muth" from *Die Winterreise*, closing phrase.

PARENTHETICAL FUNCTION

An additional formal function, found most often in the more complex forms of classical music, is what may be termed *parenthetical function*. In such phrases, a sudden or unexpected change in tonality, theme, or texture conveys a sense of being a parenthetical aside or interjection. An example may be heard in the Brandenburg Concerto No. 2, measures 71–72 (Example 5.4a). Here a sudden change in texture and dynamics, and the introduction of a dominant pedal gives the effect of an interjection or digression within a thematic restatement as Bach elaborates and varies the ritornello that opens this movement.

Example 5.4b from Symphony No. 40 by Mozart shows a phrase segment that also may be understood as parenthetical. This segment is part of the repetition of the previous phrase in the movement, an antecedent phrase. The material in measures 56–57 had previously led to a two-measure cadential progression. Measure 58 instead introduces a startling harmonic digression to V7/♭VII, which is repeated three more times before the expanded cadential progression in measures 62–66. In this case the parenthetical function of the segment is conveyed by the unexpected harmony and the insistent repetition of the motives introduced. The harmonic digression momentarily interrupts the continuity and heightens the dramatic sense of the moment, which Mozart convincingly leads to a cadence. Example 5.4c shows a brief but pronounced parenthetical interjection in music of Debussy. The material in measure 98 briefly recalls a pentatonic melody heard in an earlier section of the movement, which contrasts with the chromatic motives heard in the surrounding measures. The marked contrasts in orchestration, register, and texture contribute to the parenthetical effect.

Each of the excerpts cited in Example 5.4 differs in its effect, and it must be noted that such functional interpretations of phrases as parenthetical are often subjective and can have varied effects or meanings. In the example by Bach, the dynamics give an impression of a parenthetical interjection, though the thematic material is not new. In the Mozart example, the parenthetical quality is tonal and rhythmic in nature and is part of an expansion of a

Example 5.4 *Parenthetical function.*

a. Bach, Brandenburg Concerto No. 2, mm. 68–73.

b. Mozart, Symphony No. 40, I, mm. 56–66.

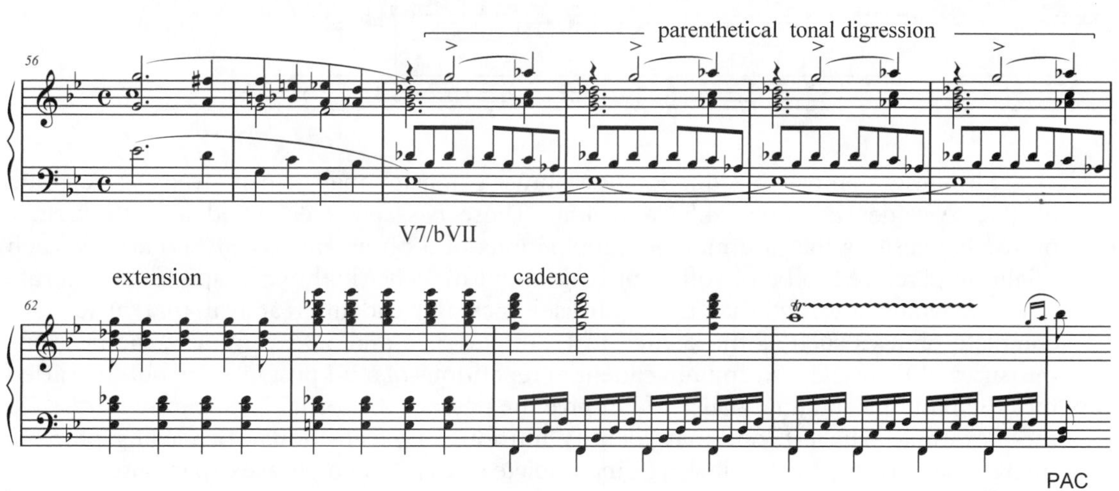

c. Debussy, "Nuage" from *Nocturnes*, mm. 96–102.

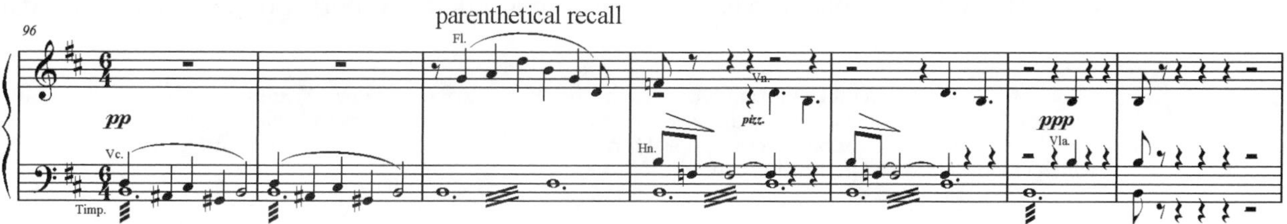

repeated phrase. In the example by Debussy, the parenthetical measure is a fleeting recall of an earlier theme, resulting in a juxtaposition of two different motivic ideas.[2]

In all of these examples, the parenthetical passages are relatively brief. It is certainly possible to have an entire phrase or section function parenthetically, particularly in episodic forms where strong contrasts in material are expected. That a passage is parenthetical does not imply that it is of secondary formal importance. Often such passages have important connections to previous themes or later developments, and they invariably create marked dramatic and expressive effects. Finally, we must keep in mind that parenthetical phrases are infrequent in most music. Not all sudden changes create parenthetical function; there must be some sense of the musical material being unexpected formally, standing apart from surrounding material.

Analytic Note: The relations between phrase connections and expansions, and the formal functions cited above, merit consideration. Consider Example 5.5 from the end of the first section of the second movement of Mozart's Symphony No. 41. Measures 43–44 are a link that returns to the opening of the movement initially. After the repeat of measures 1–44, the link is expanded in measures 45–46 (a second ending after the repeat). In both instances the connection links serve as a transition to a new key: the first time the link effects a return to tonic (F major); the second, a modulation from dominant (C major) to submediant (D minor). The second occurrence occupies four measures, and takes the form of an extension and continuation that stands apart from the cadence in measure 43 and the beginning of a development section in measure 47. Thus this passage may be viewed as a separate transitional phrase, though it is initiated as a phrase link.

Example 5.5 *Phrase link as transition*

Mozart, Symphony No. 41, II, mm. 43–47.

Similarly, a phrase introduction or a phrase extension may be perceived as a separate phrase. Consider Examples 4.5a and 4.5b. These passages were cited as introductory phrase expansions that are motivic anticipations of a phrase melody. Alternatively, each might be perceived to be of sufficient length and melodic/rhythmic shape to be separate phrases. Note, however, that these phrases lack the cadential arrival that articulates complete phrases such as those cited in Examples 5.2c and 5.3c. Similarly, the last four measures of Example 4.7a contain cadential repetitions of a V-I progression, but the varied melodic patterns and final register shift give the passage the form of a separate phrase. As these examples suggest, one may identify introductory, transitional, or closing phrases, though the phrases may be viewed as incomplete or as part of a phrase expansion.

The distinction between phrase expansions and separate phrases with related formal functions also is affected by the relative proportion and shape of the passage in question. As is so often the case, formal interpretations may vary and the context must be considered. The difference between an extension and a codetta (a short coda), or a codetta and a

[2] Recall of themes from other movements in multi-movement works is a device exploited by composers of the nineteenth-century in particular. Such *cyclic forms* will be discussed in a separate chapter. The use of parenthetical phrases and juxtapositions to create novel formal designs is one of Debussy's important formal innovations, which will be addressed in the final chapter.

coda, for example, is not necessarily hard and fast, and should be understood in terms of relative length and context. However labeled, the formal function would be that of closing. Table 5.1 gives a summary of some possible correlations between internal phrase functions and the formal functions discussed. These functions may occur within phrase segments or, as illustrated in the examples discussed in this chapter, may be expanded to be separate phrases or even sections of a work.

Table 5.1 Correlations between phrase and formal function.

Phrase Function	Formal Function
complete theme	expository
lead-in	introductory
links	transitional
continuation	transitional
extension	closing (coda)
internal expansion	parenthetical

II. Musical Texture and Form

Musical texture, broadly conceived, refers to the arrangement and quality of sounds in music. In the discussions of tonality, themes, phrase structure, and formal functions, the importance of musical texture in shaping musical form was frequently noted. Cadences, for example, often are signaled by the coalescence of parts, or by increases or decreases in the number of parts. Thematic presentations are often characterized by textures such as melody and accompaniment that give prominence to the principal melodic line. Certain textural processes also characterize various formal functions. These observations substantiate the idea that as we study a score or listen to music, we sense that different functions look and sound differently from one another, and that there is a connection between texture and form. Further, musical texture is subject to frequent changes at various levels; the textural processes involved in these changes are among the most salient aural phenomena of music.

To clarify these points, the second part of this chapter will consider musical texture and its role in shaping form. The discussion will define aspects of musical texture, examine the distinctions and relations among basic types of texture, and then briefly describe some common textural processes that generate and delineate musical form. The emphasis will be on processes or techniques that are most readily perceived and that are related to the textures prevalent in Western tonal music.[3]

TYPES OF MUSICAL TEXTURE

Musical texture is usually described in terms of general categories that indicate the density and/or the relations of lines. *Monophony* refers to texture of a single line; *polyphony* refers to a texture of many different lines or melodies that are rhythmically independent and of equal importance; *homophony* usually refers to a texture in which a melody is presented in one voice with accompaniment, sometimes in similar rhythms; *heterophony* refers to a texture of lines that contains different elaborations of the same basic melody. These categories are indeed very general and apart from monophony, a wide range of possibilities exist within the categories described.[4]

[3] Further discussion of textures will be found throughout the text, notably in Chapters 12 and 14.

[4] Traditional Western music is particularly associated with polyphony and homophony while heterophony is often associated with non-Western music. Monophony is the oldest texture, originally associated with chant.

More specifically, a musical texture is defined by 1) *density*, the number of lines or pitches in a passage *and* their range and spacing; 2) *rhythmic relations* of lines such as homorhythmic (the same) or polyrhythmic (contrasting); and 3) the *function of constituent lines* such as melody, accompaniment, imitative entry, countermelody, cantus firmus, and so forth. Closely allied to texture is the element of *timbre*, which is defined by the dynamic level, articulation, range, register, and instrumentation. Inasmuch as timbre affects the quality of sounds, it may be understood as an element of texture. Texture then is a composite element of music since it involves several different aspects and as such it is subject to change from moment to moment.

Though these categories of musical texture are widely used, the terms are somewhat ambiguous and require clarification. Monophony refers to a single line, although melodies sung in octaves, for example, might be considered monophonic since the melody is simply doubled. Conversely, a single line may be a compound melody that implies more than one line. Generally, *a texture in which a single line or a single melody is heard is monophonic*. The change to a single line of music from a multi-voiced texture is one of the most common means to signal a formal delineation or function. In many examples discussed in section I of this chapter, we observed changes to unison or octave textures, as in Example 5.1b. Listen again to Example 2.5a and Exercise 3.7 and observe the change to monophonic textures as cadences are approached. Other times, a single line may serve as a lead-in, link or transition between phrases, as in Examples 4.4c, 4.6a and 4.6b. Such changes also create anticipation of a fuller texture that will initiate the next phrase.

Polyphony is a general term that refers to music that may contain contrapuntal and homophonic textures. The term *contrapuntal*, which will be used here, more precisely describes textures in which rhythmic independence and functional equality of lines is heard. Imitation of thematic material in any line of the texture is often used to create contrapuntal textures. As lines are imitated, they continue in counterpoint to the imitating line; that is, the initial line continues in contrasting rhythms and contour as it is imitated. Non-imitative contrapuntal textures will make use of rhythmically contrasting melodic lines of equal prominence and importance. The Bach Two-part Invention in D minor cited in Chapter Two is an example of a composition composed with imitative and non-imitative contrapuntal textures. An important aspect of contrapuntal textures is that voices often drop out and reenter at different times. These changes in density help shape and articulate phrases. Listen for example, to a fugue such as Example 12.5. As voices imitate one another, drop out, and reenter, the changes of density shape the contrapuntal flow of voices.

Homophony, as noted, refers to textures made up of a single melody with accompaniment. The most important contrast with contrapuntal textures is that the lines in homophonic textures will not have equality of function or importance. One voice in a homophonic texture is usually considered the principal voice or melody while other voices are considered subordinate. As observed earlier, such textures are often used in expository presentations of themes.

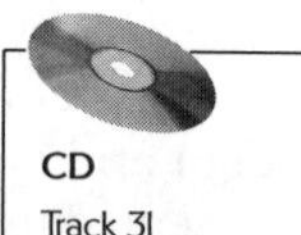

CD
Track 31

The degree of rhythmic independence in homophonic textures is quite varied and has a seemingly endless range of possibilities. At one extreme are *homorhythmic* (or chorale) textures in which a melody is supported by lines moving in identical or similar rhythms. The hymns cited in previous chapters use such a texture. At the other extreme are textures such as those illustrated in Example 5.6, in which one line may have melodic prominence, but rhythmically distinct accompaniments or brief points of imitation occur. The result is a texture that is both contrapuntal and homophonic.

The distinction between contrapuntal and melody/accompaniment textures then is not always clear. Elaborate accompaniments and countermelodies often exhibit distinct rhythmic and linear shapes in counterpoint to a principal melodic line. Even in four-voice chorale textures, good voice-leading dictates some degree of independence between the lines. Consequently, the categories of polyphony and homophony are best

Example 5.6 Wagner, Overture to *Die Meistersinger,* excerpt.

understood as a continuum of possibilities, with imitative, contrapuntal works at one end and homorhythmic chorales at the other end.

Many accompaniments in homophonic textures are easily recognized by their repeated rhythmic patterns and limited melodic interest, which provide a distinct contrast with the melody. A wide range of different figures can be found, distinguished by density, range, and spacing. Example 3.8 provides good examples of melody and accompaniment textures with characteristic accompaniment patterns. Example 3.8a uses a repeated figure in the bass voice with a simple contour and limited range typical of Classical period accompaniments. The chordal figures and afterbeats used as accompaniment in Example 3.8b are typical of much nineteenth-century music in which a wider range of motion is used. (See also Example 4.4c, beginning in measure 17, for a common nineteenth-century accompaniment figure.)

In compositions such as these, a distinct accompaniment may be maintained throughout a section or even a complete work. In other works, changes of texture and accompaniment are far more frequent. Consider the textures of the Scherzo from Piano Sonata Op. 2 No. 2 by Beethoven addressed in the exercises for Chapter 2. In this movement we hear 1) an alternation between a motivic figure in the top voice and a chordal response in measures 1–2; 2) a change to a homorhythmic chordal texture in measures 3–4; 3) an introduction of a new texture of melody and rhythmic accompaniment in measure 19; 4) another texture using sustained chords introduced in measure 25; and 4) a return to the opening texture, later varied in the closing measures of the movements. Consider also Example 3.9b from the *Nutcracker Suite* by Tchaikovsky. The opening period is a melody with accompaniment but in a homorhythmic texture. The repetition of the period that begins in measure 9 introduces distinct rhythmic and linear motion in the subordinate voices, creating a more contrapuntal texture. These two examples give some idea of the wide range of specific textures within the general category of homophony. They also show how changes in texture can distinguish phrases and sub-phrases.

In addition to the categories mentioned, the density and range of lines and pitches are important elements of musical texture subject to frequent change. General terms such as *thick, thin, high,* or *low* are used to describe density. More precisely, density may refer to the number of lines sounding over a period of time; it may also refer to the number of pitches sounding at a given point in time. These linear and vertical aspects of textural density may be identical, but they may fluctuate and are often distinct from one another. Further, the spacing and range of constituent lines affects the vertical density. This aspect of texture is influenced by the type of music being composed. In this regard, a comparison of instrumental and vocal textures is instructive.

VOCAL AND INSTRUMENTAL TEXTURES

Vocal textures traditionally are categorized by linear density. That is, we designate choral works for unison, two, three, four, or more parts or voices. Range designations also characterize vocal textures; thus we speak of four-voiced textures for soprano, alto, tenor and bass (SATB) or various combinations such as duets or trios. The number of lines is generally quite clear in vocal textures, since the limitations of the voice make compound lines impractical. On the other hand, the spacing of voices and their respective ranges may vary greatly, changing the vertical density and timbre of the textures. As will be discussed in Chapter 13, vocal forms are shaped in part by the changes in density of the vocal texture. Further, the accompaniment to a vocal texture adds an additional element that is subject to change and variation. That a vocal work may use several types of textures in succession is illustrated by the chorus "The Lord Gave the Word" from *Messiah* by Handel.

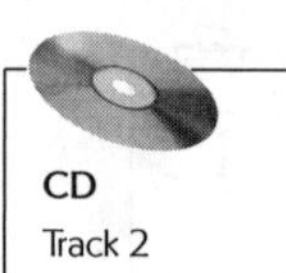

CD
Track 2

Instrumental textures, especially chamber ensembles, may also be identified by the number of parts. String or woodwind trios, quartets and quintets, for example, all have a specified number of parts. In contrast to vocal music, however, instrumental writing may draw on the capabilities of various instruments and incorporate frequent leaps, arpeggios, extensive doublings, active or extended rhythmic figures, and compound melodies. Thus instrumental textures potentially exhibit a wider range and greater variance in rhythmic activity and density, especially in accompaniments. The Scherzo from Beethoven's Piano Sonata, Op. 2 No. 2 (see Chapter 2) also illustrates this point. The principal theme is characterized by systematic changes of register, an element playfully exploited in the closing phrase. Note how the new melody in G♯ minor (measures 19–25) narrows the range and introduces a consistent rhythmic accompaniment, a contrast to the sudden changes heard elsewhere. Works for instrumental ensembles extend textural possibilities with contrasts in orchestration and a wider range of pitch space to draw on. Of importance in any work then is the influence of medium or genre on the textures that help shape the musical form.

TEXTURAL PROCESSES

The various changes in types of texture discussed above may also be described in terms of systematic changes in textural aspects—textural processes—that shape the musical form. The following processes are found in a wide range of music and may generate phrases and contribute to directed motion toward closure. Changes in one or more aspects of rhythm may also accompany these processes, including changes in harmonic rhythm, and techniques such as hemiola, syncopation, and cross rhythms. Often several processes may work together in a complementary manner.

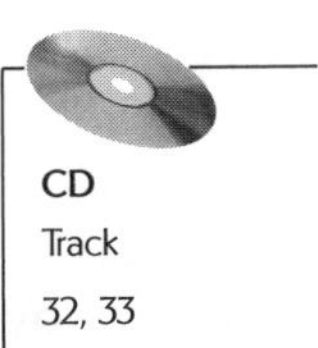
CD
Track
32, 33

Systematic ascent or descent of linear motions through several registers. Listen to the excerpts from Bach's Double Concerto and Verdi's Prelude to *La Traviata*. These excerpts offer clear examples of systematic ascending and descending gestures, respectively.

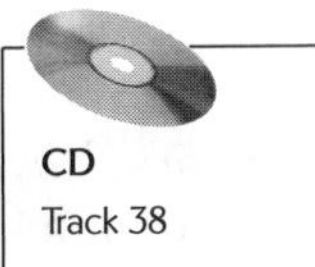
CD
Track 38

Dissolution or accumulation of textural components: *dissolution* involves a reduction, whether sudden or gradual, in the number of components. As we have observed, a reduction to a single line is not uncommon in transitional phrases or introductory phrases; *accumulation* involves gradual or sudden additions to the texture to increase density toward climax. An excerpt from Beethoven's Symphony No. 3, I, illustrates both of these processes.

Coalescence: The change from a polyrhythmic texture to a homorhythmic texture as lines coalesce or come together, notably at points of cadence. Review Examples 2.4–2.7.

Juxtaposition: Two strongly contrasting musical ideas or textures alternate with one another. The sense of juxtaposition will be conveyed by the suddenness of the alternation and the absence of transitions from one idea to the next. Timbral contrasts, including instrumentation, dynamics, and articulation, contribute to the identity of the contrasting ideas. Contrasts between solo and tutti textures found in concertos demonstrate this idea. This technique is also prevalent in much twentieth-century music and is discussed further in the concluding chapter.

Textural Inversion: The repetition of material with an exchange of registral position. This technique results when invertible counterpoint is used and is a frequent occurrence in contrapuntal genres like fugues. Example 5.7 illustrates a partial exchange of material, the cello taking the violin line in m. 16 and inverting it melodically.

Example 5.7 Haydn, String Quartet Op. 76, No. 3, III, mm. 10–20.

Antiphony: The alternation of different, spatially separated ensembles, or of different timbres, such as strings alternating with brass. This technique often involves double choirs or ensembles, but is also used in ensemble writing. Example 5.1b illustrates an antiphonal texture as strings and winds alternate.

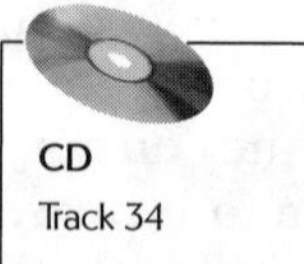

CD
Track 34

Rhythmic acceleration or deceleration: A systematic progression in *rhythmic motion* by changes in note values. Listen to an excerpt from Beethoven's Piano Sonata Op. 53, I, for a clear example of this process.

Other processes may be encountered but the ones listed here are among the most common and readily perceived. *Most of the processes described may be supported by changes in dynamics*. As lines accumulate or dissolve through changes in density, dynamics change inherently. Systematic changes in register or density are often accompanied by notated changes in dynamics.

Summary

Formal function refers to the role of a phrase or section of music in the musical form. These functions include introductory, expository, transitional, developmental, closing, and parenthetical. Each function has distinct characteristics, but in practice a phrase, phrase combination, or section of a work may exhibit characteristics of more than one function. Passages that project a single function—usually introductory, transitional, and closing functions—can be most salient in delineating the sections of a form. Expository and developmental functions are prevalent in many forms, within phrases or sections, because the presentation and variation of material is basic to generating music. Parenthetical function is perhaps the least frequently found, and is used for unexpected formal digressions. Different genres or styles will exhibit different manifestations of formal functions. Simple songs or hymns are basically expository; through-composed works such as fugues or preludes are expository and developmental; the sonata forms of eighteenth and nineteenth centuries encompass a wide range of formal functions, often presented or blended in intricate ways.

Textural processes and changes are among the most salient features of music. Changes in texture shape musical ideas and can project formal functions. Introductory or transitional phrases, for example, often use octave textures or textures of a single line. At large levels, contrasts in basic types of texture, in density, or in types of textural configuration can delineate sections of a composition. A trio that follows a minuet, for example, is usually differentiated in part by a reduction in textural density as well as the introduction of a new melody and accompaniment. The density, spacing and rhythmic motion of lines can be subject to frequent change within phrases. Systematic changes in density and register contribute to motion toward closure. Though some compositions, including instrumental preludes and many dances and songs, maintain a consistent rhythmic texture or density of lines throughout, a great variety of specific textures may be found in a single short composition. Textures may also be influenced by the type of composition, whether vocal or instrumental, solo or ensemble, and not least by the composer's imagination.

The art of composing, in part, is that of exploring the possibilities for elaboration, expansion, or transformation of material to shape musical ideas and forms in a unified and convincing manner. Formal functions provide one means of delineating and evaluating musical designs from the perspective of formal discourse, of understanding how musical ideas are shaped and related. Composers have continually demonstrated that the invention of specific textures is a basic aspect of composing music. Considering changes in texture, which shape ideas and formal designs and help generate a composition, illuminates the notion of form as process. Our ability to recognize and follow these changes enhances our ability to hear processes as parts of larger musical wholes.

SUGGESTED READINGS

For an interesting account of the inflence of the concept of formal functuion on composition, see Douglas Rust, "Conversations with Lutoslawkski," in *Musical Quarterly* 79 (1995), 207–223. See also Berry, *Structural Functions* and Levy, "Texture as a Sign" for discussions of texture and formal function.

Review and Exercises

1. **Terms:** In a concise sentence or two, describe the characteristics of the various formal functions discussed in this chapter.

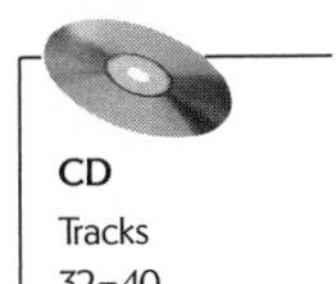

CD
Tracks
32–40

2. **Aural Exercises:** Listen to each of the following excerpts and determine the type of formal function(s) evident in each. Identify formal processes, including changes in texture, that clarify the function. Describe or identify any textural processes you hear.

   1. Bach, Double Concerto, Movement 1
   2. Verdi, Prelude to *La Traviata*
   3. Beethoven, Sonata Op. 53, I
   4. Tchaikovsky, Overture to *Nutcracker Suite*
   5. Handel, *Messiah*, "Rejoice, Rejoice"
   6. Beethoven, Symphony No. 3, IV
   7. Beethoven, Symphony No. 3, I
   8. Chopin, Ballade in G minor
   9. Schubert, Symphony No. 8

3. **Score Analysis:**
   a. Examine the Prelude in E major and the Two-Part Invention in E minor by Bach given at the close of Chapter 2. Identify as many different textural configurations as you can and note where marked changes in density or register occur. Consider the extent to which these changes align with the tonal design of each composition. Where are the points of greatest density or rhythmic activity?
   b. Formal functions are identified for the following excerpts. The function(s) listed may be evident in the entire excerpt or within a segment. Listen to and study the score of each example. Explain what attributes convey the function identified, focusing on tonal and textural elements.

Haydn, String Quartet in C, Op. 76, No 3, III, Trio: expository, transitional, parenthetical.
Mozart, Symphony No. 41, III, Minuet, mm. 1–16: expository.
Mozart, Symphony No. 41, III, Minuet, mm. 28–44: developmental.
Mozart, Symphony No. 41, III, Trio, mm. 68–79: transitional.
Mozart, Symphony No. 41, IV, mm. 282–313: parenthetical and closing.
Beethoven, Symphony No. 3, III, mm. 1–6: Introductory.
*Schubert, "Der Doppelgänger", introductory and closing functions.
*Beethoven, Sonata for Violin and Piano, Op. 24, I, mm. 1–32: expository and transitional.
+Wagner, Prelude to *Lohengrin*, mm. 13–19: transitional.
+Brahms, Sonata No. 3 for Clarinet and Piano in E♭ Major, I, mm. 162–173.

PART
2

Forms of Music

6 One-Part and Binary Forms

Introduction

Many types of musical compositions divide into a distinct number of sections or parts. Sectional forms sometimes are referred to as "part forms" to distinguish them from forms that tend to be continuous and through-composed. The most common part forms are those that divide into two or three sections, which result in *binary* and *ternary forms* respectively. In addition, some pieces are comprised of a single section, thus are labeled *one-part forms*. Other larger forms, to be discussed in later chapters, result from expansion of binary and ternary forms. Composers use themes, keys, or textures in a variety of ways to relate or distinguish the sections of these forms. Typically the ends of sections are articulated by strong closure and often by rhythmic breaks.

In this chapter we will discuss one-part and binary forms. We will examine different ways in which sections of music may be organized with regard to phrase structure, formal processes and functions. As we shall see, the processes of statement-elaboration or statement-contrast-restatement are important formal principles in most part forms. We will also continue to address points raised in Part I regarding how music is segmented and how musical forms are generated.

One-Part Forms

One-part forms consist of a phrase group or period that comprise the complete piece. One-part forms tend to be brief and are most often found in instrumental preludes and etudes, or in songs. The most important distinguishing characteristics of one-part forms include:

- continuous harmonic and rhythmic motion until the final cadence
- lack of a conclusive, PAC in the original key until the end
- frequent if not continuous use of elided cadences or connections between phrases
- absence of thematic restatements in the tonic key following contrasting phrases

To say a piece is a one-part form is not to imply that there is only a single phrase or that there are no repetitions of material within the piece. Further, some of these characteristics may be found in other part forms. *In tonal music, the most salient feature of one-part forms is continuous harmonic motion such that a conclusive cadence in the tonic key is not heard until the end of the piece*. Further, one-part forms often are both expository and developmental; the thematic ideas presented initially are continuously elaborated. A few examples will clarify these points.

The prelude shown in Example 6.1 is based on continuous sixteenth-note figures introduced in the first measure and used throughout the prelude. This type of solo instrumental prelude is sometimes referred to as a *figuration prelude*, which frequently is in one-part form. As in many Baroque compositions, statements and sequential elaborations of motives generate the piece, which thus tends to be monothematic and developmental. In this example, the modulations to closely related keys of D minor (vi) and G minor (ii) are confirmed by cadences. The points of cadence are elided and followed immediately by new tonal motions. This continuous harmonic and rhythmic motion results in a phrase group rather than periodic phrases. Finally, no restatement of the opening theme in the tonic key is heard, though a return to F major is clearly emphasized to conclude the piece.[1]

While the preceding example contained continuous rhythmic motion and elided cadences, some one-part forms are comprised of two or more phrases with distinct rhythmic deceleration at cadences or with breaks between phrases. Example 2.10 (Chapter 2) contains four phrases with implied breaks between each phrase. The piece is a one-part form since each phase modulates, creating continuous harmonic motion. The modulations and persistent dotted rhythm that is presented in varied harmonic and melodic guises conveys a developmental function. One-part forms may also have two phrases in an antecedent/consequent relation as seen in Example 3.2 (Chapter 3). The first phrase is tonally open, ending on a Phrygian HC in D minor. The second phrase, rhythmically similar but melodically contrasting, completes the piece with a return to F major and a PAC on the tonic. The two phrases comprise a single formal unit, a contrasting period. Thus this hymn may be perceived as a one-part form that is expository.

Example 6.1 Bach, *The Well-Tempered Clavier,* Book I, Prelude No. 11 in F major.

[1] Though many preludes and etudes exhibit the characteristics described, such pieces may be in two or more sections and thus take on other forms. See for example, Bach, *The Well-Tempered Clavier,* Book II, Prelude No. 5 in D.

Analytic Note: Some analysts assert that pieces comprised of periods, whether contrasting or parallel, may be understood as small binary forms. The distinction, as is often the case, will rest on one's criteria for segmenting and grouping. A period may be understood as a group of related phrases comprising a single section and thus a one-part form. Small binary forms, as defined in the next section, exhibit different designs and processes than the periodic one-part forms described here. One-part forms also are considered through-composed in most instances, since tonal/thematic restatements do not occur. It must be understood, however, that through-composed pieces are often in two or more sections.

Analytic Exercises

1. Listen to each of the works cited below and make note of the types of cadences you hear and whether modulations take place. Then, with the aid of a score,

determine formal elements in each piece that contribute to the perception of a one-part form.

a. *Bach, *The Well-Tempered Clavier,* Book I, Prelude in C major, Prelude in C minor
b. *Chopin, Prelude in C major, Prelude in G major (CD Track 1)
c. *Schumann, "War Song" from *Album for the Young*
d. +Poulenc, *Mouvement Perpétuel* No. 1

2. Schubert, "Wanderers Nachtlied." This haunting, romantic lied is a good example of a piece that is a one-part form though it divides into contrasting phrases. A complete harmonic analysis of the piece will illuminate the continuous harmonic motion that shapes the form.[2] What is the formal function of the first two measures and of the final three and a half measures of the piece?

Binary Forms

Binary (two-part) forms occur in a number of genres but are most consistently encountered in dance movements, simple songs, and variation movements. Many binary forms are readily apparent by the presence of repeat signs in the score indicating that each of the sections is to be played twice. Rather than using repeat signs for exact repetitions, composers often chose to write out a section a second time to vary the material.

Tonally, binary forms are either continuous or sectional. *Continuous binary* form refers to a form in which the first section ends in a new key. *Sectional binary* form refers to a form in which the first section ends in the original key, usually with a PAC. *These distinctions can have implications for the way material is elaborated or reprised in the second half of the form, as is discussed in the examples*. Thematically, binary forms are classified as *simple, rounded,* or *balanced.* Each of these types is distinguished by the absence or presence of thematic restatements in the second section of material from part one. The proportions and processes involved in each of these binary forms vary such that further distinctions between small and expanded binary forms may be made. It should come as no surprise that the distinction between these various categories is not always unambiguous. As always, the analysis of formal structure will clarify the specific attributes of a given piece. Each of these binary forms will be discussed separately to clarify the attributes of the various categories.

SIMPLE BINARY FORM

Simple binary form is a two-part form in which each section is normally repeated and which is represented as ‖:A:‖:B:‖.[3] The B section is related thematically to the A section, but it contains no restatement of the opening phrase of the A section *in the tonic key. This*

[2] An excellent linear analysis and discussion of text in this lied may be found in Cadwallader and Gagne, Analysis of Tonal Music, 208–214. The text of the lied with translation is given in Chapter 13.

[3] Traditional letter designations for binary forms can be somewhat misleading. The thematic material is often the same or similar in both sections of a binary form such that the designation A‖A' would seem more logical. The conventional designation of part two as the B section reflects the new elaboration of material and contrasts in keys and tonal motion.

Example 6.1 Schubert, "Wanderers Nachtlied."

absence of thematic restatement in section two is the distinguishing characteristic of simple binary forms. A continuous, simple binary form is then a two-part form in which the A section closes in a new key, and the B section contains no tonic restatement of themes from the A section. The first section of a continuous binary form in most instances modulates to the dominant or, if the piece is in a minor key, to the relative major. The B section may continue in the closing key of the A section, or begin in a key other than tonic; eventually the music modulates back to tonic. Whether the form is sectional or continuous, the B section contrasts with the A section since it will digress harmonically and then return to the tonic key.

Analytic Note: The term *restatement* refers to the return of a thematic idea in its original key following a contrasting phrase or section. It therefore differs from *repetition*, which refers to the recurrence of a thematic idea, phrase or section immediately following its presentation. The possibility of a perceived restatement occurring in a non-tonic key is a technique composers exploit in shaping their forms.

Simple binary forms are found most often in dance movements from Baroque suites, in short songs, or in self-contained themes within larger forms. Though these genres are based on the simple binary design, they exhibit a wide range of formal structures and proportions. The movements from Baroque suites are usually simple binary forms with each section comprised of two or more phrases. Example 6.2 shows an Allemande by Bach.

Example 6.2 Bach, French Suite No. VI in E, Allemande.

This movement exhibits all of the characteristics of the continuous simple binary form outlined above. Note the following:

- Repeat signs clearly divide the piece into two sections.
- The first section modulates to the dominant, concluding with a PAC in B major.
- The two sections use similar material reflecting the principle of *statement-elaboration* that generates the music.
- The second section continues to elaborate the motives of the first section, but its tonal motion and melodic content are varied, conveying a developmental function.
- No restatement of the opening phrase of section one is heard in section two in the tonic key.

Though the two sections of a simple binary dance movement may be of similar or identical length, the second section more often is longer, as illustrated in Example 6.2. This expansion may be due to the presence of more modulations or the use of a closing phrase or codetta that extends the second section. The two sections of the piece are clearly based on elaboration of the same or similar motives, a monothematic approach typical of Baroque forms. The dance movements often open each section with expository presentation of the same idea, which is subsequently developed in one or more keys with no distinct transitional phrases. Closing function is conveyed by the return to tonic and reinforced when a coda is added. In this example, the B section begins with a dominant statement of the opening measures of the movement, characteristic of many simple binary forms, followed by a new continuation. Modulations to C♯ minor (vi) and then back to E major (I) shape the tonal motion in the B section. Note the PAC in measures 24–25 that marks the last four measures as a codetta, a final cadential elaboration that closes the movement.

The modulations in Example 6.2 are to closely related keys, typical of Baroque music. While a modulation away from tonic is expected in the A section with a close on dominant, and a modulation back to tonic is expected in the B section, the tonal designs within sections will vary. The placement and number of modulations will help shape the formal structure of a specific piece. Note in Example 6.2 that the modulation to B major (V) is made rather early in the first section (measure 5) with extensive confirmation of the key in measures 6–12. Modulations to submediant (vi) in section two are common in major keys, as are modulations to IV or ii. Figure 6.1 illustrates the tonal designs of two other works to give some idea of the flexibility composers may employ.

Figure 6.1 *Examples of tonal designs in simple binary forms of the Baroque.*[4]

a. Bach, French Suite No. IV in B minor, Minuet, continuous simple binary form

measure: 1	8	16	:‖:	24	29	36:‖
key: i	i	III	III	v	i	i
cadence type:	HC	PAC		PAC		PAC

b. Handel, Sonata No. 3 for Flute, Minuet in G, sectional simple binary form

measure: 1	8	:‖:	9	16	20	24:‖
key: I	I		I	vi	(ii)	I
cadence type:	THC			PAC		PAC

Most Baroque dances in simple binary forms contain a phrase group in each section. If the first section is periodic, the second section is invariably a more extended elaboration of motives; consequently it is a phrase group that is considerably longer than section one.[5] In songs or short themes that are simple binary forms, however, the two sections may be equal in length and relatively short. Example 6.3 shows a theme that became well known as the basis for a monumental set of variations by Beethoven.

This theme contains all of the characteristics of simple binary form noted previously. In addition, another important attribute distinguishes this example of simple binary form. Note that each section is a sixteen-bar phrase (4 + 4 + 8) that comprises a large sentence. Short, simple binary forms that are comprised of a single phrase in each section result in a *small binary form*. Small binary forms are very often symmetrical though they do not always contain sentences in each section.[6] Another theme used in a set of brilliant variations by Brahms illustrates this point. (See Example 6.4)

In this example, each section consists of four measures that are repeated. In the second section, the first two measures are a continuation based on the previous motives. The final two measures, though beginning with a restatement of the first measure, have a cadential function, completing a four-measure phrase in section two. Each section then is comprised of a single phrase and the theme is a small binary form.

---

[4] Keys in ( ) are passing modulations, that is, tonicizations.

[5] See for example the Gavotte I and II from the English Suite No. 3 in G minor by Bach.*

[6] See also the theme from the Beethoven String Quartet Op. 131 in C♯ minor, IV, mm. 1–32 in which repeats are written out. (Example 3.12b gives mm. 1–16.)

Example 6.3 Beethoven, Theme from *Thirty-Three Variations on a Waltz by Diabelli,* Op. 120.

1

7

14

2nd time only

G:

PAC

20

26

1st time only

PAC

Example 6.4 Brahms, Theme from *Variations and Fugue on a Theme by Handel,* Op. 24.

BALANCED BINARY FORMS

Some binary forms such as the Courante shown in Example 6.5 use the same or similar thematic material and phrase structures at the end of each half. Here measures 21–24 are almost identical to measures 9–12, apart from the transposition and some variation in rhythm and register, with identical closing cadences. Such binary forms are referred to as *balanced binary forms*.[7] The thematic connection between the ends of each section of a balanced binary form alludes to a rhyming scheme, which vocal works often exploit. Like simple continuous binary forms, balanced forms close the first section in a new key and contain no clear restatement of the opening material in the tonic key. The balanced binary form, however, presents the same themes to close each section in different contexts: the first presentation confirms the modulation; the restatement in the second

Example 6.5 Bach, Partita No. 2 in C minor, Courante.

[7] Green observes that a balanced binary form is usually perceived only when an entire closing section is restated. See Green, 78–79. This assertion obviously is subject to varied interpretations.

section marks the return to tonic. Though the two sections of balanced binary forms are not always identical in length, as in this example, they do tend to be in similar if not identical proportions. Note how this example also begins section two with a variant of the first measure of the movement, now transposed to G major and with inversion of motives. The parallel beginnings of each section with *inversion* of motives in the second section are common in simple and balanced binary forms of Baroque dance movements.

The amount of material that is restated in balanced binary forms may vary from a few measures to several phrases. Many baroque sonatas, notably those of Domenico Scarlatti, are balanced binary forms in which much of the closing material of the A section is restated at the end of the B section. Listen to the Sonata in G major, K. 427 (Longo 286) by Scarlatti. The two sections of the sonata begin with different elaborations of related motives but the final ten measures of each half are identical apart from transposition. This passage is shown in its original form in D major (V) in Example 6.6. The "echo-like" repetitions of short subphrases, characteristic of Scarlatti and the Italian Baroque style, help to expand the passage.

Example 6.6 Scarlatti, Sonata in G major, K. 427 (Longo 286), mm. 12–22.

Exercises: Simple, balanced, and small binary forms

1. Complete an analysis of the tonal design and phrase structure of Example 6.3. Close harmonic analysis will aid in identifying the brief tonicizations in each half.

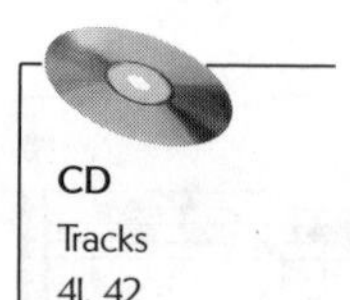

CD
Tracks
41, 42

2. **Aural Analysis.** Listen to each of the examples listed below and determine if they are small, simple, or balanced binary forms, and whether they are sectional or continuous.
   - **a.** Bach, Badinerie from Orchestral Suite No. II in D
   - **b.** Beethoven, String Quartet Op. 131, IV, Theme

3. **Score Analysis.** Examine the following pieces and determine the type of binary form that is evident. Outline the tonal design as illustrated in Figure 1.
   - **a.** Corelli, Concerto Grosso, Op. 6, No. 8, II, IV, +
   - **b.** Bach, Minuet from the *Notebook for Anna Magdalena Bach**
   - **c.** Bach, Gavotte I in G minor from the English Suite No. 3, BWV 808*
   - **d.** Scarlatti, Sonata K. 96 (L. 465) in D major*
   - **e.** Handel, Suite No. 4 in E minor, Courante+
   - **f.** Beethoven, Symphony No. 3, III, Scherzo; IV, mm. 45–59
   - **g.** Schubert, Waltz in A♭ major, Op. 9, No. 2*
   - **h.** Schubert, Waltzes, Op. 9 +
   - **i.** Brahms, "Guten Abend" (Lullaby)
   - **j.** Liszt, "Nuages Gris"+
   - **k.** Hindemith, "A Swan," from *Six Chansons**
   - **l.** Bartók, *Pentatonic Melody*+

ROUNDED BINARY FORM

Binary form in which a restatement of phrases from the A section is presented *after* a contrasting phrase or phrases in the B section is referred to as *rounded binary form*. Such forms are consistently used in the minuets or scherzo movements of Classical and Romantic instrumental works. The form is also used in sections of larger ternary forms, in short songs, in themes used for variations, and in rondo forms (discussed in later chapters). The formal design of rounded binary form is diagrammed ‖:A:‖:BA:‖. The B section is typically comprised of one or more transitional phrases that are harmonically unstable or modulatory. A half cadence in the original key normally marks the end of the B section and leads to the restatement of A material in the tonic key, the "rounding" of the form.

A critical aspect of the formal structure of the rounded binary form is that the return of the opening theme emphasizes a return to the tonic key and to harmonic stability. In continuous rounded binary forms, this means that the restatement of the A theme will be altered so as to remain in tonic rather than modulate. The restatement also signals the start of the closing section of the form though the amount of material restated will vary. Some typical models for rounded binary forms are given below in Figure 6.2.

Several common elements should be observed in studying these models:

- The A section of a rounded binary form is normally a period or sentence; it is therefore expository.
- The form may be tonally sectional but is more often continuous, with section one modulating to V or, if in a minor key, to III or v.
- The B section is transitional and may simply elaborate material using a brief sequence or dominant expansion, or may have one or more additional modulations and extensive elaborations of motives. In such cases it is also developmental.

- The end of the B section is marked by an arrival on a HC in the tonic key, emphasizing the return to tonic and to the opening theme.
- The repeats and the connection between the two parts (BA) of part two convey the binary design, but the form has three distinct formal functions: *presentation* of a distinct theme in section one; *contrasting continuation* to begin the second section; *restatement* of A material to close the second section.

The examples outlined in Figure 6.2a and b are *small rounded binary forms*, a form in which each section is comprised of two short phrases. In each case the restatement of the opening material is a single phrase that concludes on a PAC. The Beethoven Scherzo outlined in Figure 6.2c (Exercise 2c at the end of Chapter 2) is notably different from the other two examples because of the modulations and phrase expansions that occur in the B section and the restatement of the complete period of the A section. This movement offers a good example of the how the initial presentation of material in a piece has implications for later developments. The fact that the first section does not modulate means that 1) we may expect some tonal digression in the B section; and 2) that the entire period can be restated to round the form since no tonal alterations are necessary. This suggests why Beethoven consequently writes an expansive B section with two modulations and even introduces a new thematic idea and expressive character beginning in measure 18. The eventual return to the dominant of A major (I) is highlighted by the *rallentando* that Beethoven indicates, and the rest in measure 31. Finally, note the expansion of the restatement by the addition of a cadential phrase that playfully inverts the texture of the main theme and disrupts the triple meter as it closes.

Large rounded binary forms, in which one or more of the formal sections are expanded, are particularly common in the minuets and scherzo movements of eighteenth

Figure 6.2 *Rounded Binary Form: Models of formal design.*

a. Mozart, 12 Variations on "Ah, vous dirai-je, Maman," Theme.[8]

‖:A	:‖:B	A′ :‖
single phrase	expanded V	restatement of opening phrase
expository function	transitional function	expository and closing function
I----------------------I PAC	HC	-------------------------------PAC

b. *Mozart, Piano Sonata in D major, K. 284, III, Theme.

‖:A	:‖:B	A′ :‖
parallel, modulating period	modulating, sequential phrase	restatement of opening phrase
expository/trans. function	transitional function	expository/closing
I----------------------PAC	----------------------arrival on HC	------------------------------PAC

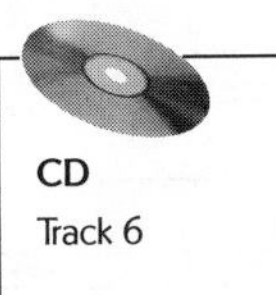

CD
Track 6

c. *Beethoven, Scherzo Allegretto from Sonata Op. 2, No. 2 in A major (Exercise 2c).

A	:‖:B	A′ **codetta** :‖
parallel period	modulating phrases	reprise of entire period
sentence in both phrases	phrase expansions	extension/codetta
	motion to expanded V7	expository function
expository function	transitional/dev. function	closing function
I----------------------PAC	I ----------------------arrival on HC	---------------------------PAC

[8] This melody is familiar to most people as "Twinkle Twinkle Little Star."

and nineteenth-century symphonies. A brief examination of the minuet from Mozart's Symphony No. 41 will illustrate some of the dramatic possibilities of the form in the hands of a skilled composer. Recall the sixteen-measure sentence structure that opens the minuet (see Example 3.11). The second part of the minuet is shown in Example 6.7.

The B section of this minuet begins with a melodic sequence over a dominant pedal using a motivic fragment of the main theme. The expansion of this fragment (measures 22–24) emphasizes the arrival at a HC. This important formal junction is stressed by the fanfare-like figure of measures 24–27 and the antiphonal orchestration—strings answered by

Example 6.7 Mozart, Symphony No. 41, III, mm. 14–59.

winds and timpani. All of these elements serve to highlight the return to the opening phrase in the tonic key. Rather than simply restating the opening phrase and leading to a PAC to close the minuet, Mozart presents a dramatic expansion of measures 1–4. Three statements elaborate the material (measures 28–39) with new contrapuntal accompaniments that serve as further development of ideas. The cadential progression of measures 40–43 might well have ended the minuet. Instead, Mozart gives a quiet, contrapuntal passage to the winds that may be perceived as a coda. In an even more surprising move, the full orchestra returns with the last eight measures of part one, now heard in the tonic key. The previous wind passage is developmental yet sounds parenthetical in retrospect, while the expository closing measures convey a sense of stability, finality and formal balance to this grand movement.

This movement offers an excellent example of how new elaborations of ideas may shape the second half of a rounded binary form. Mozart deftly shows his creativity in blending expository, developmental, parenthetical and closing functions in dramatic, unexpected ways. As in many symphonic settings, expansions, evaded cadences, and cadential elaborations are incorporated in the "rounding" of the form to dramatize the return to tonic and the close of the movement. A coda is often added as well. As in this example, many if not most rounded binary forms have a strong sense of continuity from the B section into the varied restatement of the A section. These passages consequently are grouped as a single large section, clarified by the repeats. It should also be noted that the A section often will contain phrase expansions and cadential extensions to emphasize the modulation to a new key. Additional examples for analysis are included in the exercises below.

Analytic Note: In some cases it may be tempting to analyze the second part of a small rounded binary form as a period, because the B section contains a single phrase that arrives on a HC. The restatement of the A material in a single phrase that concludes with a PAC may be interpreted as the consequent phrase of a contrasting period. The Mozart theme from the Piano Sonata K. 284, III is such a case. However, the formal function of the first phrase of the B section as a transitional, continuation phrase sets it apart from the A material that follows, and emphasizes the formal functions in the form as described above.

Another genre, the march—popularized by military bands and a staple of concert bands—also makes use of an expanded binary form. In a march, there are two large sections referred to as the *march* and the *trio*.[9] Each of these sections is based on binary formal designs. Such forms, in which one or more sections are also self-contained forms, are designated *compound forms*.[10] Each repeated phrase or section within a march and trio is traditionally referred to as a "strain." Usually the trio of the march is repeated following a transitional passage. This repetition of the trio expands the binary form.

Figure 6.3 shows a formal diagram of one of the most famous marches of John Phillip Sousa, a compound binary form used frequently in American marches. The first part is a simple binary form with each section comprised of 16 measures that are repeated. As in most marches and dances, symmetrical phrases of 4 and 8 measures are used throughout and the sections tend to be largely expository. The so-called "break strain" before the repeat of the trio (D in Figure 6.3) is in effect a *transitional* section that may use sequence, chromatic harmonies, melodic repetitions, and expanded dominant harmonies; it often ends on a HC or an elided PAC. *Forte* dynamic levels in many cases also characterize the break strain, which contribute to its often-tumultuous character.

The compound binary form of marches, illustrated here, has two distinguishing features: 1) following the repeat of the trio, both the break strain and trio are repeated again as a unit; and 2) the trio is in A♭ (subdominant) and consequently the piece does not end in the original tonic key.[11]

---

[9] The term "trio" is adopted from minuet and trio form of the eighteenth century. In a march, the trio does not always assume a lighter texture as its classical predecessor and is often in a new key.

[10] The term "composite forms" is also encountered. See the next chapter, pp. 126–143 for a discussion of compound ternary forms.

[11] This tonal design is also found in many rags as exemplified by Scott Joplin. See, for example, his "Maple Leaf Rag" and "Weeping Willow," which are compound binary forms without the repeat of the trio.

Figure 6.3 *Sousa, Stars and Stripes Forever, Formal Diagram.*

A			**B**	transition	**B′**
1–36			37–68	69–92	93–124
Intro.	A	B	C C	D	C C
March:	Simple	Binary	Trio: period		Trio
4	‖:16:‖	‖:16:‖	16 + 16	‖:8+8+8	16 + 16:‖
intro	strain 1	strain 2	strain 1 strain 2	break strain	strain 1 strain 2
E♭----------------------------------		--E♭	A♭----------------A♭	unstable--------A♭	------------A♭
I			IV		

SUGGESTED READING

An important performance issue is whether or not to take repeats in binary forms. While taking repeats that are notated would seem obligatory, in practice some performers decide not to take the repeats for various reasons. Thoughtful discussions can be found in the articles by Michael Broyles and David Smyth listed in the bibliography.

Review and Exercises

1. **Terms:** In a concise sentence or two, define the following terms:
   one-part form, simple binary, rounded binary, balanced binary
   continuous binary, sectional binary, compound forms

2. **Phrase Analysis, Example 6.7:** Consider the phrase structure of the transitional passage that begins the B section. The transition is grouped in two-measure units in which the first measure of each group can be felt as a hypermetric downbeat followed by an upbeat in the second measure. Identify where a shift in the pattern occurs, in other words, where a metric reinterpretation occurs. What does this serve to mark in the form?

3. **Aural Analysis:** Sing or listen to the pieces listed and determine what types of formal design are used. Examples of each of the forms discussed in the chapter are represented. The pieces should be matched with the list of specific forms given below. Try and determine the phrase structures and modulations that are heard in each example through repeated listening. Subsequent reference to scores can be used to clarify your analysis.

   My Country 'Tis of Thee (God Save the King)
   Old Folks at Home ($\frac{4}{4}$ meter)
   Bach, *The Well-Tempered Clavier,* Prelude in E, Book I (CD Track 5)
   Scarlatti, Sonata in E, Longo 530
   Haydn, Symphony No. 104, mm. 1–37
   Mozart, Symphony No. 41, Trio
   Mendelssohn, Symphony No. 4, III

a. One-part form with a non-tonic restatement of the opening theme in the latter half.
b. Continuous, rounded binary form with a short period in section one and an expansion of the consequent phrase of the restatement followed by a codetta in section two.
c. Sectional, rounded binary form with a complete restatement of A to close.
d. Continuous, rounded binary form with an abbreviated restatement that fuses with an expansive two-part coda.
e. Small binary form with unequal length phrases.
f. Full, balanced binary forms with more than one modulation in each half.
g. Small rounded binary form of four-measure phrases.

4. Score Analysis: Formal Design: Each of the pieces listed below is in rounded binary form. Answer the following list of questions for each work.

a. Is the piece or passage a continuous or sectional binary? Note the cadence and key, by Roman numeral, at the end of the first section.
b. What type of phrase structures are evident in the A section (sentence, period, phrase group)? Are there any phrase expansions in the A section? Give a diagram of the phrase structure.
c. Identify the points of cadential arrival in the second section, and the key and type of cadence that occurs. At each point of cadence note whether a phrase connection occurs.
d. Identify the measures where the opening phrase returns. How much of A is restated? To what extent is the restatement varied or obscured?
e. In Beethoven Piano Sonata No. 9, identify by measure numbers one instance of a phrase expansion. Give a brief description of the type of expansion. Identify a phrase in the B section that is transitional and briefly explain why.

*Anonymous, Polonaise from the *Notebook for Anna Magdalena Bach*.
*Handel, Air from Suite No. 5 in E, theme.
+Handel, Suite No. 4 in E minor, Courante.
Haydn, Symphony No. 104, III.
*Beethoven, Piano Sonata No. 9 in E, Op. 14, No. 1, II, mm. 63–100.
+Schubert, Six Waltzes, Op. 9, No. 3.
*Chopin, Mazurka in A minor, (Op. 7, No. 2) mm. 1–32.
+Chopin, Nocturne in C minor, Op. 48, No. 1, mm. 1–24.
*Brahms, Intermezzo in A minor, Op. 76, No. 7, mm. 9–32.

The following formal description of the Beethoven Minuetto from the Sonata Op. 2, No. 1 is given as a model.

a. The Minuet is a continuous rounded binary form. Section one ends with a PAC in III, the relative major of the principal key.
b. Section one is a parallel period with extensions. The first four measures, the antecedent phrase, comprise a sentence structure.
c. Section two: Cadences and Keys.
measures 20–24 PAC in B♭ minor, no connection—rests
measure 28, HC in F minor. Bass line link with octave leap
d. The piece is rounded. Following the HC in measure 28, the opening motives return in varied form in measure 29.
e. There are several expansions: Measures 20–24 are extensions that repeat the cadence in B♭ minor; measures 37–38 extend the phrase by echoing the cadence. The last two measures confirm the final cadence.

f. Measures 25–28 comprise a transitional phrase. The quick rhythms and octave texture create a sense of urgency and increased motion, and the scalar patterns introduce accidentals that lead back to the original key and the dominant.

5. Score Analysis: Phrase structure: For each piece, complete a detailed analysis of the phrase structure and formal functions. Compare the formal design and structure of each piece. Note similarities and differences in the way each of the pieces shapes the basic form. Account for the unique formal aspects in each piece. Additional comments and questions are given for individual pieces.

a. Haydn, String Quartet Op. 76, No. 3 Trio. The contrast in the length of each section of this trio results in part from a rather surprising "parenthetical" insertion in the B section of the trio. To identify this insertion, consider which passage could be omitted within the second part and still leave a well-constructed formal design. Once identified, consider why the passage may be interpreted as parenthetical and why it stands apart. Give an interpretation of the expressive effect of the passage and how it plays with our perception of the form.

Exercise 6.5a. Haydn, String Quartet Op. 76, No. 3, Trio.

(This excerpt continues on p. 118.)

(Exercise 6.5a, continued.)

b. Grieg, Holberg Suite, Sarabande. The lyric breadth of this movement is emphasized by the introduction of new ideas in the B section. How many distinct themes can you identify? What aspects of the tonal design and harmonies of this piece are characteristic of nineteenth-century music (discussed in Chapter 2)? The restatement of the opening material does not simply serve as a rounding of the form, it is also a point of climax in the movement. What elements of the music contribute to this climax?

Exercise 6.5b Grieg, *Holberg Suite,* Sarabande.

(This excerpt continues on p. 120.)

(Exercise 6.5b, continued)

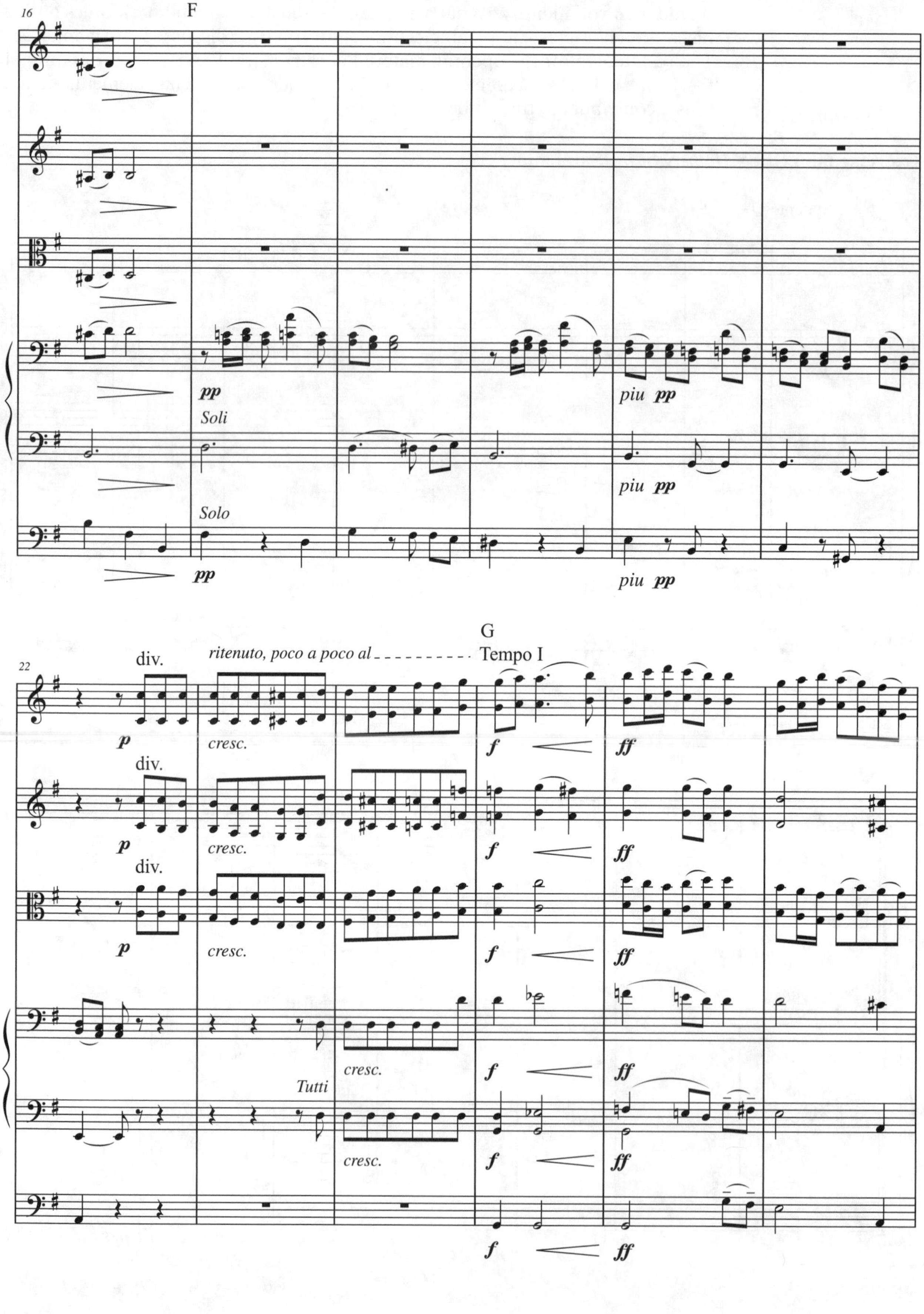

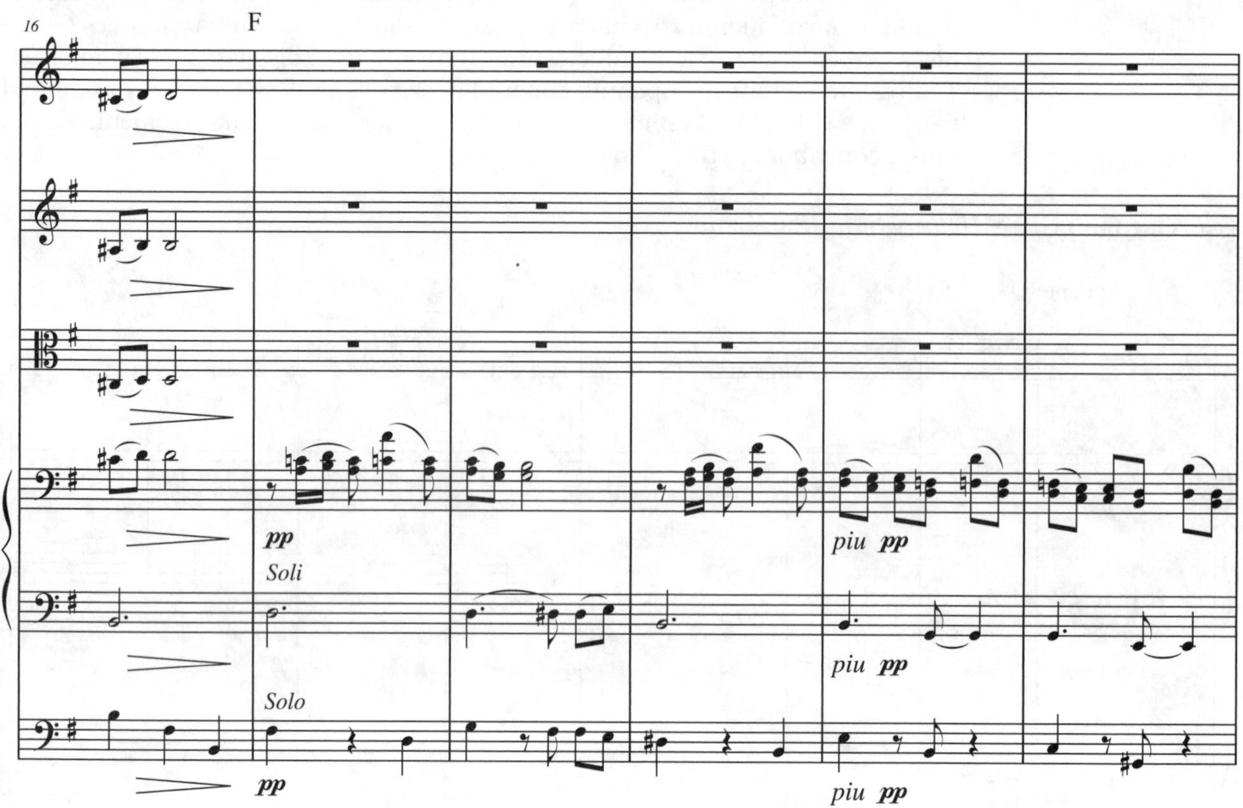

16
F
pp
Soli
Solo
pp
piu pp
piu pp
piu pp
22
div.
p
ritenuto, poco a poco al
cresc.
G
Tempo I
f
ff
div.
p
cresc.
f
ff
div.
p
cresc.
f
ff
cresc.
f
ff
Tutti
cresc.
f
ff
f
ff

c. **Brahms, Theme from *Variations on a Theme by Haydn* ("St. Anthony Chorale").** Though this theme originally was written in the eighteenth century, the textures in this setting are characteristic of Brahms. What kinds of doublings and spacing of parts does Brahms use here? What is the function of measures 23–29? Explain.

Exercise 6.5c Brahms, *Theme from Variations on a Theme by Haydn.*

(This excerpt continues on p. 122.)

(Exercise 6.5c, continued.)

25
1.
2.
p
1.
2.
p

7 Ternary Forms

Introduction

The formal principal of statement-contrast-restatement is most clearly manifested in musical forms in which there are three distinct sections. This principle results in a three-part or *ternary form* in which a contrasting middle section is followed by a restatement of the first section, usually complete and often in varied form. An important point to note is that the first and last sections are identical or quite similar in terms of key and themes. Consequently, there are only two contrasting sections of music producing a formal design designated A B A. The principle of ternary form is based on the restatement of the first section after the second or middle contrasting section. Thus a form with three contrasting sections, which might be labeled A B C, is considered through-composed, not ternary. The principle of contrast followed by restatement has also been discussed with reference to rounded binary form. In fact this form and certain simple ternary forms are in some ways similar, a point to be discussed further.

Different categories of ternary form result from the varied design of the sections within the form. As in binary forms, ternary forms may be sectional or continuous, depending on the tonal motion of the first part, and they may be small or large depending on the proportions of the sections. *Simple ternary* form results when each section is a sentence, period, repeated phrase, or phrase group. *Compound ternary* form results when one or more sections comprise a self-contained binary or ternary form. The following discussion will examine some models for the construction of ternary forms and identify other types within these two broad categories.

Simple Ternary Forms

Simple ternary forms are most commonly found in songs or in sections of larger forms, and in nineteenth-century, instrumental character pieces. In its most obvious manifestation, a ternary form will be sectional with the A section beginning and ending in the tonic key. The middle section may be tonally closed or modulatory. The form is continuous when the first section closes in a new key or ends on a HC in the original key. The contrasting middle section will then contain a modulation back to tonic. Simple ternary form is so frequently found in songs of various kinds that it is sometimes referred to as "song form."[1] The following examples address complete pieces that utilize simple ternary form. Other examples of this form will be examined in the compound works discussed in the next section and in the exercises.

In many cases songs or arias are in simple, *sectional* ternary form. Figure 7.1 outlines a model for this form, which is illustrated by an aria from Mozart's opera *Così fan*

[1] It must be understood that many songs are not in simple ternary form. Further, the simple ternary forms of "song form" are often quite distinct with regard to phrase structure and tonal motion from those found in short instrumental pieces of the nineteenth century.

Figure 7.1 *Formal diagram of simple, sectional ternary form.*

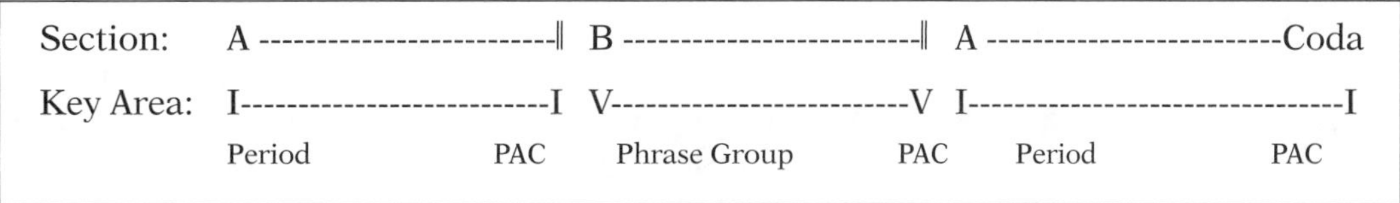

Tutte. The most salient features of the three-part division are the perfect authentic cadences that close each of the sections. The opening and closing phrases of the A and B sections are given in Example 7.1. The contrast between tonic and dominant keys in this work is a fundamental aspect of Classical period forms. The A section begins and ends in A major (I). The first part of the B section (not shown) quickly modulates to E major (V); the second part of B closes with a PAC in E major. The fact that each section of the form closes with a PAC and has no repeats of sections provides clear aural cues for the three-part division. As you listen to the aria, you may note the phrase extensions at the end of the A section, the introduction of two different contrasting themes in the B section, the evaded cadences and extensions at the end of the second A section, and the addition of a coda. The beginning of the B section also is marked by a change to an accelerated rhythmic accompaniment.

Example 7.1 Mozart, "Un auro amoroso," No. 17 from *Così fan Tutte,* mm. 18–23, 40–45.

Quite often a change in mode to the parallel key marks the beginning of the contrasting middle section. In pieces in a minor key, a direct modulation to the relative major key is another possibility, as in Example 7.2. Note that the three sections of this simple ternary form are tonally closed, each beginning and ending in the same key. This particular piece has an exact restatement of the opening sixteen-measure period in measures 41–56, not uncommon in many sectional ternary forms. The middle section of this piece is also 16 measures, but with unusual harmonic and phrase structure. This section characteristically introduces a new melodic continuation and contrasting harmonic motion. The return to the opening section is emphasized by the transitional passage in measures 33–40. A transitional phrase, here marked by the reduction in texture, the melodic repetitions, and the implied expansion of the original dominant, is often used as a way to connect the sections of a ternary work and offset the sectional nature of the form. All sections of the form may be connected by a link or transition, though the connection between the end of B and the restatement of A is most typical.

Example 7.2

Chopin, Mazurka in G minor, Op. 67, No. 2. *Simple, sectional ternary form.*

32-BAR SONG FORM

The symmetrical phrases of Example 7.2 are characteristic of many nineteenth-century character pieces[2] and of popular songs. In fact, one song form is referred to as *32-bar song form*[3] because of the frequency with which this design is found in many traditional songs and in show tunes of the twentieth century. Countless numbers of songs made use of this form, which uses four or eight-measure phrases as illustrated in Figure 7.2.

The three-part division of the form is based on the grouping of the first phrase (A) and its repetition as one section, and on hearing B as a contrasting middle section. The first section of this song form is often referred to as the *head* while the contrasting B section is referred to as the *bridge*. The single eight-measure restatement of A without the repetition

[2] A character piece is a short, lyric work for piano, intended to evoke a particular mood or character. It is usually associated with the Romantic period. Chopin's Nocturnes and Brahms' Intermezzi are examples.

[3] This form refers to the main part of the song—the refrain—which is the tune listeners generally recognize.

Figure 7.2 *Simple ternary form in a model 32-bar song form.*

	A	A	B	A (extension)
Phrase length	8 +	8	8	8
Cadence	AC or HC	PAC	HC modulatory	PAC
Key Area	I	I	x	I

completes a form made of four symmetrical phrases or a *quatrain,*[4] briefly discussed in Chapter 3. Though no repeats of the B section or of the final A section are found in this form, the entire 32 measures is often repeated to introduce a second verse of text.

The sixteen-measure A section of the 32-bar song form may take on a variety of phrase types. It can be a repeated phrase that is a sentence structure, an eight-bar repeated period, or a single sixteen-measure period as in Example 7.3. Although the A section normally closes

Example 7.3 Weill, "My Ship."

a. mm. 9–17.

[4] The quatrain illustrated in Example 3.1, "Drink to Me Only" is a sixteen-measure form of four-measure phrases. This is related to the 32-bar song form and is often found in simple tunes and folk songs. This form may also be understood as a ternary form. However, some 32-bar song forms are small binary forms, grouped as 16+16 with large sentence structures or periods. See for example "Laura" by David Raskin or "Make Believe" by Jerome Kern.

b. mm. 25–34.

in the tonic key, some songs have a sequential, modulating A section as in the Jerome Kern song "All the Things You Are" (discussed further in Chapter 13). As in the simple ternary form, the B section will introduce a new melodic continuation and contrasting harmonic motion; it may also contain brief tonicizations or a modulation confirmed by cadence. In either case, the end of the B section will turn back toward the tonic key, often with a HC connected to the return of A or an elided PAC. "My Ship" by Kurt Weill provides a clear example of this ternary song form. Weill uses some interesting harmonic progressions to mask his cadences, though the melodic patterning makes the eight-measure phrases and three-part design clear. The first eight measures of the melody and the contrasting B section are shown in Example 7.3a and b. Listen for a phrase expansion and rhythmic deceleration in the six-measure codetta that ends the piece. The song also includes a brief introduction (not shown), a feature of many vocal and instrumental ternary forms.

Continuous, simple ternary forms are those in which the initial A and the B sections are both modulatory. Like the ternary forms described above, the first section is often periodic while the modulatory B section is a phrase group that may utilize sequence. Such forms have a continuous harmonic motion that is resolved in the restatement of the first section. These two sections consequently take on a transitional as well as an expository function. The middle section may also take on a developmental function by elaborating motives from the A section. An example of this type of form can be found in the *Songs Without Words*, Op. 62, No. 1 by Mendelssohn. This work is instructive regarding the importance of tonality in delineating formal design. The piece uses a single accompaniment figure throughout (see Example 7.4), giving the impression of a continuous one-part form. Analysis of its phrase structure and tonal design shows it to be composed in three distinct sections, as outlined in Figure 7.3. The first section is a modulating parallel period that includes a phrase extension. The second section continues the accompaniment figure and uses variants of the motivic material of part one. The use of sequence and restless tonal motion contrasts with the first section. This section closes with a move back toward the original key through A minor (ii), connecting smoothly with the return of the opening theme on the dominant

Figure 7.3 *Formal design of* Mendelssohn, *Songs Without Words,* Op. 62, No. 1.

	A	B	A	
	mm. 1–10	**10–22**	**22–35**	**35–41**
	Modulating period	contrasting section	modified restatement of period,	codetta
Key area:	**I--------------------iii**	**iii-IV—(ii)-I**	**I-----------------------------------**	**-I**
	PAC			

Example 7.4 Mendelssohn, *Songs Without Words,* Op. 62, No. 1.

chord. The third section restates the antecedent phrase of the opening period, but as expected, alters the consequent to conclude in tonic. Phrase expansions and evaded cadences reinforced by dynamic contrasts distinguish the close of the piece. The design outlined here is found in many character pieces of the nineteenth century. The elaboration of related motives in the middle section and the continuous sense of rhythmic and tonal motion are in contrast with the simple sectional ternary forms describe above.

Analytic Note: The continuous ternary form, as you may have observed, is not unlike the continuous rounded binary form discussed in the previous chapter. Recall that the latter form is in two parts but had three distinct formal units and functions: an opening modulatory period or sentence; a transitional passage that returned to the tonic key; and a restatement of the opening period modified to close in the tonic key. In fact, some analysts prefer to think of rounded binary form as a small ternary form or an incipient ternary form.[5]

[5] The former term is used in Caplin, *Classical Form,* the latter is used in Berry, *Form in Music.*

While the distinctions between these two forms are sometimes elusive, they may be considered as two different types of designs based on the following criteria:

- *Repeats in the binary form*. This is perhaps the overriding factor in distinguishing the two forms. The repeat of the BA portion of the rounded binary form groups these two formal units into one section. Continuous ternary form has no repeat of the middle and third section though sometimes there may be a written out repeat of the opening period.[6]
- *Proportions*. In ternary form, the amount of A material that is restated in part three is usually of equal or greater length than the original material, rather than abbreviated as in the rounded binary form.
- *Function and length of the middle section*. The B section in rounded binary form is clearly transitional and often a simple elongation of dominant harmony in a single phrase; the middle section of the continuous ternary form is almost always a modulatory phrase group that may be developmental as well as transitional.

What is also noteworthy is how different the continuous ternary form is from other sectional ternary forms. The closed tonal sections and marked contrasts in theme and texture create a clear division into three sections in sectional ternary forms. The continuous ternary forms of the nineteenth century can be understood as a hybrid mixture of rounded binary and ternary elements, with an emphasis on continuous development of a main idea throughout a piece. This emphasis leads to creating a sense of climax late in a work, as in the Mendelssohn piece. This tendency, as Leonard Meyer observes, reflects the value nineteenth-century aesthetics placed on "openness and becoming," which in part shaped their formal designs.[7]

Compound Ternary Forms

As mentioned above, in some ternary forms one or both sections are self-contained binary or ternary form. These compound ternary forms are found in a number of genres but occur in two basic designs: *Da capo form* and *large ternary form.* In a da capo form, the first section, a binary or ternary form, is repeated in its entirety after the contrasting middle section. Usually this large-scale restatement is indicated by the designation *da capo al fine*, which specifies a repeat of the A section.[8] The middle section may also be a self-contained form, thus there are slight breaks between the sections. In a large ternary form, the sections are connected and the restatement of A is written out, frequently with elaborate embellishments and sometimes expanded. *In both of these types, the first section almost always ends in the tonic key, thus the large-scale form is sectional.* Da capo compound forms are usually associated with instrumental music. The da capo aria, a vocal form, is not necessarily a compound form, and will be discussed in the chapter on vocal forms. The following discussion will give a summary of examples of these compound forms in instrumental genres.

DA CAPO DANCE MOVEMENTS

The pairing of two related dances as a single movement originated in multi-movement dance suites, which reached their apex of popularity in the Baroque period. Typically one movement (occasionally more) would be designated by dance titles such as Gavotte I and

[6] See, for example, Brahms's Intermezzo in C major, Op. 119, No. 3.

[7] Meyer, *Style and Music, 262 ff.* See also Cone, Chapter 3.

[8] *"Da Capo,"* an Italian term, literally means *"from [the] head."* It is translated in English as *"from the beginning."* Some dance movements are followed by repeats of the same dance with embellishments. The repetition is referred to by the French term *double,* and should not be confused with the three-part, da capo form.

Gavotte II, or Minuet I and Minuet II, with a *da capo* indication at the end of the second dance. In the *da capo* restatement, the repeats in the binary form traditionally are omitted. The second dance usually will be in the same key or in the parallel key (major or minor) of the first dance. Consequently, contrasts in texture and thematic content are expected in the second dance, while maintaining the general style of the dance type. Most often the second dance has a reduction in the number of voices and a lighter texture. In Baroque *da capo* dance movements such as these, *each dance is a self-contained, binary form*; thus, the movements will always be a sectional, compound ternary form. Countless examples of such movements can be found.[9] The interest formally is in the internal forms of the individual dances.

In the Classical period, the primary vestige of the older Baroque suite was the minuet and trio found in sonatas, string quartets, and symphonies. These movements are also in compound da capo form but *both sections now are in a rounded binary form.* The minuet is often an expanded rounded binary as discussed in the previous chapter. The trio is designated as such because this section was traditionally associated with a reduction to a three-voice texture in the French courts where the minuet originated. Two trebles and one bass instrument would play and the music was meant to take on a lighter, more graceful or lyric quality. In addition to this contrast in texture, the trio is often of simpler design and proportions than the minuet. The key of the trio is often in the relative or parallel key of the minuet, thus contrast in mode is achieved. While there are usually clear breaks between the sections, some trios will close with a transitional phrase that ushers in the restatement of the minuet. (See Haydn, Symphony No. 104, III, measures 95–104, Example 5.1).

Nineteenth-century composers, beginning with Beethoven, replaced the minuet with the livelier Scherzo and also expanded the form. The da capo of the scherzo is frequently written out to allow embellishment or phrase expansions, and transitions between sections are used.[10] Compound ternary form also is used in nineteenth-century piano pieces, including waltzes and mazurkas by Chopin, and character pieces by Schubert, Schumann, Brahms and others. Normally the first section is a binary form with repeats, or a simple ternary form. The middle section will introduce a contrast in mode and character, and is often a small form with repeats; the restatement of A may incorporate embellishments. Figure 7.4 illustrates the formal design of a Chopin waltz. The first section is a rounded binary form with the repeats of part one written out. These repeats are omitted in the restatement. Characteristically, the middle section of a ternary dance is a phrase group, as in this example, or a repeated period.

Figure 7.4 *Formal design of* Chopin, Valse Op. 69, No. 2 in B minor:

	A	**B**	**A**
	mm. 1–65	**mm. 66–97**	**mm. 98–145**
	AA‖: BA :‖	C (8×4)	A‖BA
Key area	i	I	i

DA CAPO ARIAS

Arias of the Baroque period also make use of complete restatements of an opening section by the indication *da capo al fine*. Sometimes the *da capo* is written out to provide embellishments but with no change in phrase structure. A *da capo aria* may be in simple

[9] See for example the Baroque keyboard suites of Bach and Handel. For orchestral examples see Bourree I and Bourree II from the Orchestral Suite in C major by J.S. Bach, or Minuet I and Minuet II from the *Music for the Royal Fireworks* by Handel.

[10] See for example, Mendelssohn, Symphony No. 4, III; Schumann, Symphony No. 4, III; and Brahms, Symphony No. 3, III.

or compound ternary form. When these arias are in compound form, it is almost always the first section that is a self-contained form, either a simple ternary or binary form. The middle, contrasting section then is a modulatory phrase group. Example 7.5 shows a well-known aria by Handel from his opera *Rinaldo.* The two verses of text are set in two different sections followed by a *da capo* of the first section. The first part is a sectional ternary form with clear contrasts between tonic and dominant keys. The B section provides characteristic tonal contrast by moving to the relative minor (D minor) and modulating to its dominant (A minor) at its close. Many Baroque da capo arias are extensive and elaborate, but each section may be a phrase group rather than a complete small form.

Example 7.5 Handel, "Lascia ch'io pianga" (Let me bewail) from *Rinaldo.*

(This excerpt continues on p. 134.)

(Example 7.5, continued.)

They also incorporate instrumental ritornelli that frame the vocal sections, to be discussed more fully in Chapter 13.

EXPANSION AND MODIFICATIONS OF COMPOUND TERNARY FORMS

In some instrumental works additional restatements of the trio and the scherzo expand the compound ternary form to five or more sections. Notable among such works are Beethoven's Symphonies Nos. 4 and 7 and his String Quartet Op. 131, in which the additional repetition of the trio and the scherzo is followed by a brief final reference to the trio and a subsequent coda. His Symphony No. 9 expands the Scherzo into a full sonata form with lengthy development and a coda. Some works, such as Brahms Symphony No. 2, include two trios in the scherzo movement, the second trio a variant of the first trio.[11]

[11] Mendelssohn's Wedding March from *A Midsummer Night's Dream* also incorporates additional repetitions of the trio and march. Another example of a compound movement with two trios occurs in Mozart's Clarinet Quintet K. 581.

Large Ternary Form

Found most frequently in the slow movements of late eighteenth- and nineteenth-century instrumental works, the large ternary form is similar to the compound ternary of the minuet and trio, in that the first section is a self-contained form ending with a PAC in the tonic key. The middle section of both types also will be tonally contrasting and introduce contrasting textures. The large ternary, however, differs from the compound da capo instrumental forms in the following ways:

- The first section of a slow movement in large ternary form, unlike the minuet or scherzo, is not always a rounded binary form with repeats. In fact, it is as likely to be a simple binary or ternary form.
- The middle section may be a simple binary or ternary form, but may be a modulatory, developmental section as well. In either case, this section often introduces more active rhythmic textures in large ternary forms.
- The middle section of the large ternary will often shift modes like the da capo forms, but may also move to key areas IV or vi in Classical period works, or to a chromatic mediant key in later works.
- The large ternary will often include links or transitions between sections, particularly between the B section and the restatement of A. This connection gives a stronger sense of continuity not heard in the clearly separated minuet and trio.
- The restatement of the A section, unlike the literal *da capo*, is written out and usually embellished or expanded; it will often lead to a coda that recalls the middle section briefly.

The second movement of the Haydn Symphony No. 104 is an excellent example of a slow movement in large ternary form. Recall the opening of this movement (Example 3.9a), a modulating period that serves as the first part of an expanded rounded binary form (measures 1–37). Following a strong close in G major (I), the second section begins in G minor. After a recall of the first four measures of the movement, Haydn makes a dramatic shift to D minor (v) and a developmental section ensues (see Example 7.6a). As you listen to this movement, take note of the false return of the opening theme (measure 56) in B♭ major (♭III) after a full measure's rest in this development section (see Example 7.6b). A dominant preparation and reduction in texture quietly ushers in the actual restatement in the tonic key. The restatement incorporates written out repeats in part one of the rounded binary form and a large expansion of part two as well as a coda.

Analytic Note: The foregoing discussion has emphasized the contrast in tonality or mode between the outer and middle sections of a ternary form, a primary basis for delineating sections. Contrasts in thematic material and texture are also expected. The question of how unity is achieved in the midst of overt contrasts between sections also merits consideration. In some ternary forms the use of related motivic material in the middle section obviously creates a sense of unity. Such is the case in *Songs Without Words,* Op. 62, No. 1 by Mendelssohn, which also uses a continuous accompaniment figure. In ternary forms in which the contrasting middle section introduces new themes and textures, the basis for the unity within the piece is often less clear. Further analysis of underlying motivic pitch or rhythmic patterns may reveal the relation between the sections, but such thematic unity is not always present. Large-scale tonal motion, including the pattern of key successions and linear connections may also convey a unified whole. Finally, consideration of elements that reflect a consistency in style related to the composer and the general historical style will reveal an important aspect of unity. In short, while the element of contrast is often readily apparent in music, further consideration of the unifying elements will give a stronger understanding of structure and style.

Example 7.6 Haydn, Symphony No. 104, II.

a. mm. 34–46.

42
a2
Fl.
sempre ff
a2
Ob.
ff
sempre ff
Cl.
ff
Bsn.
ff
sempre ff
Timp.
ff
Vln. I
ff
sempre ff
Vln. II
ff
sempre ff
Vla.
ff
sempre ff
Vc.
ff
sempre ff

b. mm. 55–61.

Summary

- Ternary form has three sections, though the third section is a restatement, often varied, of the first. Thus the form is based on the principle of statement-contrast-restatement. It is diagrammed as an A B A form. The restatement of the A section may be a varied repetition but tends to be a complete restatement.
- The form tends to be sectional because the A sections are most often tonally closed: they begin and end in the tonic key. The B section may be tonally closed or open. When the A section modulates and ends in a new key, the ternary form is continuous; the restatement of A will be varied to close in tonic.
- Simple ternary forms are those in which each section is a period or phrase group but not a self-contained form. This form is most common in songs, or sections of larger ternary forms.

- Compound (composite) ternary forms are those in which one or both of the sections is a self-contained form. Simple ternary and rounded binary may be used for either of the sections. The compound form tends to take two guises:

  1. Da capo forms, in which A and B are both tonally closed and A is simply repeated in full, often by the designation *da capo* at the end of the B section. (Note: While minuets and trios are always compound forms, da capo arias may be simple ternary forms, with each section containing a period, phrase group, or sentence).
  2. Large ternary forms that are characteristic of slow movements in sonatas. Here the A section is quite often a simple ternary, and transitions between sections may give the effect of a continuous form.

- Continuous ternary forms, such as Mendelssohn's *Songs Without Words,* have the attributes of a continuous rounded binary. Theorists and analysts take different views of the distinctions between these two small forms. Some analysts describe rounded binary form as small ternary form. Arguments can be made for both of these descriptions. Distinctions between the two forms include the following factors:

  a. Repeats in the binary form—perhaps the overriding factor.
  b. The amount of the A material that is restated—rounded binary form has only partial restatements of the first section.
  c. The tonal structure of the B section—in rounded form is clearly transitional and often an expansion of the dominant.

- 32-bar song form consists of four, eight-bar phrases (a quatrain) but may be understood as a ternary form: aa (head)–b (bridge)–a (head).

Review and Exercises

1. **Terms:** In a sentence or two, define each of the following terms:

   simple sectional ternary form
   32-bar song form
   large ternary form
   continuous simple ternary form
   da capo form
   compound ternary form

2. **Aural Analysis:** The works listed below offer examples of the various ternary forms discussed. Prior to examining a score, listen to each of them several times. Determine what type of ternary form is being used by observing **a)** whether the first section is tonally closed or open; **b)** whether the first or second section contains repeats or is a binary or ternary form; and **c)** whether the first section is restated exactly, embellished, or varied by expansions or addition of a coda. Close listening may also reveal the theme types and phrase structure of the various sections and the changes in mode or modulations that may occur in the middle section. What types of contrast are readily apparent in the middle sections? Which elements create unity or continuity?

   Mozart, Symphony No. 40, III
   Mendelssohn, Symphony No. 4, II
   Chopin, Mazurka No. 45 in A minor
   Verdi, *Celeste Aida* from *Aida*
   Fauré, Violin Sonata No. 1, III, Allegro Vivo
   Prokofiev, Gavotte from the *Classical Symphony*

Ravel, *Valse nobles et sentimentales*, No. 1
Arlen, "Over the Rainbow"
Lennon and McCartney, "Yesterday"

3. **Phrase Analysis:** The Mazurka in G minor (Example 7.2) offers interesting examples of how Chopin maintains the phrase symmetry expected in a dance movement while incorporating creative phrase structures.
   - **a.** Consider the first eight-measure phrase: how does the phrase subdivide, where exactly is the cadence of the phrase, and what type of cadence is it?
   - **b.** Compare the subsequent eight-bar phrase with the first. What standard phrase type is evident in the second phrase?
   - **c.** The middle section contains interesting harmonic motions. What harmony begins the phrase in measure 17? How is this measure re-harmonized when the phrase is repeated?
   - **d.** Analyze the harmonies in measures 21–25. What type of sequence is used? If measure 25 begins a repetition of the previous eight-measure phrase, measure 24 should be a point of cadence. Is this the case? Should a performer slightly separate or connect measures 24–25? Explain your answer.
4. **Score Analysis:** Each of the following works is in ternary form. The questions for each work are intended to guide your analysis and draw attention to noteworthy details. Listen to each work to determine the large-scale design. Map out the cadences and, if possible, the keys that you hear. With the aid of a score, answer the questions for each work.

Mozart, Symphony No. 40, III

1. The term "minuet" is derived from "menu," which refers to the small graceful steps of this dance. This minuet is hardly in the stately or grandiose style one might expect. The minor mode, the rhythmic counterpoint between the melody and accompaniment, and the irregular three-measure subphrases of the opening give it an agitated, "Sturm und Drang" character that incorporates "learned" (contrapuntal) style. Note how the three-measure subphrases contain a hemiola in the principal melody that conflicts with the more regular rhythmic/metric profile of the lower voice. How could these three-measure subphrases be made into more regular four-measure phrases?
2. The first section of the minuet is a fourteen-measure sentence. Copy this passage and provide a phrase analysis using the models for annotation given above. Indicate where and how Mozart makes the modulation to the dominant key.
3. This movement is a compound ternary form. The minuet and trio are in the expected rounded binary form. Give a large-scale diagram of the movement that illustrates this form. Indicate the three large sections by letter name and measure numbers, the keys at the beginning and end of each section, and whether any transitions between the large sections are used.
4. Measure 15 begins a transitional phrase. Cite two techniques that convey the transitional nature of this phrase. In what measure does the opening melody return in the tonic key? The restatement of the A section is dramatically reinterpreted, as one might expect in a symphonic work. In a few sentences, describe how Mozart alters the opening phrase (measures 1–8), with consideration to texture and orchestration as well as phrase structure. What is the function of the last 6 measures of the minuet? Give an interpretation of its expressive effect as you perceive it.

5. Describe three differences between the trio and minuet with regard to formal structure and texture.

***Beethoven, Piano Sonata No. 4 in E♭ Op. 7, II**

1. What kind of cadence occurs in measure 8?
2. Where does a restatement of the opening phrase first occur?
3. In what key does the passage in measures 9–15 begin? What is the relation of the key to tonic?
4. Measure 19 appears as if it will lead to a PAC. What chord occurs instead on the downbeat of measure 20?
5. Where does the material of measure 19 recur a few measures later? To what chord do the harmonies resolve this time?
6. The entire movement is a large ternary, with the A section found in the first 24 measures. What type of form do the first 24 measures comprise?
7. In what key does the B section of the entire movement begin? In what measures and in what key do we hear a brief "false return" of the opening?
8. Where does the restatement of the large A section begin? How is this third section varied? Are the phrase structures retained?
9. Provide an analysis of the phrase structure of the coda. Which thematic motives are recalled? Which are new? How is final closure emphasized in the last phrase?

+Schubert, "Auf dem Flusse" from *Winterreise*

1. Examine the text and note which stanzas are used in the three sections of the form. How might one account for the grouping of the text in relation to the form?
2. The first section makes a surprising modulation. How is the closing key of this section reached and what is its relation to the tonic key?
3. Account for the use of major mode in this section. What is the function of measures 38–40?
4. The third section is tonally very unstable. Trace the series of brief modulations. In what ways do measures 54–70 serve as a climax to the song?

Schumann, "Vogel als Prophet," from *Waldszenen

1. The A section begins and ends in G minor. To what keys do the first two phrases modulate? Analyze the phrase structure of the A section.
2. In what measure does the B section begin? Explain your answer.
3. Cite three ways the B section contrasts with the A section. What elements of the middle section create unity?
4. The B section ends with a transition back to the original key of G minor: To what key does the music shift as a way to lead back to G minor?
5. In what measure does the restatement of the A section begin? How much of A is restated?
6. Note the ending of the A section each time. Where is the thematic material of the closing phrase of the A section first heard? Why does this closing phrase not sound like an ending?

***Gershwin, "I Got Rhythm"**

1. The refrain (the familier tune), which begins at the repeat sign after the introduction of this song, has four phrases counting the repetition of phrase one. Identify the beginning and ends of each phrase and the type of cadence that concludes each phrase.
2. What type of phrase structure is used in the first eight-bar phrase?
3. Give a harmonic analysis of the third phrase. What process generates the phrase?

4. How is the last phrase different from the first phrase?
5. What type of ternary form does this song illustrate?

ADDITIONAL EXAMPLES FOR STUDY. THOSE MARKED ** MAY BE INTERPRETED AS ROUNDED BINARY FORMS.

Burkhart: Simple Ternary

Handel, "Where'er You Walk" from *Semele*, da capo
Beethoven, Piano Sonata No. 4 in E♭, Op. 7, II mm. 1–24
Clara Schumann, No. 3 of *Quatre pieces fugitives*
Mendelssohn, *Songs Without Words,* Op. 19b, No. 1**
Chopin, Mazurka No. 37 in A♭ major. Op. 59, No. 2
Brahms, *Wie Melodien Zieht es Mir,* Op. 105, No. 1
Brahms, Intermezzo in C major, Op. 119, No. 3**
Mahler, Symphony No. 5, IV, Adagietto

Burkhart: Compound and Large Ternary Forms. The interest here lies primarily on the internal forms of each large section and the possible use of transitions and retransitions.

Bach, Minuet I-II from Suite 1 in G for cello
Haydn, String Quartet, Op. 74, No. 3, II
Beethoven, Piano Sonata No. 9 in E major, Op. 14, No. 1, II,
Chopin, Mazurka No. 6 A minor, Op. 7, No.2
Brahms, Intermezzo in A major, Op. 118, No. 2

Kostka/Graybill: Simple Ternary

Corelli, Concerto, Op. 6, No. 8, III
Bach, French Suite No. 1, Minuet II
Mozart, *The Magic Flute*, "March of the Priests"
Beethoven, Piano Sonata, No. 9 in A Major, Op. 2, No. 2, III**
Schubert, Mass in G, Kyrie
Chopin, Nocturne in C minor, Op. 48, No. 1 mm. 1–24**
Schumann, *Widmung*
Brahms, Waltz, Op. 39. No. 2
Brahms, Intermezzo, in A major, Op. 119, No. 2**
Grieg, *An der Wiege*
Britten, *Serenade for Tenor, Horns, and Strings*, Pastorale**

Kostka/Graybill: Compound and Large Ternary

Haydn, String Quartet in C major, Op. 74, No. 1, III
Mozart, String Quartet in B♭, K. 458, II
Clara Schumann, Romance, Op. 11, No. 2**

8 Sonata Form

Introduction

Sonata form, one of the most interesting and flexible forms in music, was developed in the Classical period and continued to evolve in the nineteenth and twentieth centuries. The formal structures of sonata form movements are so varied, and so often unique to a specific work, that some writers and analysts refer to "sonata forms" or to "sonata principles," rather than sonata form.[1] Other synonyms include "first-movement" or "sonata-allegro form" since the form is so often found in the first movement of multi-movement instrumental works such as symphonies, string quartets, and sonatas. It is also used in final movements, slow movements and occasionally in minuet or scherzo movements. The principles of sonata form have also been adapted in instrumental genres such as concertos, overtures, tone poems, and Classical operas.

These various terms reflect the multifaceted nature of musical form and the close relation between form and content discussed in Chapter One. This relation is nowhere more evident than in sonata form movements. The distinction between formal design and formal structure allows one to distinguish between a common large-scale design that most sonata form movements are based on and the seemingly endless ways in which the form may be structured. Thus we can identify a basic "sonata form" while recognizing the flexible principles of sonata form that shape different movements uniquely.

Historically, sonata form may be understood in part as an outgrowth of the changes in style from the Baroque to the Classical period. Among these changes was an increasing interest in writing dramatic instrumental music for performance in public concerts or private recitals. From a musical perspective the form is dramatic in several interrelated ways. First, sonata form normally contains distinct contrasts in tonality, themes, textures, and rhythmic motion. These contrasts serve to convey a sense of conflict or opposition between different elements and sections of the form. Foremost among these contrasts is the difference of character in distinct expository, developmental, transitional, and closing sections incorporated in the form. Second, these various formal functions reflect the dramatic opposition of tonal areas or keys, which thematic and textural elements reinforce. Third, these contrasts in keys, themes, textures, and functions create a fluctuating sense of stability and instability, or of tension and relaxation. The result is a form shaped by large-scale intensification toward climax and resolution of musical tension and expressions. Well-constructed sonata forms integrate these contrasting elements in such a way as to convey a sense of coherence and continuity, and what the eminent English writer Sir Donald Tovey called "dramatic fitness."

These dramatic aspects of sonata form represent some of the principles that guide the specific ways a composer will shape musical ideas. The stylistically diverse range of themes and expressive qualities found in sonata forms are indicative of the flexibility in composing a sonata form. With these principles and stylistic flexibility in mind, we can identify a large-scale design to guide the study of the unique form of a given composition or movement in

[1] See Rosen, *Sonata Forms 96ff;* Tovey, *The Forms of Music,* 208–214; and Cadwallader and Gagne, 303. Rosen, following Tovey, also discusses "sonata style" in *The Classical Style.*

sonata form. The discussion will focus on examples from the Classical period by Mozart, Haydn, and Beethoven. Examples from later periods will be considered to give some idea of how the form continued evolving to reflect different aesthetics and styles.

Large-Scale Design of Sonata Form

A useful and important point of reference for understanding the large-scale design of sonata form is the continuous rounded binary form. Recall that the latter form consists of two parts with three distinct formal functions. The first part, which is repeated, is typically a modulating period, repeated phrase or sentence structure. The second part begins with a transitional passage that normally leads to a half cadence in the original key. At that point, some portion of the opening theme, usually the beginning, is restated and leads to a close in the original tonic. Figure 8.1 gives a basic outline of a sonata form, using a key scheme associated with middle Classical period forms. Like a rounded binary form, it can be understood as a two-part structure with three sections within the design. The repeats reinforce the two-part structure of sonata form. The three sections of the form—exposition, development, and recapitulation—represent an expansion of the formal functions and proportions of the rounded binary: expansions that incorporate the dramatic and stylistic elements described above. Each formal section will be discussed separately and examined in three different works to give illustration of how they may be shaped.

Figure 8.1 *Outline of sonata form in the Classical period.*

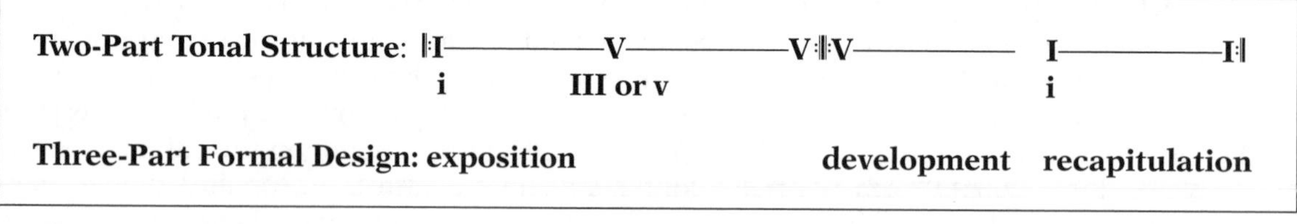

Exposition

INTRODUCTION

The exposition of sonata form begins with the presentation of a principal theme or themes in the tonic key. In most cases, a transition follows, which modulates to the new key. In the Classical period the modulation is normally to dominant (V) or in minor keys to relative major (III) or dominant minor (v). A cadence in the new key, usually a half cadence, often marks the end of the transition. Thematic presentation of material in the new key, which follows the transition, confirms the modulation and may present contrasting ideas. The end of the exposition is marked by strong cadential activity, often reiterated, in the new key. The expansion of this first section of the two-part form results from having distinct contrasting sections in the opening and closing keys or tonal areas, with a transitional passage that leads from the first tonal area to the second tonal area. The modulation to the new key and its confirmation are thus emphasized in a dramatic manner.

The broad sequence of events described above is found in most sonata form expositions. The number of themes and their character and length, the thematic processes and internal phrase structures, the length and proportions of sections, and the degree of separation or continuity within and among the sections are highly variable and reflect the composer's skill and imagination.

The diverse interplay of tonal and thematic elements found in sonata forms has resulted in a number of different terms that are used in outlining a sonata form exposition. Terms such as *first theme* and *second theme* are often used to describe the themes of each of the tonal areas in an exposition. This thematic view of the form is problematic because more than one theme may occur in any part of an exposition, and some sonata forms begin the second tonal area with a recall of the opening theme of the movement. One also encounters the terms *first group* and *second group*. The former term usually refers to everything up to the cadence that concludes the transition; the latter term to everything that follows. These terms indicate a two-part division of an exposition that is instructive, but whether they refer to groups of themes, phrases, or key areas is not always explicitly clear.[2]

The primacy of tonal design and structure in clarifying formal divisions suggest the value in using terms associated with tonality and with corresponding thematic designations. Figure 8.2 gives an outline of a sonata form exposition with terms that will be used in this text.

Figure 8.2 *Diagram of sonata form exposition.*

Principal Tonal Area		Transition	Secondary Tonal Area	
Principal Theme (s)		Counterstatement or New theme (Neutral material)	Secondary Theme(s)	Closing Theme (s)
I——————I HC or PAC	or	I——————V X——————V HC	V—————— PAC	——————V PAC

The terms *principal tonal area* (PTA) and *secondary tonal area* (STA) in Figure 8.2 reflect 1) the tonal basis of the design; 2) that the second key is secondary to the original tonic key; and 3) that the keys are established in a distinct area or section of the form.[3] The opposition of keys reflected in this terminology will be resolved in the recapitulation when secondary-key material is heard in tonic. The use of the terms *principal theme* (PT) and *secondary theme* (ST) in the diagram emphasizes the association of specific themes with specific key areas. Any reference to themes must also take into account that a number of themes may occur in the different key areas as well as in the transition (discussed later). It is often necessary to refer to PT^1, PT^2 or ST^1, ST^2 and so on, if more than one distinct theme is heard in a key area. This point will be considered further in the examples.

Figure 8.2 also shows some typical cadence patterns that articulate formal boundaries. As each section may comprise one or more phrases, additional cadences may be heard within sections. Though the placement and emphasis given the cadences will vary, directed motion toward marked cadences, as in all tonal music, is a critical aspect of the form. The functional divisions of the exposition are also subject to diverse subdivisions and

[2] Many other similar terms are to be found, including first subject/second subject, or main theme/subordinate theme. All of the terms reflect the thematic or tonal division of the exposition into two parts.

[3] The terms "region" and "zone," referring to tonal areas, are also to be found in writings on sonata form.

groupings. Quite often, the exposition can be divided into two parts, with the conclusion of part 1 marked by a half cadence in the secondary key at the end of the transition. The ST usually will end with a PAC that confirms the new key and a final PAC will close the exposition. We will examine three sonata form expositions to illustrate some common approaches to presenting ideas and articulating the form. You should listen closely to each example twice, with and without a score, before reading the analysis. Each movement will be examined in turn, followed by a summary of main points.

Example 8.1 Mozart, Piano Sonata in F major, K. 332, I, exposition.

Mozart, Piano Sonata in F major, K. 332, I (Example 8.1). As you listen to the exposition of the first movement of this sonata, in particular note the following elements as the music progresses: 1) two principal themes each closed by a PAC in the tonic; 2) a cadential extension at the end of the second principal theme, leading to a direct modulation to a minor key and a marked change in character; 3) a HC followed by a rest and a new, secondary theme that is periodic; 4) two closing themes, the first sequential; and 5) a closing phrase that contains trills.

Having listened to this movement you may have observed Mozart's skill at introducing several contrasting musical ideas in an exposition. Despite the number of different themes, Mozart's mastery of harmony and voice-leading, and his unerring sense of rhythmic motion and phrase structure allow these contrasting ideas to flow one into the other in a clearly conceived form.

The opening section contains two distinct themes, measures 1–12 and 13–22, each containing contrasting ideas. These themes confirm the initial tonic of F major and are articulated by a clear PAC. We are cued to the beginning of a transition when the cadential extensions of the second principal theme leads to a direct shift to D minor, the relative minor. The shift in key is also marked by the introduction of new material—arpeggios, full chords, and scalar passages—and an abrupt change to a "sturm und drang" (storm and stress) character. This transition concludes with a prolonged dominant harmony (measures 37–40) that expands the final phrase and emphasizes the cadence in measure 40. The tension of the transition is increased by the modulation to the dominant minor (C minor), which is followed by a shift in mode to the expected key of C major. Note as well the distinct break in rhythmic motion that clearly marks the end of the transition and beginning of the secondary theme, a characteristic strategy of Mozart. This break divides the exposition into two large sections: the PTA and transition, and the STA, including ST and *closing theme* (CT).

The secondary theme, measures 41–56, is a parallel, double period of 16 measures. Such symmetrical themes often begin a STA as they contribute to a sense of stability following the instability and drive of the transition. Complementary to this stable phrase structure is a lyric character often associated with a secondary theme, though such qualities should not be overly generalized. *When the STA begins with a self-contained, periodic theme that closes with an authentic cadence, the subsequent ideas that follow are normally grouped as a closing section to the exposition.*

In this exposition two distinct closing themes are presented beginning in measures 56 and 71, respectively. Note how CT^1 begins with two-measure repetitions that allow for a shift to dominant minor and serve as a lead-in to a sequence. Similarly, measures 67–70 extend the dominant harmony with continuous eighth-note motion that leads to the CT^2. It is just these types of phrase structures that reveal Mozart's strong sense of rhythmic motion and continuity, and which contribute to a well-conceived formal structure. The CT^3 also includes extensions using evaded cadences to emphasize the PAC in measure 86. The last eight measures of the exposition that follow are understood as a *codetta*, a short passage of 1–4 measures that prolongs a tonic chord or a cadential progression.[4] A codetta may be a single measure or as long as a four-bar phrase. It normally follows a strong PAC that could end the exposition, thus it functions to reinforce the cadence. In this example there are two parts to the codetta.

Example 8.2 Haydn, Piano Sonata No. 52 in Eb major, I, exposition.

[4] Caplin, 253.

(This excerpt continues on p. 150.)

(Example 8.2, continued.)

Haydn Piano Sonata No. 52 in E♭ major (Example 8.2).[5] Listen to the exposition of this movement and observe that the opening measure, or a variant of it, is heard several times in the exposition. Note if the continuation of this idea is based on new material or on the material of the opening theme. Why would the last 5 measures of the exposition be considered a codetta?

The first eight measures of the movement state two distinct themes in measures 1–5 and 6–8, respectively. Note how the repetitions in measure 4 expand the first theme to five measures and how the tonic harmony and cadence are avoided in measure 6. The opening measures are repeated in measures 9–10, this time in a new register and leading to a strong cadence. This musical material thus serves to close as well as initiate the PT. This reinterpretation of the formal function of a theme is a type of musical play and wit that the Classical composers explored frequently.

The transition subsequently begins in measure 11 with a restatement of the PT². Note how the change in register of this theme signals a potentially different continuation. The theme is now used in a descending sequence that modulates to B♭ minor, the dominant minor. As in Example 8.1, an elaboration of dominant (in this case over a pedal point), concludes the transition and strongly emphasizes the arrival of the STA in measure 17.

---

[5] For a description of the stylistic elements of this movement see Ratner, *Classic Form,* 412–421.

This STA in B♭ major in measure 17 begins with the motivic idea from the first measure of the movement. The nine measures after this, however, give a number of new motivic elaborations leading to a strong PAC on the downbeat of measure 27. Measures 17–27 thus are designated ST1. The next section then gives two different thematic ideas in a six-measure phrase that elides into measure 33. These motivically related ideas do not contain distinct closing characteristics and are best understood as ST[2]. The marked change in register, dynamics and character give the theme in measures 27–29 a parenthetical quality. Measure 33 gives yet another reference to the opening motives of the PT. This varied recall and new continuation leads to the strong, conclusive cadence in measure 40. Measures 33–40 may thus be designated as a CT while noting the varied use of PT material. The last four measures (40–43) function as a codetta, reinforcing the strong closure of the PAC heard on the downbeat of measure 40.

The use of principal thematic material throughout the exposition, notably at the beginning of the STA, results in what is commonly referred to as a *monothematic sonata form*. This practice is most often associated with Haydn. The term should not be taken too literally as other themes are invariably introduced in transitions or closing sections. This example also illustrates the possibilities of a continuous exposition in which a distinct break between the PT/Tr (transition) and STA/ST—a two-part division—is not heard. A certain amount of formal ambiguity results because the tonal and thematic elements are out of phase: the second tonal area is strongly established and confirmed well before a distinct new theme (measure 27) is presented. Other views of this Haydn sonata may espouse that measure 27 begins the ST with 17–27 serving as an elaboration and expansion of the PT ideas before the ST.

Example 8.3 Beethoven, Sonata Op. 14, No. 1 in E major, I, exposition.

(This excerpt continues on p. 152.)

(Example 8.3, continued.)

Beethoven, Piano Sonata Op. 14, No. 1 in E major, I. As you listen to this exposition, observe 1) how a restatement of the opening measures leads to a modulation and a pedal point in the new key; 2) the number of thematic repetitions that occur in the secondary themes; and 3) the use of the principal theme in the codetta of the exposition.

Again we see that a principal theme may contain several ideas. The first 12 measures comprise the PT and contain four distinct ideas. The restatement of the opening ideas with a shift in register (measure 13) initiates a phrase that will modulate to the dominant (F♯ major) of the dominant (B major). Note how the anacrusis in measure 22, which begins the STA and ST^1, immediately reverts to B major.

The STA in this exposition shows how more than one secondary theme may be incorporated in an exposition. The varied repetitions of the four-measure phrase in measures 23–26 and the imperfect cadences create an ongoing sense or need for continuation. A second secondary theme (ST^2, measures 39–46) is an eight-measure period that finally leads to an elided PAC and a CT (measures 46–56). Again we see evaded cadences in the closing theme as a way to stress a conclusive cadence (measures 56–57), which is followed by a brief codetta to conclude the exposition. The codetta uses PT material, now inverted, and serves as a transition to the repetition of the movement.

Each of the three expositions described vary in their expression and formal structure, as one would expect in a form as flexible as sonata form. Nonetheless, they all exhibit some general similarities in the sequence of formal functions and in the use of certain processes. The following discussion summarizes the attributes of the various sections of the sonata forms.

PRINCIPAL TONAL AREA AND THEMES

The function of the beginning section of a sonata form is to introduce thematic ideas as well as establish the tonic key. The principal theme or themes that open a sonata form movement may be as short as a single phrase, or contain several phrases and themes. Contrasting ideas or motives are often found in the principal themes as these examples illustrate. Often the theme is a sentence structure or a period, which, along with the cadences in the principal key, give an initial sense of stability. Whatever its length, the end of the principal tonal area is normally marked by a cadence, either a HC or AC in the tonic key. The manner in which this cadence may be connected to the subsequent transition and the shape of the transition may often mask this formal boundary.

TRANSITION

The preceding examples illustrate the following characteristics of transitions:

- Transitions reach a half cadence that normally concludes a prolongation of dominant harmony, which is referred to as *dominant preparation* in the new key. The length of the dominant preparation may vary from a few measures to a lengthy elaboration of cadential harmonies.
- The dominant harmony may be elided into a PAC at the beginning of the secondary theme, though it quite often is a marked point of cadential arrival at a HC, dividing the exposition into two parts.
- The accelerated rhythmic activity and changes in texture, notably the contrasts in register and range, and increased dynamic levels are characteristic of transitional passages. Such rhythmic and textural changes may be sudden, as in the Mozart sonata, or progressive. These changes, as well as the tonal instability created by modulations and changes in harmonic rhythm, create a sense of tension and instability characteristic of transitions. This cumulative tension is usually resolved as the STA begins.

Other features of these examples are indicative of varied compositional strategies that may be found in sonata form transitions. The transitions by Haydn and Beethoven begin with a varied restatement of the opening measures of the principal theme. The term *counterstatement* (abbreviated CS) is often used to identify this technique, in which the opening motives or ideas are restated with continuation that modulates. Thus it is different or "counter" to the original theme. A counterstatement is one of the most audible ways to recognize that a transition is beginning. By contrast, in the Mozart example, the shift in key and new thematic material in measure 23 mark the beginning of the transition. Though counterstatements or new material are both used to initiate transitions, the latter is perhaps more common.[6]

It is also important to note that transitions most often start in the tonic key. Although the point of modulation may be heard or identified at a specific point in the transition, *the transition as a formal unit should be understood as a phrase or phrase group that leads to a new key*. Exactly where the modulation is placed and how it is reached is a critical part of the compositional process. Many transitions are comprised of two parts: a first part that modulates, and a second part that uses dominant preparation to lead to a HC. Part 1 may make a direct and sudden move to the new key, or may first tonicize another key—most often ii or vi—before modulating to V.

SECONDARY TONAL AREA

The function of the secondary tonal area is to introduce additional thematic material associated with the new key and to bring the exposition to a decisive close in the new key. The STA may also provide further elaboration of themes or motives from the PTA. *As in the principal tonal area, the number, length and expressive character of themes and the proportions of the STA are highly variable*. Consequently, the division of the STA into secondary and closing themes is subject to different interpretations, depending on the specific thematic structure of a given exposition. Generally speaking, the closing section and themes may be understood as those that follow the first PAC in the new key. This typically would mean there is one secondary theme followed by a series of one or more closing themes. This model is most clearly the case when the STA begins with a new theme that is a period or sentence. As is evident in the Beethoven and Haydn examples, ideas from the principal themes are sometimes used in closing sections. Closing themes typically contain most of the following elements:

- repetition of short phrases or subphrases of 2–4 measures
- phrase elisions and evaded cadences
- accelerated rhythmic and harmonic motion
- phrase extensions that emphasize cadences in the new key

Elided or evaded cadences and phrase repetition create an ongoing sense of motion toward closure while delaying arrival on of a conclusive PAC in the new key. The resultant continuity of motion is characteristic of closing themes and of the STA in general.

In movements where a number of thematic ideas occur in the STA without the rhythmic and phrase characteristics of closing sections, more than one ST may be identified. Another thematic view of the STA is that it should be understood as a series of secondary themes, with the designation of closing themes reserved for those heard in the codetta of a movement. This view is reasonable when there are several distinct themes in the STA before characteristic closing material appears in a codetta or coda. The segmentation of themes and sections, however they are interpreted functionally, should be consistent if careful consideration is given to tonal and thematic elements. In other words, however one interprets the thematic functions in the exposition shown in Example 8.2, the important formal junctures occur at measures 9–10, 17, 27, 33, and 40.

---

[6] The term "dependent transition" is also used to refer to one that uses PT material; the term "independent transition" to one that does not.

Analytic Note: Wherever one interprets the beginning of the closing section of an exposition, a critical aspect of the STA is a confirmation of the new key by a strong PAC in the new key. This cadence is called the *essential expositional close* or *EEC*. Normally this is the first PAC in the new key.[7]

FORMAL BOUNDARIES AND GROUPING OF THE TRANSITION

How the transition begins and continues has a distinct role in the perception of the large grouping structure of the exposition. When a counterstatement is begun in the tonic key, particularly after a HC, it is reasonable to perceive the beginning of the transition as a continuation of the PTA since it may be heard initially as the consequent of a larger period. This perception supports the grouping of the transition with the principal theme and tonal area. When the transition begins with marked changes in theme or key, as in the example by Mozart, the transition is more likely to be heard as a separate formal event between the two tonal/thematic areas.

Many sonata forms exhibit less clear divisions because of how the principal themes and transition are connected and how the tonal motion shapes the arrival in a secondary tonal area. Consider the famous opening movement of Symphony No. 5 by Beethoven (Example 8.4). Following the dramatic introductory gesture, the PTA begins with a sixteen-measure sentence structure that reaches a HC and a pause, followed by a varied repetition of the phrase introduction. Repetition of the opening motive in a descending gesture is heard in measures 25–33, which contain a repeated V-i progression.

The subsequent fragmentation, rhythmic acceleration, and registral ascent heard in measures 34–44 increase the drive and tension of the music in the manner of a transition. However, the rhythmic continuity, the motivic repetitions, and the continued emphasis on tonic and dominant harmonies through measure 51 suggest this is still an expansion of the principal theme. It is only in the motivic repetitions in measures 52–56 that a modulation is suddenly made near the close of the entire passage. In a remarkably dramatic gesture (measures 57–62), Beethoven expands the resolution to the new key with rests, adding a bold horn call to announce the beginning of the STA.

Here then, the two formal functions of the principal theme and transition are fused such that no clear division occurs. This process of *fusion* results when two different formal functions are merged into a single unit by continuous harmonic and rhythmic motion. It is one of the most important ways of achieving continuity of motion in a form that is easily sectionalized by internal contrasts.[8]

NON-MODULATING TRANSITION

There are instances when a transition will not modulate but instead will reach a strong HC in the original tonic, followed by a direct shift to the STA and a new theme. The music will still exhibit the characteristics of a transition passage—accelerated rhythmic activity, quicker harmonic rhythms, expansion of range, and the use of new ideas—to distinguish its function from the PT. The use of a non-modulating transition is a strategy that allows for an exact restatement of the transition in the recapitulation.[9]

---

[7] Hepakoski and Darcy (1997).

[8] See Caplin, *Classical Form*, 165–67 and 209–211 for additional discussion and examples of the fusion of formal units in sonata forms.

[9] A good example of a non-modulating transition may be found in +Mozart's Piano Sonata in A minor K. 311, I.

Example 8.4 Beethoven, Symphony No. 5, I, principal theme and transition, mm. 25–64.

A final example by Haydn (Example 8.5) illustrates how dramatic changes in texture and rhythmic activity may precede the transition. Recall the graceful and subdued opening theme of Haydn's Symphony No. 104, I, Allegro (Example 4.10). This periodic theme now elides into a *fortissimo* tutti texture and a new thematic idea (PT2). These marked changes might suggest the beginning of a transition, but it is not until 18 measures later in measure 50 that another new idea initiates the transitional phrase. The transition (measures 50–64) continues the basic rhythmic motion and texture of the preceding passage. In this case, then, the principal themes are strongly contrasting in texture and rhythmic motion, while the transitional phrase is a continuation of the textures of the second principal theme.

As these examples illustrate, the length and connections of phrases, the number of themes and the placement of the modulation in the first half of an exposition are important to the shape and dramatic effect of the form. *It is these elements of the exposition that a composer will reconsider or reinterpret when the recapitulation of themes is presented.*

Example 8.5 Haydn, Symphony No. 104, I, mm. 26–64.

(This excerpt continues on p. 160.)

(Example 8.5, continued.)

Exercises: Exposition

The following exercises focus on some specific aspects of each movement though the general task is to identify the main sections of the exposition. One may distinguish the most important formal boundaries readily in some works, while others require more detailed consideration of phrase structures and tonal motions. In an exposition, the placement of modulations is critical to the formal shape and design of the music. Listen for and identify points of important chromatic motion that lead to new keys. The leading tones of the dominant key and of the V of dominant are important visual and aural cues. In the key of C, for example, the pitches F♯ and C♯ will direct a modulation to G major (V). Take note of pedal points and marked cadences as well as thematic statements and changes in texture. Close analysis of phrase structure will always give a better understanding of the work and help clarify the formal divisions and functions. The answers to the questions posed may be in the form of short essays. The essays should not only answer the questions regarding formal divisions but explain how the form is articulated. For these and subsequent exercises, access to a score is necessary.

1. **Haydn, String Quartet Op. 76, No. 3 in C major, I.** This movement is an example of Haydn's monothematic forms. The conclusion of the transition and the beginning of the STA and ST are ambiguous. The transition may be interpreted as a non-modulating one that closes with a HC in the principal key. Which measures comprise the transition? Where is the modulation to G major (V)? Where is the first cadence in this key? To what key does the music move in measure 29, and in measures 31–33? What is the function of the passage that begins in measure 38? A formal analysis of the recapitulation may help guide one's interpretation of the exposition.

2. **+Haydn, Piano Sonata No. 41 in B♭ major, I.** This work also contains an example of a non-modulating transition. What happens to the tonality briefly after the ST begins? In what key does the development begin? What is the relation of this key to the PTA and the key that follows in the development? How is the transition handled in the recapitulation? Examine how Haydn explores register for variation of material in the recapitulation.

3. **Mozart, Symphony No. 40, IV.** Listen to the exposition of the opening of the movement, which is an *Allegro assai* in *alla breve* tempo. The principal theme is a 32-measure symmetrical unit. Listen without the aid of a score and determine the relations among the four-measure phrases. What form do these 32 measures comprise? How is the close of this section connected to the transition that follows? How is the conclusion of the transition marked? The ST is periodic and begins with an eight-measure phrase. What kind of period is formed with the next eight-measure phrase? How is the beginning of the closing section clearly marked?

4. ***Mozart, Piano Sonata in B♭ major, K. 333, I, mm. 1–22.** How do measures 1–10 subdivide? Briefly explain where the transition begins. In what measure(s) does the modulation to dominant take place? How do measures 11–22 subdivide? Why might or might not measure 15 be considered a continuation of the transition? What is the harmonic function of measures 16–22? How many themes are heard in the STA? Which are closing themes? How does Mozart make clear where the codetta to the exposition begins?

5. ***Beethoven, Piano Sonata Op. 2, No. 1 in F minor, mm. 1–48.** The skillful elision of phrases may also be achieved between transitions and secondary tonal areas such that their boundaries are masked by continuity of motion. The exposition of this sonata is a case in point. In what key does the counterstatement in measure 9 begin? Most analysts cite measure 19 as the beginning of the STA. How does Beethoven maintain the tension of the transition as the ST is introduced? At what point does the music finally reach a PAC in the secondary key? What is the formal function of the passage that follows?

6. **+Beethoven, Piano Sonata Op. 31, No. 2 in D minor, "Tempest," I.** This unusual movement incorporates two strong contrasting ideas at the beginning of the exposition. Of particular interest here is the ambiguity of the thematic and tonal divisions, which are frequently out of phase. The transitions may be heard as beginning in measure 21, the STA in measure 41. What makes this division ambiguous? How does Beethoven achieve the sense that points of arrival immediately become points of continuation, a noteworthy characteristic of his music? Explain why division of the STA into ST and CT areas is not straightforward.

7. ***Beethoven, Piano Sonata Op. 53 in C major, I.** This exposition has clearly articulated divisions marked by changes in rhythmic motion. How does the transition begin? What is the function of measures 23–34? What type of phrase structure is used for the secondary theme? The closing section begins in measure 50. How does Beethoven provide continuity from the secondary theme into this section? How many closing themes can you identify? Describe the textural and rhythmic processes that he uses to shape this closing section. Where is the climax of this section? What other function does the codetta assume?

Development

INTRODUCTION

Sonata form is in essence concerned with the statement, elaboration, contrast, and development of ideas. The formal section referred to as the *development* is the central section of a sonata form in which previous themes are heard in new textures and combinations, in new keys, and in varied phrase structures. However, thematic material may be developed in any section of a sonata form, notably in transitional passages and codas. The principal tonal function of the development is to return to the tonic key. This is usually emphasized by *dominant preparation* at the conclusion. The overall effect is that of increasing tension and heightening the need for resolution back to tonic, which occurs as the recapitulation begins. The thematic and tonal design of developments is subject to such great variance that generalizations about their design are difficult. The following discussion presents some basic ideas concerning how developments begin, the compositional techniques and processes that are found in developments, and some strategies for closing a development section.

BEGINNING THE DEVELOPMENT

The development may begin with themes previously introduced or occasionally with a new theme. One common strategy is to begin with the principal theme in the secondary key and subsequently modulate. Example 8.6 gives two such examples. In the Haydn Quartet (Example 8.6a), the development starts with the motives of the principal theme but uses the counterstatement that initiated the transition. This phrase quickly modulates from G major (V) to A minor (vi) and is followed by a series of tonicizations. The development of the Beethoven Piano Sonata Op. 2, No. 1 (Example 8.6b) begins with a restatement of the principal theme in A♭ major (III), which is fragmented and modulates to B♭ minor (iv). In each of these examples, the theme is varied to modulate through a different continuation that alters its phrase structure. These changes immediately created a sense of instability and restlessness characteristic of developments. See also Beethoven Piano Sonata, Op. 14 No. 1 in which the codetta is extended through the second ending. Beethoven makes a passing motion through tonic—E major—but continues with a modulation to A minor.

Mozart will sometimes begin the development with a new theme motivically or stylistically related to the principal theme but in the secondary key. The Piano Sonata K. 332, I, illustrates this strategy (Example 8.7). The theme introduced here has the simple, *ländler*-like quality of the principal theme of the movement. The theme is a symmetrical eight-measure sentence that is repeated with a change in register. These characteristics give a brief sense of stability before the main modulatory section of the development begins. Conversely, that this new theme is perhaps unexpected increases anticipation of the actual beginning of the development. Normally the secondary theme does not open a development in the secondary key, since it has already been heard in the STA of the exposition.

The development may also begin with a transitional phrase to modulate from the secondary key to a new key that will initiate the main part of the development. The effect here is of a passage that connects the exposition to the actual beginning of the development.[10] The Haydn Piano Sonata No. 52 begins with a fragment from the closing section (see Example 8.2, measures 44–45), which immediately effects a modulation from B♭ major (V) to C major (VI). A statement of a secondary theme in this new key follows.

[10] Caplin uses the terms "core" and "pre-core" to distinguish between the main part of a development and passages that precede this. See Caplin, 147–57 for further discussion of the characteristics of a pre-core.

The beginning of the development in Mozart's Symphony No. 41, I, measures 121–123 is a similar example (see Example 8.8). Here Mozart uses a fragment of the PT to modulate from G major (V) to E♭ major (♭III). He then returns to a closing theme of the exposition. These examples reflect Haydn's and Mozart's fondness for beginning the development with a closing theme or motive of the exposition, providing a sense of continuity from one section to another.

One other strategy worth noting is that of beginning a development with a restatement of an introductory theme that opened the movement. Beethoven and later nineteenth-century composers favored this strategy. For example, see the first movements of Beethoven's Sonata Op. 13 and Symphony No. 9, Tchaikovsky's Symphony No. 4, and Schubert's Symphony No. 8.

Example 8.6 a. Haydn, String Quartet Op. 76, No. 3, I, mm. 42–50.

b. Beethoven, Piano Sonata Op. 2, No. 1, mm. 49–55.

Example 8.7 Mozart, Piano Sonata, K. 332 development, mm. 94–140.

DEVELOPMENTAL PROCESSES

While thematic patterns, tonal motions, and proportions are unpredictable in a development section, certain processes or compositional techniques are expected and are summarized in the following discussions.

Modulations The modulation to new keys and tonal instability are basic aspects of a development section. As has been discussed, modulations normally are confirmed by a cadence in the new key. An extended passage in a new key may also emphasize a modulation. Generally speaking, cadences in new keys are often followed by another modulation as the next phrase or section begins. Though some key areas will be given more emphasis than others, areas of tonal stability are not the norm. The rapid changes in key are one of the principal ways the music increases in tension. The frequent modulations or *tonicizations* will naturally entail the use of chromatic harmonies, also characteristic of developments.

Any key, however close or distantly related, may appear in a development section. In the Classical period, the submediant (vi) is one of the most frequently encountered keys, as is a change in mode from major to minor. The relatively brief development of the Mozart Piano Sonata K. 332 (Example 8.7) illustrates these features. Measure 109 returns to a sequential closing theme of the exposition. A change in mode from C major to C minor (measure 111) is followed by tonicization of G minor (ii) and then a modulation to D minor (vi). The final section (measures 123–133) returns to tonic, as discussed below.

Example 8.8 Mozart, Symphony No. 41, I, beginning of development, mm. 121–132.

More elaborate developments may modulate through several keys, often reaching a very remote key before the return to the home key of the movement. Leonard Ratner uses the term "point of furthest remove"[11] to refer to the most distant key reached in a development, which normally leads to the modulation to tonic. An outline of the tonalities and textures of the development of the finale of Mozart's Symphony No. 40 is given in Figure 8.3. This agitated and driving music relies exclusively on the principal theme of the movement in a wide range of textures. It reaches the remote key of C♯ minor (♯iv)—the point of "furthest remove"—before turning back toward tonic.

Figure 8.3 *Mozart Symphony No. 40, IV Development section, mm. 100–165.*

Section:	transition	I	II		III	retransition		
Measure:	125	135	148	161	175	191	211	215
Key:	III	v	vii	iv	♯iv !	♯iv-----V6/5 of i		
	B♭	Dm	Fm	Cm	C♯m	C♯m-----Gm		H.C. pause
					H.C. Pedal			
Texture	unison	antiphonal	fugato	stretto/strings		antiphonal	tutti	

FRAGMENTATION AND SEQUENCE

Since sonata form themes are often comprised of subphrases two to four measures in length, they naturally lend themselves to fragmentation. This in turn allows for different continuations and variations of phrase structure that are characteristic of developments. Each of the passages shown in Example 8.6, for example, uses repeated fragments of principal themes to create new continuations that effect modulations. *The fragmenting of themes into smaller units and presenting them in sequential repetitions is a basic technique of development sections.* Example 8.9 shows a passage from the development the Beethoven Piano Sonata Op. 53, I. Measure 96 continues with a compressed statement of the PT motives heard in measures 93–95. This one-measure idea is fragmented again in measure 103 using repetitions of motive *b* to accelerate the motion. The motive *a* is then presented in a *pianissimo* sequence beginning in measure 104, that uses a series of secondary harmonies. Note how the two-measure pattern is compressed to a single measure as the passage concludes (measure 109), accelerating the motion toward a HC in measure 112. This technique of compression, in which a sequential or melodic pattern is further fragmented, gives the music a sense of urgency and tension.[12]

NEW TEXTURES AND THEMATIC REORDERING

Another basic technique of developments is the presentation of thematic material in new textures and different combinations or order. Example 8.2 shows how Haydn restates the ST^2 in measures 46–47, now in C major (VI). The theme subsequently modulates to F major at which point the closing idea of the ST^1 initiates a chromatic sequence. Such passages show the composer's skill at creating new harmonic progressions and phrase continuations to connect themes in a convincing manner. The unpredictability of the continuations contributes to the interest and instability of the development.

[11] Ratner, *Classic Form,* 226.

[12] Other terms one may encounter for the compression of ideas include *"foreshortening"* and *"telescoping."*

Example 8.9 Beethoven Piano Sonata Op. 53, I, development, mm. 93–111.

The development of themes in contrapuntal textures is also an important developmental technique. Imitation and the introduction of new counterpoint against previous themes are frequently encountered in developments. Passages that employ systematic imitation of a theme or fragment in the manner of a fugue as part of the development are referred to as a *fugato*. This technique is heard in the Mozart Symphony No. 40 first movement, as outlined in Figure 8.3. Imitative textures and thematic reordering, along with fragmentation, sequence, and evaded or deceptive cadences, create irregular phrase rhythms that are characteristic of developments.

Marked changes in the dynamic and textural setting of a theme are also a way to alter the expressive character and give it new dramatic meaning. Nowhere is this more apparent than in the bold statement of a theme in an octave, *forte* texture. The development of Mozart's Symphony No. 40, I (Example 8.10a) begins with fragments of the principal theme in just such a texture, which serves as a transition from B♭ major (III) to D minor (v). Irregular phrase rhythm, chromatic harmonies, and disjunct linear motion also contribute to the intensely agitated effect of this passage. Similarly, the subdued, dark introductory theme of Schubert's Symphony No. 8 recurs in a tutti, octave texture in the development (Example 8.10b), creating a forceful declamation.

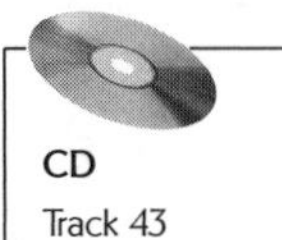

CD
Track 43

New themes are sometimes introduced in the development, although this is not a frequently encountered strategy. A famous example occurs in the first movement of Beethoven's Symphony No. 3, beginning in measure 284. This quiet lyrical theme is first heard in the key of E minor (♭ii), a very remote key from the tonic of E♭ major that marks the "point of furthest remove" in the development. Coming after a climactic and relentless dissonance in the preceding passage, the effect of this theme is that of a brief, almost

Example 8.10 *Development.*

a. Mozart, Symphony No. 40, I, development, mm. 125–141.

b. Schubert, Symphony No. 8, I, development, mm. 170–78.

mysterious release in tension. It also initiates the final stages of the massive development of this movement.

RETRANSITION

The final section of a development that leads to the beginning of the recapitulation is referred to as the *retransition.* The most salient feature of the retransition is a modulation back to the original tonic. Retransitions are often marked by a change in texture and dynamics as well as repeated melodic patterns. Example 8.7, measures 123–132, illustrates these processes. A HC in D minor (vi) in measure 123 is followed by a change in texture that initially expands the dominant of D minor. The repeated melodic motion in thirds eventually progresses to the V7 chord in F major. A quiet iteration of this harmony in root position (measures 131–32) leads to the return of the PTA and principal theme. The emphasis on the submediant key prior to or within the retransition is a favorite strategy of Mozart's.

Example 8.11a shows the second part of the retransition of Haydn's Symphony No. 104, I. This passage continues motivic statements and melodic ascent from the previous passage, reaching a climax in measure 190. The persistent dominant pedal reiterated in the timpani and bass in D major reinforces this climactic moment. A dramatic pause then ushers in the recapitulation in measure 194. Often the retransition will close with an extended passage of dominant preparation using a pedal point that begins with a marked change in texture and theme as in Example 8.11b. Such a passage may be understood as the actual retransition though it is the preceding passage that affects the modulation back to tonic. In effect the result is a two-part retransition. Note the use of tonic minor (Em) for dramatic emphasis.

Example 8.11 *Retransitions.*

a. Haydn, Symphony No. 104 in D major, I, retransition mm. 186–193.

b. Beethoven Piano Sonata Op. 14, No. 1, I, retransition and recapitulation, mm. 81–94.

Example 8.12 shows yet another strategy for a retransition: a sudden or direct modulation to the tonic key. Following a boisterous and playful passage in E major (III), Haydn switches modes to E minor and reduces the texture and dynamics in measures 75–78. As the dynamics recede to *pianissimo* the texture thins and the melodic repetitions in measure 78 seem to stall the rhythmic and harmonic motion of the passage. In a witty and quick stroke Haydn moves directly back to C major (I) and begins the recapitulation with the pickup to measure 79. These three examples give some idea of the range of proportions and expressive effects that composers might exploit at this significant formal juncture.[13]

FLUCTUATIONS IN TENSION

The development of musical material by changes in key, texture, thematic order and phrase structure, and the dramatic change in expressive character of themes all contribute to a sense of instability and tension that prevails in a development. Fluctuations in tension, however, are also important to the shape of a development. *Passages of brief stasis or repose may be introduced to augment the tension when development is renewed.* Expository techniques such as the introduction of a new theme, periodic phrases, melodic repetitions, or stable harmonic activity may create momentary repose, often complemented by dynamic recession.[14] Another developmental technique is that of a *false retransition*, in which a prolonged dominant in the wrong key—a key other than tonic—misleads our expectations of a forthcoming resolution to the original tonic. A subsequent *false recapitulation* may occur, in which the principal theme returns decisively

[13] See Shagmar, (1981) for a discussion of locating the retransitions.

[14] See for example the *cantabile pp* passage beginning in measure 274 of Beethoven's Symphony No. 9, I.

Example 8.12 Haydn, String Quartet Op. 76, No. 3, I, retransition and recapitulation, mm. 75–86.

but briefly, followed by further development. Such passages give a momentary sense of stability, which is invariably countered by further development.[15]

ANALYZING THE DEVELOPMENT

The development section can be the most challenging section of a sonata form to analyze given the fluctuations in tonality, themes and textures. Changes in these elements are often out of phase in developments, with an avoidance of coordinated closure until the recapitulation or beyond. Keep in mind that a well-composed development is clearly organized. While changes in texture and themes will give many obvious clues for segmenting the development, underlying tonal motions should guide analytic decisions. This may require detailed harmonic analysis of certain passages to clarify tonal motion.

Some basic procedures for analyzing a development include the following (not necessarily in order):

- Determine how the development begins and the degree of continuity or discontinuity, stability or instability that it effects.
- Note marked changes in texture and dynamics.
- Chart the modulations that occur and note which keys are given the most emphasis through prolongation or cadence. Which key is the most distant?
- Chart the themes that are being used. Compare the phrase structure and formal processes of thematic restatements with their initial presentation in the exposition.
- Identify the beginning and ending of sequences, instances of pedal point or reiterated bass-line motions.
- Note keys at points of cadence; melodic repetitions and cadential bass-line motions may cue these events along with changes in other elements. Is closure attenuated at points of cadence? Do changes in texture or thematic material coincide with points of cadence?
- Work backwards from the recapitulation to determine how the retransition is treated. Determine where the modulation back to the tonic occurs. Is there an expanded dominant preparation as the development closes?

Exercises: Score Analysis of Development Sections

1. ***Mozart, Piano Sonata in B♭ major, K. 333, I.** This development section may be readily divided into three sections, with the middle section serving as the core of the development. Where do these various sections begin and how are these formal boundaries made clear? The retransition is in two parts, the first containing a dominant expansion but not in the tonic key. What key is established prior to the modulation back to the tonic, B♭ major? Where does dominant preparation begin at the end of the development? What type of texture serves as a lead-in to the recapitulation?

[15] Some analysts define a false recapitulation as the appearance of the PT in the tonic key but prior to the actual recapitulation. Other analysts consider a marked appearance in a non-tonic key to be a type of false recapitulation. For an example of the former, see Haydn, Symphony No. 55, I, m. 97; for an example of the latter, see Mozart, Symphony No. 41, I, m. 161. See Rosen, *Sonata Forms* 264–268 and Caplin, *Classical Form*, 159 and 277.

2. **Mozart, Symphony No. 40 in G minor, I.** Use Figure 8.3 as a study guide to the first movement development. Analyze the harmonies of the transitional opening of the development, measures 125–135 (Example 8.10a). How do the texture, rhythm, melodic contour, and harmonic motion contribute to the agitated, stormy expression in this passage?

3. **Haydn, String Quartet, Op. 76, No. 3, I.** The point of furthest remove is the key of E major (VI). Where is this key reached? How does Haydn dramatically highlight the passage in which this key is heard? How are the various instruments used in the texture of this passage? Describe the style or character of this passage. In what way is this passage static? Does this stasis seem to increase or decrease the tension of the development? Explain your answer.

4. ***Haydn, Piano Sonata No. 36 in C♯ minor.** The development begins with the ST1 of the exposition. At what point is the continuation of this theme different from the exposition? What key is implied by the harmony in measures 41–42? How is that same harmony reinterpreted and resolved? The PT recurs in measures 44–49. Do a harmonic analysis of this passage, noting the modulation that occurs. Explain why measure 51 may be understood as the beginning of the retransition. Where does the modulation back to C♯ minor occur?

5. ***Beethoven, Piano Sonata Op. 53, I.** Beethoven makes the connection between exposition and development seamless. How is this achieved? A four-measure elaboration of a CT begins in measure 112. Trace the sequential elaboration of this idea. At what point is the sequential idea compressed? What is the harmonic goal of this passage? The second part of the retransition begins in measure 142. Describe the processes or techniques Beethoven uses to build to the climactic ending of the development.

6. ***Beethoven, String Quartet Op. 59, No. 2 in E minor.** This development, starting with the second ending, begins with a number of brief tonicizations, some of them so abrupt as to be startling. Analyze the harmonic motion of the development up to the point where a dominant pedal is reached in B♭ minor. How is this pedal point resolved? A new dominant pedal emerges from this resolution. Follow the bass line motion of this pedal point to determine its resolution. Note where the music reaches a B♭ in octaves and a *fortissimo* dynamic level. Follow the subsequent bass line motion: to what key does this passage eventually resolve with a decisive change in texture?

Recapitulation

FUNCTION

The third major section of a sonata form, the *recapitulation*, has several functions. The main tonal function is to return to the tonic key. The most important aspect of this function is the restatement of material of the secondary tonal area of the exposition in the tonic key. As Charles Rosen states, "what seems to be the one fixed rule of sonata recapitulation [is the following]: material originally exposed in the dominant must be represented in the tonic fairly completely, even if rewritten and reordered, and only material in the tonic may be omitted."[16] From this tonal perspective, the recapitulation then serves as a

[16] Rosen, *Classical Style*, 72. Of course the STA of the exposition may also be the relative major in minor keys, or other keys. In any case, this material will be restated in tonic in the recapitulation.

large-scale resolution of the opposition of tonal areas in the exposition. The beginning of the recapitulation also contributes to an immediate sense of resolution as it resolves the tension of the development by a return to the tonic key.

TECHNIQUES

Far from being simply a mechanical restatement of material, the recapitulation allows a composer to reinterpret or explore new continuations of themes. Normally the recapitulation will begin with the restatement of the principal theme. This theme or any of the sections of the exposition may be altered by 1) phrase contraction or expansion, 2) changes in rhythm, texture and dynamics, 3) fusion of principal themes and transition, 4) omission and reordering of thematic material.

Thematic compression and expansion. The reasons for thematic alterations are varied and subject to interpretation based on a given formal and expressive context. The relatively lengthy PT of the finale of the Mozart Symphony No. 40, for example, is compressed from 32 to 16 measures in the recapitulation, with no repeats of phrases. This compression seems appropriate in the new context: the theme was used throughout the development and the shorter version gives impetus to the recapitulation. Generally speaking, the compression of a PT or the transition may be related to the fact that the principal key need not be reinforced, as it will be heard in the restatement of the ST in the recapitulation. Conversely, expansion of principal themes can serve as further development of material as the composer explores new possibilities for continuation. Principal themes may also encompass new tonicizations or tonal digressions. The recapitulation of the PT of the Beethoven Piano Sonata Op. 53, I, discussed in Exercise 5, interpolates new material and unexpected harmonic turns before returning to the tonic key to begin the transition.[17] Such formal surprises often serve as the basis for later developments in the coda of the movement.

Changes in rhythm, texture and dynamics may be used to change the expressive qualities of the principal theme. The beginning of the PT of the Beethoven Piano Sonata shown in Example 8.3 has a lyric, restrained quality. When it recurs to begin the recapitulation (Example 8.11b), the thicker textures, *forte* dynamics, and more active left-hand scalar passages give it a triumphant, exuberant quality. Such changes often serve to dramatize this critical juncture in the form.

The most significant changes in phrase structure or tonal motion in the recapitulation normally will be in the transition since it is this section that returns to tonic rather than modulating as it did in the exposition. This transition often tonicizes new keys or introduces secondary chromatic harmonies as it presents a varied restatement of the transition heard in the exposition. *Consequently the tonal unrest that characterizes the transition is maintained or intensified, though it will normally resolve in the tonic key at its conclusion*. Tonally, then, this transition is not needed, but dramatically, it is essential to articulating the return of the ST in the tonic key.

An example of an expanded transition can be seen in the recapitulation of the Mozart Sonata K. 332, I (Example 8.13). The PT is restated exactly but the transition is expanded by an additional four-measure statement (measures 163–166) that turns briefly toward the subdominant key of B♭ minor (iv). The transition then continues to a close in tonic minor and a HC in measure 176. A modulation to subdominant in the recapitulation is a frequent tonal strategy, as it leads strongly back to tonic by way of dominant.[18] Note also the use of modal mixture in this example.

---

[17] See also, for example, Beethoven, Symphony No. 3, I, mm. 391–424.

[18] This tonal digression may be toward other related keys such as ♭III, ♭VI, or even ♭II, as well as IV. These are referred to as "flat side" keys, that is, keys that introduce chromatic notes that are lowered scale degrees in relation to tonic.

Example 8.13 Mozart, Piano Sonata K. 332, I, transition in recapitulation, mm. 155–176.

Fusion of principal theme and transition is a vital means of achieving continuity and offsetting the stability encountered at the beginning of the recapitulation. This technique results in dramatic reinterpretations of material that intensifies the recapitulation. The Mozart Symphony No. 41, IV provides an interesting example of this fusion of formal units (see Example 8.14). The PTA of the exposition consists of a periodic theme (measures 1–19) followed by a fanfare-like theme that leads to a number of cadential repetitions, closing on a HC. A fugal elaboration of these motives follows, leading to a transitional section beginning in measure 53. The recapitulation begins with the expected eight-measure antecedent phrase of the PT. The parallel consequent phrase (measure 233), however, introduces a startling new continuation, using the four-measure opening idea of the PT in chromatic sequences and in stretto. As this highly charged and agitated passage closes, the music reaches the subdominant key and the modulatory section of the transition suddenly appears. A large portion of the PTA (measures 13–55) is thus supplanted by this new developmental passage and the fusion of the two formal units.[19] The beginning passage of the transition is also eliminated as part of the process of fusion. This deletion is not uncommon, as transitions normally begin with emphasis on tonic harmony, an emphasis not necessary in the recapitulation.

Example 8.14 Mozart, Symphony No. 41, IV, PTA, recapitulation, mm. 233–256.

[19] For a famous example of expressive reinterpretation and fusion of PT and transition see Beethoven's Symphony No. 9, I, mm. 301–339.

While the restatement of the STA themes in the tonic key is of large-scale significance, the secondary themes and closing material are least likely to be altered substantially *apart from the transposition*. This is especially true in the works of Mozart and, to a lesser extent, Beethoven. Mozart's Piano Sonata K. 332 for example, restates the STA exactly as in the exposition simply transposed to tonic. When the STA is altered, it is usually through phrase expansions or by extensions of the closing material that reinforce the final closure of the movement. The close of the exposition in the Haydn Piano Sonata No. 52, I, (Example 8.15), shows how some witty interpolations enliven the PT closing section of the recapitulation. (Compare the same passages of the exposition, given in Example 8.2.)

Example 8.15 Haydn, Piano Sonata No. 52, I, recapitulation, mm. 78–87, 104–116.

(This excerpt continues on p. 180.)

(Example 8.15, continued.)

Haydn, more than Mozart or Beethoven, will often have significant changes in the recapitulation, including the STA. In the first movement of Haydn's String Quartet Op. 76, No. 3, for example, the end of the transition (measures 10–12) and the beginning of the STA (measures 13–17) are eliminated. The passage in measures 13–17 contained a statement of the PT motives in the dominant key to mark the beginning of the STA. This passage would be tonally redundant in the recapitulation, and Haydn skillfully fuses the transition and the first phrase of the STA. Significant reworking of the closing themes is also heard in the conclusion of this movement (see Exercises).

Omission and reordering of thematic material. One encounters instances when the principal theme is omitted at the beginning of the recapitulation. This is of course not an arbitrary notion though the reasons, as always, must be inferred and interpreted from the context. In some cases the ST will begin the recapitulation and the PT will be heard in the closing section. This reordering results in what is sometimes termed a *reverse recapitulation*. The Mozart Piano Sonata K. 311 contains an example of this type of recapitulation. In the first movement the PT has the character of a cadential, closing theme, a function it assumes when it is clearly restated near the end of the recapitulation. In other movements the PT may have been elaborated extensively in the development and its recurrence is delayed until a coda that is appended to the recapitulation. The first movement of Chopin's Piano Sonata No. 2 in B♭ minor is a good example of this type of omission. The development focuses on the motives of the principal theme with continuous and rapid modulations through many remote keys. The entrance of the broad and lyrical ST at the beginning of the recapitulation provides a sense of stability and breadth that relieves the intense tonal instability and tension of the development.[20]

Exercises: Recapitulation

Comparing the recapitulation with the exposition facilitates analysis by broadening our understanding of a composer's variation and reinterpretation of ideas. The recapitulation of any of the movements of the previous exercises may be considered in light of the analysis of corresponding expositions. These exercises pose questions for select movements.

1. **Haydn, Symphony No. 104, I.** The transition of this movement is playfully altered in the recapitulation. Identify the measures where the most obvious changes take place. Compare the beginning of the STA of the recapitulation (starting in measure 247) with that of the exposition (see Example 8.5). What thematic material is used and to what extent is it altered compared to its original presentation in the movement?

[20] See also the Haydn, String Quartet in E♭, Op. 50, No. 3, I; Schubert, Quartetsatz in C minor, I; Mendelssohn, Symphony No. 4, IV; and Chopin, Sonata No. 3 in B minor, I.

2. **Haydn, String Quartet, Op. 76, No. 3, I.** The fusion of transition and the beginning of the STA in the recapitulation has been discussed. Compare mm. 93–94 with the corresponding passage in the exposition (measures 21–22). At what point does the subsequent closing section of the recapitulation dramatically depart from that of the exposition? How is the passing modulation in the closing section of the exposition (G-E♭-G) treated in the recapitulation?

3. ***Haydn, Piano Sonata No. 36, in C♯ minor, I.** What is the formal function of measures 7–11, and 12–16 in the exposition? How are these measures treated in the recapitulation? Identify instances of phrase expansion in the recapitulation of the PT and ST.

4. ***Mozart, Piano Sonata in B♭ major, K. 333.** How is the counterstatement of the exposition altered in the recapitulation? Which closing theme is expanded in the recapitulation?

5. ***Beethoven, Piano Sonata Op. 53, I.** Toward what keys or harmonies does the PT turn before the elided cadence that begins the transition in measure 174? Compare the proportions of the transition with the transition of the exposition. How is the transition in the recapitulation altered to modulate to a different STA? What is the key of the ST when it is first restated in the recapitulation? How does the move from the tonic to this new key in the recapitulation mirror the relation of tonal areas in the exposition?

6. ***Beethoven, String Quartet Op. 59, No. 2, I.** This quartet contains an excellent example of the fusion of PT and transition in a recapitulation. Analyze the phrase structure of measures 1–38. Compare this passage with the recapitulation of this material.

Coda

In a sonata form a coda is a section that *follows* the restatement of the closing section of the recapitulation. The formal functions of a coda may include a) a reinforcement of closure through a series of cadential phrases that give a more dramatic ending to a movement; b) further development of ideas, particularly those that may have been harmonically unresolved or incomplete in earlier presentations; c) a recall of themes that had been omitted in the recapitulation; and d) a recall of themes one final time in the context of more marked closure. Of these interrelated functions, the recall of developmental passages and of themes not previously resolved to closure in the tonic key are prevalent in lengthy codas. Beethoven's Symphony No. 3 provides a famous example of a lengthy coda that returns to the principal theme for further development and final resolution. The principal theme and its various statements at prominent formal junctures are shown in Example 8.16. The theme contains harmonic digression in earlier statements, avoiding a strong sense of closure and tonal stability. This stability is reserved for the end of the coda, which emphasizes tonic and dominant harmonies using the principal theme. The result is a dramatic and heroic sense of resolution and closure.

Analytic Note: The terms *coda* and *codetta* are used and distinguished in different ways. As discussed in Chapter 5, they may be distinguished on the basis of relative proportions. As used here in reference to sonata form, they refer to different parts of the form. A codetta in a sonata form is an internal part of the exposition and thus is restated in the recapitulation.

Example 8.16 Beethoven, Symphony No. 3, I, principal themes.

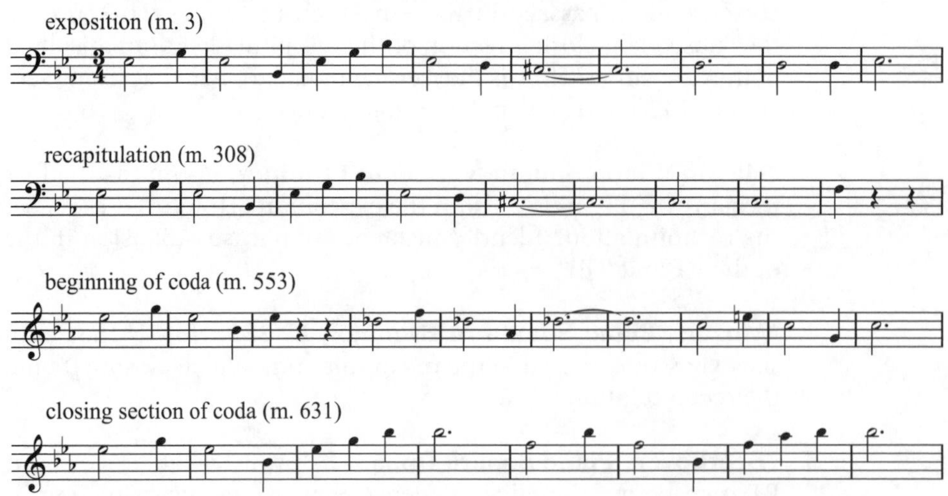

(See for example, Mozart, Symphony No. 40, IV, last 8 measures.) A coda may follow the strong cadence that closes the recapitulation, or it may emerge from an extension to the codetta of the exposition. In either case it is heard as a new section that follows the recapitulation and thus occurs at the end of a movement.[21]

Exercises: Codas

1. ***Beethoven, Sonata Op. 53, I.** This movement raised the technical demands on the pianist to new levels, which is nowhere more evident than in the coda to this movement. To what key does the coda initially turn as it restates the PT? How does the recapitulation of the PT foreshadow this key? What function or character, associated with the soloist in a concerto, does this coda take on as it progresses? The ST makes a final appearance in measures 284–292. Compare the first three measures of this restatement with measures 196–199 of the recapitulation. Why do you think Beethoven made this final presentation of the ST? What musical or expressive intent does it convey?

2. **Listening. Mozart, Symphony No. 41, IV, and Beethoven, Symphony No. 3, I.** Both movements contain celebrated codas that function as secondary development sections and brilliant conclusions to these great movements. Listen to Tchaikovsky, Symphony No. 4, I for an example of a coda that incorporates progressive changes in tempo toward forceful final closure. The coda in Brahms Symphony No. 3, I, incorporates gripping, contrapuntal textures and cross rhythms that lead to a tranquil close.

[21] See Caplin, 179.

Nineteenth-Century Sonata Form

INTRODUCTION

The nineteenth-century composers of the Romantic period continued to write sonata form movements, though the handling of formal design evolved to reflect stylistic tendencies of that era. As in the Classical period, any nineteenth-century sonata form has unique formal attributes. The following discussion introduces certain basic tendencies that are found in many nineteenth-century sonata form movements and presents some salient features of a few exemplary works.

EXPANDED TONAL RELATIONS

The nineteenth-century tendency to modulate to keys a third away and the use of modal mixture are frequently evident in sonata form movements. Such tonal motions are not new to this period—the Beethoven Piano Sonata Op. 53 is one well-known example of a Classical work that utilized this strategy. In the works of Schubert and later composers, this practice became more common. Schubert's Symphony No. 8, the "Unfinished Symphony," for example, begins in B minor and modulates to G major for its STA, creating a large i-VI tonal motion in the exposition. The recapitulation presents the ST initially in the key of D major (III), a mirror of the tonal move from the exposition. That is, the exposition modulates to a third below the tonic key, while the recapitulation modulates to a third above the tonic key.[22] The subsequent closing section moves to B major (I) and then to B minor for the coda. These tonal relations are outlined in Figure 8.4.

Figure 8.4 Schubert, Symphony No. 8, I, sketch of tonal design.

Exposition		Development		Recapitulation			Coda
Bm----------	G----------	Em----------	(D)----	Bm----------	D----------	B----------	Bm
i	**VI**	**iv**		**i**	**III**	**I**	**i**

The move to keys a third away is often colored by a change of mode in the new key. The resulting *chromatic third relations*, discussed in Chapter 2, are encountered frequently in nineteenth-century sonatas. Brahms' Symphony No. 3 in F major, I, for example, modulates to A major (III) for the STA. An expected complementary move to D major (VI) is made in the recapitulation of this movement, followed by a closing section in the tonic, F major.

THREE-KEY EXPOSITIONS

While the Classical sonata form contrasts two different keys in an exposition, some expositions in the Romantic period have three distinct tonal areas with corresponding themes. The term *three-key exposition* is used to refer to such expositions, which are encountered in works by Romantic composers, notably Schubert and Brahms. Precedents for this expansion of keys and themes can be found in some Classical works.[23] The idea of an intermediary

---

[22] Such tonal relations are sometimes referred to as *axial* relations since the tonic key acts as an axis from which the two secondary keys are equidistant.

[23] For example, see Beethoven, Piano Sonata Op. 10, No. 3, I, Beethoven, Symphony No. 8, I, and Beethoven Piano Concerto No. 5, I.

key within a transition is discussed in the Analytic Note below. In a three-key exposition, the second key is clearly established by presentation of a new theme and often by a conclusive cadence. A subsequent transition to the third key and another new theme will follow the second key. Schubert's *Quartetsatz* in C minor is an excellent example of this approach. A decisive modulation is made from C minor to A♭ major, which is confirmed by an expansive period of 34 measures. Another transition follows, leading to a third key in G major, rather than the more predictable G minor. Generally three-key expositions have the following design:

- The second key corresponds to the ST and is in a third relation with tonic.
- The third key corresponds to the CT and is the expected dominant of the principal key.
- There are very brief or no transitions between S and C keys, contributing to a sectional rather than continuous motion.

An additional example of a three-key exposition by Brahms is given in Exercise 3 at the end of this chapter.

Later nineteenth-century composers expanded tonal areas even further, particularly in large-scale symphonic works. The symphonies of Bruckner and Mahler, for example, contain multiple tonal areas in their expositions.

Analytic Note: The notion of a three-key exposition raises questions about the formal functions of the various key areas. In some instance, such as the Brahms Symphony No. 3 in F, I, a second key—D♭ major—is established but seems to be part of a larger transitional passage on the way to the STA of A major. This second key makes use of PT motives and a transitional motive first presented in tonic. It may be reasonable to speak of an *intermediary key* in such cases, with the third key serving as the real STA. Conversely, in movements such as the Schubert *Quartetsatz*, one may identify principal, secondary, and closing tonal areas, since each of the keys is strongly established and a new theme is presented in each key. The labeling suggested here reflects the possible formal functions of the various keys, which must be carefully considered in any sonata form.

EXPANSION AND COMPRESSION OF FORMS

The noted musicologist Friedrich Blume observes that "two points may strike us in Romantic music: on the one hand, a preference for arching melodic lines that begin hesitantly, unfolding slowly, over and over . . . and, on the other, the markedly songlike character of these melodies."[24] This Romantic interest in lyric melodies led, in sonata form movements, to broader and more expansive themes, with greater degrees of contrast among themes and keys. The idea of a three-key exposition, with a distinct closing tonal area and themes, complements this tendency. The contrasts among themes and keys may be emphasized further by the absence of integrated transitions, which are sometimes brief, abrupt or nonexistent.

The Tchaikovsky Symphony No. 4, I, offers an excellent example of expansive, contrasting themes and a three-key exposition. The movement opens with a declamatory gesture by the brass that recurs at the beginning of the development, recapitulation, and coda. This theme thus serves as the "motto" for the movement, framing the large-scale design.[25] The restless PT in F minor is tonally active, modulating to A minor as it unfolds "over and over" before a return to F minor. Such tonal unrest is found in the openings of many Romantic works. This section ends with a forceful and reiterated plagal cadence followed

---

[24] Blume, *Classic and Romantic Music*, 142.

[25] This motto theme also recurs in the last movement, a cyclic recall of the theme that will be discussed in the next chapter.

by an abrupt change in texture, key, and thematic material that begins a transition to an STA. The remainder of the exposition moves from A♭ minor to B major, each key introducing a new theme. (It should be noted that the transition to B major is less abrupt, with the ST moving to B major before a CT in that key is introduced.) Each of these tonal/thematic areas has a different tempo and different character with transitions in tempo articulating the new themes.[26]

Figure 8.5 outlines the tonal design of the movement to show the pattern of keys. The series of chromatic third relations in the exposition continues through the whole movement. The development goes through a wide range of keys in broad sequential motions until arriving at the motto theme in D minor. This leads to a brief recapitulation of the PT and a full recapitulation of the ST, both in the "wrong key" of D minor. The recapitulation eventually returns to F major and then F minor, completing the large-scale ascending tonal motion of the exposition. This movement shows how far removed later nineteenth-century works became from the Classical sense of sonata form. In fact, one might assert that no real recapitulation occurs since the PT and ST are not restated in the tonic key.

Figure 8.5 Tchaikovsky, Symphony No. 4, I, tonal design.

Exposition				**Development**	**Recapitulation**		**Coda**	
27	**104**	**116**	**134**		**282**	**295**	**313**	**355**
PT	**tr.**	**ST**	**CT**		**PT**	**ST**	**CT**	
Fm---(Am)---Fm	**---A♭**	**A♭m---**	**B**	**-----------------------**	**Dm------**	**Dm------**	**F----**	**Fm**
I	**III**	**iii**	**♯IV**		**vi**		**I**	**i**

A contrasting tendency that may be found in some nineteenth-century sonata forms is the compression and overlapping of formal units, producing a greater sense of tonal fluctuation and instability throughout a movement. The opening movement of Franck's Violin Sonata in A major offers an excellent illustration of this formal strategy (Example 8.17). This movement begins with a quiet introduction using a prolonged V9 chord. As the PT progresses it soon cadences in the principal key of A major (measure 8), followed by a continuation that modulates immediately to C♯ major (♯III). The continuation of the PT thus functions as part of the transition. The close of the transition (mm. 28–30), which elides into the ST, is a dominant preparation for the secondary key of E major (V).[27] Similarly, the secondary theme, which begins at a climactic moment, is only briefly elaborated before leading to the development. The formal boundaries of the design here are blurred by the absence of any prolonged tonal stability or closure. The continual unfolding of the lyrical principal theme through motivic repetitions and elaborations also gives a Romantic breadth of line to the music.

These examples by Tchaikovsky and Franck are indicative of the importance of *contrast* to nineteenth-century composers. Edward Cone's remarks on this tendency are worth noting:

---

[26] These tempo and character contrasts are designated in the score as follows: Motto Theme, *Andante Sostenuto*; Principal Theme: *Moderato con anima (In movemento di Valse)*; Secondary Theme: *Moderato assai, quasi Andante*; Closing Themes: *Ben sostenuto il tempo precedente . . . stringendo . . . Moderato con Anima (Tempo del comincio)*.

[27] An earlier example of this strategy may be found in Beethoven's Piano Sonata in A major, Op. 101, I. As Tovey notes in his *Companion to Beethoven's Pianoforte Sonatas*, "there is no point in arguing where the PT ends and the transition begins," which are clearly brought together in a continuous passage.

> **The tendency of the nineteenth century is increasingly to emphasize the forces of contrast over those of unification; and this applies not only to tempo but to thematic material, harmonic progression, rhythm, and mood. . . . The principle of contrast obtains, too, not only within individual works, but also among the works of one composer, and above all among composers.[28]**

Example 8.17 Franck, Violin Sonata in A major, I, exposition and beginning of development.

[28] Cone, *Musical Form and Musical Performance*, 82.

Another important principle of form in the nineteenth-century noted by Cone is the unwillingness to restate a theme in a new key without some important alteration in texture, tempo, rhythm, or harmonic progression.[29] Liszt, as he points out, is perhaps the most notable composer in this regard. Liszt's Piano Sonata in B minor is a large, single–movement work with contrasting sections in different tempos. He employs recurring themes in the contrasting large sections but they are transformed by notable alterations. The thematic transformation creates an underlying sense of thematic unity that counters the marked contrasts of the work.

---

[29] Ibid, 84.

Exercises: Each of the Examples Cited Below Offer Examples of Characteristic Nineteenth-Century Themes from Sonata Form Movements

1. **Schubert, Symphony No. 8, I, mm. 13–38.** The principal theme is a good example of the Romantic interest in lyrical melodies. The theme is a large period, with the consequent phrase containing several internal expansions. The antecedent phrase contains an extension (measures 20–21). What is the harmonic function of this extension? How is the consequent phrase expanded? What is unusual about the proportions and phrase structure of the transition compared to the Classical models discussed?
2. **Schubert, Piano Sonata in B♭, D. 960, I.** The principal theme is periodic. What kind of period does this theme comprise? How is the phrase rhythm and expressive tone of the antecedent phrase disrupted? To what key does the music modulate at the end of this first period? Where does the PT return in the tonic key? This PTA may be understood as an A B A section followed by two additional keys and themes, beginning in measures 48 and 80 respectively, which complete a three-key exposition. Determine the keys and their relation to tonic. Identify how the various modulations take place and where additional tonal "wanderings" take place within the second and third tonal areas.
3. **Dvorak, Symphony No. 8, I.** The exposition of this movement offers a good example of an introductory section in the principal tempo of the movement, which anticipates and gradually leads to the principal tonal area and themes of the movement. Are these formal boundaries clearly articulated, or is fusion and overlap of sections evident? Explain your answers. To what key does the exposition modulate? What is the relation of the second key to the principal key?
4. **Borodin, String Quartet No. 2 in D major.** Analyze the phrase structure of the principal theme, measures 1–36. Are four-measure phrases used throughout? How is this melody expanded upon its repetition?

Sonata Form in the Twentieth Century

While composers explored new harmonic languages in the twentieth century, they continued to draw on the principles of contrast and development of ideas found in sonata form. In the absence of clearly defined tonalities, contrasts in thematic areas, texture, and rhythm took on greater importance in shaping the form. Some composers expanded traditional harmonic language through the use of modality and extended harmonies, but retained tonal designs related to sonata form. An example of this approach is found in the first movement of the Sonatine for Piano (1905) by Ravel. This movement is in F♯ minor and has a distinct close in A major at the end of the exposition. Ravel's use of modal and parallel harmonies mask these keys and creates tonal ambiguity at times, as in the beginning of the secondary theme (see Example 8.18). Additional aspects of this harmonic approach are addressed in exercises A and B.

Other twentieth-century works incorporate tonal and chromatic writing that conveys a sense of pitch centers in various sections without a clear sense of tonality. One well known work, the Piano Sonata by Barber (1949) is noteworthy for its use of tonal and atonal elements. The music is generally dissonant and chromatic with a blend of dramatic and lyric elements. The first movement begins with a key signature of E♭ minor that is abandoned when a secondary theme is introduced with twelve-tone rows as accompaniment. Serial composers, including Schoenberg, Berg, and Webern also wrote works and movements that drew on elements of sonata form design. The diversity of styles in these various works is indicative of the flexibility of sonata form principles and the continued evolution of the form in post-tonal music.

Exercises

Works by twentieth-century composers that incorporate sonata form are given below, with some study guidelines included for select works. As with any work, it is important to listen closely and consider how various aspects of the music delineate the form.

A. **Ravel, Sonatine for Piano.** Study Guidelines. The exposition of this work is shown in Example 8.18. Consider the phrase structure of the exposition. What kinds of cadences are evident? In what way do the phrases differ from traditional themes and what processes are used to generate themes? Where does the transition of the exposition begin? What is the function of measures 24–28? What aspects of the performance are important in conveying the form of the movement?

Example 8.18 Ravel, Sonatine for Piano, exposition.

(This excerpt continues on p. 190.)

(Example 8.18, continued.)

B. Barber, Sonata for Piano, Op. 26, I. Study Guidelines. After careful listening and with the aid of a score, consider how the various sections are delineated. In the absence of traditional cadences, how is closure created at various points? How are the various formal functions conveyed? How is material in the recapitulation reinterpreted or varied? Identify the beginning of the coda and determine what processes shape the coda. An outline of the form follows.

Figure 8.6 Barber, Sonata for Piano, Op. 26, I, form outline.

Exposition: PT mm. 1–8, Tr. 9–22, ST 23–35, CT 35–42–50

Development: 51–74, 75–109

Recapitulation/Coda: 148–167

C. Additional Twentieth-century works for study.

Stravinsky, Octet for Winds, I
Bartók, Music for Strings, Percussion and Celeste, II
*Schoenberg, Klavierstücke, Op. 33a
+Shostakovich, String Quartet No. 3
Hindemith, Piano Sonata No. 2

Conclusion

The foregoing discussion of sonata form is intended to present some analytic concepts that can be applied to any movement one may choose to study. The discussion, though at times detailed, is not intended to be comprehensive. As we have noted, gifted composers invent new strategies, expressions and musical structures each time they write a composition, and this is nowhere more true than in a form as potentially rich and complex as a sonata form.

As the examples discussed here suggest, any well-conceived sonata form will have unique formal and expressive qualities. When analyzing a sonata form, as in all analysis, one should be concerned with discovering these unique aspects of the work, not merely how it adheres to some conventional design. Though the large-scale design is often readily apparent, the study of detail and its connections or relations to the large-scale design must be carefully considered to find the unique aspects. Further, we should not be interested in simply tabulating formal segmentation and functions. Rather, having determined how the movement is organized, we should ultimately focus on how compositional choices evident at a given point reflect a particular expressive or musical intent. We might ask, for example, why a sudden, tonal digression takes place, or why a theme is expanded, abbreviated, or omitted, and consider the expressive effect or intent. Though admittedly subjective, carefully considered interpretation of the composer's intentions and the expressive effect of the music will extend one's understanding of a work in the most meaningful way.

Summary

Sonata form is a flexible, dramatic form that emerged in the Classical period. The form is an outgrowth of rounded binary form, in which a first part modulates to a new key followed by a second part that modulates back to the tonic key and subsequently restates material from the first part. In sonata form, this two-part tonal structure is expanded into three distinct sections: *exposition, development*, and *recapitulation*. Part one, the exposition, modulates to dominant or relative major keys in the Classical period; modulations to other keys are found in later sonata forms. The development elaborates thematic material through one or more keys and eventually modulates back to tonic. The recapitulation is marked by the return to the tonic key and restatements of the material of the exposition.

The exposition of a sonata form is comprised of:

- a *principal tonal area* (PTA) that presents one or more principal themes (PT) in the tonic key.
- a *transition* that contains a modulation to a new tonal area, or that reaches a HC in the principal key followed by a direct modulation to a secondary key.
- a *secondary tonal area* (STA) that presents one or more secondary themes (ST). A strong authentic cadence in the new key will usually close the ST. This cadence, usually the first PAC in the new key, is referred to as the *essential exposition close* (EEC).
- An EEC normally marks the beginning of the closing section. One or more *closing themes* (CT) will be presented to close the exposition.

Each of these formal units within the exposition normally concludes with a decisive cadence, which may be separated or elided with the next section. The principal tonal area and transition often are grouped together with a marked HC at the end of the transition preceding the STA. This strategy creates a two-part division of the exposition. Continuous expositions that lack a clear dividing point are also to be found. *Three-key expositions*, in which a third tonal area and a new theme are presented, are often found in nineteenth-century sonata forms, notably by composers such as Schubert, Brahms, and Tchaikovsky.

The number, length, and character of principal, transitional, secondary, and closing themes in the exposition is highly variable. The transition may introduce new material or may begin with a *counterstatement* based on the principal theme. It normally begins in tonic, though a modulation to an intermediary key at or shortly after the beginning of the transition is not uncommon. Neutral material such as scales and arpeggios are typical of many transitions, emphasizing the harmonic and rhythmic motion of the music rather than new thematic elements. Transitions frequently close with *dominant preparation* (an expanded dominant) to reinforce the modulation.

The STA may have one or more secondary themes and one or more closing themes. Passing modulations to other keys may also be found in the STA before the close in the secondary key. The secondary theme that initiates the STA is normally a new, contrasting idea that initially may serve as a point of repose and stability following the tension of the transition. Symmetrical periods or sentence structures may reinforce this stability. Some sonata forms make use of the principal theme or motives for the first secondary theme in the STA. Such forms are referred to as *monothematic forms*. The first authentic cadence in the STA normally marks the beginning of the closing section. Accelerated rhythmic motion, short repeated phrase segments, and cadential harmonic progressions characterize closing themes. They often employ deceptive or evaded cadences to delay and thus reinforce the eventual close of the exposition. The closing section of an exposition may recall themes or motives from the PTA as well. A *codetta* may present the final, cadential phrase or phrases of the exposition.

The *development* section of a sonata form is subject to a wide range of designs. Its main function is to increase the tension of the music and lead to a return to the tonic key of the movement. Frequent modulations, chromatic harmonies, fragmentation and sequence of thematic ideas, new textures, and reordering of thematic ideas characterize a development. Imitative textures are likely to be used in development sections, often with a fugal section—a *fugato*—serving to develop ideas. Phrase elisions and irregular phrase rhythms also characterize development sections.

The *recapitulation* is marked by a return to the tonic key and the varied restatement of the sequence of musical ideas of the exposition. Themes may be expanded, shortened, omitted, fused, or on occasion reordered. The principal theme typically begins the recapitulation. It is often abbreviated and may be fused with the transition. In the recapitulation the transition may contain a modulation, often to the subdominant key, but closes in the tonic key. The STA of the recapitulation is in the tonic key, and is often subject to only minor changes in phrase structure.

A *coda*, comprised of one or more phrases, may follow the recapitulation. It may restate themes, especially those omitted in the recapitulation, and reinforce final closure. Lengthy codas may serve as a second development section that leads to the final closure of the movement.

SUGGESTED READINGS

An excellent study on the origins and evolution of Classical sonata forms is Charles Rosen's *Sonata Forms*. William Caplin's *Classical Form* offers an exhaustive discussion and detailed classification of thematic types, formal functions and strategies in the Classical instrumental repertoire of Haydn, Mozart, and Beethoven. James Webster's *Haydn and the Farewell Symphony* offers insight into Haydn's compositional techniques and his approaches to sonata form as a through-composed form. Leonard Ratner's *Classic Form and Style* offers an invaluable discussion of expressive topics and ideas in Classical style music. His ideas contain useful tools for identifying the style and expressive content of sonata forms. See also Robert Hatten, *Musical Meaning in Beethoven,* Chapter III. For a thorough reconsideration of the sonata principle cited above, see Hepokoski, "Beyond the Sonata Principle" and Hepokoski and Darcy, *Elements of Sonata Theory.*

For a discussion of the secondary theme as parenthetical insertion, see G. Cook Kimbell, "The Second Theme in Sonata Form as Insertion." For a study of the sources of the three-key exposition, see Rey M. Longyear and Kate R. Covington, "Sources of the Three-Key Exposition." For further discussion of the reverse recapitulation, see Timothy Jackson, "The Tragic Reversed Recapitulation in the German Classical Tradition."

Review Questions

1. Give the probable key for the secondary tonal area of the exposition of a sonata form for each of the following principal tonal areas (keys):
   a. E major: __________
   b. D minor: __________ or __________
   c. D♭ Major: __________
2. What harmonic device is characteristic of the retransition of a sonata form?
3. Briefly explain where a counterstatement most likely may be used in a sonata form exposition.
4. Describe three different characteristics of a development.
5. Describe two ways in which the form of a recapitulation will most likely differ from the exposition.
6. What is the location and function of a codetta in a sonata form?

Exercises: Analysis of Complete Movements

The previous exercises focused on passages or sections with specific formal functions to facilitate an understanding of various ways these functions may be realized. Any of the works addressed in the previous examples may be examined as complete movements. The following exercises, varied in approach, are intended to give consideration to complete movements. Focus questions are given to address one or more unique attributes of a given movement. A more detailed analysis of the formal structure of each movement is encouraged and will reward study.

1. ***Beethoven, Piano Sonata Op. 13 in C minor, "Pathetique," I.**
   a. The second theme (tonal area) begins in measure 51 in the key of __________. How is this different from the expected key?
   b. The exposition closes in the key of __________, though after the second theme begins there is a brief modulation to the key of __________.
   c. Identify, by measure number, the beginning of the closing section of the exposition. Briefly justify your answer.
   d. What thematic material is used to begin the development? What key is it in? What developmental technique is used in the ensuing phrase?
   e. In what measure does the retransition begin? What in the music signals this event?

f. The recapitulation surprisingly moves to the key of __________ to begin the second theme before moving to the expected tonic key.

g. What thematic material is interpolated between the end of the exposition and the beginning of the development and in what key is it? Where else does this material subsequently occur? Speculate on the expressive intent and effect of these events.

2. Schubert, Symphony No. 8, I.

a. This symphony is passionate, expressive and full of memorable melodies. Make a list of expressive terms to describe the emotional affects or states that may be perceived. Such interpretation is of course subjective, but nonetheless reveals salient features of the music. The point is to characterize the themes and textures as one way to interpret the dramatic musical story that unfolds. Connections between emotional descriptions and musical content are needed to make the interpretation persuasive. You may draw on the following list of expressive ideas:

mysterious, dark, tragic	peaceful, joyful
painful suffering, pathos	transcendent, triumphant
agitated, anxious	serene

b. The opening theme is an example of an introductory theme that becomes an integral part of the movement, unlike a slow introduction that is heard in many Classical symphonies. The quiet and mysterious opening, taking a cue from the opening of Beethoven's Symphony No. 9, is also a Romantic gesture: the inchoate opening. Find other occurrences of this theme in the movement and determine the following:

1. In what key is the theme?
2. Is its character retained or altered? If altered, how?
3. What is its formal function?
4. Is it fragmented or expanded?

c. The secondary theme starting in measure 44, one of the most famous melodies of Classical music, is also an asymmetrical period. Note the construction of the four-measure antecedent: one-measure statement/one-measure response/two-measure response continuation-cadence.

1. How is the parallel, consequent phrase expanded from a four-measure phrase to a six-measure phrase?
2. How is this phrase connected to the next phrase, a repetition of the period?
3. Why might the conclusion of this repeated period be characterized as an abandoned cadence?
4. How is this lyric, "serene" theme transformed in the closing section?

d. Determine the keys through which the development modulates. What key is emphasized before the final part of the retransition? What expressive character does this passage seem to convey?

e. Compare the recapitulation with the phrase structure of the exposition. Where are phrase structures altered? What theme is used to close the movement? How is it varied? Does the movement seem to end tragically or triumphantly? Explain how elements of the music convey your interpretation.

3. *Brahms, Sonata for Clarinet and Piano, Op. 120, No. 1 in F minor, I. This movement offers an example of a "three-key" exposition. The additional modulation, the great number of themes, the many contrasts in rhythmic textures, and the diverse interplay between the clarinet and piano makes this a very rich and complex movement. Begin by marking the following points of formal divisions in the exposition on the score:

- measure 25: beginning of transition
- measure 38: beginning of the intermediate tonal area
- measure 53: beginning of second tonal area and themes
- measure 77: beginning of closing section
- measure 90: beginning of development
- measure 138: beginning of recapitulation
- measures 206, 214: coda

NOTE: This is one interpretation of the formal functions of sections in the exposition; others are possible.

Read through the questions below and then listen to the movement at least twice, marking any further subdivisions that you may note. Keep in mind that the clarinet is tuned in B♭ so the notated pitch in the clarinet actually sounds a whole step lower. Then answer the following questions.

a. The first four measures present important thematic material but also serve as an introduction. What gives the passage an introductory quality? What chromatic scale degree is used to inflect the cadence at the end of this introductory theme?

b. Notate the clarinet part from measures 5–12 in *concert pitch.* The first note is the C above middle C. Try to sing the melody as you play it at the piano. What gives this principal theme an instrumental rather than vocal quality, that is, why is the melody hard to sing?

c. What is the key to which the music has modulated in measures 38? (Hint: analyze the harmony in measure 37—the B♭ in the melody is an appoggiatura). What is the relation of this key to tonic? What thematic material is being used in the left hand of the piano part?

d. What is the key of the second tonal area from measures 53 onward? (Hint: analyze the harmonies in measure 53 and measures 76–77 downbeat.) What is the relation of this key to tonic?

e. What rhythmic device is used in measures 75–76 and 79–80? (Hint: consider how the rhythmic/melodic patterns group together in terms of the number of beats per group.)

f. What thematic material begins and ends the development section (measures 90–135)? What is the harmonic function of the chord in measure 137? (Hint: what is the interval D♭-B?) What is unusual about the resolution of this chord?

g. At the point of recapitulation, what thematic material is being restated? Identify one way in which it is varied compared to its original presentation.

h. Brahms was fond of syncopation and displaced accents as a way of creating rhythmic tension. How are these techniques reflected in the notation of the clarinet part in measures 147–151?

i. In what measure does the intermediary tonal area section begin in the recapitulation? What is the key? Where does the secondary tonal area and secondary theme begin in the recapitulation? What is the key? (Hint: look for the return of the themes and tonal areas of the exposition outlined above.)

j. What thematic material closes the movement? What does the expressive marking *sotto voce* mean in the last ten measures of the movement? What type of cadence closes the movement?

k. Cadences. You may have noticed that the cadences in this work are at times very subdued and weak sounding. At some points Brahms seems to actually abandon the cadence. In other words, the cadential motion seems to stop before reaching its goal and there is no sense of resolution—a new section just begins. Can you identify two such weak or abandoned cadences in the exposition of this movement? Briefly explain your answers.

l. Identify and describe three different expressive topics in this movement, citing passages by measure number.

9 Modification of Sonata Form and Cyclic Forms

Introduction

The basic design of sonata form—exposition, development, and recapitulation—is subject to modifications. Most common is the addition of a coda, which, as discussed earlier, is initiated as an extension of the recapitulation and thus may be understood as a part of the sonata form proper. Other modifications result in significant additions or departures from the basic formal outline of a sonata form, which will be discussed here. These include the addition of a slow introduction, sonata form without development, and concerto sonata form. We will also discuss cyclic forms that extend the thematic elements of a sonata form movement to other movements, and the related concept of arch forms.

Slow Introduction

A slow introduction often precedes the exposition of a sonata form whether in an overture or a movement of a multi-movement work. Though the length of slow introductions may vary widely, they are normally perceived as separate sections that precede the actual beginning of the sonata form. Slow introductions may be found in solo sonatas and chamber music, but they are particularly characteristic of symphonic works. The inclusion of a slow introduction may be related to the opening slow section that was used in opera overtures of the eighteenth century. It served the practical function of a "noise killer" or "curtain raiser," alerting an audience that the work was beginning. As music for public concerts emerged in the Classical period, the slow introduction may have served a similar purpose. For this reason, a slow introduction is most likely to occur in the first movement.[1] From a purely aesthetic viewpoint, a slow introduction will provide a dramatic pronouncement and create anticipation as a listener awaits the faster tempo that will follow. The slow introduction may also anticipate motives of the sonata allegro, though this is not a requisite feature of the introduction.

As in a sonata form, the formal structure of slow introductions varies considerably. Douglass Green identifies four types of gestures that may be heard in a slow introduction: heraldic, melodic, motivic, and cadential.[2] All of these types of passages may not be present and they may be used in varied combinations.

The opening of Beethoven's Symphony No. 1 (Example 9.1) illustrates these introductory functions. The movement begins with a heraldic gesture characteristic of many symphonic openings: a tutti, chordal, texture. The use of a sustained dominant seventh chord, (C7=V7/IV) for the first entrance gives harmonic tension to this opening, and its resolution gives the surprising sense that a cadence begins the movement. Beethoven magnifies this

[1] It is worth noting that Haydn often used a slow introduction in part because his principal themes, though well suited to development, were not particularly effective in opening a movement.

[2] Green, *Form in Tonal Music,* 221–222. These gestures are not exclusively introductory in function, but are common in introduction to sonata forms. Heraldic gestures, in a musical context, give notice that a work is beginning through the use of tutti textures, *forte* dynamics, slow tempos, and sustained or repeated rhythmic figures.

surprise by the two repetitions of this gesture that lead to the THC in measure 4. The strong harmonic and linear direction of this powerful opening phrase leads convincingly to a lyric, melodic passage in measures 5–7 generated by motivic repetitions. The two gestures alternate in measures 8–9 leading to a DC and an expansive cadential progression that elides with the opening of the *Allegro con brio*. The asymmetrical, short phrase structures and themes, marked contrasts in textures and dynamics, and harmonic instability of this example characterize slow introductions.

Example 9.1 Beethoven, Symphony No. 1, I, mm. 1–17, introduction.

(This excerpt continues on p. 198.)

(Example 9.1, continued.)

An introduction closes most often with arrival on a cadential dominant harmony that resolves as the *allegro* begins. Sometimes, however, the close of a slow introduction will delay the resolution to the tonic harmony until after the *allegro* has begun. This may be the case if the principal theme begins on a non-tonic chord, or if the principal theme is delayed. Beethoven's Symphony No. 4, after an elongated dominant chord in the last three measures of the slow introduction, changes to an *Allegro vivace* that continues the dominant harmony and the previous motives at a quick tempo. The dominant resolves to tonic four measures later when the principal theme begins. Another interesting example that overlaps the slow introduction with the subsequent introduction is the Berlioz *Symphony Fantastique*. The introduction, like the entire work, is novel and fascinating. It begins very quietly with solo winds and sparse textures (see Example 9.2). The lengthy introduction progresses through many climactic moments in several contrasting sections before a PAC marks the beginning of the *allegro*. This fast section begins not with the principal theme but hammered chords that reiterate the cadential progression and serve as an introductory phrase to the famous principal theme, the *idée fixe* of the symphony.[3]

INTRODUCTORY PHRASES

Slow introductions are heard as separate sections that precede the sonata allegro form that follows. A different type of introduction is that of a brief heraldic gesture, motivic anticipation, or theme that opens a sonata movement in the principal tempo. These types of introductions, unlike slow introductions, often introduce motives or ideas that will be incorporated in the movement. The opening of the Beethoven Symphony No. 5, mentioned in the discussion of phrase introductions (Chapter 4, Example 4.5a), is one

[3] The recurring idea or principal theme is referred to as the *idée fixe* (fixed idea) by Berlioz, which reflects the programmatic notion of a young artist's fixation on his beloved.

Example 9.2 Berlioz, *Symphony Fantastique,* mm. 59–69.

example.[4] This type of gesture serves as a phrase introduction. By contrast, the opening of Schubert's Symphony No. 8 begins with a complete introductory phrase that presents a theme that will be used as one of the principal themes of the movement. (See the discussion of this theme in Chapter 5.) Many works like the Schubert use an introductory theme at major formal junctures, incorporating the theme in the various sections of the work, as noted in the exercises.

[4] Beethoven's Symphony No. 3 offers a similar brief introduction: two short, forceful tonic triads are heard before the principal theme begins.

Exercises

In addition to the works listed below, Haydn's Symphony No. 100+, Mozart's Symphonies Nos. 38 and 39, and Beethoven's Symphonies Nos. 2, 4, 7, and 9 contain interesting, diverse examples of slow introductions. Berlioz' *Symphony Fantastique* offers an example of an extended, fantasy-like introduction.

1. **Haydn, Symphony No. 104.** This symphony begins with a slow introduction that contains characteristic gestures as discussed. Identify the types of gestures, the number of phrases and the tonal motions of the introduction. What do you notice about the voicing of the very first harmony? How does modal mixture play a part in this introduction? How does the material of the first two measures function to articulate the form of this introduction?

2. ***Beethoven, Piano Sonata Op. 13, I.** The slow introduction to this movement is particularly noteworthy for its chromatic harmonies and bold modulations. Analyze the harmonies and modulations of this introduction. Where else in the movement does this introductory material recur? How is it varied?

3. **Dvorak, Symphony No. 8, I.** Although this movement begins in the principal tempo of the movement, *Allegro con brio*, the opening section functions as an introduction. What elements of the music convey the introductory function? Where exactly does the introduction end and the exposition begin? Explain your answer.

Sonata Form Without Development

Some movements are constructed in the manner of a sonata form but with only a short link or brief retransition between the exposition and the recapitulation. There is no unequivocal, concise term for this type of form. It is sometimes referred to as *sonatina form.* This term, however, more accurately refers to sonata forms of modest proportions that are also lighter in expressive character and that may have brief development sections. The *sonatina form* is consequently different from many sonata forms with no development. The latter form is so often found in slow movements of Classical works that Rosen refers to it as slow movement form.[5] As he observes, however, the form is also common in opera overtures, such as Mozart's *Marriage of Figaro* and many Rossini overtures.[6] In the absence of any generally accepted term, "sonata form without development" is the most accurate description.

Sonata form without development normally has an exposition of contrasting keys, themes, and textures, as expected. The recapitulation, which may at first sound like a repeat of the exposition, also displays the characteristic alterations and presentation of secondary and closing themes in the tonic key.[7] The form in fact does occur most often in

[5] Rosen, *Sonata Forms*, 120–21.

[6] While sonata form provides flexible principles for presenting contrasting themes, keys, and textures appropriate to an opera overture, the absence of a development avoids a full-scale dramatic form that may impinge on the forthcoming opera.

[7] A few instances of abbreviated recapitulations are found in sonata forms without development. See for example Haydn's String Quartets, Op. 33, No. 5–6, II, and Mozart's Clarinet Quintet in A, K. 581, II.

slow movements in which lyric expression is given dramatic form. One characteristic of this slow movement form is the omission of repeats of each part. This omission, apart from avoiding movements of excessive length and duration, avoids excessive repetition of themes that would be conspicuous in a form with no development. Another feature of certain slow movement sonata forms with no development is an abbreviated recapitulation. It is of interest that the majority of slow movements in sonata form without development occur in solo sonatas and chamber works. Symphonies with slow movement sonata forms normally contain development sections.[8]

ANALYTIC EXERCISES

Listen to and study the slow movement of the Beethoven* Piano Sonata Op. 10, No. 1. Where and how does Beethoven return to the tonic key and PT after the STA? What material is recalled in the coda? How is it reinterpreted? See also Haydn's String Quartet, Op. 76, No. 4, II, and Mozart's Symphony No. 39, in E♭, K. 543, II.

Sonata Form in Concerto Movements

INTRODUCTION

In earlier chapters we have noted that second and third movements of concertos may use binary, ternary, rondo, or variation forms, or, in Baroque concerti grossi, fugal forms. The opening movements of concertos, however, contain a specific formal model related to the interaction or opposition of soloist and orchestra. The Baroque concerto used a form based on alternation between ritornello material played by the full ensemble and solo sections in which the orchestra accompanied. Beginning in the Classical period, the first movements of concertos used elements of the Baroque concerto, in conjunction with the emerging sonata form of the Classical style. In order to understand this integration of formal styles, a brief review of the ritornello forms used in the Baroque concerto will be useful.

RITORNELLO FORMS

The word "concerto" originates from one word with two different meanings: the word "concertare" in Italian means "to come together or arrange," whereas in Latin it means "to fight or contend." The former usage was applicable to concertos of the early and middle seventeenth century, in which vocal soloists and an orchestra were brought together in a work. The latter meaning is more applicable to the concertos of the late seventeenth and early eighteenth century in which the soloist would "contend" with the orchestra for prominence. Whether a vocal work, a *concerto grosso* (a concerto with a concertino of soloists) or a solo concerto, *the contrast between solo and tutti textures was a basic element of the form.* The extent to which such works embody one or both meanings of the term is subject to interpretation and will vary, a point to which we will return.

The concerti grossi of Corelli, and later Handel, usually in four or more movements, showed no set approach to the number of tutti and solo sections, and the sectional forms of the movements varied widely. Conversely, Vivaldi, in his solo concertos, established a three movement format, with the first movement based on an alternation of solo sections with four to five tutti sections. It was this form that influenced Bach and later composers in the

[8] Beethoven, Symphony No. 8, II is a sonata form without development. See also Schubert, Symphony No. 8, II. Mozart, Symphony No. 41, II is a good example of a full-scale sonata form in a slow movement. For a list of Classical movements in sonata form without development see Caplin, 217.

composition of concertos. The designation "tutti" (Italian for "all") referred to passages played by the entire ensemble. These passages also presented recurring thematic material referred to as the *ritornello*.[9] The form based on the alternation between solo and ritornello (tutti) sections is designated *ritornello form.*

THE BAROQUE SOLO CONCERTO

A common outline of the ritornello form that emerged in the early and mid-eighteenth century is shown in Figure 9.1. The opening ritornello, which established the key and thematic material of the movement, recurs in abbreviated form and alternates with modulatory solo sections. The ritornello sections normally serve to confirm keys to which the soloist has modulated. Solo sections may be virtuosic figurations or material derived from the opening ritornello. After a modulation to dominant (V) or relative major (III), the subsequent sections would modulate to other closely related keys (CRK). The final ritornello was usually the most extensive restatement, bringing the movement to a close by reaffirming the tonic key.

Figure 9.1 *Ritornello Form of the Baroque solo concerto.*

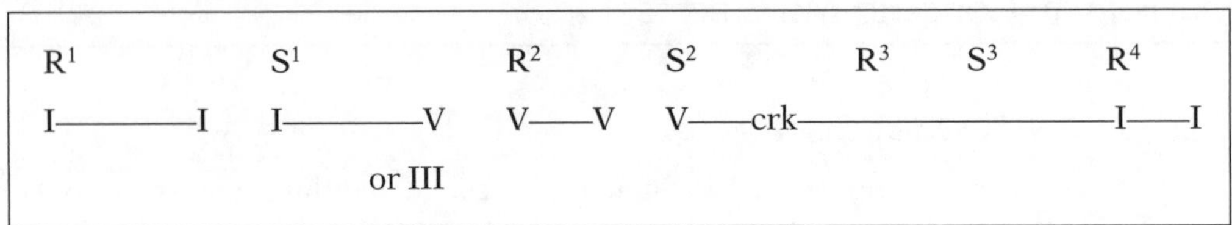

This form is flexible, particularly with regard to the entrance of ritornello material. The ritornello sections specified in Figure 9.1 refer to those marked by cadential closure that confirms a previous modulation. Within solo sections there may be *interjections* of the ritornello in tutti textures. Furthermore, it must be understood that the orchestra is playing during solo sections. While the orchestra may be relegated to simple accompaniment, it may also provide counterpoint with the soloists. In solo concertos, the distinction between solo and ritornello sections is usually quite clear. In concerti grossi, the varied interaction of soloist and orchestra was often more elaborate. This is particularly true in Bach's Brandenburg Concertos, a set of six concerti grossi, each scored for a different ensemble.[10] The interaction of solo and orchestra in diverse contrapuntal textures reaches a new level of sophistication in these justly famous works.

CONCERTO SONATA FORM

The ritornello model of alternation is also used in the Classical period concertos, but elements of sonata form are infused in the form.[11] The resulting *concerto sonata form* is not a fusion of the two forms; rather it draws elements from each to create a distinct form. The concerto sonata form incorporates the dramatic contrasts and opposition of keys and themes found in sonata forms along with the basic contrast between soloists and orchestra. It is used in the opening movements of concertos and sometimes in slow movements. The formal design is best understood as a sonata form with orchestral ritornello used to

[9] Review the concept of ritornello in Chapter 3. One will encounter diagrams that use Tutti-Solo or Ritornello-Solo to outline concerto forms. While 'tutti' is a textural designation and 'ritornello' a thematic one, the terms usually refer to the same passages in a work, i.e. tutti sections function as ritornellos.

[10] Numbers 1, 3, and 6 of the Brandenburg concertos are *ripieno concertos* in which there are no designated soloists but contrasts between tutti and solo textures are explored. Numbers 4 and 5 give prominence to the solo violin and solo harpsichord, respectively, combining characteristics of solo and concerto grosso.

[11] Ritornello forms were also used in the Baroque da capo aria, discussed in Chapter 13. As Rosen has observed, the aria was an important influence on the concerto as well. See Rosen, *Sonata Forms*, 84–85.

Figure 9.2 *Concerto Sonata Form.*

R^1 Orchestral Exposition S^1 Solo Exposition $\leftarrow$ R^2 $\rightarrow$ S^2 Development (retrans)

I I I I V V modulatory I

PTA PTA STA

PT Tr. ST CT ‖ PT Tr. ST CT

$\leftarrow$ (R^3) $\rightarrow$ S^3 Recapitulation R^4 (solo cadenza) R$^{4 \text{ or } 5}$

combined cad. 6/4 ----------------- V-I

articulate large-scale form. A diagram of the form, which was fully developed by Mozart in his piano concertos of the 1780s is given in Figure 9.2. A brief description of each section and its formal functions will explain the elements of the combined forms.

Ritornello^1—Orchestral Exposition. The first ritornello[12] is also an orchestral exposition but it does not modulate. The secondary theme occasionally moves briefly into a new key (for example, Mozart, Piano Concerto No. 20, in D minor, K. 466) or begins with a non-tonic harmony but then cadences in the tonic key. The modulation, a dramatic event in a sonata form, is reserved for the soloist. Although the orchestral exposition lacks this key ingredient of a sonata form, it will contain distinct contrast in themes, textures and rhythmic motion characteristic of a sonata exposition. New themes are presented for each section, including the transition, which in concertos always presents a new idea rather than a counterstatement.[13] In the Classical concerto, unlike most Baroque concertos, the soloist is silent, making the first solo entrance all the more dramatic.

Solo^1—Solo Exposition. The solo exposition will almost always present new thematic material as well as use themes from the opening ritornello.[14] Though a variety of thematic plans may be found, a few common tendencies can be cited. The principal theme of the solo exposition is often the same as the orchestra with a *new* transitional theme then introduced. If a *new* principal theme is introduced the transitional theme from the orchestral exposition is often used. The secondary tonal area will generally introduce a new theme and, after another transitional passage, restate the orchestra's secondary theme. The closing section will normally include brilliant, virtuosic passage work for the soloist with expanded and evaded cadential activity a hallmark of the classical concerto. The close of the solo section is normally highlighted by an expanded cadential trill leading to R^2.

An example of a thematic design for two expositions is given in Figure 9.3 based on Mozart's Piano Concerto No. 17, in G, K. 453. Here the soloist uses the principal themes (PT^1 PT^2) of R^1 and introduces a new transitional passage (Tr^2). The soloist then introduces a new

---

[12] The term *ritornello*, though originally associated with Baroque music, is used to designate tutti statements by the orchestra in post-Baroque concertos. The differences between the two types of ritornello are significant, though both types serve to delineate form and recall thematic material.

[13] Some writers downplay the idea of two expositions in a classical concerto, preferring to call the first orchestral section simply a ritornello or an introduction. This viewpoint understates the contrasts in length between a concerto exposition and most Baroque ritornelli as well as the important differences in style and formal design. In the mature concertos of Mozart and the concertos of Beethoven the opening orchestral material is clearly shaped in the manner of a sonata exposition. The notion of a double exposition is viable in such works as long as the differences between the two expositions are acknowledged. See Rosen, *Classical Style*, 197–98 for elaboration of this point.

[14] Mozart, Piano Concerto No. 23, in A major, K. 488, in which the solo exposition basically restates the themes of the orchestral exposition with elaborations and the requisite modulation, is one notable exception.

Figure 9.3 Mozart, Piano Concerto No. 17, in G, K. 453, exposition.

R^{1}Orchestra Exposition								
PT^1	PT^2	Tr^1	ST^1	CT^1	CT^2	codetta		
1	16^{elided}	22	35	57	^{evaded}65	69		
I			**(vi)-I**					
S^1	**Solo Exposition**							
PT^1	PT$^{2\ elided}$	Tr^2	ST^2	ext→Tr^3	ST^1	CT^3	CT^4	PT^2
75	94	100	110	124	139	153	160	
I			**V**					

secondary theme (ST^2), followed by a new but related transitional passage (Tr^3) and a restatement of the orchestral secondary theme. The new closing material allows the soloist to introduce virtuosic passage work, new harmonic elements, and drive toward closure.

Example 9.3 shows the beginning of the solo exposition, which uses the principal theme of the orchestral exposition. This example shows two important aspects of a concerto: 1) the solo sections do not merely restate the themes with simple orchestral accompaniment, they may elaborate *and* expand the themes; 2) the orchestra will not simply accompany, it will interact in a variety of ways. Listen to the recording of Example 9.3. Note how the intermittent entrances of the orchestra articulate the first phrases of the principal theme as presented by the soloist. The orchestra subsequently *initiates* the PT^2, then doubles the melody and takes it over once the soloist begins the elaborations in measure 97. These passages give some idea of the flexibility involved in the relationship between the orchestra and soloist. Additional formal elements of a concerto exemplified in this work are addressed in the exercises at the end of the chapter.

***Ritornello^2*.** The second ritornello is signaled by a tutti texture in which the full orchestra enters and the soloist rests. This ritornello reinforces the modulation to the secondary key usually with full dynamic levels and with thematic material drawn from the orchestral exposition. Though any thematic material may be recalled, it is normally that which was omitted by the soloist, which is often the transitional or closing theme. The arrows in the diagram (Figure 9.2) also indicate the flexible formal function of this ritornello: 1) it may close the exposition with a PAC allowing the soloist to begin the development (see Mozart, Piano Concerto No. 20, in D minor, K. 466); or 2) it may close the exposition but lead to HC or even a DC that elides with the solo entrance (see Beethoven, Piano Concerto No. 4, and Mozart, Piano Concerto No. 17; or 3) it may start out sounding as if it will close the exposition, but lead to a new key to initiate the development, usually closing with a HC (see Beethoven, Piano Concerto No. 3 in C minor).

***Solo^2—Development*.** The development section of a concerto usually brings the soloist to the forefront, even though interaction with the orchestra may be part of the development of the material. A common aspect of this section is the soloist's virtuosic passagework including scales, arpeggios, rapid sequences, and use of the full range of the instrument. The emphasis on improvisatory, fantasy-like writing precludes extensive motivic development of ideas. This section will still retain many of the formal features of a development as discussed in the previous chapter.

***Ritornello^3*.** The end of the development is signaled by a marked entrance of the orchestra in another tutti-like texture. Because this entrance can be very brief and integrated with the retransition or the recapitulation, it is sometimes not perceived as a "formal" ritornello.

Example 9.3 Mozart, Piano Concerto No. 17, in G, K. 453, solo exposition, mm. 74–101, PT[1] to beginning of Tr[2].

(This excerpt continues on p. 206.)

(Example 9.3, continued.)

Example 9.4 shows the tutti entrance at the end of the development of the Beethoven Piano Concerto No. 4, I. In this case the orchestra entrance is quite marked but simply states a two-measure cadential pattern that ushers in the recapitulation by the soloist. In many cases, however, the orchestra enters at the point of recapitulation and restates the first principal theme of the movement. The arrows in the diagram (Figure 9.2) again suggest the two possible functions of this ritornello: *it may close the development or begin the recapitulation*.

Example 9.4 Beethoven, Piano Concerto No. 4, in G, Op. 58, I, mm. 251–254.

R³–S³ Recapitulation. The concerto recapitulation is not intended to be a recapitulation of one or the other of the expositions: *it is meant to bring back elements of both in a single, unified, section*. It is this section of the form, as Rosen notes, with "the most frequent interruptions from the orchestra."[15] This, in part, results from the merger of the two expositions.

Recall from our discussion of recapitulations that themes may be omitted, fused, expanded, or reordered, and that the most significant changes in phrase structure often take place in the first half of an exposition, the PT and Tr. These aspects of a recapitulation are also important in a concerto, as is the reinterpretation of thematic order. Given the great variation in the thematic design of concerto expositions, generalizations about the recapitulation are difficult to make. The recapitulation may 1) present themes from the orchestral exposition that were omitted in the solo exposition (often the ST¹ or orchestral closing themes), even replacing those of the soloist; 2) omit or fuse transitional material if more than one transition was used in the solo exposition; 3) reorder the secondary themes. Generally, the presentation of themes will vary according to the thematic design of a given exposition, and as with any recapitulation, careful comparison of the two must be made.

R⁴—Cadenza. The fourth ritornello functions as a closing section to the recapitulation and, in most concertos, serves as a lead-in to the solo cadenza.[16] Like other formal

[15] Rosen, *Sonata Forms,* 94. He also cites Tovey's observation that in Mozart, the recapitulation of a concerto was a fusion of orchestral and solo exposition.

[16] Haydn places his cadenzas at the end of the recapitulation. Mozart and Beethoven place their cadenzas after R⁴ has begun, thus the cadenza is framed by ritornellos.

ritornellos, it is characterized by full textures and *forte* dynamic levels. It may use any material from the original ritornello, including themes that may have been omitted. Closing or transitional material is often used to intensify toward closure, leading convincingly to the cadential 6/4.

The R^4 varies in length from a short phrase to a phrase group. Often this ritornello follows a cadential trill by the soloist and initiates a new phrase and theme. In other instances it is a continuation of the soloist's previous phrase. An example of the latter case is illustrated in Example 9.5. Here the orchestra continues the phrase initiated by the soloist, which also parallels the close of the solo exposition. A salient formal element of R^4, illustrated here, is that it *pauses on a cadential 6/4*, thus it does not reach cadential closure. The ensuing cadenza then serves not only as a virtuosic, improvisatory elaboration of thematic material, but also as an expansive cadence that ends with an elided PAC. At that point the ritornello returns.

Example 9.5 Beethoven's Piano Concerto No. 4, I R^4, mm. 341–350.

Whether the final entrance of the orchestra is heard as a continuation of R^4 or as a fifth ritornello is subject to interpretation. The ritornello may continue the thematic material of the previous ritornello, or the soloist may continue playing with the orchestra. In such cases, we may perceive the cadenza as an event within R4.[17] In other instances, such as Mozart's Piano Concerto in D minor, the orchestra enters with an extensive recall of thematic material that closes the movement without the soloist. In such cases a fifth ritornello is perceived.

THE NINETEENTH CENTURY AND BEYOND

After Beethoven, a tendency toward a single exposition in a concerto emerged, with the soloist entering immediately or shortly after a brief orchestral introduction. Example 9.6 shows one of the earliest instance of this approach, in Mendelssohn's Violin Concerto in E minor. The orchestra provides a simple accompaniment figure as lead-in to the violin's lyric principal theme. This approach in part reflects the nineteenth-century interest in lyric melody and in giving the soloist the "leading role" in the concerto. In the single exposition the orchestra and soloist may alternate or share thematic presentation.

Composers such as Schumann, Grieg, Dvorak, and Tchaikovsky followed this model. The expected development, recapitulation and cadenza were included in the form, influenced by the tendencies of nineteenth-century sonata forms outlined in the previous chapter. Brahms, in his two piano concertos and violin concertos, continued to develop the concerto sonata form with two expositions, while expanding the form and exploring new virtuosic demands on the soloist. The emphasis on virtuosity saw the introduction of more than one cadenza-like passage in a movement, a trend foreshadowed in the works of Beethoven.

Example 9.6 Mendelssohn, Violin Concerto in E minor, Op. 64, I, mm. 1–5.

The role of the soloist as virtuosic performer is epitomized in the piano concertos of Chopin and especially Liszt. Chopin's two concertos began with orchestral ritornellos but the orchestra primarily serves an accompaniment role. While Chopin for the most part follows the concerto sonata form, a freer approach is evident in the two concertos by Liszt. He connected the movements of his concertos, a precedent set by Mendelssohn in the violin concerto, and used cyclic forms (discussed below). His concertos also placed extreme demands on the soloist. Extended cadenza-like passages without orchestra are heard throughout and the works contain many changes in tempo. Consequently, the form is often influenced more by virtuosic display than discourse between soloist and orchestra.

---

[17] See Mozart's Piano Concerto in G, K. 453 for an example of the former, and Beethoven's Piano Concertos Nos. 4 and 5 for an example of the latter.

In the twentieth century, many concertos continued the traditions of the nineteenth-century forms with an emphasis on the virtuosic role of the soloist and expansive themes. At the same time, an interest in the earlier models of Baroque concertos is heard in works such as Stravinsky's Violin Concerto and the two concerti grossi by Ernest Bloch. In these works, as in any concerto, the relationship between soloist and orchestra is an important element of the formal conception of the composition.

Analytic Exercises

A. **Mozart, Piano Concerto No. 17 in G major, K. 453, I.** The formal outline of this movement is given in Figure 9.3. Several noteworthy features of the formal structure can be observed through close listening. To aid your listening, select themes are reproduced here. Without the aid of a score, attempt to answer the following questions. A score may be used to corroborate answers.

Exercise 9.1 Mozart, Piano Concerto in G, K. 453, I, principal themes.

1. The PT^2 might be considered the beginning of the transition. What elements of the music increase the tension at this point?
2. The orchestra transition (Tr^1) has three distinct phrases, the first initiated by continuous sixteenth notes in the melody. What type of cadence ends the first phrase, eliding with phrase two? What elements mark the closing phrase of the transition?
3. The ST^1 begins with a restless, repeated note motive. Conduct the phrase rhythm of this theme in $\frac{4}{4}$, with the measure equaling one beat. What do you observe about the connection of the phrases as the theme repeats?
4. The repetition of the ST^1 ends with a *deceptive cadence* that introduces a new motive as part of a phrase extension. What specific harmony is used at the DC?
5. The closing section has three distinct themes, including the codetta. Where is an evaded cadence heard within this section?
6. The solo sections make use of sequences at several points. Which formal functions make greatest use of sequence? Can you identify the types of sequence?
7. Note the cadence that closes R^2. What is the harmony used at that point?
8. Attempt to outline the recapitulation in a manner similar to Figure 9.3. In what order are the various themes and sections restated? What material omitted in the solo exposition returns in the recapitulation?
9. Is the final ritornello a continuation of R^4 or a new ritornello? Explain your answer.

B. The relationship between soloist and orchestra can take many forms. From a purely musical viewpoint it might be considered in terms of phrase structure and function. The following list provides some relations that may be encountered.

1. Orchestra provides accompaniment to a solo theme.
2. Soloist provides accompaniment (often very elaborate) to an orchestra theme.
3. Orchestra and soloist alternate phrases in the presentation of a theme.
4. Orchestra and soloist are in dialogue, alternating phrase segments or phrases.
5. One or the other enters intermittently in a passage or section.
6. One or the other rests during a thematic statement.
7. One initiates a phrase that is then continued by the other.

This aspect is a key element of any concerto, and other relations may be found. You may also consider the roles of the soloist and orchestra in more subjective terms, such as collaborative, confrontational, reciprocal, and so forth. Tchaikovsky, for example, famously observed that a concerto is a struggle between "the powerful, inexhaustibly richly colored orchestra and its small, insignificant, but strong-minded adversary."[18] The slow movement of Beethoven's Piano Concerto No. 4 offers one of the most noteworthy examples of a seemingly adversarial relationship between soloist and orchestra. Listen to the movement, then write a narrative or dialogue that interprets the drama of the music.

C. The slow movement of Mozart's Piano Concerto in G is unusual in that it opens with a short phrase that is an introduction and that serves as a ritornello throughout the movement. The orchestra then begins what will be the first exposition of a sonata form movement. Listen closely to what follows the opening ritornello each time it returns. This movement contains some striking modulations and some of Mozart's most dramatic and expressive music in the genre. As in any concerto, careful attention to the thematic plan is required to understand the form.

---

[18] Cited in Joseph Kerman, *Concerto Conversations*, 21.

D. Listen to the opening exposition of Beethoven's Piano Concertos Nos. 4 and 5. What departures from concerto sonata form do you hear at the beginning of the concertos? Are full orchestra expositions heard?

E. The concertos listed here offer additional examples of concerto first movements in sonata form. Prior to study with a score, listen for the types of phrase relations between soloist and orchestra and the treatment of formal ritornellos with regard to placement and function. Note that the Mozart Clarinet Concerto does not have a cadenza.

+Mozart, Piano Concerto in B♭ Major K. 450
*Mozart, Clarinet Concerto in A major, K. 622
Haydn, Trumpet Concerto in D major
Mendelssohn, Violin Concerto
Brahms, Violin Concerto

SUGGESTED READING

A concise summary of the history of the concerto can be found in *The Harvard Dictionary of Music,* 4th ed., edited by Don Michael Randel. John Roeder's *A History of the Concerto* offers an extensive survey of the genre. Joseph Kerman's *Concerto Conversations* is a thoughtful and engaging examination of the various roles and relations between soloists and orchestra from the Baroque to the present day. Tovey's *Essays in Musical Analysis, Vol. III* contains analytic commentary on several important concertos. See also the books and articles by Lindeman, Stevens and Swain listed in the bibliography.

Cyclic Form

A multi-movement musical work that uses the same thematic material in more than one movement is referred to as a *cyclic form*. Note that the term does not refer to the form of a single movement, but of an entire work in which movements are thematically interrelated. Cyclic form is often associated with nineteenth-century instrumental music. However, precedents for the recall of material in later movements of a work are found in the cyclic Masses of the fifteenth and sixteenth centuries, in which the same cantus firmus is heard in each movement, or each movement begins with the same motives. This idea of thematic recurrence at the end of a multi-movement work also is evident in certain works of the Baroque period, including suites and sacred works such as chorale cantatas. Many of Bach's chorale cantatas, particularly those of his Leipzig period, use the original chorale at the beginning and end of the cantata. Similarly, his setting of the *Magnificat* in D major for soloists, chorus, and orchestra uses the same musical material in the opening and closing movements.

The eighteenth-century classical composers generally did not employ cyclic forms; each movement of their multi-movement works is a self-contained form without overt cyclic connections. It was in the nineteenth century that composers began to draw on the cyclic recall of themes in later movements of instrumental works. This tendency reflected the Romantic emphasis on melody and thematic transformation. The cyclic use of material would take on various guises and have different functions in different works. The most prominent manifestations are in instrumental works, in particular symphonies, which will be the focus of this brief discussion.[19]

[19] Nineteenth-century song cycles display a different approach to cyclic form, usually relying on poetic connections, and a tonal design that runs through an entire cycle of songs. Thematic cyclicism is not always evident. Motivic recurrences can be significant features of operas, most famously in the operas of Richard Wagner.

The recurrence of themes from earlier movements of a multi-movement work normally involves thematic material from the first movement, which is recalled in new contexts. In most cases it is the final movement in which themes are recalled. Beethoven was the first composer of instrumental sonata forms to use such cyclic forms. In his Symphony No. 5, a fragment of the scherzo returns in the finale, a theme using repeated notes that also recalls the opening motive of the symphony. Perhaps the most famous example of cyclic recall is Beethoven's Symphony No. 9, in which fragments of each of the first three movements are recalled in the introduction of the last movement. After a dissonant fanfare that begins the movement, a recitative by the contrabasses is repeatedly interrupted as quotes from each movement are heard as follows: 1) introduction to movement I, measures 30–37, 2) PT of movement II, measures 48–55, and 3) PT of movement III, measures 63–64. These recurrences are not integrated into the movement; they are, in effect, parenthetical quotes that simply make fleeting reference to the expressive ideas of previous movements before the Finale proper begins.[20]

Less than a decade after Beethoven's Symphony No. 9 was completed, Berlioz composed the *Symphony Fantastique,* which relies on a recurring thematic idea throughout its five movements.[21] In this work, the theme is used as a quotation and integrated as a theme in new contexts. Berlioz's cyclic restatements of the *idée fixe* make use of *thematic transformation.* This technique entails a change in character or expressive effect resulting from rhythmic, metric, dynamic and timbral changes in a theme, as illustrated in Example 9.7. The first phrase of the original theme is shown in Example 9.7a. It occurs as a fragmentary quotation, suddenly interpolated in the coda of the fourth movement, the "March to the Scaffold." Here the theme is heard before the hero is beheaded—a faint recall of his beloved (Example 9.7b). At other recurrences, the theme is transformed and serves as integrated thematic material. In Examples 9.7c–e it appears in the guise of a waltz theme in movement two, as a recitative-like passage in the coda of the third movement, and is transformed as part of the "Dream of a Witches' Sabbath" in the last movement. The programmatic and cyclic use of the fixed idea throughout the entire work is one of the unique aspects of this symphony.

Example 9.7 Berlioz, *Symphony Fantastique,* fixed idea.

a. I, mm. 72–80.

b. IV, mm. 164–169.

c. II, 120–128.

---

[20] The earliest example is found in Haydn's Symphony No. 46. See also Beethoven's Piano Sonata in A major, Op. 101 for cyclic recall as quotation. Rosen describes cyclic thematic relations among different movement as either explicit or implicit, defined as thematic quotation or thematic integration, respectively. See *Sonata Forms,* 320–321.

[21] Beethoven's Symphony No. 9 was completed in 1824; Berlioz's *Symphony Fantastique* was completed in 1830.

d. III, mm. 89–92.

e. V, mm. 21–25.

After Berlioz, many composers, notably Liszt and Franck, wrote cyclic works using thematic transformations. Many cyclic works by Romantic composers recall a theme from the first movement in an integrated manner, often in the finale as part of the conclusion of the work. Tchaikovsky's Symphony No. 4 in F minor is a case in point. The first movement's introduction is a bold fanfare that occurs at the main formal junctures of this expanded sonata form movement. It also anticipates a motive of the principal theme. The initial fanfare motive is repeated several times before quietly resolving, as shown in Example 9.8a. Note the unusual harmonic motion that precludes a strong cadence. This theme appears again prior to the coda of the fourth movement. This reappearance asserts the forceful expression that had been heard throughout movement one, emphasizing its function as a motto for the work. The final phrase of this recurrence resembles the close of the introduction from the first movement, but is extended. This extension prolongs an augmented sixth chord that eventually resolves to the dominant as the coda begins (Example 9.8b). This cyclic recurrence, which serves as a point of climax for the finale, thus serves to provide the strong closure that had been withheld each time the theme was presented in the first movement. The theme thus functions in the last movement as a quote as well as a formally integrated idea.

Example 9.8 Tchaikovsky, Symphony No. 4.

a. I, mm. 16–20.

b. IV, mm. 208–222.

Arch form, a multi-movement form related to cyclic form, refers to a work in which motivic and formal relations exist between symmetrically corresponding pairs of movements. The patterns of movements one encounters usually are either an A B A or an A B C B A. This approach to multi-movement form is most often associated with certain works of Bartók. In the first pattern, exemplified in Bartók's first two piano concertos and the violin concerto, the third movement is a freely varied restatement of the first movement. The five-movement arch form is found in his fourth and fifth string quartets. In the fourth quartet, the fast outer movements use similar thematic material, the second and fourth movements are scherzos, and the middle movement is a large ternary form in slow tempo. This approach goes beyond the cyclic recall of a single theme, but is related to cyclic form in its use of the same thematic material in more than one movement. Bartók and other twentieth-century composers also use five-part arch form in single movements. The first movement of Bartók's *Music for Strings, Percussion, and Celesta,* for example, is a fugal movement shaped in the manner of an arch form.

SUGGESTED READING

Charles Rosen provides a useful discussion of the formal effects of cyclic recall of themes in *The Romantic Generation,* 88–98. See also Dahlhaus, *Nineteenth-Century Music,* 274–276.

Analytic Exercises

These works contain cyclic use of themes to varying degrees. Brief descriptions of this approach, and how it is rendered for each work, are given to guide listening and analysis. Among the composers listed, Franck makes the most extensive use of cyclic forms, often based on subtle thematic transformations rather than recall as quotation. The analysis of the score may focus on comparison of cyclic themes with regard to phrase structure, harmony, and cadences. The larger question of expressive effect or intent of the cyclic recall of themes will of necessity require interpretation of the alterations and context of the theme.

A. **Beethoven, String Quartet Op. 131 in C♯ minor.** The final phrases of the coda to this work recalls the opening fugue subject of movement one. Consider how the subject is altered and how its texture and expressive context is changed in the coda.

B. **Schubert, Wanderer Fantasie in C major for Piano, D. 760.** This four-movement work is to be performed without pause between movements. The slow movement of this fantasy is a set of variations on Schubert's song "The Wanderer" (1816), but the theme is used in the other three movements as well.

C. **Liszt, Sonata for Piano in B minor.** This one movement sonata is in effect a four-movement work that embraces a complex sonata form. Thematic transformation of the principal theme occurs throughout the work. What other elements, in addition to the thematic transformation, articulate the internal movements of this work?

D. **Brahms, Symphony No. 3 in F minor.** The opening theme of the first movement is used in the coda of the last movement and closes the symphony. The harmonic content and texture of each presentation should be examined. Interpretation of the expressive effect of the cyclic return can then be considered.

E. **Franck, Symphony in D minor.** This three-movement work makes cyclic use of the main themes of the first and second movements. The second movement has a secondary theme that is related to the secondary theme of movement one. In the last movement the development recalls the principal theme of movement two, which was first heard on the English horn. The coda of the last movement recalls both the principal and secondary themes of the first movement. To what extent are the first movement themes transformed?

10 Rondo Forms

Introduction

The principle of statement-contrast-restatement, which was discussed as a basis for ternary form, is often expanded to create larger forms referred to as rondos. In a *rondo form*, contrasting sections alternate with restatements of an initial theme to create forms that are most often in five or seven sections.[1] Formal diagrams of five-part and seven-part rondos are given in Figure 10.1. The letter schemes traditionally used to designate these forms reflect the contrasts in key, mode, thematic material, or texture among the sections. Note that the seven-part rondo expands the five-part form by the addition of a third episode. Rondos of nine or more parts are sometimes found, though they are exceptional. In any case, the rondo always closes with a presentation of the refrain or a coda that makes reference to the refrain. Often the final refrain is fused with a coda.

Outline of Rondo Form

The first section of a rondo, the opening theme, is referred to as a *refrain* because it recurs several times in the form. As Figure 10.1 illustrates, the refrain, or A section, is characterized by the presentation of its thematic material *in the tonic key*. The contrasting sections that occur between statements of the refrain are referred to as couplets or *episodes*. These episodes are in contrasting keys, most often closely related keys (CRK), or they may be in the parallel minor or major mode of the tonic key.[2] Episodes, which are generally expository, may also be modulatory and present material in more than one key. In most seven-part rondos of the classical period, the first episode is in the dominant key. The second episode may present a new theme or development of earlier thematic material. The third episode is then a restatement of the first episode but in the tonic key. The return of episode 1 material in the tonic key for episode 3 corresponds to the recapitulation of a ST in sonata form. Thus this form may take on characteristics of both a rondo and a sonata form and is designated a *sonata-rondo form*, discussed later in this chapter. The seven-part rondo with a third new theme in episode 3 (D) is less common. Other variants one may encounter include A B A B′ A and A B A C B A, the latter a scheme favored by Mozart.

The rondo form is used in keyboard suites of the Baroque period; it also is used in the slow movement or finale of sonatas, symphonies, chamber music, or concertos of the Classical period. Sonata-rondos are almost exclusively found in the finales of multi-movement works. After Beethoven, sonata-rondo movements are encountered more often than rondo forms, particularly in the finales of concertos. Solo works designated as a rondo also have

[1] Some texts refer to sectional ternary form as "first rondo form," five-part rondos as "second rondo form," and seven-part rondos as "third rondo form." This terminology ignores the contrast between other ternary forms and rondo forms and is no longer current.

[2] As in the contrasting middle sections of ternary forms, the terms *minore* and *maggiore* sometimes appear in the score to designate modal contrasts of key in an episode.

Figure 10.1 *Five-part rondo and seven-part rondo forms. (CRK=closely related keys)*

Five-part Rondo

Refrain 1	Episode 1	Refrain 2	Episode 2	Refrain 3 (Coda)
A	**B**	**A**	**C**	**A**
Tonic	CRK	Tonic	CRK	Tonic

Seven-part Rondo

Refrain 1	Episode 1	Refrain 2	Episode 2	Refrain 3	Episode 3	Refrain 4	Coda
A	**B**	**A**	**C**	**A**	**B′**	**A**	
Tonic	Dominant	Tonic	CRK	Tonic	Tonic	Tonic	
Refrain 1	Episode 1	Refrain 2	Episode 2	Refrain 3	Episode 3	Refrain 4	Coda
A	**B**	**A**	**C**	**A**	**D**	**A**	
Tonic	CRK	Tonic	CRK	Tonic	CRK	Tonic	

been composed, notably piano works by Mozart, Beethoven, and Mendelssohn.[3] The rondo forms found in Baroque music have attributes distinguishing them from rondo forms that emerged in later music. The following discussion first will consider the earlier rondo form used by Baroque composers.

Baroque Rondeau

The historical precursor of the Classical rondo was the French *rondeau* of the Baroque period in which a refrain alternated with *couplets*.[4] Such forms were found frequently in the keyboard suites of French composers including Lully and Rameau, and most notably in the suites or *Ordres* of François Couperin. The *rondeau* was cultivated by other composers of the Baroque era as well. Example 10.1 shows a well-known rondeau by the English composer Henry Purcell. Several features of this work are characteristic of the Baroque rondeau form:

- The refrain is tonally closed, normally ending with a PAC in the tonic key.
- The refrain is a short, self-contained theme, in this case a ritornello-type phrase of eight measures. Periodic phrases are also common in a rondeau.
- Each time the refrain recurs it is in the tonic key and is unaltered.
- The couplets are in contrasting keys but make use of similar or related thematic material from the refrain.

[3] See for example Mozart, Rondo in F, K. 494, and Rondo in A minor, K. 511; Beethoven Rondo Op. 52, No. 1 and Op. 129, and Mendelssohn, Rondo Capriccioso Op. 14.

[4] The terms “refrain” and “couplet” are literary terms used with reference to poetry in which a refrain alternates with a pair of successive lines of verse called “couplets.” This practice was applied to music in the rondeaux of the medieval and renaissance periods. The setting of refrains and verses to music will be discussed in Chapter 13.

In this example, the first couplet makes use of the motivic elements of the theme but is now in the contrasting, closely related key of F major (III). This couplet is also tonally closed and is followed by a direct modulation back to tonic for the refrain. Note that the second couplet, which began in A minor (v), ends with a phrygian HC that leads to the final statement of the refrain in the tonic key. The modulation conveys a transitional function that may be incorporated at the beginning and ending of episodes. The decisive cadences and breaks between refrains and episodes give the form a decidedly sectional nature. The brevity of the sections and the monothematic tendencies are characteristic of the *rondeaux* of that period.

A rondeau may have as few as three sections—thus resembling ternary form—or seven or more sections. Couperin's most famous and monumental *rondeau*, the *Passacaille* from his *Ordre VIII*, has eight couplets alternating with nine refrains, totaling seventeen sections. The beginning of a seven-part *rondeau* by Couperin is shown in Example 10.2. His keyboard compositions usually had programmatic titles; in this case the title *La Bandoline* is thought to refer to a woman from the town of Bandol.

Example 10.1 Purcell, *Abdelazer,* "Festival Rondeau."[5]

(This excerpt continues on p. 220.)

[5] The refrain of this Purcell rondeau is used in Benjamin Britten's well-known work *Young Person's Guide to the Orchestra,* a set of orchestral variations on the refrain.

(Example 10.1, continued.)

30
Refrain (A)
HC
36
PAC

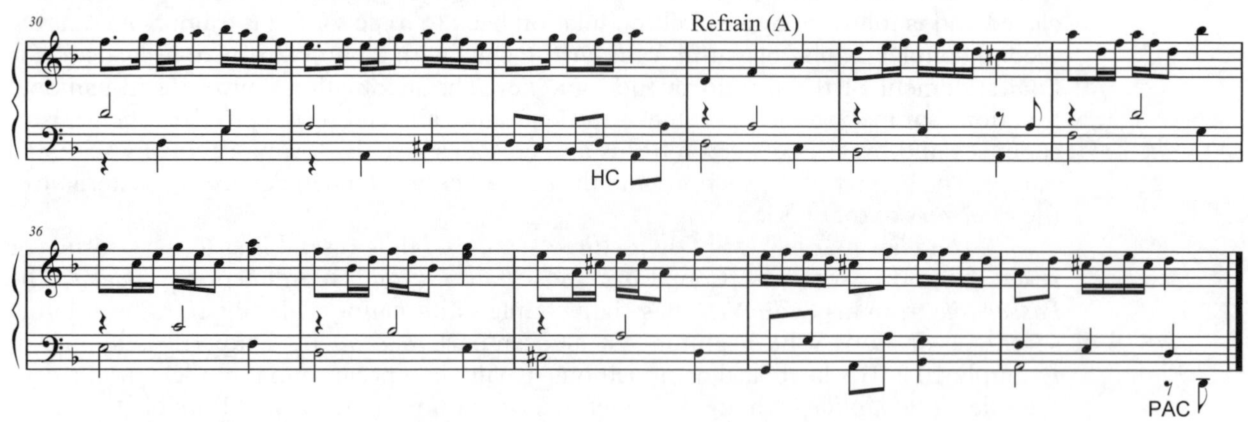

Example 10.2 Couperin, *La Bandoline,* rondeau.

HC
6
1.
2.
Fine
PAC
Couplet 1
13
18
3.
Couplet 2
22

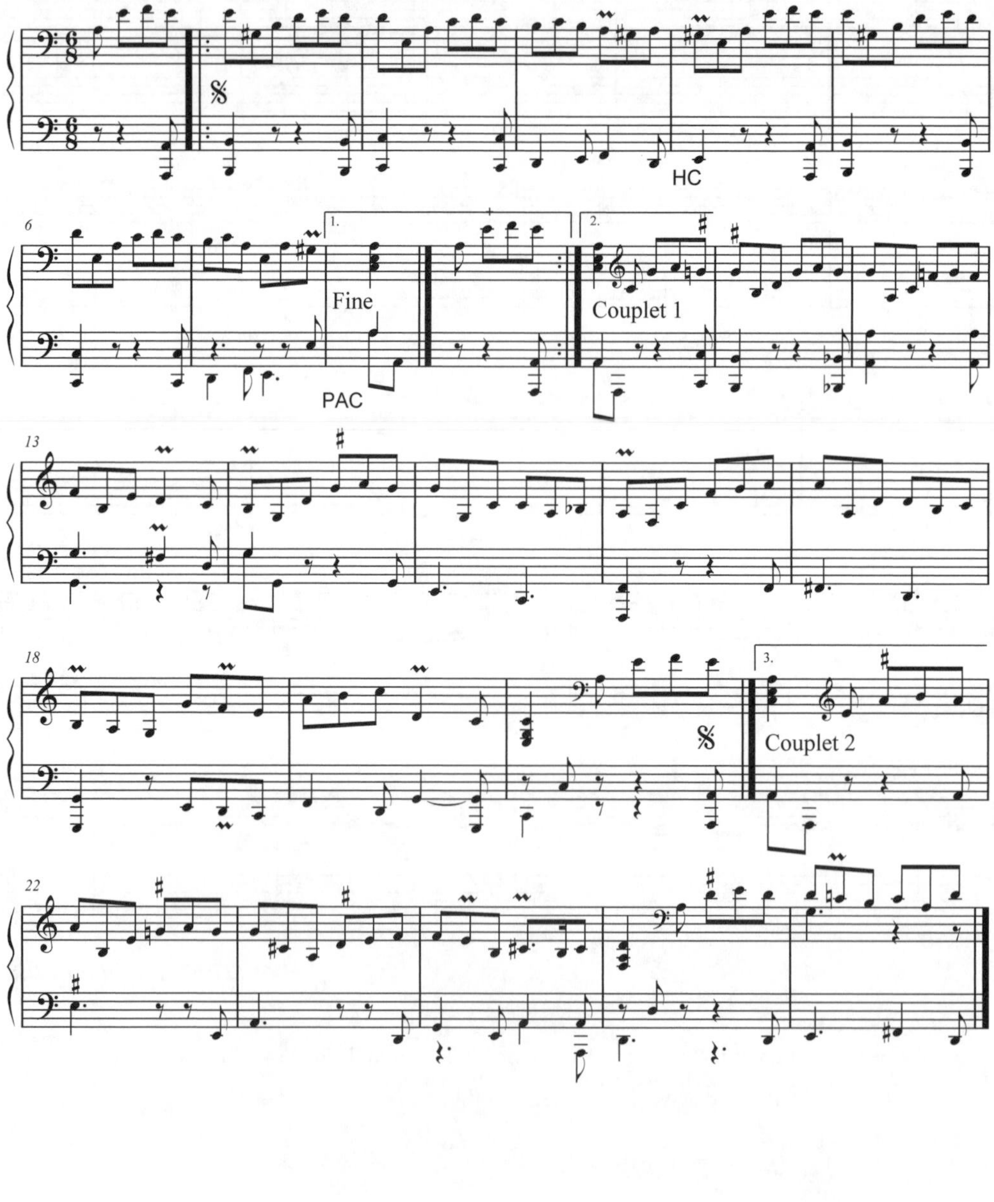

This composition, as in many rondeaux, uses the *dal segno* sign to indicate that the refrain is to be repeated after each couplet. The performance practice was to do so without repeats within the refrain, but with possible ornamentations, especially in a longer rondeau. The refrain, as in this Purcell example, is a short eight-measure theme, though in the form of a parallel period. The couplets continue to elaborate the motives of the refrain with contrasts in harmonic progressions and tonality. They are also varied in length and make use of sequential phrases. These varied elements contrast with the unaltered recurrence of the symmetrical refrain. The result of these processes is a clearly articulated and perceivable form, both predictable and surprising at turns.

Exercise

Analyze the form of the rondeau **Les Moissonneurs* (The Harvesters) from the *Sixième Ordre* of François Couperin.

1. In addition to identifying the tonal design, consider the motivic derivations and phrase structures of the couplets. In what way is the phrase structure of the first couplet simpler than the refrain? Where is its principle motive used in the refrain?
2. Consider the two phrases of the second couplet. How are they related to the first couplet and to the refrain?
3. The third couplet begins as a restatement of the refrain. How is it different from the refrain? At what point does it deviate from the refrain?
4. The third couplet is also much longer than the first two. How many phrases are in this couplet? How do you account for its length?
5. Finally, what type of dance style is used in this rondeau? How might the style relate to the title?

Five and Seven-Part Rondo

Rondos of the Classical era use the basic formal principles of the Baroque *rondeau* but with greater contrasts of themes and textures in the episodes. The refrain, frequently a short binary or ternary form, is often longer than Baroque refrains. Furthermore, the Classical rondo is more likely to incorporate distinct transitions and retransitions to effect modulations and provide continuity. Transitions will lead to episodes, while retransitions return the music to the tonic key and the restatement of refrains. These attributes distinguish the rondos of Classical composers from the more sectional rondeaux. Five-part rondos sometimes occur in final movements, notably by Haydn, and are also used in slow movements as well as operatic arias.[6] Seven-part rondos, with a few exceptions, are used in finales.[7] Examples from various works will illustrate the characteristics of the sections of a rondo form. Complete movements will be addressed in the exercises that follow.

Refrains typically are self-contained, symmetrical themes that end with a PAC. These elements of symmetry and stability result in part from the dance-like and tuneful quality that is typical of many rondo themes. Such qualities not only contribute to the recognition of the refrain when it returns but also provide the potential for contrast with the intervening

[6] See for example "E amor un ladroncello," No. 28, from Act II of *Così fan Tutte* by Mozart; and "Che farò senza Euridice" from Act III of *Orfeo* by Gluck. The adaptation of the form in these vocal works will be discussed in Chapter 13.

[7] There are a few instances of nine-part forms by Mozart, including the Serenade in D ("Haffner"), K. 520, IV; the Rondo in F major, K. 494; and the Piano Sonata K. 281, III.

episodes. Two example are given in Example 10.3a and b. The opening theme of the Beethoven Piano Sonata Op. 13, II (10.3a) is a contrasting period, which is repeated with embellishments to complete a sixteen-measure refrain. In contrast, Example 10.3b shows Haydn's use of a sectional rounded binary form with an extensive dominant preparation in the B section and complete return of the eight-measure sentence that opened the refrain. Both of these refrains are from five-part rondo forms, though the use of a repeated period, a sentence, or a rounded binary form is typical of most seven-part rondo refrains as well.[8] When the refrains or the episodes are self-contained forms, the result is a compound rondo form. Repeats of complete phrases or sections in the opening refrain, whether written out (as in the Beethoven) or notated, are characteristic of the rondo form.

The restatement of refrains may be complete or abbreviated, and may include embellishments and new textural settings of the principal theme. (Recall that the symbol A′ is used to designate a varied restatemant.) The partial restatement of the theme is often heard in slow movements when the theme is a repeated period or a small form. In such cases a single statement of the opening period is all that is recalled. Another possibility is a restatement of the opening phrase of the refrain, which subsequently fuses with the ensuing episode. This technique is found most often in sonata-rondo forms and is discussed in that section of this chapter.

Example 10.3a Beethoven, Piano Sonata Op. 13, II, refrain.

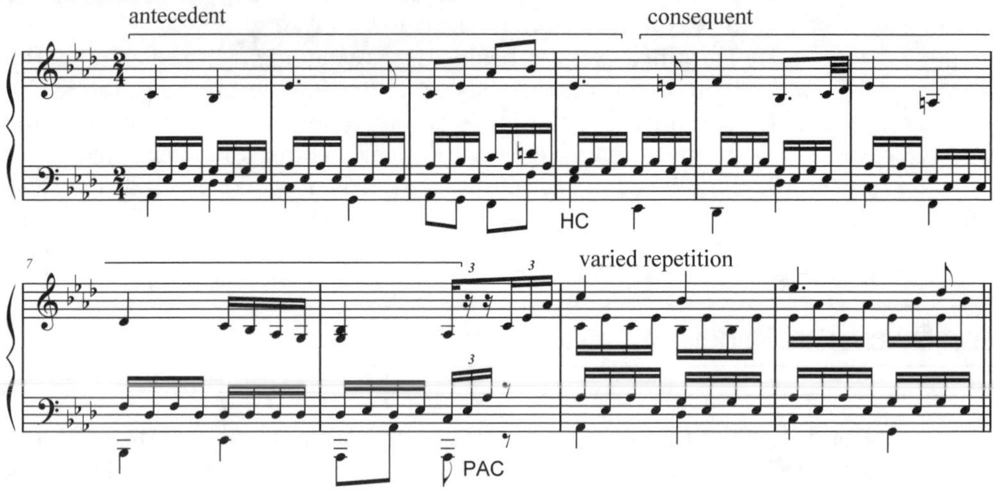

Example 10.3b Haydn, String Quartet Op. 33, No. 2, Finale.

[8] For an example of a refrain in simple ternary form see Beethoven, Sonata Op. 90, II.

(This excerpt continues on p. 224.)

(Example 10.3b, continued.)

In finales, where quicker tempos are used, the complete refrain will more likely recur. If it is a binary form, repeats may be omitted since the refrain has been well established and is familiar to the listener. When the refrain is presented with changes in texture or rhythm, or with melodic embellishments, the form takes on the character of a set of variations with episodes between the variations. The alternation of theme and episodes retains the principles of rondo form; thus such forms are best understood as *rondo variations*.[9]

Episodes, particularly the first one, usually introduce a new theme that is self-contained, defined by a distinct beginning and strong cadential closure in a new key. Sometimes the new theme and key are introduced directly after the close of the refrain, emphasizing the sectional nature of the form. Example 10.4 shows the start of a first episode, which is stated directly following the close of the refrain. Note the presence of repeat signs, a clear indication that the episode is a self-contained formal unit, in this case a continuous binary form. The episode begins and ends in G minor (i) and is followed by a direct modulation to G major (I) as the refrain returns.

Example 10.4 Mozart, Piano Trio in G major, K. 564, III, end of refrain, episode 1.

More often, transitions and retransitions are used between refrains and episodes. These phrases serve to lessen the sectional nature of the form and to create a sense of anticipation of a new theme or a the return of the refrain. Transitions are more common in seven-part rondos and sonata rondos, though retransitions are employed in all types of rondos. Example 10.5 shows the end of a first episode and a retransition that leads to the

[9] See the Haydn, Piano Trio No. 15 in G major, II; and Beethoven, Symphony No. 9, II.

return of the refrain. The retransitional function of measures 24–27 is evident because the passage follows a PAC in C minor (vi), makes use of repeated melodic patterns, modulates, and concludes with an arrival on a V7 chord in the original key of E♭ major.

Example 10.5 Mozart, Piano Sonata in B♭ major, K. 570, II, mm. 23–28, retransition.

An episode may be modulatory, blending developmental and expository functions. Example 10.6 shows the first episode of the Beethoven piano sonata movement shown in Example 10.3, a five-part rondo form. A direct modulation to F minor (vi) and a new thematic idea are introduced in measure 17 immediately after the close of the refrain. The new key is never confirmed; rather the phrase leads to a PAC in E♭ major (V) in measure 23. The subsequent phrase elaborates E♭ major with a new idea but also serves as a retransition that leads to the refrain. As a result of the modulatory harmonic motion the episode is an open-ended, developmental, formal unit rather than a self-contained theme. This technique, especially favored by Beethoven, gives a sense of contrast between stable, closed refrains and unstable, harmonically open episodes.

Example 10.6 Beethoven, Sonata Op. 13, I, mm. 17–26, modulatory episode.

(This excerpt continues on p. 226.)

(Example 10.6, continued.)

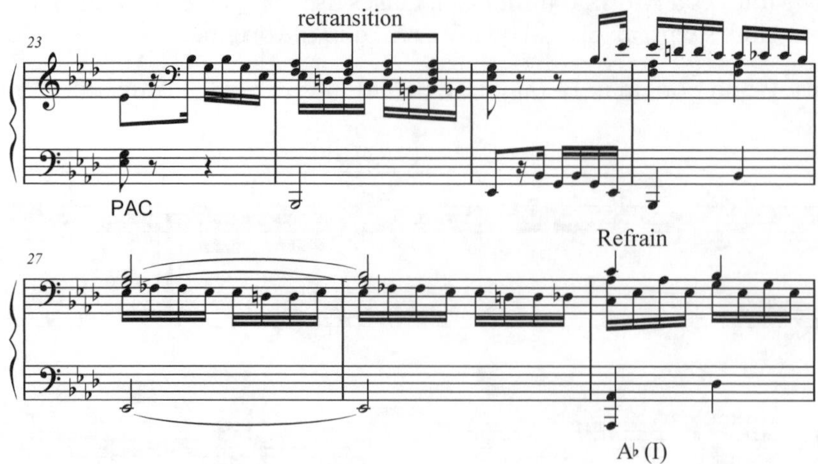

Final Refrain and Coda. Although the final refrain may be presented in its entirety to conclude the form, two other possibilities are common: 1) a codetta or coda may follow the complete refrain, or 2) the refrain may be abbreviated and lead directly into a codetta or coda. In the first case the coda is perceived as a distinct section that follows the refrain. In the second case, the first phrase or two of the refrain is heard to confirm its function as a final return of the theme but is fused with a subsequent coda. In either case, a coda may present further development of any of the previous themes or may simply elaborate the final cadential closure of the form. Examples of these possibilities are explored in the exercises.

Romantic period rondos, like the sonata form, are often expansive or compressed with abrupt contrasts and tonal fluctuation. A miniature five-part rondo by Schumann illustrates some of these characteristics (see Example 10.7). The refrain is a brief, six-measure phrase that initially modulates. Note how the refrain starts on a dissonant harmony, prolonging the dominant chord. Its subsequent recurrences are varied in phrase structure, each time closing in the tonic key of D minor. The direct move from F major to A major (V), rather than to the expected A minor (v) for the first episode produces a bold change in tonality, a chromatic third relation using modal mixture. The brevity of each section gives the movement a restless quality typical of many brief, nineteenth-century character pieces.

Example 10.7 Schumann, *Papillons* No. 6.

Exercises

Listen to the various works listed below. The theme of the refrain for each movement is given in the examples listed for each exercise. In addition, a formal description of each movement is given to guide your listening. As you listen, try to recognize the following formal elements:

- What form does the refrain take? Is the refrain restated completely, varied, expanded or abbreviated in its subsequent recurrences?
- Are the refrains followed by direct modulations to a new key and theme?
- Are transitions or retransitions apparent between refrains and episodes?
- Are the episodes self-contained themes or developmental?
- Are the refrains or the episodes grouped or fused with the transitional passages?
- If there is a coda, does it follow or incorporate the final refrain? How much of the final refrain is heard?

1. **Haydn, String Quartet Op. 33, No. 2 in E♭ major, "The Joke," IV (A B A B'A) Example 10.3b.** This celebrated movement resulted in the nickname for this quartet. Listen for the way he shapes the final refrain, including a parenthetical phrase. Note also the monothematic tendency of the work, characteristic of Haydn, and his clever use of pedal points throughout. How does Haydn tease the listener's expectations that the work is about to end? What is surprising about the ending?

2. **Haydn Piano Trio No. 24 in G major, III.** This movement, entitled *Rondo alla ongarese*, is from Haydn's best known piano trio. The lively tempo and rhythms, repetitive four-measure phrases, and contrasts in *maggiore* and *minore* sections are indicative of the Hungarian qualities suggested by the title. Though clearly a rondo form, its design—A B C A D A—is a departure from the standard rondo. The refrain

is a rounded binary form. What kind of phrase structure is used in the first part of the refrain shown in the music? The first episode is unusual in that it remains in the tonic key. How does Haydn create contrast in this episode? Each of the episodes contains more than one theme. Do any of the episodes comprise a complete binary or ternary form? Which of the episodes departs from the tonic key of G?

3. **+Mozart, Piano Sonata in A minor, K. 310, III.** In this rondo finale, Mozart eliminates the return of the final refrain, creating an A B A C A B form. The episodes are unusual in that they are all modulatory. Where do transitions and retransitions occur within the first episode (B)? How does Mozart clearly delineate episode two (C)? How is episode three (B′) altered when it recurs? After studying the form carefully, speculate as to why Mozart may have made the alteration. Consider also how Mozart uses the various registers of the piano to shape the music.

4. **Beethoven, String Quartet Op. 18, No. 4 in C minor, IV.** This is a seven-part rondo (A B A C A B′A) in which each of the first two episodes are closed forms in A♭ major (VI) and C major (I) respectively. The third episode (B′) recalls the theme of Episode I (B) but is varied. How much of this B theme is heard and at what point does the episode take on a retransitional function? How does Beethoven intensify the anticipation of the final entrance of the refrain? A dramatic coda closes the movement: what material is used? Observe the many phrase expansions and how Beethoven uses modal mixture as well as stark contrasts in texture and dynamics to create a dramatic close to the movement.

5. **Tchaikovsky, Violin Concerto in D major, III.** Many finales of solo concertos use rondo forms. The refrain of this exhilarating movement is a Russian-like tune. On initial listening, without a score, attempt to outline the form based on thematic layout. How does Tchaikovsky depart from the standard rondo form? What is the function of the opening section of the movement? What other aspects of the music, apart from changes in themes and keys, delineate the form? Of particular interest in such movements is the role the soloist and orchestra take in the form. One assumption might be that the orchestra presents the refrains while the soloist presents episodic material, but such a simple approach is seldom found. In this regard, review some possible relations outlined in Chapter 9. What role does the orchestration play in delineating the form?

6. **Stravinsky, Octet, III.** The finale of this work for flute, clarinet and pairs of bassoons, trumpets, and trombones is a five-part rondo. The score gives rehearsal numbers, for example R1, continuously through all three movements; this movement begins four measures after R57. A broad outline of the movement is as follows:

A	B	A	C	A′	coda
R57+4	R61	R62+4	R66	R69	R73

Consider how thematic material and orchestration delineate the sections. How is the A material varied each time it recurs? Brief transitional passages may also be identified. Both the C episode and the coda make use of a samba rhythm based on a syncopated rhythmic grouping. The coda uses this rhythm as an ostinato, giving a static quality that is a trademark of Stravinsky's codas.

7. **The following works also offer excellent examples of five-part and seven-part rondos.**

Five-Part Rondos

*Haydn, Piano Sonata No. 37 in D major, III

+Mozart, "Mi tradi quell' alma ingrata" from *Don Giovanni*

+Beethoven, Piano Sonata in A major, Op. 2, No. 2, II

*Beethoven, Sonata Op. 13, II

Beethoven, Symphony No. 3, II, with Fugal Development

Mendelssohn, Concerto for Violin, finale

Schumann, Aufschwung from Fantasiestücke Op. 12 for Piano

Brahms, Trio Op. 40 for piano, violin, and horn, IV

Ravel, String Quartet, IV

Berg, *Lyric Suite*, II

Seven–Part Rondos

*Mozart, Sonata in B♭ major, K. 570, II

+Beethoven, Piano Sonata in A major, Op. 2, No. 2, IV

Mozart, Piano Trio in G, III, K.564

Beethoven, Violin Sonata in A minor, Op. 23, III

Sonata-Rondo Form

While seven-part rondos with three contrasting episodes can be found, most seven-part rondos in the Classical period and thereafter are in *sonata-rondo form*, outlined in Figure 10.2. The distinguishing characteristics of a sonata rondo are as follows:

- The use of transitions and retransitions, often quite elaborate and with distinct thematic material.
- A second episode that modulates and is developmental.
- A return of the first episode in the tonic key, in the manner of a ST recapitulation.

Figure 10.2 *Sonata-rondo form.*

Refrain 1	Episode 1	Refrain 2	Episode 2/Development	Refrain 3	Episode 3	Refrain 4 Coda
A	**B**	**A**	**C**	**A**	**B′**	**A**
Tonic	Dominant	Tonic	Various	Tonic	Tonic	Tonic

With few exceptions, the sonata rondo form is found in the finales of multi-movement works.[10] The refrain is not unlike that of a regular rondo, with symmetrical periods or rounded binary forms being most common. When all of the characteristics cited above are incorporated, the sonata-rondo emerges as one of the most intriguing and elaborate of musical forms. Most theorists assert that a true sonata-rondo form must have all of these characteristics, in particular a central developmental or modulatory episode. The developmental function of this episode is most important in distinguishing a sonata-rondo from a seven-part rondo. When a seven-part rondo has a closed theme in a small form for its central episode (C), as in the Mozart Piano Sonata in A minor, K. 310, III and the Beethoven String Quartet, Op. 18, No. 4, IV, the form is best understood as a seven-part rondo form, even with the return of the B material in tonic. Each of the characteristics of sonata-rondo form will be discussed with examples to illustrate some common formal strategies.

FIRST EPISODE: TRANSITIONS AND RETRANSITIONS

After a PAC to close the refrain, a sonata rondo will continue with a transitional passage that will modulate to the dominant and lead to the main theme in the first episode (B). The main theme of the episode will often be periodic. The transition may be heard as a separate passage between the refrain and episode, or may be linked to and considered a part of the episode. A distinct closing theme may follow the main theme of the episode, followed by a retransition to close the episode. Both the transition and retransition may use neutral figuration but are just as likely to present their own distinct themes. Example 10.8 shows how Mozart incorporates all of these formal elements in episode 1 (B) of a sonata-rondo movement. Note how Mozart shapes this entire episode in the manner of the STA of a sonata exposition:

- After an eight-measure period is repeated to conclude the refrain, a transition presents a distinct new theme (measures 16–39) whose consequent phrase modulates to the dominant.
- A decisive arrival on V/V is prolonged (measures 32–39) to confirm the new key of B♭ major (V) and lead to a new periodic theme in the episode (measures 40–51).
- A distinct closing theme is presented (measures 51–63) followed by a retransition (measures 63–70) and a return to the refrain.

With distinct themes marking each function, the use of a periodic secondary theme in V, and a closing section with an expanded cadence, a listener may rightly perceive the movement as a sonata form up to this point. It is only with the return of the sixteen-measure refrain followed by a new episode that the rondo aspects of the movement become evident.

Because the initial transition and retransition often present distinct new themes, the material will be used in the subsequent episodes. As a result, these passages may

---

[10] See Beethoven's Symphony No. 4, Op. 60, II and String Quartet Op. 18, No. 3, II for examples of sonata-rondo forms in slow movements.

comprise a relatively large proportion of a sonata-rondo form movement. They will also contain rhythmic contrast and expanded cadential harmonies that infuse the music with tension, making the form more continuous and dramatic.

Example 10.8 *Mozart, Quintet for Piano and Winds in E♭ major, K. 532, III.*

a. Refrain, mm. 1–40.

(This excerpt continues on p. 234.)

(Example 10.8a, continued.)

fp
f
p
Ped. ❊
ii6
V/V
V
dominant preparation
B♭:
Episode 1 (B)
expanded upbeat
legato
HC

b. Episode 1, mm. 41–70.

(This excerpt continues on p. 238.)

(Example 10.8b, continued.)

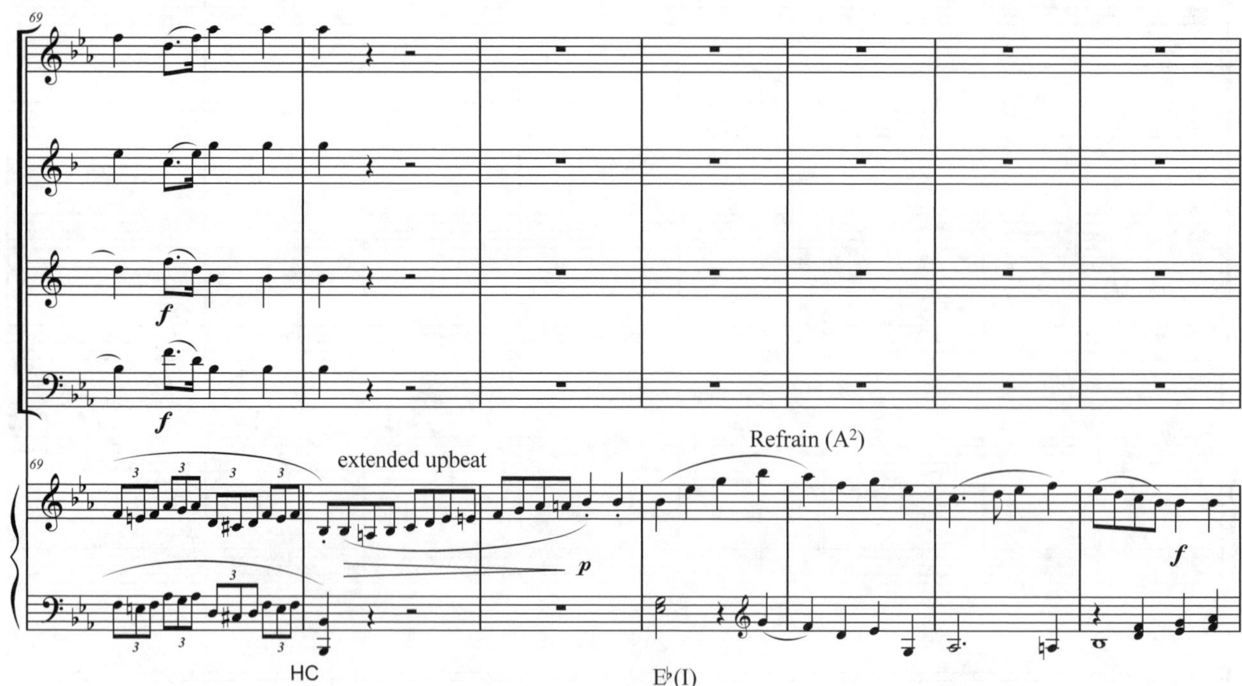

CENTRAL EPISODE

The second episode (C) of a sonata rondo will be modulatory. It may take on the character of a sonata form development by elaborating the previous themes and motives of the movement, present new themes in different keys, or combine these two approaches. Of particular interest is the manner in which this episode begins. It may, as previously mentioned, begin with transitional material that modulates to a new key and theme. (See Mozart Sonata in B♭ Major, III, Exercise 1.) Another technique is to begin the episode with a direct shift to tonic minor or a new key. (See Example 10.9a and Example 10.4.) The second refrain may also be abbreviated and fused with the beginning of the second episode. The finale of the Mozart Symphony No. 35, the "Haffner," uses just such a technique. The original refrain is an asymmetrical, contrasting period: an eight-measure antecedent phrase for strings only, followed by a ten-measure, consequent phrase for full orchestra. When the refrain returns for the second time (Example 10.9b), the consequent phrase is altered after the fourth measure to initiate the developmental episode.

Example 10.9a. Haydn, Symphony No. 101, IV, mm. 134–139.

b. Mozart, Symphony No. 35, IV, mm. 77–96.

A developmental episode (C section) will almost always close with a distinct retransition, which may or may not be new material. As in sonata form developments, expanded dominant harmony, melodic repetitions, and distinct breaks in texture are characteristic of the retransition. These passages generally create a strong sense of anticipation of the restatement of the refrain, heightening the dramatic qualities of the form. Sometimes the third refrain will be omitted, notably in the works of Mozart, as discussed in the exercises. The result is an A B A C B A design that compresses the form into six sections. The implications of this strategy for concluding the form will be discussed in the section on Final Refrain and Coda.

EPISODE 3: RECAPITULATION OF EPISODE I

The third episode (B′) will usually begin with a restatement of the transition that followed the first refrain, now altered to conclude in the tonic key. *The theme or themes of the first episode will then be heard in the tonic key*. As in the sonata form recapitulation of the ST, this recapitulation will often simply restate the theme, unaltered or only slightly varied apart from the transposition. Whether this section is abbreviated or not, it is the following retransition that must be recomposed since no modulation back to tonic is required. This retransition may be expanded to create even greater anticipation of the final refrain or may even introduce new material to heighten this dramatic juncture. Sometimes it leads to the subdominant key and an apparent return of the refrain but in the "wrong" key. This technique results in a false recapitulation of the refrain, which subsequently will be altered to return to tonic and the close of the movement.[11]

FINAL REFRAIN AND CODA

Given the scope and complexity of many sonata-rondo forms and the fact that they conclude an entire work, a coda is almost always incorporated. A complete or abbreviated refrain that elides with a separate coda is one possibility. But if the composer wishes to avoid the predictability of a simple restatement of the refrain, he or she may delay, vary, or even omit the final refrain. A few common strategies may be identified.

- A coda follows the third episode (B′) using motives of the main refrain, and the movement closes without a separate restatement of the refrain.
- Variants of the refrain, with accelerated rhythmic activity and new continuations using cadential progressions will be presented. The final refrain is altered and becomes a coda to conclude the work, a fusion of final refrain and coda.
- The close of the third episode (B′) may lead to a section that sounds like a coda, with extensions and cadential reiterations. At some point a recall of a segment or phrase of the refrain is incorporated in the coda.

Mozart's Quintet for Piano and Winds (Example 10.8) illustrates a creative blending of these techniques. As the third episode (B′) closes, he uses a strategy encountered in several of his rondo and variation movements: a written out cadenza leading to expanded cadential phrases that suggest a coda is under way. This relatively lengthy passage, encompassing about fifty measures of music, builds to a climax and a strongly marked cadence emphasized by cadential trills (see Example 10.10). This cadence elides with a brief recall of the refrain; the consequent phrase is altered to create strong closure. A separate coda of reiterated cadential activity closes the movement. In cases where an abbreviated refrain follows coda-like closing material, the refrain may be perceived as occurring within the coda, or even as a parenthetical insertion.

Whether the final refrain is complete, abbreviated, or subsumed as part of a coda, some recall of the refrain is expected to close the movement. At the same time a sense of strong closure and finality must be conveyed, which a simple recall of the refrain may not achieve. It is this point in the form, therefore, that is often of greatest formal interest and which especially challenges a composer's skill and imagination.

---

[11] See for example the Beethoven Piano Sonata Op. 28 in D major, III, mm, 160–192.

Example 10.10 Mozart, Quintet for Piano and Winds, K. 452, III, close of cadenza and beginning of final refrain, mm. 197–217.

(This excerpt continues on p. 242.)

(Example 10.10, continued.)

Conclusion

On the surface, a rondo form is a rather straightforward design. Seemingly simple, tuneful and readily perceived, it is a sectional form that can easily lack formal complexity or interest. But in the hands of skilled composers, a rondo will present alluring themes, skillful connections between sections and surprising turns that can create a work of great interest. Frequently characterized as a form that is lively and lighthearted in its expressions, a rondo may exhibit pathos and drama as well as charm, wit, and exuberance.

SUGGESTED READINGS

For additional discussions of the treatment of rondo form in various eighteenth-century genres, see Fischer, "Further Thoughts on Haydn's Symphonic Rondo Finales," Galand, "Form, Genre, and Style in the Eighteenth-Century Rondo," and Neville, "The Rondo in Mozart's late Operas."

Review of Terms: In a sentence or two, define each of the following terms:

Rondeau Rondo Refrain Couplet Episode

Five-Part Rondo Seven-Part Rondo Sonata-Rondo

Exercises: Sonata-Rondo Forms

The guidelines for analyzing rondo forms (Exercises for Rondo Forms) should be used in analyzing sonata-rondo forms as well. Particular attention should be paid to the expected transitions and retransitions between sections. These passages can contain distinct themes and may be more extensive and elaborate than the main themes of the refrain and episodes. As in a sonata form, the themes of a sonata-rondo form may be shortened, expanded, omitted, or may recur in new contexts. The recapitulation of episode 1 (B) in episode 3 (B′), and the way the final refrain is treated offer possibilities for the reinterpretation of themes and formal functions. The works for these exercises are drawn from diverse examples found in the classical literature. Additional examples of rondo and sonata-rondo forms found in vocal music, concertos, and post tonal music will be discussed in later chapters.

AURAL ANALYSIS

1. **Mozart, Symphony No. 35, "Haffner," III.** This movement is one of Mozart's most exuberant sonata-rondo finales. Based on your listening, make a sketch or diagram of the form. Some points to listen for: a) the transition starts as an extension of the refrain and ends with a rhythmic break on a HC, thus it may be perceived apart from the first episode; b) a 16-measure periodic theme opens the first episode followed by a lively closing section that begins like the transition and ends with a DC; this DC marks the beginning of the retransition; c) within the central developmental episode (the beginning shown in Example 10.8b), Mozart elaborates both the refrain and the main theme of the other episodes; d) when the episode theme appears it is prepared and initially presented like a "false recapitulation," that is, an unexpected and premature return of this theme; e) each of the episodes closes with a different retransitions, the third retransition being especially playful; f) the final refrain begins as a clear restatement but leads to a formal reinterpretation of the transition theme as the coda begins.

2. ***Beethoven, Piano Sonata Op. 13, III.** Several features of this work should be noted in analyzing the formal design: a) the refrain is an asymmetrical period with several interesting phrase extensions. Take note how these extensions are handled in subsequent refrains; b) the first episode incorporates several themes in a complex thematic group. Where exactly does the main theme of the episode and the retransition begin? c) The retransition is emphasized with distinct rhythmic and textural processes that lead to a HC; d) the third refrain and transition are fused, drawing on a technique used in sonata form recapitulations; e) the coda makes a surprising modulation marked by a parenthetic insertion before a brusque final cadence.

3. ***Haydn, Symphony No. 101 in D major.** This movement presents a refrain in a straightforward binary form, while the first episode is an expansive secondary theme group. Nonetheless, the formal boundaries within the episode are clearly articulated by strong cadences. a) Which themes of this episode contain material related to the refrain? b) Trace the modulations of the central developmental episode, beginning in measure 138. c) The return to tonic and the beginning of the third refrain are marked by a decisive break in rhythmic motion and texture, but the refrain is recalled in a surprising new texture. d) The return of the first episode also is treated in a creative manner; find the phrase connection between the refrain and this third episode. e) Finally, consider whether Haydn's subdued recall of the main theme of the refrain may be perceived as an insertion within the coda or as a distinct restatement followed by a separate coda.

4. **+Beethoven, Piano Sonata in G major, Op. 31, No. 1, III.** This movement is a reasonably clear example of a sonata-rondo form. The B sections are relatively brief, comprised of a repeated phrase. Of interest here is Beethoven's handling of

the final refrain and coda, which incorporates elements of a cadenza while fusing prior material.

5. **Additional movements for analysis.** The following movements offer contrasting examples of how a sonata-rondo form may be structured. The Mozart Quintet eliminates the second refrain. The Brahms Quartet is an extended rondo with four episodes and a cadenza. The Haydn Symphony is noteworthy for the absence of a coda. The finale of Beethoven's Symphony No. 2 contains an unusual phrase structure for the lively and playful refrain, a great number of different themes, and an exceptionally long and dramatic coda.

   Mozart, Quintet for Piano and Winds in E♭, K. 532, III
   Haydn, Symphony No. 88, in G , IV
   Beethoven, Symphony No. 2, in D major, IV
   Brahms, Piano Quartet Op. 25, in G minor, I

ANALYTIC EXERCISE

6. ***Mozart, Piano Sonata in B♭ major, K. 333, III.** This rich movement illustrates most of the formal characteristics and strategies of sonata-rondo Forms. After analyzing the phrase structure of the refrain (measures 1–16), listen to the movement at least twice without a score. Take note of any passages that strike you as interesting or surprising. Listen for recurring transitional and retransitional themes, note the number of themes and keys in the central episode, and consider how the final refrain is approached and treated. Using a score, answer the following questions about the tonal design and thematic elements. The answers should lead toward an understanding of the design of the movement. In addition to completion of a formal diagram, a description of the some of the salient features of the formal structure should be included.

   a. **Tonal Design:**

      1) The opening 16-measure refrain is in B♭ major. The refrain returns in the same key beginning in measures __________, __________, and __________.
      2) The phrase beginning in measure 16 modulates to the key of __________
      3) A new theme is stated beginning in measure 24 in the key of __________.
      4) The cadence in measures 35–36 is a __________ cadence in the key of __________.
      5) The phrase beginning in measure 36 modulates to __________.
      6) The phrase beginning in measure 56 modulates to __________.
      7) A modulation takes place in measures 72–75 to the key of __________.
      8) The opening measures of the refrain recur beginning in measure 91 in the key of __________.
      9) After measure 91, dominant preparation for the return to B♭ begins in measure__________.
      10) Measure 148 begins a restatement of the theme from measure __________, now in the key of __________.

11) The thematic material beginning in measure 164 is in the key of __________ and recalls the material first heard in measures__________. The harmony that concludes this passage in measure 171 functions as a __________.

b. Thematic design, formal functions, and phrase structure:

1) Describe how the refrain is varied, if at all, when it is restated.
2) What is the formal function of measures 16–24? How many times does this passage recur and which recurrence is expanded?
3) What is the formal function of measures 36–40? In what measures does this passage recur?
4) The main theme of Episode 1 (B) is expanded when it recurs in Episode 3(B♭). In what measure does the expansion begin and where does it reach a PAC?
5) What type of passage precedes the final refrain? When does the coda to the movement begin?

c. Formal Diagram: Mozart, Sonata K. 333, III. Complete the diagram below:

Section	Measures	Key(s)	Comments
A (Refrain)	1–16	B♭ (I)	8-measure parallel period, varied repetition
Transition			
B (Episode 1)			
Retransition			
A			
Transition			
C			
Retransition			
A			
Transition			
B			
Retransition			
Cadenza			
A-Coda			

11 Ostinato and Variation Forms

Introduction

The term "variation" in music may refer to a fundamental compositional technique or to a formal genre. The technique of variation is a basic formal process by which musical ideas are embellished or elaborated. Variation techniques are wide ranging and may include ornamentation or rhythmic elaboration of melodic ideas, motivic manipulations, re-harmonization, changes in phrase structure, and changes in texture and timbre. Previous chapters have addressed the techniques of variation in many different contexts and formal levels. We noted how motivic variation, using techniques such as sequence, embellishment, and fragmentation, is used to develop or extend ideas. The processes of varied repetition, response, continuation, and expansion illustrate how variation of ideas is important to shaping phrase structures. Variation of musical ideas is also essential to conveying developmental functions. In the discussion of rounded binary and ternary forms, we observed how restatements of phrases or complete sections often entailed variation of previous material. Similarly we observed in sonata form that a recapitulation can be understood as a varied restatement of the exposition. The concept of variation is also essential to cyclic form, arch form, and to modification of other forms, as in the rondo variation. In short, the concept of variation is basic to musical form and applicable to a wide range of music.

While we will address certain techniques of variations, this discussion will focus on variations as a formal category and genre. *Theme and variation* form refers to a work or movement in which a self-contained theme or musical idea is stated and then repeated several times in varied form. The formal design of variations tends to be additive in that the form results from a succession of variations, one added after another. The theme and each variation comprise a section of the form, which might be designated A^1 A^2 A^3 and so on. The number of variations is not set; a composer may write as many variations as he or she sees fit. Consequently, there is no prescribed formal hierarchy or contrast in formal function between sections. There are, however, ways to shape the variations so that larger sectional designs are created, a point to be discussed further.

Two general types of variation forms are commonly used in music: ostinato variations and theme and variations. The term *ostinato*—Italian for *obstinate*—refers to any musical figure or idea that is continuously repeated within a phrase, section or entire composition. *Ostinato variations* are composed over a bass line or harmonic progression that is repeated continuously throughout a composition. Varied musical ideas and textures are presented with each repetition. The ostinato is usually 4–8 measures long, in the form of a single phrase or period. Ostinato variations are continuous in that the phrases tend to elide one into the other. Conversely, *theme and variations* tend to be sectional because the theme is normally a small binary or ternary form of 2–4 phrases. Because the theme is a self-contained, closed form there are slight breaks or pauses after each variation. The basis of a theme and variations is the original melody of the theme and its harmonic and formal structure.

Both types of variations are often written for solo instruments, in particular solo keyboard. Ostinati were also used in vocal works of the Baroque era as well as movements from suites. They serve as a basic compositional technique in many types of music in the nineteenth and twentieth centuries as well. Multi-movement sonatas, chamber music, and symphonic works frequently incorporate theme and variations. Because ostinato variations are based on shorter themes they often contain a great number of variations. For example, Bach's monumental Chaconne in D minor for unaccompanied violin contains thirty-two statements of the eight-measure ostinato. Theme and variation compositions tend to have four to ten variations, although some monumental variations, such as the *Goldberg Variations* by Bach or the *Diabelli Variations* by Beethoven, have over thirty variations.

Ostinato variations developed and flourished from the sixteenth to eighteenth centuries. Theme and variations developed in the the eighteenth century. Various mixtures of these types may be found in latter periods. Within these two categories, types of variations may be identified depending on the nature of the theme, the genre in which is it used, and the manner in which elements of the theme are retained or varied. The following discussion will address approaches to composing variations in different styles and genres. It will also cover the general use of an ostinato as a constructive device.

Ostinato Variations

GROUND BASS

Ostinato variations, often identified as *continuous variations*, are constructed over a repeated bass line referred to as a *ground bass* or *basso ostinato* (Italian). The ostinato may incorporate a recurring harmonic pattern. Both the bass line and the harmonic progression may be subject to variation. Over the "obstinate" bass line a composer writes a succession of varied textures and melodies. Large-scale shape is often achieved by gradual increases in rhythmic motion and changes in density, dynamics, and range. Baroque ostinato variations normally remain in a single key throughout, though a change in mode may provide contrasts between groups of variations.

The precedent for the basso ostinato lies in Renaissance dances based on repeated harmonic progressions using root position triads. The bass lines were characterized by a consistent rhythm and a simple diatonic pattern. An example of such a basso ostinato is heard in the well-known Canon in D major for three violins and bass by Johann Pachelbel, written in the late seventeenth century (Example 11.1a). The ground bass is a sequence of descending thirds ending on the dominant chord, a characteristically simple but strong bass line. The canon occurs in the three violins that continue throughout the composition in strict imitation over the repetitive bass line. Though titled a canon, the work is, in effect, an ostinato variation. As the canon progresses, the rhythmic motion and range gradually increase, giving shape to the entire movement. The changes counter the consistent use of diatonic harmony and a single key throughout.

Example 11.1 *Ostinato bass lines.*

a. Pachelbel, Canon in D.

b. Buxtehude, Ciaccona.

c. Pachelbel, Ciaccona.

While a number of different bass-line patterns may be found in Baroque basso ostinato, ascending or descending tetrachords are often used. These tetrachords may be minor or major as illustrated in Examples 11.1b and 11.2a. The step-wise motion of these patterns leads to the fifth scale degree and may arrive at a HC or be extended to close on a PAC. Example 11.1b shows a descending minor-scale tetrachord with slight embellishment in measures 2–3. In some ostinato variations the bass line will remain unchanged throughout while in others it will be subjected to varied elaborations. Example 11.1c shows a basso ostinato stated at the outset of a Ciaccona by Pachelbel and an elaboration of the ostinato used in one of the variations. In many works using ground basses, the bass line remains unaltered, though changes in specific harmonies may occur.

Composers of vocal works would use ostinato bass lines to provide a harmonic foundation, allowing the vocal parts to develop ideas freely in response to the text. For example, a simple descending tetrachord serves as an ostinato throughout the first section of the closing duet from Monteverdi's opera *The Coronation of Poppea* (Example 11.2a). The well-known lament from Purcell's opera *Dido and Aeneas* is based on a descending tetrachord elaborated with chromatic passing tones (Example 11.2b). This chromatic *ground bass* was associated with an expression of grief. "Dido's Lament" is an example of a vocal work that repeats the ground bass throughout but can be viewed in terms of a larger formal design when the vocal parts are considered. Analysis of the textual phrases, thematic repetitions and contrasts, and cadences reveals a two-part division of the entire aria. This is addressed in the exercises that follow.

Example 11.2 *Ostinato bass lines in vocal works.*

a. Monteverdi, *The Coronation of Poppea,* closing duet.

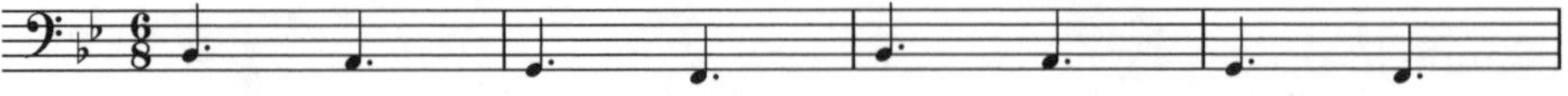

b. Purcell, "Dido's Lament" from *Dido and Aeneas.*

PASSACAGLIA AND CHACONNE

Two closely related genres of the Baroque era are particularly associated with ostinato variations, namely the *passacaglia* and the *chaconne*.[1] These instrumental genres are similar in that 1) they make use of ostinato bass lines or harmonies; 2) they are typically in slow or moderate tempos and triple meter; and 3) they originally were types of dances. Sets of variations on these dances were composed and published for solo string instruments and keyboards beginning in the early seventeenth century.[2] Chaconnes tended to be in a major key and to present a complete harmonic progression at the outset. Passacaglias were in minor key and used a basso ostinato stated unaccompanied at the outset. In practice, the use of the terms was often indiscriminate. Many chaconnes were composed over a continuous ground bass. Conversely, works titled *passacaglia* would sometimes begin with a full harmonic texture that could vary in the course of the movement. Over time, the distinctions between the two types became blurred.

The most famous examples of each of these genres are two expansive works by Bach: the Passacaglia in C minor for organ, and the Chaconne in D minor for violin. The professed distinctions between a chaconne and a passacaglia are likely based on these well-known examples. The basso ostinato in a passacaglia may take the form of an original bass line such as that which begins Bach's Passacaglia for organ. Like the stock ground basses one encounters, this basso ostinato is a diatonic pattern that clearly establishes the key. In the course of the variations, Bach places this melodic bass line in an upper voice, thus introducing variations in the bass line itself.

Example 11.3 Bach, Passacaglia in C minor for Organ, basso ostinato theme.

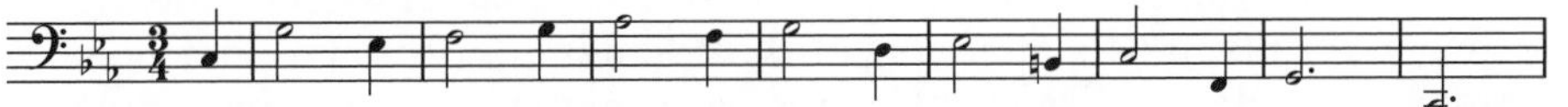

By contrast, Bach's Chaconne is based on a harmonic progression presented at the outset of the movement. The triple meter, dotted rhythm, and emphasis on the second beat of the measure are often cited as characteristics of the sarabande, a slow stately dance of the seventeenth and eighteenth centuries associated with the chaconne. Here it is the underlying harmonic motion from tonic to dominant rather than a basso ostinato that is repeated throughout. An analysis of the recurrences of this harmonic ostinato shows variations in the specific harmonies with changes in the bass line. In the course of the movement Bach uses descending major, minor, and chromatic bass lines as he varies his textures and the specific harmonic progression (see Example 11.4).

Example 11.4 Bach, Chaconne from Partita No. 2 in D minor for unaccompanied solo violin, BWV 1004.

a. Theme, mm. 1–4.

b. mm. 21–25.

[1] The terms *ciaconna* (Spanish) and *passacaille* (French) are also encountered.

[2] The chaconne and passacaglia were the basis for variations played by Spanish guitarists in the early seventeenth century. The chaconne was originally a Latin American dance; the passacaglia was a strolling dance that preceded or followed songs and other dances.

c. mm. 57–60.

d. mm. 133–37.

One very basic step in analyzing a chaconne or passacaglia is to identify and number the statements of the ostinato. One may then consider how the variations may be grouped into larger sections within the continuous form. Both of these relatively lengthy works by Bach can be divided into sections that group variations together in different ways. In the Passacaglia in C minor, the ground bass is transferred to the uppermost line beginning in variation 11 and even disappears briefly in variation 15. It is restored to the bass line in variations 16–20. Thus the first half of the movement divides into three sections on the basis of the disposition of the bass theme (Vars. 1–10, 11–15, 16–20). Each group of variations presents varied textures and increases in rhythmic motion and range. Following these 20 statements, the first part of the bass theme is used as the subject for a double fugue that leads to a final statement of the bass theme in the top voice and a coda that contains the most elaborate rhythmic textures of the movement.

In the Chaconne in D minor there are 32 statements of the eight-measure theme, which results in 64 statements of the opening four-measure harmonic progression. The movement clearly divides into three parts on the basis of a change in mode to D major in measures 133, returning to D minor in measure 209. In the course of the movement Bach exploits the wide range of techniques available to a virtuosic violinist including brilliant passage work, compound melodies, double stops and chordal textures, wide-ranging, rapid arpeggios, and repeated notes using *bariolage*.[3] These various instrumental techniques provide one way to consider the grouping of variations. Contrasts in rhythm, texture, and harmonic progressions also shape the succession of variations. The shape and subdivisions of the three large sections are addressed in the exercises that follow.

Ostinato as a Constructive Device

The ostinato variations prevalent in Baroque music were displaced by theme and variations in the late eighteenth century, though some noteworthy examples are found in the nineteenth and twentieth centuries.[4] The use of an ostinato as a constructive device in sections of a work remained a viable compositional technique, however. Various examples of ostinati used in nineteenth- and twentieth-century works are shown in Examples 11.5a–d.

[3] *Bariolage* refers to rapid alternation between open and stopped strings, usually on the same pitch, producing a contrast in tone quality.

[4] For example, see Beethoven, 32 Variations in C minor, WoO 80 for solo piano and Brahms, Symphony No. 4, IV, each of which is a chaconne based on an eight-measure harmonic progression. See also the passacaglias in the Fourth Sea Interlude from Britten's opera *Peter Grimes*, Op. 33b, and Berg's opera, *Wozzeck*, Act IV, scene 2, and the Prelude No. 12 from *24 Preludes and Fugues*, Op. 87 by Shostakovich.

Nineteenth-century composers often used ostinato figures for their expressive effect or as a compositional device. In the Beethoven Symphony No. 9, a sudden appearance of a chromatic bass ostinato imports a tragic expression to the close of the first movement (Example 11.5a). Chopin's Berceuse (Lullaby) for piano is based entirely on a harmonic ostinato of a single measure using only tonic and dominant harmonies. The undulating motion of this figure is part of the calming effect of the lullaby (Example 11.5b). Over this ostinato Chopin elaborates a variety of pianistic melodic figures. In vocal works such as Schubert's lied "Gretchen am Spinnrade," a persistent ostinato rhythm is used in the accompaniment to convey an element of the text. Though harmonic changes and slight variants in melodic contour occur, the persistent rhythm and narrow range of the figure convey the monotony of the spinning wheel and the hopelessness of the lovelorn singer (Example 11.5c).

Example 11.5 *Examples of ostinati in nineteenth-century music.*

a. Beethoven, Symphony No. 9, I, Coda.

b. Chopin, Berceuse.

c. Schubert, "Gretchen am Spinnrade."

d. Bizet, "Carillon" from *L'Arlésienne Suite No. 1.*

Ostinato figures may also take the form of a repeated melody or an insistent rhythmic figure. Bizet's "Carillon" from the *L'Arlésienne Suite No. 1* is in a ternary form whose first section uses the simple, three-note ostinato shown in Example 11.5d. This figure is given to the horns and imitates the pealing bells of a carillon, a background to the principal melodic line.

Example 11.6 *Ostinati as the basis of an entire composition.*

a. Grieg, "In the Hall of the Mountain King," *Peer Gynt Suite.*

b. Ravel, *Bolero.*

Some works employ an ostinato as the primary basis of an entire movement. Grieg's "In the Hall of the Mountain King" from the *Peer Gynt Suite* is based on a two-part melodic ostinato (Example 11.6a). The melody begins in the bass instruments and is gradually taken up by other instruments in higher registers. As the binary melody repeats relentlessly, the dynamics and tempo progressively build to a climax, depicting the accelerating race through a mountain hall as trolls chase Peer Gynt. Similarly, Ravel's well-known orchestral work, *Bolero,* shows the hypnotic effect of a persistent rhythmic ostinato, which accompanies two alternating melodies. The result is a sectional variation form with ostinato (Example 11.6b). Changes in orchestral color and continually increasing dynamic levels and density are important factors in shaping the music.

Ostinati are frequently encountered in music of the twentieth century. In the absence of traditional tonal progressions, ostinati proved a useful means of establishing a pitch collection and a metric/rhythmic background for a work, or for passages within a work. Composers as diverse as Stravinsky, Bartók, Britten, and Shostakovich made effective use of ostinati. Britten, for example, uses an ostinato in one section of his music drama *Noye's Fludde* as a constructive and pictorial device (Example 11.7c). The metrically displaced rhythm of the bass, the dissonant cross relations, and the undulating contours convey the tumultuous motion of Noah's Ark as it fights the stormy seas.

Stravinsky's works make frequent use of ostinati. A technique he favored was the use of several ostinati of irregular length superimposed upon one another. This technique is used extensively in *The Rite of Spring* (Example 11.7d). In the excerpt shown, we hear 1) a rhythmic ostinato on a single pitch that conveys a consistent pulse (bassoons and timpani); 2) a four-measure melodic ostinato in the tubas; 3) a horn melody that is metrically displaced as it is repeated; and 4) a bass drum part that is in a conflicting triple meter. The dissonant pitch relations and cross rhythms create a layered texture of competing or conflicting ostinati.

Example 11.7 *Ostinati in Twentieth-century works.*

a. Britten, *Noye's Fludde.*

b. Stravinsky, *The Rite of Spring, Part I, R67.*

Such complex, polyrhythmic textures using several different ostinato rhythms are also found in African drumming music, which has been an influence on many contemporary composers, notably those of minimal music.[5] Composers as diverse as Ligeti and Reich have used ostinati in a new constructive manner based on metric transformations and cycles, which will be addressed in a later chapter. Finally, the prominence of ostinati can be observed in jazz and rock music, where improvisation and repetitions over repeated harmonic progressions abound.

[5] Minimal music refers to compositions based on persistent repetition and very gradual changes, often using simple, diatonic ostinati. The use of ostinati in twentieth-century music in general reflects an increased interest in non-western music and cultures.

AURAL ANALYSIS

Listen to the musical examples prior to studying the score. Note the following aspects as you listen.

1. Is the ostinato in the form of a ground bass or a harmonic/melodic idea? If a ground bass, is it stated alone at the outset?
2. Does the ostinato arrive at a HC or is it elided to a PAC?
3. Is the bass line ostinato consistent throughout or is it varied? Do these changes introduce variations in the harmonic progression?
4. If the composition is a vocal work, listen again with a focus on the vocal line(s). Do the cadences in the vocal line coincide with those of the ostinato? Identify repetitions, restatements, and contrasts in the vocal line.
5. If the work is instrumental ostinato variations, are there any large sections evident? Are variations grouped together on the basis of systematic increases in rhythmic motions or changes in texture and dynamics?

SCORE ANALYSIS

Listen to the composition using a score and reconsider the items noted above. In addition, note any marked changes in texture or rhythm, registral transfer of an ostinati bass line, and the embellishments or variations on the bass line. The analysis of variations tends to be largely descriptive. Focus your descriptions by considering the basic compositional issue of how to give larger shape to the variations as a whole and how continuity from one variation to another is achieved. Specific questions are given for individual pieces.

1. **Purcell, "Dido's Lament" from *Dido and Aeneas* and Bach, "Crucifixus" from the *Mass in B minor*.**

   a. These two celebrated vocal works use a descending, chromatic ground bass to reflect the expression of grief and sorrow. Complete a harmonic analysis of each of the initial statements, including roman numerals and figured bass. What similarities or differences do you observe in the bass lines and their harmonization in the two compositions? Listen to each composition and mark the beginning of each ground bass repetition and the cadence at the end of each repetition. Note any marked changes in the harmonic progression. Why do each of the final presentations of the ground bass stand apart from the others? How are the two compositions different in their treatment of the final statement?

   b. Now study the vocal lines. Consider how the vocal phrases fit with the repetitions of the ground bass. Note the length of phrases and the cadences in the vocal parts. Do the vocal cadences coincide with the bass line cadences? How do the relations of the parts serve to articulate the form of each composition? Consider the formal design of the vocal parts on the basis of text, thematic repetition and contrast, and cadences. The two compositions are obviously contrasting in the number of vocal lines. In the *Crucifixus,* observe how changes in texture and the overlapping of vocal entrances shape the form and divide the movement into sections.

   c. Write a short essay summarizing your findings and comparing the two compositions. You may wish to include a chart to illustrate your formal analysis, and musical examples to compare the harmonization of the ground within each movement.

2. **Bach, Chaconne from the Partita No. 2 in D minor for unaccompanied solo violin, BWV 1004.**

   a. The theme and representative variants on the bass line were illustrated in Example 11.4. In the variations, structural harmonies are maintained—particularly the initial tonic and the cadential harmonies—while varied bass lines or harmonies occur frequently. Find three variations that use different elaborations of the underlying descending bass line. Complete a harmonic analysis of these variations and observe the similarities and differences among them and in relation to the original bass line. You may wish to analyze other variations to note additional elaborations of the bass line, particularly in the major section.

   b. Figure 11.1 gives an outline of the possible subdivisions within each of the three large sections. What is the basis for these divisions? Consider the various rhythmic textures, types of figures (scales, arpeggios, compound lines, chords), and changes in range and density. Does contrast in rhythmic activity group variations on the basis of accelerated motion from one variation to the next? The relationship between the changing melody and recurring bass line is another perspective to consider. Are other divisions (larger or smaller) possible? Do changes in character play a role in shaping the succession or division of variations?

Figure 11.1 *Bach, Chaconne: outline of variation groupings.*

A:	**D minor** **mm. 1–24**	**25–48–88**	**89–132 (theme restated)**
B:	**D major** **mm. 133–148**	**149–176**	**177–208**
A:	**D minor** **mm. 209–228**	**229–248**	**249–257restate theme with extension**

   c. In this work Bach explores the technical capabilities of the violin. Identify various techniques or textures related to the instrument, i.e. contrasts in register and range, compound lines, double stops, arpeggiated chordal textures, and bariolage. Do some variations group together on the basis of these techniques?

   d. Which variations have the most complex textures and elaborate harmonization? Are there climaxes within large sections? If so, how are they marked? Where are the most climactic moments? What do the endings of the three large sections of the composition have in common? How is each unique?

   e. Finally, consider how these various factors may influence the use of dynamics and pacing in a performance. Listen to 2–3 different performances of the work noting similarities and differences in interpretative decisions. Drawing on your analytic findings, discuss aspects that may have influenced the interpretation.

3. **Holst, Chaconne from the *First Suite in E♭* for Band.** A piano reduction of this composition is reproduced here. In this staple of twentieth-century wind literature, Holst draws on the Baroque variation techniques of ground bass. What alternate and perhaps more accurate title might have been used for this movement? To what extent is the bass theme altered in the course of the movement?

The movement and theme is in E♭ major. Where is that key confirmed by strong cadential activity? What key is tonicized in variations 2–3 (measures 17–32)? Carefully compare the statement in variation 9 (measures 73–80) with the original theme. What technique does Holst use to vary the theme and how does it affect the tonality in these measures?

As in previous works, consider how the variations group into larger sections. Holst shapes the composition to reach a climactic final statement of the ground bass theme in the original key. Where does this climactic point occur and how is this emphasized? Speculate as to why Holst indicates *ritard al fine* near the end. What becomes of the bass theme in the closing measures of the movement (measure 122–end)?

First Suite in E♭.

I. Chaconne.

pesante
C
p
dim.
p
D
p
pesante
E
cresc. poco a poco
F
ff
maestoso

ADDITIONAL WORKS FOR STUDY

The following works are ostinati variations or make use of an ostinato as a compositional device.

+Handel, Passacaille from the Suite No. 7 in G minor for Harpsichord
Beethoven: Thirty-two Variations in C minor for Piano
*Schubert: "Der Doppelganger" for voice and piano
Mussorkgsky, Introduction, Act I, and "Warlaam's Lied" from *Boris Godunov*
Brahms, Symphony 4, IV
Brahms, *Variations on a Theme of Haydn*, Finale
Shostakovich, Prelude in G♯ minor for Piano from the *Preludes and Fugues*.
Stravinsky, Passacaglia from the *Septet*
Berg. *Wozzeck,* Act I, Scene IV, Passacaglia
Britten, Fourth Sea Interlude from *Peter Grimes*
Holst, *The Planets: Mars*
+Corigliano, *Fantasia on an Ostinato*
Pärt, *Frates*

Theme and Variations

INTRODUCTION

The theme of a composition in theme-and-variations form is usually a small binary or ternary form, and there are normally pauses or slight breaks between variations. Consequently the term *sectional variation* is used to describe this type of variation form. This form was particularly prevalent in music of the Classical and Romantic periods. The source of the theme was an important influence on the general approach to the variations. Variations on a preexisting melody generally drew on tunes well known to an intended audience and were likely to be a separate solo piece. The titles usually indicated the source of the theme's melody, such as *Seven Variations on the Volkslied "God Save the King"* by Beethoven. More importantly, variations on popular tunes tended to be improvisatory in style and placed emphasis on varying the familiar melody. The results were often light in character and expression and readily accessible to listeners. Conversely, variation movements within multi-movement works such as sonatas or symphonies were normally based on original themes and were more likely to present complex variations and a wide range of expressive effects, often serious, dramatic or reflective.

Exceptions are found to these distinctions, most famously in three masterpieces of the genre for solo keyboard: Bach's *Goldberg Variations*, Beethoven's *Diabelli Variations*, and Brahms's *Variations and Fugue on a Theme by Handel*. Each of these solo keyboard works is an extended set of technically and interpretively demanding variations, containing a wide range of variation types.[6] Notable examples in the chamber music repertoire are two works by Schubert: the Piano Quintet in A major, Op. 114, D. 667 (nicknamed the "Trout"), and the String Quartet in D minor (nicknamed "Death and the Maiden"). These works draw on Schubert's own lieder for theme and variation movements.

A basic aspect of analyzing theme and variations is recognizing the *fixed and variable* elements of a theme; that is, which features of the theme are retained and which are varied, replaced, or eliminated. Generally speaking, in theme and variations through the eighteenth and nineteenth centuries, the formal design, phrase structure, and harmonic structure were the most important elements of the theme to be retained. The melody of the theme is frequently the most salient feature of a set of variations, although it may sometimes be omitted while other elements are retained and varied. The following discussion addresses general types of variations and basic techniques. The various types are not necessarily exclusive, and a particular variation might employ two or more different approaches.

MELODIC VARIATIONS

Melodic variations are those in which the melody is retained in its original or varied form. Many variations of the late eighteenth and early nineteenth century relied a great deal on this approach. If a melody is varied, the extent to which it is recognizable will, of course, vary. While the formal structure and tonal design of the theme is also retained, melodic variations often incorporate embellishments or variations on the specific harmonic progressions as well as new accompaniments. Several types of variations may be identified that can be understood as melodic variations.

Cantus firmus variation. In this type of variation, the melody is unchanged or in slightly simplified form throughout a variation. This approach may be understood as a contrapuntal type of variation since the emphasis is on creating countermelodies or new accompaniments around the fixed theme. The theme may be placed in a different register or instrument but is clearly recognizable. The earliest instances of this variation technique are found in chorale variations, choral preludes, and chorale cantata movements of the Baroque era.[7] One well-known variation movement by Haydn, his String Quartet Op. 76, No. 3, II, uses this technique for each of the variations. Schubert also favored the use of a fixed melody in his variations, though not exclusively.

Figural variation. A figural variation presents the melody with diminutions (melodic/rhythmic elaborations) that make use of a consistent rhythmic and/or pitch pattern—"figures"—for example, dotted rhythms, scale patterns, running triplets or sixteenths, and so forth. Mozart's set of variations on a melody now familiar as "Twinkle Twinkle Little Star" illustrates this type of variation. Example 11.8 shows the first short section of the theme and two of the subsequent variations.

---

[6] See also *Variations on a Theme by Haydn* by Brahms and *Enigma Variations* by Elgar, both of which are large-scale sets of variations for orchestra.

[7] Cantus firmus techniques originated in Renaissance masses and motets in which composers would often set a well-known hymn tune apart from the other voices in longer note values. They could then compose new counterpoint or counterpoint based on the cantus firmus motives against the cantus.

Example 11.8 Mozart, *Variations on "Ah, vous, dirai-je, Maman."*

a. Theme, mm. 1–8.

b. Variation I. Figural variation.

c. Variation VII, *Minore*. Contrapuntal and skeletal variation.

Variation I (Example 11.8b) is based on a continuous sixteenth-note figure that elaborates the melody. While a single pitch pattern is sometimes used in a figural variation, often more than one pattern is used in response to the shape of the original melodic line and to give breadth to the figural melody. In this example there is a neighbor note figure **a** followed by a leap/scalar figure **b.** Successive variations will sometimes present figural variations in increasingly shorter durations, creating a gradual rhythmic acceleration from one variation to the next. This technique may also include inversion of the textures (see Chapter 5) in successive variations.

Contrapuntal variation. Variation VII of the Mozart work (Example 11.9c) provides an example in which the melody is treated in imitation followed by a series of suspensions and an active bass line. Such *contrapuntal variations* may also employ fugal and canonic procedures as well as embellishments of the melody.

Simplification or skeletal variation. Variation VII also shows the technique of simplification of the melody in measures 3–8. In this type of variation pitches are removed from the melody, hence it is sometimes called a skeletal variation. This variation also is a *minore*, a change in mode that inflects the variation with an obvious change in character. A *maggiore or minore* variation is typical of many sets of variations.

Embellishment variation. A technique in between the cantus firmus and figural variation is the embellishment of some segments of the melody while retaining others. This technique is seen in Example 11.9b, which is based on another well-known tune set to variations by Beethoven (Example 11.9a). In an embellishment variation the melody is readily discernible and the rhythmic motion will be more varied than in a figural variation. As in most all types of melodic variations, changes in the rhythmic accompaniments are also found.

Example 11.9 Beethoven, *Variations on "God Save the King."*

a. Theme.

b. Variation I. Embellishment variation.

c. Variation VI. Character variation.

Character variation. In most variations changes in rhythm and texture are found such that the general character is inevitably changed. Some variations, however, convey a change in character related to a specific conventional style or dance. Variation VI in the example by Beethoven (Example 11.8c) uses a persistent dotted-rhythm figure and a change in meter that sets the original melody in the character of a March. While this variation could be considered embellishing or figural, its clear march-like elements make it a good example of a character variation. The change in meter and tempo is indicative, though not requisite, of character variations. Another type of character variation entails setting the theme in the style of an aria, which would usually result in a slower tempo, legato articulations, and conventional ornamentation such as trills and turns.

FIXED FORM VARIATIONS

Another approach to variations that developed in the nineteenth century was composing new melodic ideas and textures using the form and tonal structure of the theme. Phrase structure, cadences and harmonic underpinnings were retained, but specific harmonic progressions and voice leading, rhythms and textures would be varied widely. Although motivic elements of the original theme may have been used, the overall melody of the theme was discarded in such variations.

Beethoven was a notable innovator in this regard. As early as the String Quartet Op. 18, No. 5, slow movement, he incorporated variations with marked contrasts in character and melodic content. His late works, in particular the Piano Sonatas Op. 109 and Op. 111, and the String Quartets Opuses 127, 131, 132, and 135, make extensive use of this type of variation in slow movements. The fourth movement of the String Quartet Op. 131 in C♯ minor illustrates this approach well. Recall the theme, a small binary form with a varied repetition of each eight-measure sentence discussed in Chapter 3 (see Example 3.12b). Although remnants of the melodic theme are heard in some of the variations, Beethoven recasts the theme in a wide range of textures and contrasting expressions that retain the formal and harmonic structure but little else.

Example 11.10 shows the opening measures of variations 2 and 5. In each of these variations the sentence structure of the opening phrase and the structural harmonies of the theme are retained, but in strongly contrasting textures and with new melodic ideas. Variation 2 adds a one-measure introduction that establishes a simple, rather rustic accompaniment. A new melody is then stated by violin I and cello in turn. Variation 5 illustrates a feature of Beethoven's late variations: a reduction to a bare outline of the harmonic elements of the theme also evidenced in variation 6. Another feature of this set of variations is the *varied* repetition of phrases in each of the two parts, which allows for variations within each variation. This technique is sometimes referred to as a *double variation*.[8]

Example 11.10 Beethoven, String Quartet Op. 131 in Cs minor, IV.

a. Variation 2.

b. Variation 5.

Schumann and Brahms were influenced by Beethoven's approach to variations, departing from the typical melodic variations that were popular in the nineteenth century. Schumann criticized the triviality of variations that relied on melodic variation of popular themes. His *Symphonic Etudes* for piano, a set of twelve etude-style variations, uses the harmonic structure of the theme in a wide range of pianistic textures. The variations sometimes use the simple opening melody as a bass line or as background to the elaborate new texture. Other variations present new material that can be understood as counterpoint to the original theme, even though the theme is not always present.

[8] This technique is usually apparent by the absence of notated repeat signs originally seen in the theme. In this case, Beethoven also wrote out repeats in the original binary theme as well.

Example 11.11 shows the first phrase of the theme and Etude I (Variation I). The new idea that begins variation I is a counterpoint to the original theme, which is made clear in measure 5: the opening measure of the theme is heard above the new melody, now in the bass line.

Example 11.11 Schumann, *Symphonic Etudes.*

a. Theme, mm. 1–4.

b. Variation I, mm. 1–5.

Brahms, who wrote several masterpieces in theme-and-variation form, also stressed the importance of the bass line and harmonic structure in exploring the theme. He states in a letter of 1869 that "in a theme and variations it is *almost* [emphasis added] only the bass line that actually has meaning for me . . . If I vary only the melody then I cannot be more than clever or graceful . . . On a given bass I discover new melodies in it, I create."[9] An example of Brahms's variation techniques is addressed in the exercises.

FREE VARIATIONS

Variations of the nineteenth and twentieth centuries often departed from or abandoned the theme's formal structure. Melodic themes were subject to motivic fragmentation and transformation, while the phrase structure, textures, and form were subject to reinterpretation in any given variation. The general term *free variation* (or fantasy variation) is used to describe this type, in which a strongly contrasting expressive character is typical among the variations. Many fixed form variations are similar to free variations, though in the former the formal outline remains faithful to the original theme. Free variations, on

[9] Quoted by Elaine Sisman in "Variations," *The New Grove Dictionary of Music and Musicians*, 2nd edition, Vol. 26, edited by Stanley Sadie and John Tyrell.

the other hand, may make clear or fleeting reference to motives of the theme, but new phrase structures, meters, and tempos often mask any resemblance to the complete original theme. In many instances the theme is simply a source of material that is freely extracted and developed.

Elgar's *Enigma Variations,* fourteen variations on an original theme for orchestra (1899), is a well-known example of free variations. Each of the variations is meant to characterize a friend or colleague of the composer, thus the inspiration for the work is in part programmatic.[10] The theme is a short ternary melody (Example 11.12a) that incorporates a change in mode in the brief contrasting middle section.

Excerpts from two of the fourteen variations will give an idea how the theme is subjected to different transformations and characterizations. Variation 1 (dedicated to Elgar's wife Alice) initially presents the melody in a rhythmically altered and more continuous guise with delicate and wide-ranging accompaniments. Note that the pitch sequence and contour is maintained, ensuring the theme's identity. Though the ternary form of the theme is followed, the outer sections are expanded and the variation begins with a two-measure introduction. The original theme appears briefly in the third section of this variation, but it is set against a soaring countermelody. Variation XI, dedicated to the organist George Sinclair, presents an even more radical transformation of the theme. As in many of these variations, an introductory measure presents a new figure. What follows is a rapid juxtaposition of the two principal ideas of the theme, with the A theme compressed to two measures. The alternation of the two ideas and the combination of them with the new figures produces an entirely new formal structure, 41 measures in length.

In the course of the variations, Elgar incorporates contrasts in key, tempo, and mode, with variations in C major, C minor, and E♭ major. Two of the titled variations—Variation X, an Intermezzo, and Variation XIII, a Romanza—provide only fleeting reference to the theme, while others maintain the basic formal outline of the theme. Like many free variations for orchestra, marked contrasts in orchestration, articulation and dynamics contribute to the character of individual variations. The blend of programmatic inspiration and musical invention makes this one of the enduring works of the genre.

Example 11.12 Elgar, *Enigma Variations.*

a. Theme.

[10] Elgar titled the work, which refers to 1) the puzzle of whom the various movements characterize—they are indicated only by initials in the score; and 2) cryptic comments by the composer that the theme is in fact a countermelody to an existing popular theme. The first of these enigmas has been solved; the second remains a source of speculation.

b. Variation I (C.A.E), mm. 1–4 melody.

c. Variation XI (G.R.S.), mm. 1–6.

Many twentieth-century composers found free variations attractive because, like ostinati variations, they provided a formal framework conducive to diverse styles and harmonic languages. Orchestral variations, a genre firmly established by Brahms and then Elgar in the nineteenth century, are prevalent. Some twentieth-century variations take a traditional approach in using a tonal theme but make use of novel textures, harmonies, and orchestrations to create fresh approaches to the genre. For example, Britten's *Young Person's Guide to the Orchestra*, a set of orchestral variations on a theme by Purcell, is shaped by the systematic presentation of all of the instruments of the modern orchestra on variants of the refrain.[11] Other variations stress continuous development of pitch material, an approach favored by serial composers. Schoenberg's Variations for Orchestra, Webern's Symphony Op. 21, II, and Berg's opera *Wozzeck* are among the most notable serial works that incorporate a recurring twelve-tone row as a theme for variations.

A particular theme may simply serve as a store of harmonic, melodic, rhythmic, and textural resources which a composer extracts, transforms, and develops in fantasy-like variations. Bartók favored such variations, as exemplified by the Violin Concerto No. 2, slow movement. Works such as this often use a collection of pitches as the basis for variations that often seem far removed from the formal structure and melodic content of the original theme. Hindemith's *Symphonic Metamorphoses on a Theme of Carl Maria von Weber* (1934) is a four-movement symphonic work in which each movement draws on a theme by Weber, freely transforming and adapting it to a different form.

[11] See Chapter 10, Example 10.1.

Organization of Variations

A given set of variations may incorporate many different basic approaches as outlined. Furthermore, the order and grouping of variation types within a set will vary widely. Nonetheless, some patterns can be identified. In *tonal variations* of the eighteenth century, variations in successively smaller note values often shape a series of variations, particularly at the beginning of a set.[12] In addition to these *division variations*. Ratner observes that Classical variations normally incorporate 1) a *minore* or *maggiore* variation; 2) an *adagio* in the manner of an aria; 3) a contrapuntal variation, and 4) brilliant style variations, often as a finale. The most elaborate full-textured variations may occur as the finale while some well known examples conclude with a fugue.[13] Changes in mode if not key provide tonal contrast, though some variations will incorporate changes in key using relative as well as parallel keys or more remote relations. Beethoven's String Quartet Op. 127 in A♭ major, for example, has a slow variation movement that uses the remote keys of E major/F♭ major (♭VI), and C♯ minor/D♭ Major (IV) in two of the five variations.

In contrast to the standard additive variations, some sets of variations incorporate two different themes. This approach was favored by Haydn, notably in symphonic and string quartet movements, using five or seven variations on alternating themes (A1-B1-A2-B2-A3, or A1-B1-A2-B2-A3-B3).[14] One of his best known sets of alternating variations, the *Andante varié* in F minor for solo piano adds an elaborate and expressive coda to the six-part pattern. This approach is sometimes referred to as a *double variation* but should not be confused with the double variations described in the previous section. A more accurate term is *alternating variations*. Related to alternating variations is the rondo variation (see Chapter 10) in which the refrain is routinely varied with different episodes between the refrain and its variants, e.g. A1 B A2 C A3. Notable examples of rondo type variations include the slow movements of Beethoven's Symphonies Nos. 5, 7, and 9, each with unique designs and developmental episodes.

Any set of variations might draw on a number of different approaches as described, and composers often organized the set in highly individual manners. Bach's *Goldberg Variations*, for example, is a set of thirty variations on a lyric theme (an aria) in binary form, using the basic approach of a ground bass variation. In each variation it is the bass line of the theme that is retained rather than the melody. The thirty variations are organized in groups of three: first, a variation in a particular style (invention, gigue, French Overture, and so on), second, a virtuosic variation exploiting two keyboard manuals and crossing of hands, and third, a canonic variation in which each of the canons increases the interval of imitation from unison through a ninth. The thirty variations conclude with a simple restatement of the original theme.

Beethoven's theme-and-variation movements in his symphonies and string quartets creatively address the challenge of creating large-scale dramatic shape and continuity in a form that is sectional and additive in nature. His String Quartet, Op. 131, uses rhythmic connections or phrase overlap between most all of the variations. This technique gives a semblance of continuity amidst the dramatic contrasts among the variations. It also requires careful consideration by the performers of phrase connections and changes in tempo. The fantasy-like coda of this movement presents fragmentary restatements of the

[12] Ratner refers to this technique by the term "division variation in *Classic Music*, 256."

[13] Examples include the Brahms, *Variations on a Theme by Handel* and the Britten *Young Person's guide to the Orchestra*.

[14] See for example the slow movement of Haydn's Symphony No. 103, the "Drumroll Symphony."

melodic ideas of the theme while incorporating changes in key and tempo as well as cadenza-like passages for each of the players. Variations are found in the finales of two of Beethoven's most famous symphonies, Nos. 3 and 9. The finale of Symphony No. 3, which will be addressed in the exercises, presents two different but closely related themes, incorporates transitions, formal expansions, contrasts in tempo, and an introduction and coda, all organized to give a progressive dramatic shape appropriate to a symphonic movement. The finale of his Symphony No. 9, a more complex mixture of formal principles and styles, incorporates variations on the well-known "Ode to Joy" theme throughout the movement.

The fixed form and free variations that have predominated since Beethoven show a wide mixture of approaches to individual sets of variations. Stravinsky, who made use of variation movements in seven different works, including *Variations* for orchestra ("Aldous Huxley in Memorium"), approached each set of variations in a unique manner. His *Octet for Winds* includes a set of alternating variations diagrammed in Figure 11.2.

Figure 11.2 *Stravinsky, Octet for Winds, II: Tema con Variazoni.*

Theme	Var A	Var B	Var A	Var C	Var D	Var A	Var E
		March		Waltz	Can-Can		Fugue

The fixed element throughout the movement is Stravinsky's use of a pitch collection ordered as shown in Example 11.13.[15] This pattern from the opening of the theme is treated as a type of cantus firmus typical of many of Stravinsky's variations. It is subjected to transposition, registral displacement, re-orchestration, and varied rhythms but is used in all sections. The designations of Var. A and so forth, given in Figure 11.2, are indicated in the score by Stravinsky. Variation A presents a series of transposed versions of the thematic pitch pattern in various instruments accompanied by rapid scales and ostinati. What is noteworthy is that A is essentially unaltered in its restatements and thus serves as a ritornello. The episodes make use of the thematic pitch patterns but in distinct character variations as indicated in Figure 11.2.

Generally speaking, twentieth-century variations, though widely contrasting in approach, maintained stricter adherence to the pitch collections of a theme than the free variations of the late nineteenth and early twentieth centuries. Many of them, such as the works by Bartók, Seeger, and Walton listed in the aural exercises, make use of thematic transformation that results in continuous development of material and a less sectional, additive approach to the form.

Example 11.13 *Stravinsky, Octet for Winds, II, principal pitch motive of theme.*

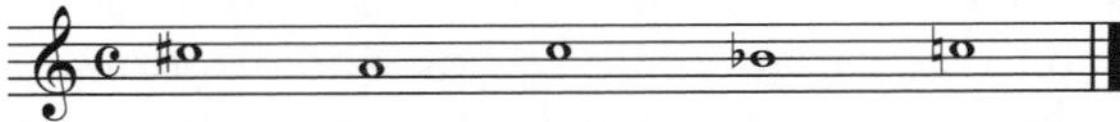

[15] The four notes of this pattern are part of an octatonic scale favored by Stravinsky in many works. Note that the four notes or tetrachord, when put in normal (step-wise) order, is built on alternating half steps and whole steps related to the octatonic scale. Stravinsky describes this pattern as two minor thirds, separated by a major third, that is, A–C/B♭-D♭ (C♯). See Chapter 14 for discussion of the octatonic scale.

Conclusion

The number and types of variations in a given set are defined by the style and genre in which the variations occur, the nature of the theme, and the design a composer has in mind for a particular set of variations. In ostinato variations, the harmonic progression and structural bass line are most important, and are retained through each variation. Theme and variations often emphasize retention of basic melodic content and shape as well as phrase structure and harmonic design. Even in melodic variations, only skeletal remnants of a melodic theme may be retained. Variations beginning with those of Beethoven blend a variety of types but often retain only the form and tonal structure of a theme, or use motives of the theme freely in varied forms and strongly contrasting characterizations.

The various types and approaches described above provide general descriptions of variations, but only close analysis of the theme will reveal the specifics of a particular variation. For a given set of variations, the harmonic progression, phrase structure, melodic shape, and form of the theme should be analyzed carefully and compared with the variations that follow. In twentieth-century variations, the pitch collections of a theme are frequently the unifying element and must be codified. The order and grouping of variations also plays an important role in variation form. As in all analyses, consideration of the large-scale organization will be helpful in clarifying detail. In the case of variations, this may entail simple consideration of the number of variations and any obvious groupings as well as more careful interpretation of the sequence and types of variations.

Exercises

Terms: In a sentence or two, define each of the following terms.

ostinato variations	ground bass	chaconne	theme and variations
melodic variations	figural variation	cantus firmus variation	embellishing variation
character variation	fixed-form variations	free variations	alternating variations
double variations	rondo variations	continuous variations	sectional variations
passacaglia			

AURAL ANALYSIS

For a given set of variations, determine the number of phrases, the cadences, and the basic form of the theme. Then listen to the variations as a whole and determine 1) the number of variations, 2) any changes in key or mode that you hear, 3) whether a given variation fits a general category or specific type of variation, 4) whether any of the variations depart from the form of the theme, and 5) descriptions of specific techniques that you hear, for example, textural inversions, transfer of register of a theme, motivic variation, changes in tempo and meter, and or additions of new accompaniments or counterpoint to a fixed melody.

*Handel, Air from the Suite No. 5 ("The Harmonious Blacksmith")
Mozart, *Twelve Variations on "Ah, vous dirai-je Maman."*
*Mozart, Sonata in D major, K. 284

+Mozart, Variations on "Unser dummer Pöbelmeint," K. 455
Mozart, Sonata K. 331 in A Major.
Beethoven, *Variations on "God Save the King"*
Haydn, String Quartet Op. 76, No. 3, II
Haydn, Piano Trio No. 25 in G major, I
Schubert, Quintet for Piano and Strings in A major, Op. 114, D. 667, Andantino.
Brahms, *Variations on a Theme by Haydn*, Op. 34.
Rachmaninoff, *Variations on a Theme by Corelli.*
Rachmaninoff, *Rhapsody on a Theme of Paganini* for Piano and Orchestra
Bartok, Violin Concerto No. 2, II
Britten, *Young Person's Guide to the Orchestra*, Op. 34.
Ruth Crawford Seeger, *Kaleidoscopic Changes on an Original Theme*
Walton, *Variations on a Theme by Hindemith*

SCORE ANALYSIS

1. **Haydn, *Andante varie* in F minor for piano.** The melody of the first theme from Haydn's *Andante varié* in F minor for piano is given below, as well as the first variation on the same melodic phrase. Both versions retain the same harmonic progression, shown below by roman numeral designations. Compare the two melodies. Apart from the obvious differences in rhythms, how else is the melodic theme varied? Consider how the variation is an analysis of what the structural pitches of the theme are. What elements of the theme are retained?

Exercise 11.1 Haydn, Theme and Variation 1.

a. Theme, mm. 1–6.

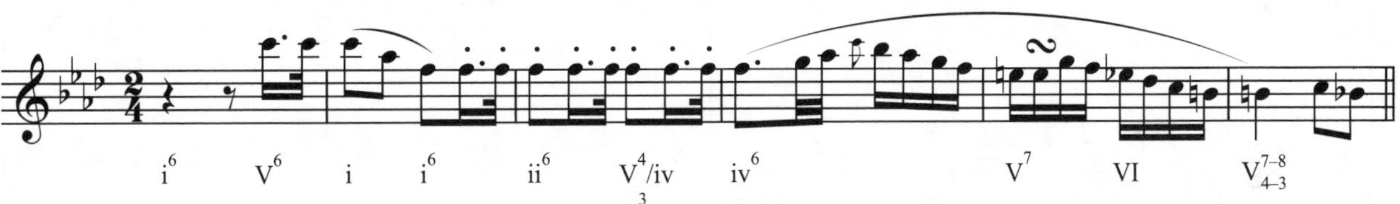

b. Variation 1, mm. 1–6.

2. **Brahms, Variations on a Theme by Haydn.** Analyze the phrase and harmonic structure of the first phrase of the theme set by Brahms in this version for two pianos. Determine what elements of the theme have been retained and which altered or abandoned in the variation given. Compare the melodies of the theme and the variation. To what extent does the variation retain or depart from elements of the theme?

Exercise 11.2 Brahms, Theme and Variation 6.

a. Theme, mm. 1–10.

b. Variation 6, mm. 1–10.

3. **Haydn, Symphony No. 104, II.**[16] This slow movement is a large ternary form. As in many of his works, Haydn incorporates variation techniques in the restatement of the opening section after the contrasting middle section. Compare the first and third sections of the work and distinguish the fixed and variable elements in the varied restatement.

[16] This exercise assumes that the instructor and students have access to the full score.

4. **Beethoven Symphony No. 3, IV.** The finale of this symphony is a set of variations built on the following themes: a) a bass-line theme introduced in measures 12–43 and b) a melodic theme, for which the first theme is the bass line. The first phrase of each of the themes is shown here.

Exercise 11.4 Beethoven, bass theme and melodic theme.

a. Bass theme.

b. Melodic theme.

a. Listen to a recording of movement four of Beethoven's Symphony No. 3 and compare the form of the bass-line theme as first presented in measures 12–43 with the first variation in measures 44–59. What is the form of each? Are the basic forms and phrase structure the same? Now consider the form of variation 3, which first introduces the melodic theme. Is the same basic form retained? When considering the forms take note of the manner in which repeats of phrases are handled.

b. The movement begins with a dramatic outburst from the orchestra—note the tonality of this introduction as it begins. The overall design incorporates ten variations and a lengthy coda, which may be outlined as shown in Figure 11.3. Complete the chart by determining the keys of each section and writing a description of the thematic content and basic types of variation. Note which variations are modulatory, which passage or passages are transitional, which developmental, and when, if ever, the two themes are combined. Are the themes ever truncated or expanded? Some sample descriptions are given and should to be matched with the appropriate variations. Also consider how the variations could be grouped into larger sections, apart from the coda. Finally, what factors determine how the coda is divided into the grouping shown in the chart? What other divisions or groupings of the coda are possible?

Figure 11.3 *Beethoven, Symphony No. 3, outline of Finale.*

Measures	Section	Tonality	Description
1–11	Introduction	?——I HC	brilliant unison passage
12–44	Bass theme	________	octave doublings of theme
45–59	Var 1	________	________
60–75	Var 2	________	________
75–107	Var 3	________	________
107–116	?	________	________
117–174	Var 4	________	________
175–210	Var 5	________	________
211–256	Var 6	________	________
257–277	Var 7	________	________
277–348	Var 8	________	________
348–380	Var 9	________	________
380–396	Var 10	________	________
CODA			
396–404	SEC. 1	________	________
404–420	SEC. 2	________	________
420–430	SEC. 3	________	________
431–435	SEC. 4	________	________
435–473	SEC. 5	________	________

c. **Descriptions (in random order).** Match the following descriptions with the variations and coda sections outlined in Figure 11.3.

1. Bass theme first time in sustained notes with counterpoint.
2. Brilliant flourishes on motivic fragments, emphatic repetitions, *sf* dynamics.
3. Syncopated oboe solo on second half of variation on melodic theme.
4. Bass theme inverted with new counterpoint in E♭.
5. Long dominant pedal but embellished in full texture and wide-ranging string parts.

6. Dramatic HC in E♭ followed by aria-like setting of melodic theme.
7. Melodic theme now in bass in E♭, chorale and march-like, majestic.
8. Turkish march over bass theme.
9. Melodic theme, antecedent only, C minor.
10. Fugato on bass theme, related to Var. 1 in C minor.
11. Abrupt shift to B minor then D major, melodic theme.
12. Transition from E♭ to HC in C minor.
13. Trumpets play bass theme, basses and cellos in brilliant style, violin on melody.
14. Bass theme now in melody with rapid counterpoint.
15. Move to A♭ after coda has begun melodic antecedent disguised in violin 1.
16. Introductory fanfare makes a dramatic return.

Additional works for analysis. All of the works listed in the exercises or in the course of this chapter offer excellent examples of the wide range of specific variation techniques composers have employed. Sets on familiar tunes are good examples for first analyses of variations.

12 Contrapuntal Genres

Introduction

A general category or type of musical form is recognized as such because it is found in many works. Although different works have unique formal structures, they may exhibit similar or identical large-scale formal designs that represent a category of musical form. Conversely, some types of music are categorized on the basis of the compositional techniques and formal processes that are used rather than recurring formal designs. Works based on an ostinato, discussed in Chapter 11, are one such category. Another category includes works based on contrapuntal techniques and textures, which tend to be continuous and through-composed, and in which formal designs vary widely. The most common contrapuntal genres that will be discussed here include canon, invention, fugue, and chorale prelude. They are characterized by contrapuntal textures resulting from the combination of independent, equally important lines. The most prevalent techniques of such genres are the imitation of a thematic idea in different voices, or the combination and development of contrasting themes. The discussion of these genres will clarify some of the compositional techniques employed in contrapuntal writing and the specific formal processes associated with them.

Imitation

Imitation is one of the most characteristic techniques of contrapuntal genres. In music, imitation refers to the repetition of material in a different voice or part[1] at different times. It is a widely used technique for elaborating musical ideas, and is found in many different styles and genres; however, it is especially associated with contrapuntal genres and textures. One voice presents a theme, after which a different voice repeats the same material at varied time intervals. As the second voice imitates the first, the first voice continues with different material, creating counterpoint with the second voice. The entrance of an imitating voice is referred to as a *point of imitation*. The imitation may involve two or more voices, and may last only a few beats or continue extensively.

Imitation may be characterized in different ways. The two basic characterizations of imitation are the pitch interval and the time interval. The pitch interval refers to the intervallic distance between voices. In imitation at the unison the imitating voice repeats material at the same pitch; in imitation at the perfect fifth, the second voice repeats material a perfect fifth above or below the first voice, and so forth. The time interval refers to the duration or distance in time between the entrances of voices. Imitation at the beat, half measure, measure, or longer time intervals describes the metrical duration before a point of imitation. Other techniques of imitation involve variation in the shape of the imitative

[1] The terms "voice" and "part" are used to refer to the lines in a musical work. Though typically "voice" is used with reference to vocal music and "part" with reference to instrumental music, in practice, the terms are interchangeable. The neutral term "line" is also used in this text.

line as described in the following paragraph. *Strict* imitation refers to retention of the intervallic quantity and rhythm throughout, while *free* or *modified* imitation will show some variance in interval succession, rhythm, or contour.

Canon

One of the oldest imitative genres and techniques is the *canon* (Greek for "rule" or "law"), a composition or passage in which strict imitation of a melody is used. Canons composed as separate works are generated entirely through strict imitation. The *rule* of a canon refers to the pitch and time interval at which a melody is subject to canonic imitation. A canon may also incorporate alterations of the melody when it is imitated (such as, inverted, backward, slower, or faster). The use of the same melody in all voices ensures unity and equality, while the contrasting rhythmic motions or contours that occur simultaneously ensure the independence of lines.

LEADER AND FOLLOWER

Traditionally, the leading voice in a canon, the part that presents the melody first, is called the *dux;* the *following voice* is referred to as the *comes*. The terms *leader* and *follower* will be used here. Canons may have two voices—one leader and one follower—but three or four-voice canons with 2–3 followers are not uncommon. Some canons will have two or three leading voices and following voices and are referred to as double or triple canons. Canons may also be accompanied by a separate voice that serves as counterpoint to the canonic imitation, sometimes referred to as an *accompanied* or *mixed canon*. The canons found in the *Goldberg Variations* by Bach are all of this type.

ROUND

The simplest type of canon, a *round*, is a melody that is sung by different voices beginning at different times, with the number of repetitions and voices left to the discretion of the performers. A round consequently entails canonic imitation at the unison.[2] The song "Row, Row, Row, Your Boat" is a familiar example of a melody that is treated as a round. Other well known rounds include hymns such as the one illustrated in Example 12.1. A canon may be

Example 12.1 *Canon by Thomas Tallis.*[3]

[2] The English writers of the sixteenth and seventeenth centuries referred to a round as a "catch." It is also referred to as a circular canon.

[3] This melody is used for the hymn, "All Praise to Thee."

notated as a single melodic line, as in this example. Numbers shown above various points in the melody indicate when each successive voice begins to sing the melody. In this example, the numbers indicate that the melody may be performed as a two-, three-, or four-voice canon at time intervals of four beats. *In a round, as in all canons, the different parts of the melody must align to produce correct harmonic progressions and voice-leading.*

BACH AND BEFORE

The earliest known canon written for four voices is a famous, thirteenth-century composition entitled "Sumer is icumen in." Canons were used in various genres in the fourteenth century, but it was in the Renaissance period that canonic writing began to flourish, notably in sacred works. In the fifteenth and sixteenth centuries, composers of masses and motets often included sections or movements in canonic imitation. In the eighteenth century it was Bach, as one might expect, who composed some of the greatest canons as he continuously explored the art of counterpoint. Among his many compositions that incorporate canons are the *Canonical Variations on the Christmas Hymn* "Vom Himmel hoch" (BWV 769),[4] the series of canons in the *Goldberg Variations, A Musical Offering* (BWV 1079), and *The Art of the Fugue* (BWV 1080). Canons from these works are shown in Example 12.2 to illustrate several categories of canonic imitation.

Example 12.2 *Types of canonic imitation in works by Bach.*

a. *Goldberg Variations,* No. 12, a mirror canon at perfect fourth with accompaniment.

b. *A Musical Offering,* Retrograde (Crab) Canon.

[4] *Einige canonische Veranderungen uber das Weihnachtslied.* "Vom Himmel hoch da komm' ich her" (BWV 769).

c. *Art of the Fugue* (BWV 1080), Canon 4, canon in augmentation and contrary motion.

A mirror canon in which the follower is a *melodic inversion* of the leader, is shown in Example 12.2a. *Melodic inversion* results when a melody is restated with the contour reversed, that is, as a mirror of the original contour. This example also illustrates a canon with an accompaniment—in this case a bass line that is used throughout the variations.[5]

A retrograde canon is a melody that is performed forward and backward simultaneously. Consequently there is no leader and no follower. These canons are sometimes referred to as "crab canons" ("canon cancrizans") because one part moves backward in the manner of a crab. The retrograde canon in Example 12.2b is notated as a *riddle canon*, which provides hints as to how the canon should be performed (the upside-down clef sign at the end) but no explicit instructions.

Riddle canons appear in works as early as the fourteenth century, and reflect composers' interest in enigmatic and hidden techniques that show their skill and cleverness. In this example, one must note the backwards clef that Bach put at the end of the notated canon melody. This indicates that one performer should play the melody in that clef but read the notation from the end to the beginning. Each performer could then reverse their part. Sometimes an upside-down clef would occur at the beginning, indicating an inverted canon. Other riddles might be in the form of verbal clues.

A mensuration (or proportional) canon is one in which the following voices perform the canon melody in augmentation or diminution, as shown in Example 12.2c. In this case the following voice states the subject in contrary motion and in augmentation, combining two different contrapuntal techniques. In some mensuration canons the voices begin at the same time, presenting the same melody at different speeds. Renaissance composers produced some notable examples of mensuration canons. Most famous among these is the *Missa prolationum* by Ockegham, in which each of the movements is a double mensuration canon.

BEYOND BACH

Composers after Bach continued to write canons, often as separate vocal works. (See the following exercises.) They would also use canons within instrumental movements, notably

[5] Bach used this bass line in another extended canonic work, *Fourteen Canons on the Goldberg Ground* (BWV 1087).

in minuet movements and in variations. One well-known example is Haydn's minuet from his String Quartet Op. 76, No. 2 in D minor (Example 12.3). The entire minuet is written as a strict two-voice canon that adheres to the expected binary form of a minuet. The minor mode and the unexpected, restless nature of the canon led to the nickname *Witches' Minuet*.

Canonic writing is often found in development sections of sonata forms, but may also occur in other passages. One interesting occurrence of a canon as an expository theme can be heard in Franck's Violin Sonata in A major, movement IV. The first thirty-six measures are an extended canon that comprises the principal theme of the movement. Composers of the twentieth century, particularly serial composers, showed a renewed interest in canons. Two famous works that incorporate canonic writing are Webern's Symphony Op. 21 and Berg's Violin Concerto; the latter incorporates a four-part canon for solo violin and strings in the second movement.

Example 12.3 Haydn, String Quartet Op. 76, No. 2, III Minuet in canon, mm. 1–11.

ANALYTIC EXERCISES

Exercises 12.1a and b show two well-known canonic hymns with the rules removed. Bearing in mind that the canonic imitation must result in good harmonic progressions and voice-leading, see if you can determine the rule, that is, the point of imitation, for each voice. Analysis of the implied harmony and phrase structure of the melody will help determine the rule. How many parts can each hymn use in canon? The manner of composing the canon can then be considered. Is the complete canonic melody composed as a single line, or must it be composed in fragments? If so, how would this be carried out? Writing out the canon in score format will help explain this process.

Exercise 12.1 *Canons for analysis.*

a. Traditional, "Dona nobis pacem."

b. William Billings, "When Jesus Wept."

Additional canons for analysis are listed here. Canons from *A Musical Offering* by Bach are also found in the Burkhart *Anthology for Analysis*, 6th edition.

1. **Mozart, *Così Fan Tutte*, Act II Finale, the "Toast Canon" Scene xv, mm. 173–203.**
   Trace the entrance of the three voices beginning with Fiordiligi. What type of canon does Mozart use in this scene? How does Mozart's use of a canon correspond to the text he is setting here?
2. **Loesser, *Guys and Dolls*, "Fugue for Tin Horns."**
   Sing through each of the parts in this playful tune. What would be a more appropriate title for this song?

Inventions

A genre unique to Bach's oeuvre is the *Invention* for keyboard. Bach's set of two-part "Inventiones" and three-part "Sinfoniae" are now commonly referred to as his "Two- and Three-Part Inventions." These collections are, in effect, teaching manuals in which different types of themes are "invented" and elaborated by various contrapuntal techniques. The inventions thus serve as models of various compositional and keyboard techniques. The following discussion will briefly address the two-part inventions, focusing on some basic compositional approaches found in many of these works.

Many of the two-part inventions are imitative pieces that sound similar to a fugue (discussed later). Like fugues, the inventions are based on contrapuntal elaboration of themes using imitation. The principal theme of a fugue or invention is referred to as the *subject*; a recurring theme used as counterpoint to the subject is referred to as the *countersubject*.[6] The two-part inventions differ from fugal writing in the following ways: (1) they often start with both voices rather than a single voice; (2) they tend to be shorter and less elaborate than many fugues, with fewer numbers of themes, modulations, and voices; and (3) the subject of an invention tends to be more concise and is often imitated at the octave. The inventions are meant to illustrate the use of various types of figures—scales, arpeggios, leaping figures, and so forth. The subjects normally begin on scale degree 1 or, in three of the inventions, scale degree 5.

Two basic approaches to beginning an invention can be identified. Eight of the fifteen two-part inventions begin with points of imitation that are followed by and alternate with episodes. Example 2.11 (Chapter 2) illustrates an invention that begins with three statements of the subject, using tonic and dominant harmonies. Each point of imitation is at the octave, a characteristic of the Inventions. Note how the third statement inverts

[6] The terms "motive" and "countermotive" are also encountered in writings on the inventions to refer to subjects and countersubjects. These terms also reflect the differences cited between fugues and inventions.

the texture of the previous statements. In the Invention in E minor (Chapter 2, Exercises) the subject is presented with a brief accompaniment at the onset. The brevity of the subject results in four statements of the subject, two on tonic, then two on dominant.

The other approach in the two-part inventions is the use of a subject and a countersubject at the onset, which are then repeated with an inversion of the texture (Example 12.4). Such use of *invertible counterpoint* is a characteristic of these inventions. Note that the subject is a complete phrase rather than a short motivic idea as found in the more imitative inventions. Of the seven inventions that begin in this manner, five present four-measure subjects, while two present two-measure subjects. *Textural inversion*, as observed in Example 12.4, occurs with the immediate repetition of the opening themes.

Example 12.4 Bach, Two-part Invention No. 9, mm. 1–8, textural inversion.

The inventions are based on alternation between expository statements of the subjects and developmental episodes that are usually modulatory and involve the use of sequence. Each invention is unique in its specific formal structure. In the Invention in E minor, we observed that the formal structure is clarified in large part by the tonal design—the pattern of keys and modulations as outlined in Figure 2.4. As is expected in Baroque music, the modulations go to closely related keys, even though the pattern of keys and the number of distinct modulations or tonicizations will vary widely. Invention No. 8 in F major is shown in Example 12.5. Figure 12.1 shows its tonal design.

Figure 12.1 *Tonal design of Invention No. 8 in F major.*

Measures:	1→12	12→15→18→25	26→31→35
Key	I→V	V → ii → vi → IV	IV→I→I
Cadences	PAC		PAC

Example 12.5 Bach, Two-Part Invention No. 8 in F major, mm. 1–10, canonic.

(This excerpt continues on p. 282.)

(Example 12.5, continued.)

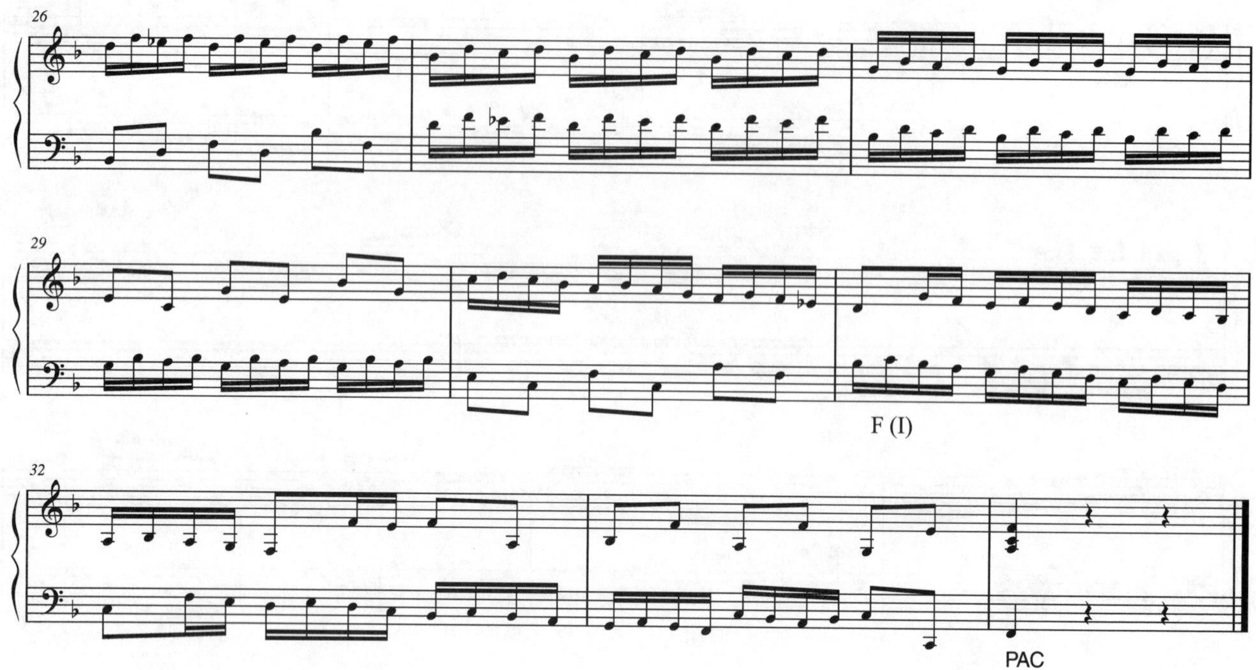

The F major Invention is one of two inventions that use extended imitation at the outset in the manner of a canon. An additional point of imitation begins in C major (V) in measure 12, where Bach exchanges the registral position of the follower and leader. The tonal design of this invention, in contrast to the E minor Invention, contains only two strong cadences and several tonicizations within its single episode (measures 15–25). The opening canonic section from measures 4–12 returns to initiate the close of the invention in measure 26, now beginning in the key of B♭ major (IV). This move to subdominant allows a modulation up a perfect fifth to tonic that parallels the tonal motion of the opening canonic passage. Notice how Bach skillfully weaves these partial restatements into a continuation phrase, avoiding a restatement of the opening point of imitation. This strategy gives a strong sense of continuity and drive to the close of this piece.

Analytic Exercises

The Two-Part Inventions are generally less complex than Bach's fugues, largely because they involve only two voices. They serve as excellent models for the analysis of tonal design, sequence, and imitation. The discussions and exercises for analysis of the D minor and E minor Two-Part Inventions presented in Chapter 2 provide models for analyzing tonal design. The following exercises address the elements discussed in this section.

1. **Points of imitation.** The following harmonic patterns are evident in the eight inventions that begin with points of imitation (Nos. 1, 2, 3, 4, 7, 8, 10, and 13). Identify which patterns are used. Two of the patterns are used only once; the

others are each used in two inventions. Consider the musical reasons for the pattern of imitative entrances at the beginning of each invention.

a. I–I V–V or i–i–V–V
b. I–I
c. i–i–i
d. I–V
e. canonic

2. **Two-Voice Invertible Counterpoint.** The repetition of the opening subject and countersubject in inverted textures, used in seven of the inventions (Nos. 5, 6, 9, 11, 12, 14, 15), occurs at either the dominant or tonic pitch level. Identify the harmonic pattern in each statement repetition and consider the musical reasons for the type of pattern used.

   a. I→V
   b. I→I

3. **Formal structure.**

   a. Cadences. Where are points of cadence in each invention?
   Which cadences are most clearly articulated?
   If cadences are masked, how is this achieved?
   b. Sequences. Identify the beginnings and endings of sequences and the types of sequences involved.
   Consider where each sequence leads: to another sequence, to a cadence, to a new key, to an entry of the subject, or to some combination of these events.
   c. Elaboration. Where is fragmentation or compression of motivic ideas used?
   What is the effect or function of such passages?
   d. Identify the uses of pedal points and consider their placement in the form.

4. **Conclusion.** How does the invention conclude?

   a. with a final statement or point of imitation
   b. with an elaborate cadential passage
   c. with a deceptive or evaded cadence that leads to a final authentic cadence
   d. with the most rhythmically active, harmonically complex textures
   e. with other techniques that emphasize final closure

Fugue

The most widely found contrapuntal genre in tonal music is the fugue. Originally the term *fuga* (literally, *flight*) was used in the thirteenth century to refer to a piece in which two voices were sung in canonic imitation accompanied by a third voice. The title reflects the sense of one part "flying" or chasing after another in imitation. During the Renaissance, sacred works were identified as fugal if they used strict (canonic) imitation in the initial presentation of a melody. In the Baroque period and after, the term *fugue* referred to pieces that employed systematic imitation and contrapuntal elaboration of themes, which may be developed in a variety of ways. Writers of the eighteenth century described fugues variously as a conversation, an argument, or a debate among voices. Works titled "fugue" are primarily instrumental works, although many vocal works are fugues, they are not titled as such.[7] Instrumental fugues normally are preceded by a prelude in the same key as the fugue.

As a contrapuntal genre, the fugue is not a form, since the formal design will vary widely. In fact, some scholars regard the fugue as only a description of a compositional technique as fugal style is found in a wide number of genres. While this point is valid to an extent, works entitled "fugue" will contain enough basic similarities in the contrapuntal techniques and processes in their formal structures as to constitute a genre or type of composition. Typically, a fugue, like an invention, will alternate *expository* passages that present the fugue subject and *developmental* episodes. The length and number of these sections varies widely.

In the Baroque period, the composition of fugues reached an apex in the works of J.S. Bach. The details of fugal processes will be examined with reference to examples from the two volumes of *the Well-Tempered Clavier* of Bach, hereafter referred to as WTC I or WTC II. Each volume of this renowned work for keyboard contains twenty-four preludes and fugues, one in each major and minor key.[8] The fact that Bach composed *two* volumes of preludes and fugues is yet another indication of his ceaseless interest in exploring the craft of musical composition. The following discussion will focus on instrumental fugue as a genre with a subsequent discussion of other uses of fugal techniques.

SUBJECTS AND ANSWERS

A fugue typically begins with an unaccompanied statement of the subject, or principal theme of the work. Fugue subjects vary widely as to length, phrase structure, and style. The distance between the entrance of the first voice (the subject) and the second entrance (the answer) normally defines the length of a fugue subject. In Example 12.6, the fugue subjects are understood to be one measure, two measures, one and a half measures, and four measures respectively. The metric placement of the fugal entrances is consistent in these initial statements. Note, however, that the fugue subject may continue to a more stable point once the second entrance is heard. For example, the subject in Example 12.6a continues to the more stable D quarter note, which sounds like a stronger point of closure. Such overlap gives continuity to the rhythmic texture and is typical of the continuous motion of contrapuntal genres. Nonetheless, it is the actual distance between subject and answer that is the basis for length of subject and countersubjects. It is this distance that is used to determine a technique called *stretto* (Italian for *close*), in which imitative entries overlap at closer time intervals.

From one perspective, fugue subjects may be distinguished as either vocal or instrumental in style. These basic categories are a reflection of the sixteenth-century origins of the fugue—the imitative *ricercare* that was derived from the vocal motet, and the instrumental *canzona*. As Bach continuously demonstrates, fugue subjects may take on a variety of shapes, styles, and expressive idioms. Example 12.6 shows four different subjects from the WTC of Bach. The D major fugue subject (Example 12.6a) exhibits two distinct motives that demonstrate fragmentation as a means of episodic development—the two motives might be used separately or in counterpoint to one another. This subject also uses the persistent dotted rhythm that is characteristic of French Overture style. Example 12.6b illustrates a toccata-like fugue that uses a continuous rhythmic motion while incorporating three different motives. By contrast, Example 12.6c shows a fugue subject with sustained

[7] A notable exception is the "Geographical Fugue" (1930) a movement from *Spoken Music* by Ernst Toch.

[8] Vol. I of the WTC was completed in 1722; Vol. 2 was completed in 1742.

note values, which clearly relate it to the vocal style of a ricercare. The subject shown in Example 12.6d is a three-part subject using a pattern of statement–varied repetition–continuation. It is also in the style of a lively gigue with its duple compound meter and running (scalar) figures. Example 12.6e is an example of a two-part subject in which two different ideas separated by rests are presented. The two parts in this type of fugue subject are sometimes described as "head and tail." These examples are by no means exhaustive but give some characteristic types of fugue subjects. Additional subjects, discussed below will demonstrate other possibilities.

Example 12.6 *Fugue Subjects by J.S. Bach.*

a. Fugue 5 in D major, WTC I, brilliant style and French Overture.

b. Fugue 10 in E minor, WTC I, toccata-like, continuous.

c. Fugue 7 in E major, WTC II, vocal, ricercare style.

d. Fugue 11 in F major, WTC II, gigue-like, three-part subject.

e. Fugue 13 in G minor, WTC I, "head and tail" subject.

Fugue subjects tend to emphasize primary scale degrees and the tonic and dominant triads because they must clearly establish the key of the fugue. Subjects tend to begin with the scale degree 1, and end on scale degree 3 or 5, though other tonic and dominant-related scale degrees are encountered. The imitation in a fugue is based on alternation between tonic and dominant statements of a fugue subject: the subject establishes the tonic while the answer establishes the dominant. Occasionally one will encounter answers at the subdominant.[9] An answer that uses the same intervals as the subject throughout is a called a *real answer*. It is an exact transposition of the subject. Sometimes the beginning of the fugue subject is modified slightly to adjust for the harmonic motion; this is called a *tonal answer*. The adjustment usually involves only a single note, thus tonal answers sound quite close to an exact transposition of the subject. Example 12.6d contains a tonal answer. Note that the first downbeat of the answer is the pitch F rather than G. The remainder of the answer continues exactly as the subject did, transposed to the dominant. See also Example 12.6e.[10]

EXPOSITION

The beginning of a fugue, in which voices enter one by one with a statement of the subject or the answer, is referred to as the *exposition*. The contrapuntal textures of a fugue foster continuous motion such that the end of the exposition and beginning of the middle section can be an ambiguous formal boundary. A clear cadence may mark the completion of the exposition, but the ending may be masked by phrase overlap. In any case, *the fugue exposition is completed when all of the voices have presented the entire subject or answer*.

Whether instrumental or vocal, the parts of a fugue are normally identified by vocal ranges. A four-voice fugue, for example, will contain four voices or parts designated S-A-T-B. Three-voice fugues will normally contain S-A-B parts. In the WTC, three and four-voice fugues are the norm, though one two-voice and two five-voice fugues are found. Figure 12.2 gives a model diagram of an exposition of a four-voice fugue. A three-voice fugue would simply eliminate the fourth entry shown.

Figure 12.2 *Diagram of a fugue exposition in four voices: S= subject, A=answer, CS=countersubject.*

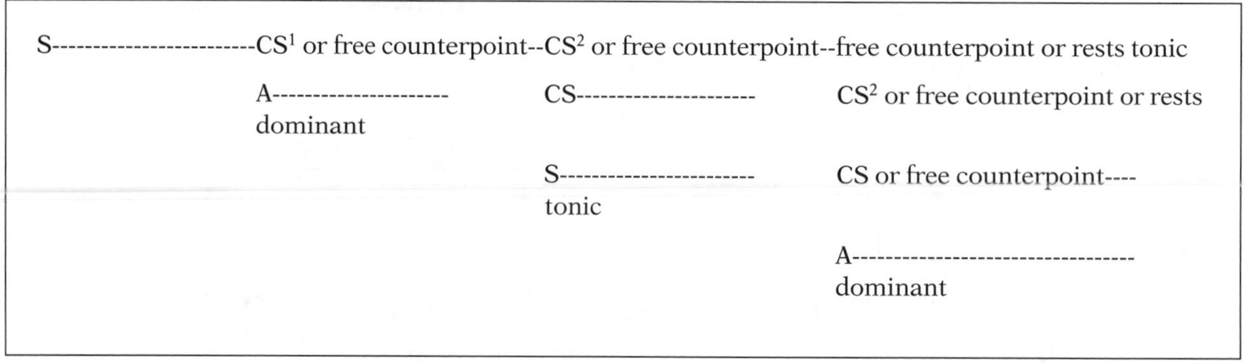

Several points should be observed concerning this diagram:

- The order in which the voices enter will vary. For example, the Fugue in E major (WTC II) presents the subjects and answers in B-T-A-S order. Three-voice fugues typically present S-A-B or A-S-B orderings.[11]
- Very often, a short modulatory episode is placed before the third entry of a fugue to allow a return to the tonic before the next subject. This passage is an *extension* as it lengthens the phrase to lead convincingly to the next entrance.[12]

---

[9] See for example Bach's G♯ minor Fugue, WTC 1, and Beethoven's String Quartet Op. 131, I.

[10] See the E♭ major Fugue WTC 1 for an answer that has tonal adjustments at the beginning and ending of the subject. A detailed discussion of tonal answers, including modulating subjects, is beyond the scope of the present discussion.

[11] Of the twenty-six three-voice fugues in the WTC, S-A-B ordering is found 12 times, A-S-B 10 times, B-A-S and B-S-A two times each.

[12] Some writers refer to this passage as a *codetta* since it is added to the answer, or as Episode I since it has characteristics of episodic writing. The term "extension" is used here to reflect the function of the passage.

- When an answering voice enters, the first voice may present a new idea, or an idea that is derived from motives of the subject, as counterpoint to the answer. If this idea is used as counterpoint to the subject throughout the fugue it is referred to as a *countersubject*. Some fugues have two countersubjects, while others simply use free counterpoint that is usually related to the subject motivically.
- While all of the fugues in the WTC begin with a single voice, some will begin with a subject *and* a countersubject. These may be perceived as having two subjects. Such fugues are referred to as *double fugues* by some writers. Occasionally one will encounter a fugue with two expositions of two different subjects separated by an episode. Such a fugue is also referred to as a double fugue. Eventually the subjects of the two fugues are presented together in counterpoint in the later stages of the fugue.[13]

EPISODES AND MIDDLE ENTRIES

Following the exposition of a fugue, the middle section of a fugue begins. In the middle section, the thematic material of the exposition is developed in passages referred to as *episodes*. In an episode, motivic fragments of the subject or countersubject are heard, but complete statements will not be presented. Episodes are usually modulatory and make frequent use of sequence. Alternating with episodes are complete statements of the fugue subject, referred to as *middle entries*. Sometimes a single middle entry of a fugue subject is followed by a new episode; two or more successive statements of the fugue subject in a new key, normally an alternation of subject and answer, may also occur.[14] While episodes are developmental in function, middle entries are expository. These entries serve to confirm new keys to which the episodes have modulated.

The number of middle entries and episodes varies widely, as will the number of modulations and keys in which the material is presented. Some fugues tend to be more expository and "subject structured" with many middle entries, while others, more developmental or "episode-structured," will have lengthy or more frequent episodes. Consequently the proportions of the sections of a fugue will also vary widely. In this regard each fugue must be examined on an individual basis. Many fugues are through-composed and have few strongly coordinated cadences in all voices. Further, elision and overlapping of phrases, typical of contrapuntal textures, contributes to continuous rhythmic motion. Some fugues, however, may have distinct formal sections within the ongoing elaboration of material.

CLOSING SECTION

The closing section of a fugue usually incorporates one or more of the following techniques:

- a return to the tonic key with a final presentation of the fugue subject
- pedal point: either a dominant pedal that leads to the closing section upon resolution, or a tonic pedal that occurs in a final statement or cadential phrase
- an increase in density and often a move to more homorhythmic textures
- a presentation of the fugue subject in stretto or augmentation, though this is not a requirement of, nor limited to the closing section.

---

[13] See for example the last movements of Brandenburg Concertos Nos. 2, 4, and 5 by Bach. A double fugue in which the second subject enters slightly after the first subject is found in the Kyrie from the *Requiem* by Mozart.

[14] The terms "subordinate exposition" and "re-exposition" are sometimes used to refer to the presentation of the subject in non-tonic keys.

ANALYSIS OF FUGUES

The study of several fugues will reveal seemingly endless variations on the processes outlined in the foregoing discussion. Each fugue will have a unique formal structure based on how the composer shapes his themes (subjects and countersubjects) and develops them contrapuntally. An examination of a fugue from Bach's WTC will provide some examples of how a fugue subject may be developed and of various techniques of fugal composition.

The Fugue in E major from the WTC I (Example 12.7) is a relatively short fugue with a brief, one-measure subject. A real answer follows—an exact transposition to the dominant. While the answer enters at the same metrical position, the subject completes its tonal motion on the third beat of measure 2, eliding with the beginning of the countersubject (CS). It is interesting that both motives of the subject begin with upbeats, which gives a strong impetus to the rhythmic motion of this fugue. The CS gives further rhythmic drive to the fugue with its extension of the sixteenth-note motion of the fugue subject. Note that the second half of the CS doubles the second half of the fugue subject in the initial presentation. The downbeat emphasis of the CS contrasts with the subject. Bach's exploitation of the rhythmic characteristics of the S and CS is evident in the relentless sixteenth-note motion of the fugue. Finally, the CS uses motives from the S, connecting the two ideas, resulting, in this instance, in the doubling of lines in thirds and sixths. While a CS may be entirely independent from the S, a sharing of motivic ideas is a common technique used to relate or connect the two ideas.

In analyzing a fugue, basic steps include identifying complete entries of the fugue subject, distinguishing the beginning and endings of episodes, and determining the tonal design of the fugue. These elements are marked on the score in Example 12.7. Of interest are the various placements of entries and episodes. In this fugue additional entries in the form of subject–answer–answer occur in measures 6–8 before confirming a modulation to the dominant key. Additional entries in the tonic or dominant keys after the initial statements by all voices are referred to as *redundant entries.*[15] Subsequently, single entrances of the fugue alternate with episodes of varied length, even though the only key besides tonic and dominant established in the course of the fugue is C♯ minor (vi).

A thorough understanding of a fugue will entail examination of each line with regard to its linear shape and points of closure or cadence, and its textural and motivic relations with other lines. In this regard, several observations may be made about this fugue that are instructive in the analysis of fugues in general.

- **Overlapping phrases.** In fugues and contrapuntal textures in general, cadences are often masked by overlapping phrases, an important technique that contributes to the through-composed nature of fugues. For example, in measure 5, beats 1–3, the upper voices make a clear authentic cadence in the dominant key. At the same time, the bass voice continues with the CS.
- **Expansion and fragmentation of subject and countersubject.** The entrance of the answer in measure 10 not only eliminates the expected A♯ but also expands the subject by repeating the second motive in measure 11. This effects a modulation to C♯ minor (vi), confirmed in the next two measures. In measure 20, the upper voice feigns entrances of the fugue subject by using only the second half. A comparison of various statements of the countersubject shows similar use of repetitions or fragmentation of motives (compare measures 3–4, 11–12, 18–19). Fragmentation is characteristic of episodes, particularly sequential passages.

---

[15] See also the F major Fugue, WTC I. Some writers use the term "double exposition" to refer to a series of redundant entries, though the term usually refers to an exposition of a second subject after one or more episodes.

Example 12.7 Bach, Fugue 9 in E major, WTC Book I.

- **Re-harmonization of the fugue subject.** Another way to elaborate the fugue subject is through re-harmonization. Though not extensively used in this fugue, measures 10–11, as noted, offer a good example of this technique.
- **Varied phrase placement and metric position of the subject.** The third entrance of the subject in measures 3–4, though in an expected weak/strong metrical position, is delayed two beats to allow a modulation back to tonic. The entrance in measure 16 is partially masked by the absence of the initial eighth rest. More importantly, the subject continues right through the cadence on the downbeat of measure 17. The subject is thus used at the end of a phrase rather than the beginning, effectively overlapping the phrases. The last partial reference to the fugue subject, in measure 28, shifts the metric placement to allow for a strong point of cadence on the downbeat of the last measure.
- **Textural Inversion.** Fugues are usually based on the motivic ideas of the subject and countersubject. One way the recurring material is varied is by restating passages with themes reassigned to different voices. For example, the S/CS in measures 7–8 reverses the registral position of two voices heard in measures 2–3; the countersubject is now above the answer. This *textural inversion* results from writing *invertible counterpoint,* in which the lines are written so that inverting their position in the texture will still produce a harmonically sound progression. Invertible counterpoint is a common feature of fugal writing. Compare the upper voices in measures 13–16 and 22–25 for another example of textural inversion.
- **Fluctuations in density.** A basic technique of fugal writing is varying the number of voices sounding at a given time. One reason a voice will rest periodically is to allow a restatement of the fugue subject or re-entry of voices to be emphasized. For example look at the bass line in measure 9. Variation in the number of voices also reflects the interest in exploring different textures. For example, the two-voice texture in measures 20–21 presents a new texture in which the voices are in *dialogue*—the upper voice mimics or responds to the lower voice.[16] The absence of the third voice helps emphasize the relation of the two voices. Final cadences may add additional voices, as in the C minor Fugue of WTC I, to emphasize closure.
- **Varied linear relations.** While the use of subjects and countersubjects in all parts conveys the equality of voices, varied relations or functions of voices are part of fugal elaboration. Rests in a voice are one way to achieve variety, as the two-voice texture in measures 20–21 mentioned previously illustrates. In measures 5–6, all three voices are sounding, but the upper voices are in a dialogue while the lower voice serves as a bass line that continues the contrasting sixteenth-note motion. Conversely, the three-voice textures in measures 13–17 and 23–27 show three distinct lines, contrasting in register, rhythm, and melodic shape.

Because a fugue is a genre or compositional technique and not a *form,* we can expect each fugue to have unique attributes while drawing on the processes and techniques described. A summary of some noteworthy attributes of this fugue, based on the discussion above, include:

- The upbeat motion of the subject and the continuous sixteenth-note motion of the CS, which permeate the fugue and give it a relentless rhythmic drive; the absence of any pedal point contributes to this effect.
- A single modulation to the relative minor, C♯ minor.
- The relatively lengthy episode in measures 11–16 that, rather than modulating, elaborates and cadences in C♯ minor; the middle entry in measure 16 emphasizes the key of C♯ minor.

[16] The term "dialogue" is used here to refer to the use of close, repeated imitation between two voices. The term is used to convey a connection between two lines analogous to a conversation between two people.

- A return to E major in measure 18 that is marked by S-A-S entrances of the subject in measures 19–21, followed by an episode that briefly tonicizes subdominant key in measures 22–25. In many fugues, restatements in tonic will signal the beginning of the closing section.
- A closing section that is initiated by a final entry of the full subject in measure 25; the final cadence is marked by a partial statement of the answer that finally leads to cadential repose!

In sum, this fugue has a judicious balance of expository and developmental (episodic) writing, and a variety of two- and three-voice textures. It is also relatively short, perhaps due to the rhythmic nature of its principal ideas. Fugues of moderate length such as this are referred to as *fughettas*. Many fugues are of far greater length, notably the great organ fugues by Bach, whose proportions are no doubt influenced by the wide range of timbres and registers that can be exploited on the organ.

ANALYTIC NOTE

To bring out the fugue subject or not to bring out the fugue subject, that is the question! A common rule of thumb when performing fugues is that the fugue subject or answer should be brought out over the other voices. While this notion is certainly valid, in many instances it is worth considering when it is not valid. A critical aspect of fugal composition is the writing of interesting counterpoint to a given subject. This observation suggests that voices should be equally balanced in many instances. Second, a fugue subject may often be masked by the position of its entrance in the phrase and the prominence of another voice or voices. For example, in the Fugue in E major, measure 20, the upper voice brings in the fugue subject on beat 3, apparently omitting the eighth-note pickup. The missing pitch can be found in the left hand (B^3 on the second half of beat two) in the expected metrical position. However, it is registrally displaced and, unlike measure 2, Bach does not notate an additional eighth-stem to indicate a doubling of voices, which suggests that he does not want the pitch brought out. Moreover, accenting the pitch (B^3) would interrupt the flow of the line and the motion between the two voices. Similarly, one would not accent the $G\sharp^4$ or E^4 in the right hand in the second half of beat two. Rather, the performer should let the remainder of the subject, beginning with the quarter note C♯, enter without undue preparation. A slight emphasis on the $C\sharp^5$ would allow the listener to realize how seamlessly the entrance is woven into the rhythmic texture.

OTHER FUGAL TECHNIQUES

Additional compositional techniques mentioned previously, though not illustrated in the E major fugue, include: melodic (mirror) inversion, stretto, and augmentation or diminution. Melodic inversion, illustrated in Example 12.8, is a common means of developing the fugue subject. Example 12.9 shows the opening of the C major fugue from the WTC I and subsequent entries of the subject and answer in measure 7. The re-entries in measure 7 illustrate a stretto, as the time span between entries is shorter than their original presentation. Figure 12.3 outlines the formal structure of the fugue and presents one model for plotting its formal organization. As the diagram illustrates, this particular fugue is largely expository in that the fugue subject enters repeatedly with extensive use of stretto. At the same time, the various stretti modulate and present varied temporal relations and textures,

Example 12.8 Fugue No. 15 in G major, WTC I: melodic inversion of fugue subject.

Example 12.9 Fugue in C Major, WTC I, mm. 1–8.

Figure 12.3 *Fugue in C major, WTC I, formal outline.*

Key: S = Subject, A = Answer, Numbers in ( ) = Beat numbers, ↓ = Cadences

m.m.	1	2	3	4	5	6	7	8	9	10	11	12	13
			A(V)——(1)				S(I)——(3)						
S	S(I)——(3)								A(V)——(3)A(V/V)——(2)				
A				A(V)——(3)			A(V)——(4)					A(V/vi)——(3)	
T						S(I)——(1)					A(V)——(1)		
B													
	EXPOSITION——→						| STRETTI ——→						

m.m.	14	15	16	17	18	19	20	21	22	23	24	25	26	27
		A(V)—S(1)—(4)						A(V)——(2)						
S	S(I)——(3)		A(V)——(1)			A(iii)——(4)					A(IV)——(1)			
A	A(V)——(1)			A(V/ii)——(3)				A(?)——(1)			S(I)——(3)			
T						A(ii)——(1)								
B	↓(1)										↓(1)			↓(3)
	A minor (vi) PAC										C major (I) PAC			PAC
	——→									| CLOSING SECTION	——→ |			

which become more complex as the fugue progresses. In a "subject-oriented" fugue such as this, the stretti thus serve as a means of development analogous to an episode. The emphasis on continuous elaboration of the subject may account for the absence of a countersubject.

Some fugues such as this one exploit stretto throughout, while others make no use of the technique. Stretto, like diminution, can create a sense of accelerated motion; thus it is often found in latter stages of a fugue as a way of building toward the close of the fugue.

The diminution of a fugue subject entails uniform reduction of note values;[17] augmentation of a fugue subject entails uniform increase of note values. Example 12.10a shows the opening of the first movement fugue from the String Quartet in C♯ minor, Op. 131 by Beethoven. The answer is unusual as it is on the subdominant, a tonal relation exploited throughout the quartet. An intensely expressive passage, beginning in measure 99, presents 1) the original fugue subject in the first violin; 2) a complete statement of the fugue subject in augmentation in the cello, which begins in stretto with the first violin and 3) diminution of fragments of the original subject, the quarter notes now eighth notes. The beginning of this passage is shown in Example 12.10b. The combination of these techniques creates a relentless but slow build to a climax in measure 113 of this fugue.

Example 12.10 Beethoven, String Quartet Op. 131, I.

a. Opening of first movement fugue, mm. 1–8.

b. Fugue subject (violin) with fugue subject in augmentation (cello) mm. 99–103.

[17] Diminution is used here in the specific sense described rather than the general sense of rhythmic elaborations of simpler ideas.

As Example 12.10 demonstrates, fugues are sometimes incorporated into multi-movement works. Although the fugue seems to have reached its apex in the truly remarkable output of Bach, it remained a technique to which composers were drawn as a way of developing ideas and displaying their technical skill. Beethoven was particularly drawn to fugal writing in his late works. His piano Sonatas Op. 101, 106, and 110, for example, all make use of large-scale fugal movements, as do his late quartets, such as Op. 131. After Beethoven, separate fugues or fugal movements were not prevalent in the nineteenth century, although many Germanic composers drew on the genre. Brahms, for example, concludes his Variations on a Theme of Handel with a fugue on the original theme.

Other genres also incorporated fugal style in the context of larger works. Two notable examples are the Baroque overtures, orchestral introductions to operas or oratorios, and sacred choral music. One standard overture type in the Baroque period was the so-called "French Overture" introduced by Lully. This type begins with a slow introductory section in dotted rhythms followed by a fast fugal section. A famous example is the Overture to *Messiah* by Handel. The introduction, discussed in Chapter 3, ends on a Phrygian HC. The allegro then begins with a canzona-type theme that is treated in fugal imitation (Example 12.11). The remainder of the overture presents only two separate middle entries and a final statement near the close, relying more on episodic development of motives in its 85 measures.

Example 12.11 Handel, *Messiah,* Overture, Allegro, mm. 14–18.

Choral music, with its long-standing tradition of contrapuntal and imitative textures, often has movements that are fugal. This is particularly true in sacred works such as masses and oratorios. Two of the best known fugal movements in choral literature include the Kyrie II from the *Mass in B minor* by Bach and the Kyrie from Mozart's *Requiem* (Example 12.12). The subject of the Kyrie by Bach is very much in the vocal style of the motet with its stepwise pitch motion and simple rhythmic motions. Note the striking use of the ♭2 scale degree (G natural). By contrast, the subject from the Mozart Kyrie has an angular contour and varied rhythmic motions. The second subject of this double fugue is also shown.

Example 12.12 *Vocal fugue subjects.*

a. Bach, Mass in B minor, Kyrie II.

b. Mozart, *Requiem,* Kyrie, double fugue, opening.

The Neo-classic trends of the twentieth century resulted in a renewed interest in fugal writing. Shostakovich and Hindemith both wrote collections of fugues for keyboard in the tradition of the WTC by Bach. Shostakovich wrote a collection of Preludes and Fugues while Hindemith wrote a work entitled *Ludus Tonalis* (Play of Tones). Hindemith's work is a collection of twelve fugues connected by interludes, and framed by a prelude and postlude. Both of these works demonstrate the continuing vitality of contrapuntal genres in the twentieth century. Two other well-known instances of fugal movements in twentieth-century works include the *Symphony of Psalms* by Stravinsky and *Music for Strings, Percussion, and Celesta* by Bartók, addressed in the exercises that follow.

Analytic Exercises

Bach's WTC, Books I and II, provide a remarkable collection of fugues in diverse styles, proportions, and formal structures. The following list of fugues from these collections provides examples of different approaches to fugue writing and strongly contrasting subjects. After identifying the subject statements throughout the fugue and the tonal design, consider the various textures and individual lines of each fugue. A diagram of a fugue, as illustrated in Figure 12.2, is one way to show the formal organization of a fugue.

As noted previously, a detailed analysis of a fugue will entail careful study of individual linear shapes, and the analysis of phrase structures. Any fugue will offer good examples of motivic variation; consider when and how such variations are used. Also consider the significant attributes of a fugue, including the rhythm, contour, linear shape, and style of the subject, the use or absence of specific fugal techniques, the relative proportions of various sections, and the manner in which the fugue is concluded. Interpret how the various attributes you identify shape the course of the fugue and influence its character and expressive effect.

1. ***Fugue in C Major, Book 1.** This fugue makes extensive use of stretto and, as some writers note, approaches a binary form. To what extent is this latter observation valid? Study the diagram of the fugue provided in Figure 12.3. Compare the various harmonic settings of the many entrances of the subject.

2. ***Fugue in F major, Book 1.** The distinct points of cadence make the tonal design of this fugue clear.

   a. What part of the countersubject helps mark cadences?
   b. Where is the strongest point of cadence other than the final cadence?
   c. Where does the exposition end?
   d. How is it extended?
   e. This fugue also makes use of stretto. Where is the most extensive use of stretto and how is it emphasized in the music?
   f. Identify instances of textural inversion. Can you find the hidden, final entrance of the fugue subject beginning in measure 64?

3. **+Fugue in G minor, Book 1.** This fugue offers a good example of a two-part head-and-tail subject.

   a. What is the relation of the CS to the subject?
   b. Consider the various textures with regard to pairing of voices. Identify instances of duets and dialogues between pairs of voices. At what points are four independent voices heard?
   c. Consider the harmony and texture of the last two measures. How are they unique to the fugue?

4. **Fugue in D♯ minor, Book I.** This three-voice fugue presents a lyrical, "stile antico" subject with no extended episodes. The subject is varied through inversion, canon, augmentation, and stretto. Which of these techniques is used most often?

WORKS FOR FURTHER STUDY

The following fugues or fugal sections of larger works will reward study:

Bach, Mass in B minor, Kyrie II. Two distinct subjects may be identified in this towering fugue; the second subject is introduced midway through the fugue (measure 35). Trace the presentation of these subjects in the various voices. Which passages are episodic? There is frequent use of deceptive cadences or overlapping phrases to convey a somewhat relentless sense of continuation. Note where all voices coalesce at a point of cadence before the final cadence. Which modulations, if any, are marked by strong cadences?

Mozart, Symphony 41, Coda. This symphony is often referred to as the "fugal symphony" on the basis of its fugal writing in the last movement, most famously in the elaborate coda. How many different ideas are used in this passage, beginning in measure 372?

Beethoven, Diabelli Variations, Nos. 19 and 24. Compare the theme, shown in Chapter 11, with these two fugal variations.

Verdi, *Falstaff*. The conclusion of this opera is built around an elaborate fugal section involving the main characters, beginning at the *Allegro brioso*. To what extent is this section expository or episodic?

Stravinsky, *Symphony of Psalms*, II. The slow movement of this work is a double fugue with an instrumental and then a vocal exposition of two different subjects. Consider the extent to which the subjects are tonal and compare the relation of the points of imitation to traditional tonal fugues. To what extent are the motives of the various subjects combined? Study the text and consider whether specific instances of text painting can be found in this movement. Where is the final statement of the first subject?

Bartók, *Music for Strings, Percussion, and Celesta*, I. Trace the entrance of each statement of the fugue subject. What type of symmetrical pitch pattern do the entrances outline?

Chorale Preludes

Chorales, which are German Protestant hymns, emerged during the late Renaissance and the Baroque period as a vital part of Protestant church services. They are short pieces in homophonic textures that were meant to be sung by the congregation. As the practice of congregational singing of chorales emerged in Protestant services, organists developed various ways of presenting the chorale beforehand as a prelude to the singing of the hymn. These organ pieces, which present a chorale melody in simple or elaborate forms with contrapuntal textures, are referred to as *chorale preludes*. A variety of techniques for setting chorale melodies led to various categories of chorale preludes including the following types:

- **Melody chorale.** The melody is presented *continuously* in the soprano part in simple or slightly elaborated form with contrapuntal accompaniment. Often the additional parts were based on repeated figures.
- **Ornamental chorale.** Similar to a melody chorale but elaborate ornamentations or diminutions of the chorale melody are presented.
- **Cantus firmus chorale.** The melody is used in long durations (often in the bass) or in simple, unembellished form. Each phrase of the melody is introduced and separated by figural material, sometimes treated as a *ritornello*.
- **Chorale canon.** A canon among two or more voices accompanies the chorale melody. This type may incorporate *cantus firmus* techniques or use the chorale melody in canon.

The chorale prelude is one prevalent type of organ chorale.[19] Inasmuch as works designated *chorale prelude* use techniques drawn from a variety of types, *chorale prelude* is sometimes used as a general term for contrapuntal works using chorale melodies. As in many Baroque genres, the best and most celebrated examples are those by J. S. Bach. An examination of select examples will clarify some of the techniques mentioned and the forms chorale preludes may take.

Bach's collection of chorale preludes in the *Orgelbüchlein*, BWV 599-644 (Little Organ Book) illustrates a number of types. Most frequently encountered in the collection is the melody chorale or ornamental chorale. Example 12.13a shows a well-known chorale melody

[19] Additional types of organ chorales include: 1) *chorale motet*, in which each phrase melody of the chorale is used as a point of imitation and then elaborated in the manner of a vocal motet, 2) *chorale fugue*, in which the first phrase melody is used as the basis for a fugue, 3) *chorale fantasie*, which is a free, extended elaboration of the chorale melody, and 4) *chorale variations*, a series of separate variations on the chorale melody in a variety of contrapuntal settings.

and Example 12.13b shows Bach's setting. This chorale melody illustrates one of two basic forms a chorale would take: a short, through-composed piece of varying length, usually 8–16 measures.[20] The cadences of the short phrases were, by convention, marked in the music by fermatas. The chorale prelude on this chorale presents the chorale melody in the soprano in continuous motion, with at least two significant changes: 1) some of the pitches of the chorale melody are elongated through augmentation of note values and metrically relocated and 2) some pitches of the melody are elaborated rhythmically (diminution). As a result of these changes in the melody, the phrase structure is expanded from eight to ten measures.

Example 12.13 *Bach,* "Vom Himmel Hoch" and Chorale Prelude.

a. Chorale melody, "Vom Himmel Hoch."

b. Chorale prelude.

[20] Some chorales are as long as 25–30 measures. See *371 Harmonized Chorales and 69 Chorale Melodies with figured bass*, edited by Albert Riemenschneider (New York: G. Schirmer, Inc. 1941).

A different setting of this chorale melody is found in a set of canonic variations, one of four sets of chorale variations Bach wrote. The beginning of variation 1 is shown in Example 12.14a. Here, each phrase of the chorale melody is presented unembellished in the bass but not in continuous phrases. The canon at the octave is in the other voices, which introduce and separate the entrances of the chorale melody. Note that the meter has been changed, a change not uncommon in chorale preludes. Variation 5 (Example 12.14b) shows a different approach to the canon. Here the chorale melody is used in a mirror canon with a continuous bass line motion. In fact, this variation, the most complex and longest of the five, presents the chorale melody in four mirror canons at different intervals. In the process, the registral placement of the canonic voices and accompaniment is varied, and additional voices are added in the final section.

Example 12.14 Canonic variations on "Vom Himmel Hoch," variations 1 and 5.

a. Variation 1, beginning.

b. Variation 5, beginning.

The other formal design most frequently encountered in chorales consists of a repeated first section, which may close with a PAC in tonic or in a new key, followed by a longer second section. While relatively short and usually through-composed, the length of each section varies. This form is diagrammed as A A B and is referred to as a *bar form*. A well-known chorale in this form is "Wachet auf" ("Awake"), shown in Example 12.15. The bar form, which originated in medieval German poetry, consists of two parts: 1) a *Stollen*, which is the first two stanzas sung to the repeated A part and 2) an *Abgesang*, which is the third stanza heard in the B section of the form. In this example, the phrases in each section are designated as A1, A2, A3, and so forth, while the pattern of thematic content is designated by lower case letters. Note that the last phrase of each section is identical, creating a rhyme scheme found in some bar forms. Bach's use of this chorale tune is addressed in the exercises that follow.

Example 12.15 Chorale melody "Wachet auf, ruft uns die Stimme."

Aural Exercises

Consult a collection of Bach chorales and familiarize yourself with the chorale melodies for each of the chorale preludes listed below. Take notes on the number of phrases, modulations or tonicizations, and cadences in each chorale. Then listen to the chorale preludes listed to determine 1) the basic approach to the chorale prelude based on the types identified above and 2) the relation of the form of the chorale to the form of the chorale prelude. Closer analysis with a score should reveal details of melodic and harmonic variations that are evident in the chorale prelude. BWV 668 is from *Eighteen Chorale Preludes* and the others are from the *Orgelbüchlein.*

Ich ruf zu dir, Herr Jesu Christ
In dulci jubilo
Wenn wir in höchstein Nöten sein
+Das alte Jahr vergangen ist
+Nun Komm, der Heiden Heiland
*Vor deinen Tron tret' ich hiermit, BWV 668

Analytic Exercises

I. Among the most famous sets of chorale preludes by Bach is a group of six, published by Schübler in 1747, and often referred to as the "Schübler Chorales." One of the best known of these chorales is the one based on "Wachet auf." This chorale prelude was originally used in the Chorale Cantata of the same name, Cantata No. 140. It is the central movement of the seven-movement cantata and is set for strings and tenor. Bach later set it for organ as part of the Schübler Chorales. The opening of the chorale prelude is shown in Example 12.16. The first twelve measures serve as a ritornello that will frame and accompany the various entrances of the chorale melody. The ritornello contains four distinct two-measure ideas plus a two-measure cadence figure to close. These are labeled a b c d on the score and in the formal diagram given in Figure 12.4. Listen to a recording of this work and compare the original chorale melody to the presentation of the melody in the chorale prelude. Without the aid of a score, complete the diagram of the form given below with repeated hearings as needed. Give particular attention to different elements each time you listen, including 1) the ordering of the phrases of the chorale in relation to the original, 2) the presentation and reordering of the ritornello segments, 3) where modulations occur, and 4) the entrance and cadences of the chorale phrases in relation to the ritornello.

Further analysis with a score should address other aspects of the piece, including 1) a harmonic analysis of the opening ritornello (Bach's elegant melodic line is a compound melody with interesting use of non-chord tones), 2) the re-harmonization of the opening Rit-a segment each time it returns, and 3) the keys to which Bach modulates (note the chorale entrance in measure 63 and its role in the modulation back to tonic).

Example 12.16 "Wachet auf, ruft uns die Stimme."

Figure 12.4 *Formal Diagram Chorale Prelude "Wachet auf," first section.*

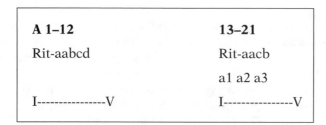

A 1–12	**13–21**
Rit-aabcd	Rit-aacb
	a1 a2 a3
I----------------V	I----------------V

II. An additional example of a ritornello approach to a chorale setting is heard in what is perhaps Bach's most famous composition "Jesu Joy of Man's Desiring." This chorale was used in the Cantata BWV 147 *Herz und Mund und Tat und Leben (Heart and Lips, Thy Whole Behavior)*. This cantata is in two parts; a chorale setting of this melody ends each part. An analysis of any of these settings will reveal certain similarities with the formal design and use of the ritornello procedures found in *Wachet auf*. Close analysis of the opening ritornello will reveal its relationship to the chorale melody.

13 Vocal Forms

Introduction

Many of the forms used in vocal music have been discussed in previous chapters, including one-part, binary, ternary, rondo, and ostinato forms. The manner in which these various forms are used merits further discussion, however, because the forms are often adapted in specific ways in vocal music. Perhaps the overriding reason for these adaptations is the obvious fact that vocal music is sung and thus incorporates text. The forms of vocal music have been influenced by traditions and considerations of setting text and performance. This chapter will address some of the specific ways that forms in vocal music are shaped and, particularly in the case of art songs, how the composer's interpretation of text influences the formal structure of the song. Hymns, popular songs, art songs, arias, and choral music will each be surveyed.

Hymns and Traditional Songs

The simplest vocal forms are found in hymns, traditional songs, and folk melodies. As observed in Chapter 3, such simple vocal pieces are often eight to sixteen bars long and comprised of four-bar phrases.[1] One of the most common designs is the sixteen-bar *quatrain*, which contains four, four-bar phrases. Two examples of quatrains are given in Examples 13.1a and b. Figure 13.1 illustrates the formal design of these quatrains. These examples show characteristics of many quatrains:

1. They begin with a repeated phrase (Ex. 13.1a) or parallel period (Ex. 13.1b), followed by a contrasting phrase and then a (varied) restatement of the first phrase to close.
2. The phrases make use of statement/continuation.
3. The B phrase ends on a half cadence.
4. They remain in the tonic key, although tonicizations of dominant sometimes occur at cadences.

We may also observe some common variables in these examples. First, if a parallel period begins the quatrain it is the second phrase (A′) that is restated at the end, as the song must close in tonic. Second, the B phrase may use varied repetition or new ideas, though the phrase melodies are often closely related rhythmically. The B phrase contrasts tonally with the A phrase and the harmonic motion will vary.

[1] See Chapter 3, Examples 3.1 and 3.2.

Example 13.1

a. German folk melody, "Es flog ein kleines Waldvögelein."

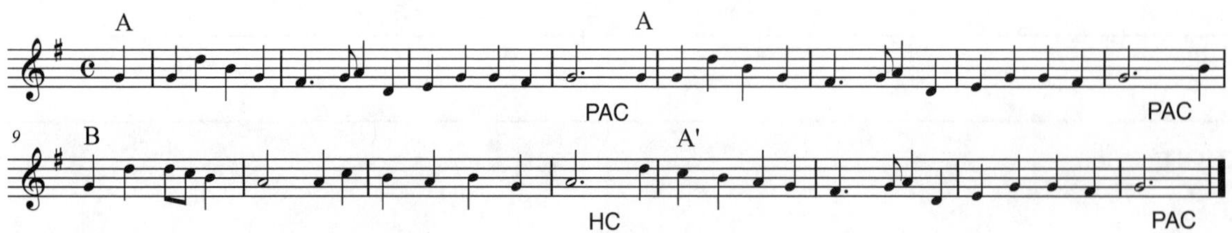

b. Holst, "In the Bleak Mid-winter."

Public domain melody from the Hymnal 1982 © 1985 The Church Pension Fund, New York.

Figure 13.1 *Formal designs of Examples 13.1a–b.*

a. "Es flog ein kleines Waldvögelein"				b. "In the Bleak Midwinter"				
A	**A**	**B**	**A′**	**A**	**A′**	**B**	**A′**	1–8=Period
ab	ab	a′b′	ab	ab	ab	a′c′	ab	
2+2	2+2	2+2	2+2	2+2	2+2	2+2	2+2	
PAC	PAC	HC	AC	HC	PAC	HC	AC	
I	I	I	I	I	I	I	I	

The form of most musical quatrains may be interpreted two ways. Many writers consider them to be in ternary form as there are no repeats that divide the form into two halves and because the B phrase functions as a contrasting middle section. On the other hand, they could be in rounded binary form if the first two phrases are paired as a larger unit that divides the form in two, and the B section is considered a transition that groups with the partial restatement of A.[2] This may be a matter of perception, but the absence of repeats in each eight-bar unit suggests a stronger case for small ternary form.[3] Some quatrains are in simple binary form (AB) with each half comprised of two four-bar contrasting phrases. Further, there are quatrains that are expanded by repeats of sections, as noted in the examples below, making them more binary-like.

Another form encountered in songs is that of the small binary form, each half containing a single phrase. This form was seen in Example 3.2, a short hymn comprised of two four-bar phrases, a common form in many short hymns. Other small binary songs are comprised of two eight-bar sentence structures as illustrated in Example 13.2. In

[2] See Chapter 7 for a review of the distinctions and overlap between these two forms.

[3] See Caplin, 71–73, for further discussion of this issue.

some cases, songs contain two eight-bar phrases that comprise a contrasting period. If the harmonic motion is continuous in any of these cases, it may be considered a one-part form.[4]

Example 13.2 Wareham, Hymn 137: small binary form using sentence structures.

From Hymns Ancient and Modern, 1875.

Another factor influencing the design of songs is the arrangement of text. In the examples cited thus far, two or more verses of text are set by repeating the entire song or hymn with a different text each time. The term *strophic form* refers to this treatment of text in a musical setting. It must be understood that the actual form of the hymn does not change and that strophic form only refers to the repetition of the complete song with different text.

Many songs incorporate a strophic setting of verses with a refrain, the latter referring to a musical phrase or section that always repeats with the same text. *The placement of the refrain will vary.* As outlined in Figure 13.2, the familiar "Old Folks at Home" by Stephen Foster is a quatrain, which repeats the opening eight-bar period. The repeated period is set to different verses while the B and restatement of A act as a refrain with the same text each time. The entire song is repeated twice more, thus six verses of text (two each time with the repeat) are heard in the verse. The song, with the distinction between verse and refrain and the repeat of the verse section, takes on characteristics of rounded binary.

Figure 13.2 *Foster, "Old Folks at Home," formal design.*

Verse		**Refrain**		
𝄆A	A′ 𝄇	B	A′	1–8=Period
ab	ab′	c′c′d	ab	rounded binary with repeats of AA′
2+2	2+2	1+1+2	2+2	
HC	AC	HC	AC	
I	I	I	I	

[4] See Example 3.2 and the analytic note in Chapter 6 concerning small binary and one-part form.

The reverse arrangement, refrain–verse is heard in another familiar strophic song, "Swing Low, Sweet Chariot" (Figure 13.3). In this case, the refrain begins the piece, and is repeated with the same text each time. The entire song is repeated twice more (three verses of text) with a final restatement of the refrain creating a small ternary form. Another variable here is the distinction between soloist and chorus. The "b" material of each phrase, which is used in both the refrain and the verse, repeats the same music and the same text ("comin' for to carry me home.") each time. Thus there is a refrain *within* the verse. Each time this text and music return, it is designated as a chorus, while the other parts of the verse and refrain are sung by a soloist. In many songs, the refrain is called a "chorus."

Figure 13.3 *"Swing Low, Sweet Chariot."*

Refrain		**Verse**		***da capo* Refrain**
ab	ab′	a′b′	a′b′	NOTE: ab alternates solo/chorus
2+2	2+2	2+2	2+2	
IAC	PAC	IAC	PAC	
I	I	I	I	

Two additional forms that are found in short songs have been discussed in earlier chapters. One is the A A B design or bar form, discussed in Chapter 11 with reference to chorale preludes. Many hymns in bar form are also strophic forms that use verse and refrain in the setting of the text. The refrain is the "B" section of the form, which concludes the hymn. Hymns may also be through-composed, often with each phrase using similar rhythms. The form is therefore A A′ A′ or A B C, and so forth, depending on the number of phrases.

Exercises

A. Aural Analysis. Each of the songs in the following list (which are presumed to be familiar), makes use of one of the forms discussed above. Sing or think through each song and match the song with the appropriate formal description. You may need to consult a score to determine text settings. Make a formal diagram of each song similar to Figures 13.2 and 13.3 to show the details of the phrase structure.

1. Twinkle, Twinkle Little Star	**a.** quatrain, small ternary
2. The First Nowell	**b.** one-part, parallel period
3. Auld Lange Syne	**c.** quatrain, simple binary
4. Eternal Father (Navy Hymn)	**d.** quatrain, simple binary, verse/refrain
5. America the Beautiful	**e.** bar form, verse/refrain
6. On Top of Old Smoky	**f.** through-composed

B. Score Analysis: Hebrew melody, Leoni. Analyze the phrase structure of the following hymn melody. Use small letter designations for phrase components and label all implied cadences. Which type of small form does this hymn exhibit? Is more than one reasonable interpretation of the form possible?

Hebrew melody, *Leoni*.

Popular Song

The genre of popular song embraces a wide range of repertoire from show tunes, jazz standards and ballads, to folk, rock, and country songs. Of these types, many display ternary or binary forms that are based on eight-bar phrases of music. This is particularly true of show tunes, jazz standards, and ballads. Verses, refrains, and interludes may be incorporated in many songs as well. The discussion here will elaborate on some of the prevalent forms in these types of popular songs.

Literally hundreds of American popular tunes have been written in 32-bar song form (introduced in Chapter 7), particularly in the first half of the twentieth century. This vocal form is typically a quatrain in a small ternary form. The tunes "My Ship" by Weill and "I Got Rhythm" by Gershwin illustrate one standard version of this form: a repeated, eight-bar sentence followed by a contrasting eight-bar phrase ending on a HC, and a restatement of the first phrase. This pattern is an enlarged version of the quatrain illustrated in Example 13.1a and Figure 13.1. Notable in these examples is the retention of the tonic key, with harmonic digression in the contrasting B section. The first sixteen bars may also comprise a repeated period as in the well-known song "Over the Rainbow" by Harold Arlen. As in the quatrains discussed above, this gives the form characteristics of a rounded binary form. Finally, some song forms may take 16 or 64-bar forms, depending on the tempo and style of the piece. The number of phrases remains the same. As in sentence structures, it is the proportional relations, rather than the number of measures, that characterize the form.

Popular songs often begin with an introduction that may take two forms. Many songs in a broad range of styles begin with an introductory phrase that establishes the tempo and key for the singer. In some songs, such as "My Ship," this instrumental introduction leads directly to the main melody. More often there will be a verse that presents introductory text in repeated phrases, each phrase containing new text. The verses normally keep the same melodic pattern although modulations or tonal digressions may occur in varied repetitions. The verse also has introductory musical qualities, notably inconclusive cadences. Verses are typically in four or eight-bar phrase pairs, though phrase extensions may be added.

The verse helps establish the subject of the song leading to the principal melody and text, which is the *refrain. In popular songs, the verse normally precedes the refrain.* As in any refrain, those in popular songs are characterized by the use of a single verse. The refrain also may be referred to as the "chorus" in some scores, even though the song is for solo singer. In concert performances of many popular songs, the verse is sometimes considered optional. This is one reason why the refrain is what most listeners associate with the song.[5]

A diagram of a complete song with introduction, verse, and refrain is shown in Figure 13.4. Note that the refrain is usually repeated. Recall that the refrain—the 32-bar form—contains a *head* (first two phrases), a *bridge* (contrasting B phrase), and a restatement of the head. In many performances with a singer, the head of the refrain is presented by the instrumentalists at the repeat, often in varied improvisatory form. The singer then comes back in after the bridge. As in many forms, a coda may close the piece. The coda often takes the form of an instrumental closing phrase, called a *postlude.* Similarly, instrumental phrases within the form are called *interludes.*

Figure 13.4 *Verse/Refrain form of popular songs.*

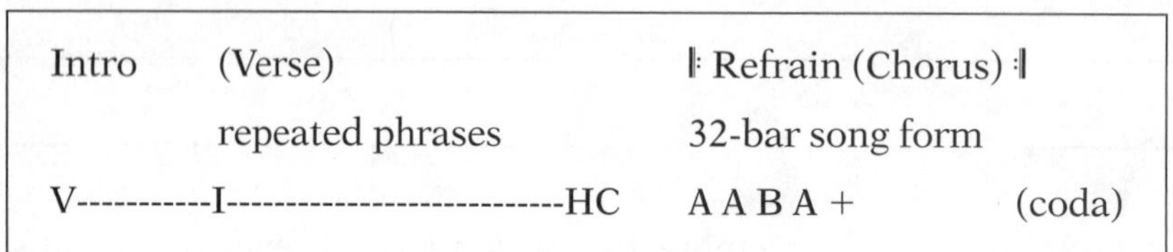

One important variable in the 32-bar song form is the tonal design. The B section, or *bridge,* is expected to have harmonic digression, which will vary from song to song. Normally this section concludes with a half cadence, although exceptions do occur. Typically, as in the songs cited above, phrases in the A section cadence in the tonic key. The verse and refrain, however, may also digress from the tonic key. Example 13.3 illustrates a noteworthy example of such digressions. "All the Things You Are," one of Jerome Kern's best loved and most admired songs, contains a rich tonal design. The introduction and verse are in the key of G major, but the end of the verse makes a surprising pivot to F minor at the beginning of the refrain. This turns out to be a non-tonic opening that leads the first phrase of the refrain through A♭ major to close in C major. The repeat of this phrase begins in C minor, passes through E♭ major and closes in G major, a transposed version of the first phrase. The head of the melody thus uses sequences and descending fifth progressions to provide unusual tonal motions to this striking melody.[6] The bridge continues in G major but modulates to E major. The recall of the head (restatement of A) creates a climax melodically and harmonically to finally close in the tonic key of A♭ major, which emphasizes the text in an eloquent manner. Note how the expansion of the closing phrase supports this dramatic close. In spite of the rather square phrase structure through much of this song, the subtle harmonic and melodic qualities and the treatment of text approach the sophistication of art songs.

[5] In fact, verses of popular tunes are often not familiar or as memorable as the refrains, making an interesting game of "name that tune" based on a given verse.

[6] This melody offers excellent opportunity for re-harmonization using tritone substitutes and is a favorite of jazz musicians.

Example 13.3 Kern, "All the Things You Are" (1939), refrain.

The 32-bar song form usually is a small ternary form. Some 32-bar songs, however, are clearly in simple binary form based on two, 16-bar sections in A B/A B or A B/A C formal designs. The refrain of the song "Laura" by David Raksin is an example of the A B/A B form, which is based on two large sentence structures, each 4+4+8 bars long. Example 13.4 shows the first eight bars of the refrain. Not unlike the example by Kern, this refrain contains sequential, modulatory harmonic progressions. It also begins with a non-tonic progression around G major, V of the principal key of C major. The progressions are outlined in Figure 13.5. Also, like the Kern song, the modulations of the first 16 bars are resolved in the varied restatement of A which turns to tonic in the last subphrase and adds a phrase extension to emphasize closure.

Example 13.4 Raksin, "Laura" (1944), mm. 21–36.

Figure 13.5 *Tonal design, "Laura," mm. 21–36.*

Measures:	**21**	**25**	**29**	**32**	**34**	**36**
Progressions:	**G: ii^9–V^9–I^{9+6}**	**F: ii^9–V^9–I^{9+6}**	**E♭: ii^9–V^9–I^{9+6}**		**G: V–III**	**V/ii**

One other well-established form is the 12-bar blues form. This form can be traced back to nineteenth-and twentieth-century African-American poetry that was often sung. Even though the blues originated as a vocal form, it has been widely disseminated in instrumental and vocal styles. These styles include boogie- woogie, jazz, rhythm and blues, soul, rock, and country music. The most common design of the form is given in Figure 13.6. The three phrases reflect an A A B or bar form pattern that is evident in the text. The harmonies shown are the standard blues progressions which are modified in different styles. Melodic inflection using the ♭3, ♭5, and ♭7, so called "blue notes," is a defining characteristic

Figure 13.6 *12-bar blues form.*

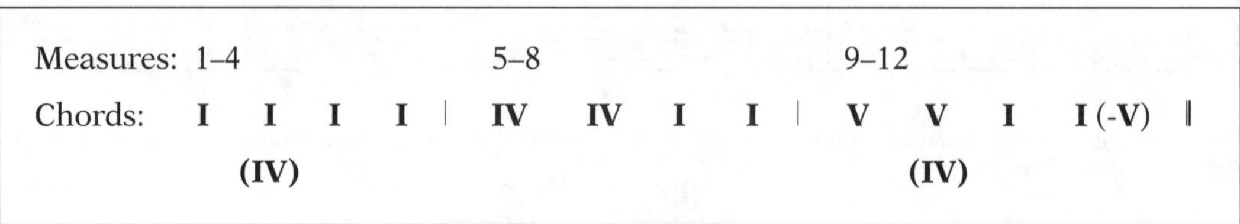

Measures:	1–4				5–8				9–12			
Chords:	**I**	**I**	**I**	**I**	**IV**	**IV**	**I**	**I**	**V**	**V**	**I**	**I (-V)**
		(IV)								**(IV)**		

as well. Jazz performers will often perform blues with secondary progressions, extended chords, and substitute harmonies to elaborate this harmonic structure. Eight- and 16-bar blues progressions are also found, but the 12-bar blues is the primary form. Vocal blues forms will also employ verses and refrains to expand the 12-bar forms. Examples are listed in the exercises that follow.

ANALYTIC EXERCISES

The various songs listed below contain instances of the popular song forms described above. Most of them should be familiar or readily available in recordings. Listen to each of the songs and observe the length of phrases and the cadences. Listen for verses, refrains, interludes, and postludes. Some of these songs expand or modify the forms described above, especially in the case of those marked with **.

Harold Arlen	"Blues in the Night" (1941)**
John Cander	"When You're Good to Mama" (*Chicago,* 1975)
Billy Joel	"She's Always a Woman" (*Stranger,* 1977)**
Elton John	"The Morning Report" (*Lion King,* 1997)
Jerome Kern	"Make Believe" (1937)
B.B. King	"How Blue Can You Get?" (1963)
Paul McCartney	"Yesterday" (1965)
J. King Oliver*	"West End Blues" (1928)
Meredith Wilson	" 'Til There Was You" (*Music Man,* 1957)
Son House	"Death Letter Blues" (1965)
Carole King	"So Far Away" (1971)**
Chris Thomas King	"Come on in My Kitchen" (2001)

Art Songs

Art songs refer to solo vocal compositions in which existing poetry is set to music. The art song flourished in the nineteenth century, notably in the German *lieder* and French *mélodie.*[7] Turning to the great Romantic poetry of writers such as Goethe, Heine, and Schiller, German composers, including Schubert, Schumann, Brahms, and Wolf, wrote many outstanding lieder. French art song is exemplified in the works of Berlioz, Fauré, and Duparc. In the early twentieth century, composers such as Mahler, Strauss, Debussy, Ravel, Schoenberg, Webern, and Berg (followed later by composers such as Britten, Vaughn Williams, Barber, Ives, Copland and Rorem), contributed significant works to the art song repertoire. Art song composition continues to the present day, though not as prolifically as in the nineteenth and early twentieth centuries.

The choice to set poetic text is in contrast to popular songs, where the text is referred to as the *lyrics* of the song. Lyrics may be written by the songwriter (composer), but often in popular song, a songwriter and lyricist collaborate. The composer of art songs, on the other hand, carefully chooses poetry, and then sets it to music. The primary task of the composers is to convey an interpretation of the poetry in musical terms. Given the subtlety and richness of language in poetry, art songs, while frequently based on common formal designs, are often quite elastic in their treatment of musical form. Some select examples will illustrate this point.

---

[7] The German term "lied" means song of any kind, although it has come to refer specifically to art songs. Similarly, the French "mélodie" (melody) refers to French art songs.

ONE-PART FORM: SCHUBERT, "WANDERERS NACHTLIED"

We turn first to a song in addressed in the exercises in Chapter 6, Schubert's "Wanderers Nachtlied" (Example 13.5). As indicated earlier, the piece is in one-part form, not only because of its brevity but more importantly because of its continuous harmonic motion. The first two measures comprise a small introductory phrase, the final three and half measures echo the previous phrase, and the last measure echoes the cadence heard in measures 2, 10, and 13. These phrases are expansions of the form, with measures 3–11 forming a continuous line. What merits further consideration is the phrase structure of measures 3–11 and the text.

Example 13.5 Schubert, "Wanderers Nachtlied."

The analysis of art songs must include consideration of the text to fully understand the formal structure. The text to this lied is given in Figure 13.7 with the translation.

A central concern of both the composer and the singer is the meaning and expressive intent of the text. One way of addressing this concern is to decide "who is speaking," which in a song is referred to as the *vocal persona*. Generally, a song may be 1) a narrative in which a story is being told, 2) a dialogue between or among characters, 3) reflective: the singer is a single character speaking to him or herself (or to an unseen character), or 4) a combination of these types (for example, a poem may include dialogue and a narrator). Another concern is the mood or psychological state of the vocal persona. In this poem the persona is an expressive archetype of Romanticism: the lonely wanderer who is drawn to nature and its solitary beauty and yearning for a peaceful death.[8] In short, it is a poem of expressive imagery and mystery. This perspective may account for the slow tempo (*Lento*), the opening chorale-like texture, the sometimes restless rhythms (syncopations), and the restrained dynamics.

Figure 13.7 *Wanderers Nachtlied (Goethe/Schubert).*

Über allen Gipfeln	Over all mountaintops
Ist Ruh,	Is peace.
In allen Wipfeln	In all treetops
Spürest du	you feel
Kaum einen Hauch;	Scarcely a breath;
Die Vöglein schweigen im Walde.	The little birds are silent in the woods.
Warte nur, balde	Wait now, soon
Ruhest du auch.	Rest you also.

The brevity of the poem by Goethe is one factor in setting the text in a one-part form. In addition, the lines of text are quite short, even as they create a rich setting. The text divides neatly into two quatrains based on the rhyme scheme; however, the poem's meaning is not arranged in that manner.[9] Lines 1–6 describe a scene in nature, grouped as 2+3+1 lines. The brevity of the first five lines creates a sense of mystery, and the more elaborate sixth line conveys a yearning for quiet and solitude. The last two lines foreshadow a peaceful death.

Now examine the musical setting of this text. If one sings through the vocal line, the short and unequal length phrases should be apparent, as indicated by the brackets in Example 13.5. The unequal phrase lengths can be understood as a reflection of Goethe's unequal lines of text. The musical phrases also articulate the lines of text. Another important point we should notice is that Schubert has choosen to repeat the last two lines of text in measures 11–13. This repetition emphasizes the importance of these lines in Schubert's interpretation. Now consider the groupings of these phrases. Arguably, the change in accompaniment in the middle of measure five, to a more agitated rhythmic texture,

[8] The symbols of the wanderer, the evocative, mysterious world of nature, the solitary forest, and yearning for peaceful death are commonly cited in descriptions of German Romanticism.

[9] A discussion of the prosody—the stress, sound, and length of syllables—is beyond the scope of this discussion. See Stein and Spillman, 45–51, for a discussion of prosody in Schubert's "Wanderers Nachtlied."

groups measures 5–8 as a short section. However, the melodic and harmonic motion in measures 5–6 suggests a HC within measure 6. This analysis is also supported by the punctuation of the text. The change back to the opening texture in measure 10, the PAC in measure 11 reiterated in measure 13, and the text repetitions, set measures 9–14 apart from the previous passages.

What can be observed here is that the textural and tonal elements are out of phase in measures 5–8, creating a sense of continuing motion. The continuation of dominant harmony in measures 7–8 contributes to this continuity. The piece might be labeled an A(3–8) B(5–8) C (9–13) design. Even though we can divide this short piece into small sections, the harmonic motion clearly conveys measures 3–11 as a continuous line. The piece can be understood as a through-composed, one-part form. The delay of harmonic resolution until the last phrases of the piece confirms this sense of its form. In the absence of any clear restatements of material, motivic repetitions unify the piece. In regard to this we can note the dotted rhythms, the recurring cadence from measure 2, and the motivic doublings of thirds and sixths between voice and piano. Finally, the importance and diversity of the piano textures is indicative of the nineteenth-century developments in pianistic textures, which support the setting of the text.

TERNARY FORM: SCHUMANN, "ICH GROLLE NICHT"

It was observed in Chapter 7 that ternary form is so often used for songs of various types that it is sometimes described as "song form." Though clearly there are other types of song forms, a great many songs are in simple ternary form. This points to the need for restatements of material to create musical closure, a need that often influences the treatment of text. Schumann's song "Ich Grolle Nicht," from his song cycle *Dichterliebe* (1840), illustrates this point.[10]

The text by Heinrich Heine is given along with Schumann's setting in Figure 13.8. This poem is in two stanzas sung by a reflective vocal persona who ponders a lost love. What we see here is Schumann's well-known penchant for altering the text for musical and interpretive reasons. Text in **bold face** type indicates Schumann's relocation or repetition of text, which should be compared with the original poem.

Schumann's alteration in text placement clearly emphasizes what he must have considered the main thrust of the poem: the vocal persona is heartbroken but will "bear no grudge." Just how Schumann interprets the state of mind of the vocal persona is a point we will return to.

The three parts of the song are relatively clear: measures 1–10 (A) complete the first stanza and close with a PAC in the tonic key of C major; measures 13–18 (B) begin in A minor and through a rising sequence returns to C major; the opening musical material returns in measure 19 (A). At this point of musical restatement, Schumann brings back the same text of this music, the opening line. To do this, he uses the first line of the second stanza to close the middle section. The musical principle of restatement with the associated text may inform this choice by Schumann, but it also emphasizes the repeated text, "Ich grolle nicht."

The restatement of A, as is often the case in nineteenth-century ternary forms, is varied in significant ways. The text is different, beginning in measure 20, requiring changes in rhythm. This phrase corresponds to the phrase that began in measure 5 given in Example 13.6a. This restatement is altered and expanded, not only because of the different text, but to create a musical climax in measures 27–29 given in Example 13.6b. Here, the vocalist dramatically sings of the "devoured heart" and misery of his lost love, made all the more forceful when the optional pitches are taken. The point of the phrase expansion, it seems, is to stress

[10] A song cycle is a group of songs composed and meant to be performed as a set in the specified order. Unifying elements may include text (a cyclic group of poems on a general theme), tonalities (an ordered sequence of keys), and recurring musical motives.

Figure 13.8 *"Ich Grolle Nicht," text by Heinrich Heine.*

Ich Grolle Nicht, und wenn das Herz auch bricht, Ewig verlor'nes Lieb! ich grolle nicht.	**I bear no grudge**, even though my heart may break, eternally lost love! I bear no grudge.
Wie du auch strahlst in Diamantenpracht, Es fällt kein Strahl in deines Herzensnacht.	However you may shine in the splendor of your diamonds, no ray of light falls in the darkness of your heart.
Das weiss ich längst. Ich sah dich ja im Traum, Und sah die Nacht in deines Herzens Raum,	**I have long known this.** I saw you in a dream, and saw the night within the void of your heart,
Und sah die Schlang', die dir am Herzen frisst, Ich sah, mein Lieb, wie sehr du elend bist.	and saw the serpent that is eating your heart— I saw, my love, how very miserable you are.
Setting by Robert Schumann (1840)[11]	
A	
Ich Grolle Nicht und wenn das Herz auch bricht.	m.1: I bear no grudge, even though my heart may break,
Ewig verlor'nes Lieb, ich grolle nicht.	m. 5: eternally lost love! I bear no grudge.
B	
Wie du auch strahlst in Diamantenpracht,	m. 13: However you may shine in the splendor of your diamonds,
Es fällt kein Strahl in deines Herzens Nacht.	no ray of light falls in the darkness of your heart.
Das weiss ich längst	m. 17: **I have long known this.**
A′	
Ich Grolle Nicht Ich sah dich ja im Traume,	m. 19: **I bear no grudge.** m. 23 I saw you in a dream,
Und sah die nacht in deines Herzens Raume,	m. 24: and saw the night within the void of your heart,
Und sah die Schlang', die dir am Herzen frisst,	m. 26 and saw the serpent that is eating your heart-
Ich sah, mein Lieb, wie sehr du elend bist.	m. 28: I saw, my love, how very miserable you are.
Ich Grolle Nicht, Ich Grolle Nicht.	m. 30: **I bear no grudge**

the pain of the vocal persona and his lost love. This sentiment is reinforced by the final phrase expansion by the vocalist and the dynamic postlude. The thick and continuous rhythmic texture of the accompaniment gives added weight to the passion of this song. Such alterations in musical restatements are not uncommon in art songs and invariably serve the composer's interpretation of text.

A final question might be posed here: Is the vocal persona expressing resignation, pity—for himself and his lover—or even anger? The answer will be left to the reader to ponder, but Schumann's poetic alterations and musical setting suggest that there may be more than one viable interpretation of the expressive intent in this well-known lied.

---

[11] Schumann also changed "Traum" and "Raum" to "Traume" and "Raume" for the sake of rhyme scheme and rhythm.

Example 13.6 Schumann, "Ich Grolle Nicht" from *Dichterlieb.*

a. mm. 5–12.

b. mm. 23–32.

EXPANDED SONG FORM AND REFRAINS: WOLF, "IN DEM SCHATTEN" (1889)

The previous examples give some idea of the varied phrase rhythms and flexible forms one may encounter in art songs, which sets them apart from most popular songs. Their formal types, nonetheless, were relatively clear. A final example by Hugo Wolf will show how a composer's setting of text can result in an expanded "song form" whose formal design may be ambiguous.

Again we begin with the text (Figure 13.9), in this case a verse from a Spanish traditional song translated to German by Heyse and set to music by Wolf. The vocal persona in the song "In dem Schatten" is a woman in love who is alternately agitated and tender as she reflects on her sleeping love. Note that each of the three stanzas ends with the same text, thus a refrain is evident in the poem. The first stanza is noticeably shorter than the next two. Measure numbers are given to show the position of the text in the musical form indicated by letters. Unlike the previous example, there are no alterations of text. After obtaining a score and a translation as needed, it is of value to mark textual divisions and musical divisions. Observe that in Wolf's setting the formal divisions of the music do not align with the three verses of the poem.

Figure 13.9 *"In dem Schatten," text.*

In dem Schatten meiner Locken	In the shade of my tresses	mm. 1	A
Schlief mir mein Geliebter ein.	My darling went to sleep.		
Weck ich ihn nun auf? Ach nein!	Shall I wake him now? Oh, no!		
Sorglich strählt ich meine krausen	I carefully comb my tangled locks	m. 12	A′
Locken täglich in der Frühe,	Each day in the morning,		
Doch umsonst ist meine Mühe,	But my effort is all in vain	m. 16	B
Weil die Winde sie zersausen.	For the wind tumbles them about.		
Lockenschatten, Windessaussen	Shading tresses, whistling wind	m. 23	
Schläferten den Liebsten ein.	Soothed my darling to sleep.		
Weck ich ihn nun auf? Ach nein!	Shall I wake him now? Oh, no!	m. 27	A″
Hören muss ich, wie ihn gräme,	I must bear it when he is morose,	m. 34	C
Dass er schmachtet schon so lange,	That he has suffered so long,		
Dass ihm Leben geb und nehme	That they given and take from him life		
Diese meine braune Wange.	These my dark cheeks.		
Und er nennt mich seine Schlange,	He calls me his serpent,	m. 43	A
Und doch schlief er bei mir ein.	Yet he went to sleep by my side.		
Wech ich nun auf? Ach nein!	Shall I wake him now? Oh, no!		

On hearing this song one is struck by the sudden changes in dynamics and expression, the sudden modulations to modal harmonies or chromatic third relations, and the dance-like rhythm that suggests a bolero. The many rolled chords and homorhythmic textures in the accompaniment suggest the sound of a guitar, which, like the rhythms, give a Spanish flavor to the setting. Figure 13.10 provides a diagram of the form and outlines several elements that shape the formal design. A few points of explanation may clarify its details:

Figure 13.10 *Wolf, "In dem Shatten," formal design.*

Sections	A		(A′)______	B		A′	C	A		
Measure	1–4	5–10–12	12–15	16–20	20–23–26 ‖	27–32–34	34–41–42 ‖	43–47	53–47–55	55–58
Melody	a	b	c	d	e	b′	d′	a′	b′	a
Phrase length	**4 +**	**7**	**4 +**	**4 + 3 + 4**		**4 + 3**	**2 + 2**	**1+4**	**7**	**4**
Function	intro	refrain	refrain/	episode	ext----	refrain	episode	intro	refrain	postlude
Expression	tender			agitated	tender	tender	agitated	conflicted		tender
Dynamics	*p>ppp*		*mf<f*	*sf-p*	*ppp*	*P*	*mf<f*	*p<mf>p*		
Keys	B♭--F ‖	D-G♭-B♭	B♭--F ‖	Cm(Gm)	D ‖	B♭-D♭-F	F7/D-F♯‖	B♭-V7 ‖	D-G♭-B♭	
Cadences	HC	PAC	PAC	sequence PC			PAC	PAC	PAC	PAC
Tonal Design	**a.** I-‖ III♯---(♭VI)—I III♯		I---V	ii----(vi)	III♯	I—♭III---V F: ♭VI-I	♭VI I-------III♯	I–V ‖ III♯---♭VI—I		
	b. I__________			I	III♯	I	♭VI		IIII♯	I

- Where measures are repeated, elisions take place (measures 12, 34, 55).
- Expressive characterizations are one interpretation of the basic conflict experienced by the vocal persona.
- Points where direct modulations take place are indicated with ‖; measure 16 may be understood as part of a larger sequence.
- The F7/D starting in measure 34 indicates the juxtapositions of the two harmonies.
- The modulation to F♯ major to conclude the C section may be understood as enharmonic ♭VI but also as III♯ in relation to D major, similar to the B♭-D motion of the other sections.
- The modulation in measure 20 is to G minor, although its dominant, D major, prevails as tonic.

The form of this song may be viewed several ways, depending on which aspect of the music is being considered—text, tonality, accompaniment, or vocal line. The divisions shown in Figure 13.9 emphasize the tonal motions with particular attention to the return to tonic. The vocal line gives some indication of being through-composed, although the setting of text "Weck ich ihn nun auf? Ach nein!" serves as a kind of refrain and always returns in the tonic key. At first glance, the sectional designations may suggest a rondo form. The vocal line and harmonic motion of the opening section never return exactly however, and Wolf reinterprets the textual divisions for musical and expressive purposes. These factors may reflect the conflicting emotions of the vocal persona. The two episodes (B and C in the diagram) have different text and vocal lines, but in terms of expressive quality, use of dynamics, and rhythmic motives, they are similar. Note how episode B groups with measures 12–15 sequentially. A large ternary form of A(1–26) B(27–42) A(42–58) might be a reasonable interpretation since measure 42 is a varied return of the opening section. Some writers have described it as a five-part song form. In any case, the formal ambiguities and marked contrasts in expression and tonal areas seem to convey the ambiguous feelings of the vocal persona.

The three works discussed here illustrate the importance of considering several elements when interpreting an art song, particularly the text. They also—in varying degrees—point to the importance of the piano part, which often has a persona of its own. Of the forms employed in songs, the ternary form is the most common. The ternary form with a repetition of the first A—A A B A—is also found in art songs; an expanded B section is another common modification. Some ternary forms also incorporate a refrain, as illustrated above. Finally, simple and rounded binary forms and rondos may be found, the latter also incorporating refrains. These forms are addressed in the following exercises.

Exercises

A. Analytic Exercises. The songs listed below demonstrate various forms, which are identified for you. For each piece consider the following questions:

1. Read through the text and a translation. Is the text narrative a dialogue, reflective, or a combination of types?
2. What is the attitude, mood, or psychological state of each persona? Is this mood clear or ambiguous?
3. Using letter designations and measure numbers, determine the form of each piece, including tonal design. Note the use of interludes, postludes (codas), and transitions. Is the basic form modified in a significant way?
4. Compare the form of the music with the form of the poem. To what extent do they match? How is text repetition treated in the music? Does the composer make any alterations?
5. If a contrasting section begins, how does it effect contrast and at what point does it begin in the text? Consider why the composer chose that point to introduce contrasting material.
6. If there are restatements of material, are they varied? Do the variations reflect the text?
7. How does the musical setting convey the expression, mood, and persona of the text? Does the accompaniment reflect the vocal persona or an individual persona of its own? To what extent is "text painting" (the use of musical techniques to convey or highlight textual images) evident?

Composer	**Song Title**	**Form**
+*Schubert	"Der Erlkönig"	through-composed with rondo and refrain elements
Schubert	"Der Tod und das Mädchen"	simple binary
Schubert	"Morgengruss" from *Die Schöne Mullerin*	rounded binary, strophic
+Schumann	"Widmung"	ternary
Schumann	"Am leuchtenden Summermorgen" from *Dichterliebe*	simple binary
Fauré	"Toujour"	through-composed with elements of ternary form
+Brahms	"Wenn du Nur Zuweilen Lächelst"	simple continuous binary
Brahms*	"Wie Melodien zieht es mir"	simple ternary
Wolf*	"In der Frühe"	simple continuous binary
+Strauss	"Morgen"	simple binary
+Lili Boulanger	"Elle était descendue au bas de la prairie"	through-composed
Amy Beach*	"Dark is the Night"	simple continuous ternary
+Ives	"The Things Our Fathers Loved"	simple binary
Copland	"The World Feels Dusty"	continuous ternary form

B. Compare Musical Settings. The text of Mignon's song "Kennst du das Land" from Goethe's *Wilhelm Meister*, was set to music by three composers—Schubert in 1815, Schumann in 1849, and Wolf in 1888. Comparing different settings of the same text is an invaluable way to study art song composition. You may also wish to compare Brahms's setting of "In dem Schatten" (Op. 6, No. 1, 1852) with Wolf's setting.

Da Capo Aria, Ritornello, and Rondo Forms

An *aria* (Italian for "tune") is a song for solo voice with instrumental accompaniment. While concert arias have been composed, most arias are found in operas, oratorios, and cantatas. Thus the accompaniment is intended to be an orchestra or chamber ensemble. Arias are normally preceded by recitatives, which establish the dramatic action or conflict surrounding the aria. An additional feature of many arias is the use of an instrumental ritornello, which was common in the Baroque era. Ritornellos frame the sections of an aria and expand the vocal forms described previously. Basic forms, notably in opera, are sometimes modified based on conventions and dramatic context. A brief discussion of select examples will give an idea of the types of formal designs one may find in these genres.

BAROQUE DA CAPO ARIA

The arias of the Baroque period, discussed briefly in Chapter 7, were usually compound ternary forms with the indication *da capo* at the end of the B section, indicating a complete restatement of the opening A section. An important element of the aria form is the use of orchestral ritornellos. Arias began with orchestral ritornellos that would recur at various points in the form. The opening ritornello establishes the key and principal melodic ideas of the aria. When restated within the aria, only a portion of the ritornello is heard. Its function is to confirm a modulation to a new key: normally dominant or, in minor keys, relative major. A complete ritornello statement normally closes the first A section of the aria. A general outline of the Baroque *da capo aria* is given in Figure 13.11.

Figure 13.11 *Basic Baroque da capo aria.*

A				*fine*	B	A *da capo*
Rit[1]	Solo[1]	R^2	S^2	R^3	‖ S^3	
	Strophe[1]		St[1*]		St^2	
I	I-[V]	[V]	I-I [V-I]	I	closely related keys	

As the diagram indicates, the second and third ritornellos confirm the keys in which the soloist has cadenced. R^2 will often conclude the cadence initiated by the soloist and therefore may continue the phrase. S^2 may move directly to tonic or modulate from V to I near the beginning. The third ritornello is more extensive than the second, as it closes the A section and the aria at the end of the *da capo*. It often is a complete ritornello restatement framing the entire aria.

NOTE: [V] refers to a modulation to dominant; * refers to an optional cadenza; a strophe is a unit of text comprised of two or more lines.

Ritornello themes may present several motives, ending with a cadential passage that typically recurs in all ritornellos.[12] The thematic and textural relations between the ritornello and solo is variable, as are the relative proportions of the sections . The vocal part often elaborates ritornello motives but may also introduce new ideas. The close of each strophe, particularly the second one, tends to be florid and may incorporate a cadenza-like passage. The B section of the form is usually shorter and contains no ritornello. The text is a single strophe, usually with repetitions. This section may be in any closely related key and normally modulates through one or more keys.

Handel's well-known aria "Let the Bright Seraphim," from his oratorio *Samson* (1741), gives some idea of the flexibility within the formal design outlined above. The text, in two strophes of two lines each, is as follows:

Let the bright Seraphim in burning row
Their loud, uplifted angel trumpets blow

Let the Cherubic host in tuneful choirs,
Touch their immortal harps with golden wires

The opening ritornello is given in Example 13.7. Each of the motives of the ritornello, labeled Ra through Rd, is used in the solo sections in restatements and elaborations. Of particular interest is Handel's use of a solo trumpet, reflecting not only the text but providing interesting possibilities for varied textures. As you listen to this you will hear antiphonal textures as the trumpet and voice alternate florid singing, during which the trumpet is silent, and imitative textures. The ritornellos are, as expected, tutti textures using the full accompaniment. Listen to the two formal ritornellos after the opening, which are abbreviated. Which part of the ritornello is used each time? The B section begins in B minor and modulates through E minor, D, B minor, A, and ends in F♯ minor. Consider the differences in orchestration, text setting and texture between the A and B sections. Are there motivic connections between these two main sections?

Example 13.7 Handel, "Let the Bright Seraphim," mm. 1–8.

The da capo aria may be expanded if 1) the solo sections in the A part are repeated or 2) when the B section incorporates ritornello statements. An excellent example of an elaborate interaction of ritornellos and solo material is found in an aria from Bach's Cantata No. 140, III. The movement is scored for piccolo violin, soprano and bass duet, and

[12] Review the construction of ritornello themes in Chapter 3.

Figure 13.12 *Bach, Cantata 140, III.*

A

m. 1	**9**	**18**	**28**	**33-**
Rit. abcd	**A**	**A′**		**Rit.[2] ac**
8 (2+2+2+2)	**10**	**10**	**4 ext**	**4**
Cm———PAC	**cm**	**gm**	**DC**	**gm—PAC**
i	**i**	**v**		**v**

B

m. 37	**47**	**51**	**61**
B	**Rit.[3] bd′**	**B′**	**Rit.[4] a**
10	**4**	**10**	**2**
(fm)———E♭	**E♭—PAC**	**(fm)-A♭**	**A♭—IAC**
iv———III	**III**	**(iv) VI**	**VI**

A

m. 63	**66**	**69**	**76**	**81**
A	**A′**	**(Rit. abcd)**	**A″**	**Rit.[5]** ***(dal segno)***
2	**12**		**4 ext.**	**8**
Fm———	**Cm**		**DC**	**Cm—PAC**

continuo.[13] The ritornello passages, outlined in Figure 13.12, are scored for instruments alone framing the large sections of the aria. The violin ritornello is in the elaborate and virtuosic style of the Baroque Italian solo sonata, an ornate instrumental obbligato found in many of Bach's solo arias (see Example 13.8). The vocal parts make extensive use of the opening motive, which often initiates phrases. Of particular interest is Bach's use of ritornello material in the violin to accompany the vocal duet. The vocal parts are often in an imitative dialogue, creating an imaginative contrapuntal texture with the violin.

Example 13.8 Bach, Cantata 140 (1727), III, ritornello, mm. 1–8.

[13] The piccolo violin is tuned a P4th higher than a normal violin, which gives a brilliance to the sound and allows easier execution in certain keys. The continuo specified is *fagotto* (bassoon) and organ.

A diagram of this aria's form is shown in Figure 13.12. The internal ritornellos that articulate the form are, as expected, partial restatements. The fourth ritornello uses the opening motive as a lead-in to the written-out *da capo*, thus seamlessly connecting the two sections. The restatement of A begins in F minor before quickly modulating to the tonic key of C minor. The entire piece has a continuous tonal motion that counters the sectional nature of the form. In addition, the return of the A section incorporates a complete statement of the ritornello, indicated as Rit. abcd in the diagram, in measures 69–76. This ritornello is a counterpoint to the vocal phrases of A′, which are expanded and now in C minor instead of G minor. The voice parts conclude with an extension following a deceptive cadence (measure 76) and the violin closes with a complete ritornello. The elaborate contrapuntal textures and strong sense of continuity are characteristic of Bach's finest writing.

CLASSICAL RONDO ARIAS

The da capo aria of the Baroque period gave way to modifications influenced by the emerging Classical style. Arias might adhere to clear simple ternary form, such as "Un auro amoroso," No. 17 from *Cosí fan tutte* by Mozart, discussed in Chapter 7. The sectional form was still common, but the reprise of A, now written out, was often followed by an extensive coda that gave a dramatic close to the aria. Another variation was the reprise of only a phrase of the A material after a half cadence at the end of the B section, followed by a coda. This formal process creates a sense of a rounded binary form. A good example of this type is soprano Despina's first aria, No. 12 "In uomini" (Fidelity in men?) from Act I of *Cosí fan tutte*. Generally, the designations *da capo* and *dal segno* gave way to written out restatements that allowed for dramatic variation and expansion of material that was typical of the Classical opera.

The Classical rondo also adapted the ritornello as a passage that was heard at both the beginning and at the end of an aria. However, the ritornello functions as an introduction of the principal melodic line of the refrain that was subsequently sung by the soloist. The closing ritornello extended the refrain as an instrumental coda, rather than simply restating the entire ritornello. This is a departure from the ritornello procedures of the Baroque period. The refrains within the rondo would return to the tonic key and original text, fulfilling its formal and poetic functions.

Gluck's celebrated aria "Che farò senza Euridice?" (What shall I do without Euridice?), from the opera *Orfeo ed Euridice*, offers a well-known and clear example of the rondo form with framing ritornellos. The aria is sung by Orpheus after he has regained and then lost Euridice forever. This lament is a five-part rondo (A B A C A) with three stanzas of text. The accompaniment is for strings only, and Orpheus seems to have misplaced his lyre. The refrain (presented in the opening ritornello in an abbreviated form), an elegant melody, is an expanded sentence structure (Example 13.9). As you listen, note the changes in tempo during the recitative-like C section. The final statement of the refrain is dramatically expanded with a repeat and extension of the continuation phrase.

Example 13.9 Gluck, "Che farò senza Euridice," ritornello melody.

OPERATIC RONDÒ

A different form labeled *rondò* refers to an extensive operatic aria that is in two parts: a slow section and a fast section, each expressing a different emotion. This operatic rondò emerged in the eighteenth century and began to displace the large da capo aria during the 1770s. Its basic form is outlined in Figure 13.13. Usually, an orchestral interlude, even if only briefly, separates the two main sections. The diagram shows the most basic outline; in practice the aria was often expanded. Each of the two parts may be shaped according to a familiar form, for example, rounded binary, simple ternary, or rondo. Thus the operatic rondò is a large composite binary form. These internal forms allow for textual contrast and repetition within sections. A coda may be added in a quicker tempo, bringing the aria to a rousing close.

Figure 13.13 *Basic design of an operatic Rondò.*

Slow		| **Fast**		
R^1	S^1	R^2	S^2	R^3
I	I-V-I	I	I trans V-I	I

Mozart's opera *Così fan tutte* provides an example of an operatic rondò in one of his most dramatic and virtuosic arias, "Per pieta." (See Figure 13.14.) In this aria, the soprano character Fiordiligi expresses her torment at being in love with two different men. In the first part, the *Adagio*, she expresses remorse for her unfaithful thoughts and pledges to be faithful to her fiancé. In the second part, in a more animated tempo and character, she chastises herself and reaffirms her fidelity. The middle section of the *Allegro moderato* brings back the text from the *Adagio*, a characteristic practice in the operatic rondò that alludes to the textual refrain of a standard vocal rondo.

Figure 13.14 *Mozart, Cosí fan tutte, No. 25, rondò, "Per pieta."*

Adagio									‖**Allegro Moderato**						
(R^1)	S^1	R^2	S^2	R^3	S^3	R^4	S^4	R^5	S^5	cadenza	S^6	R^7	S^7		R^8
mm.	1		11		20 ‖		35		50	59	67	80	105	112	122–127
theme	A		B		A ‖		C		D—E		C	Coda	*rall.*		*a tempo*
stanza	st^1		st^2		st^1 ‖		st^3		st^{1+2}		st^3		accomp cadenza		st^3
E major	I	vi		V I	I	IV-V- I	HC	I	I	DC		I			

As you listen to the aria, note that the ritornellos are short transitions or links that connect sections rather than complete phrases that separate sections. This approach gives a greater fluidity and continuity to the form, especially in the hands of a skilled composer like Mozart. The coda displays Mozart's flair for writing brilliant virtuosic vocal lines and creating dramatic closure. Also note Mozart's use of evaded cadences in the coda, and the DC and *rallentando* at measures 104–105 highlighting the final drive toward closure.

NINETEENTH-CENTURY EXPANDED RONDÓ

In the nineteenth century, binary, ternary, rondo, and strophic forms were still common in operatic arias. Formal designs ranged from simple strophic songs to short through-composed arias and long sectional forms with contrasting tempos.[14] The rondò was the norm for large, dramatic arias, especially in Italian opera of the first half of the century. This form was expanded, as illustrated in Figure 13.15. In the early nineteenth-century rondò the two sections were labeled *cantabile* (or *cavatina*) and *cabaletta*.[15] The cantabile, a moderate or slow tempo aria, is preceded by an orchestral introduction and a recitative by the singer. The recitative, as is usual, outlines the dramatic conflict or situation facing the character. In addition, a transitional episode normally occurs between the slow and fast sections, appropriately labeled *tempo di mezzo* (middle tempo). In this episode, the emotional situation takes a turn; for example, the character may make a decision about her dilemma, or a messenger may bring important news. To shape the drama, the recitative and tempo di mezzo employ modulations and modal mixture. The tonally-closed main sections provide stability.

Figure 13.15 *Nineteenth Century Expanded Rondò, basic outline.*[16]

Orchestra Introduction	**Recitative**	‖ **Cantabile (Cavatina)**	**Tempo di Mezzo**	**Cabaletta**	**Orchestra**
		A B A B	(cadenza) transition–(cadenza)	A B A	Coda

The nineteenth-century operatic rondò, in its expanded form, could shape an entire scene. Excellent examples of this convention can be found in Verdi's opera *La Traviata* (1853), in which each character is given a scene in this form. Perhaps most famous is Violetta's aria "Ah fors'e lui ("Was this the man"—cantabile) . . . "Sempre Libera" ("Forever Free"—cabaletta), which concludes Act I. After pondering (in the cantabile) the love offered her by Alfredo (*Andantino*, F major/minor), she reprimands herself for such foolish interest in love in the *tempo di mezzo* section. Her dramatic cadenzas before the cabaletta highlight her resolve. In the cabaletta (*Allegro brilliant*, A♭ major), Alfredo's voice interjects with a refrain from an earlier duet. Violetta rejects this voice and Verdi uses virtuosic singing in the second half of the cabaletta and coda to express Violetta's passionate desire for freedom.

The second half of the nineteenth century saw great changes in opera, spearheaded by Wagner. He abandoned the separate recitatives and arias of traditional opera in favor of endless melody and a continuous drama that blurred distinctions between recitative and aria. Verdi's style also continued to evolve. He moved away from the cabaletta and adapted the Italian and French conventions of opera in innovative ways suitable to his dramatic purposes. At the same time, many composers continued the use of operatic conventions and wrote in symmetrical phrases and forms that dominated much music of the nineteenth century. The twentieth century continued exploration of vocal and operatic forms in which distinct arias played a less prominent role. The extremely varied approaches to composing operas in the twentieth-century reflects the diversity of styles that influenced musical developments, including serialism, neoclassicism, and minimalism.

---

[14] Various terms associated with modes of expression can be found, such as *arietta*, *romanza* and *cavatina*. "Celesta Aida" from Verdi's opera *Aida*, for example, is a simple ternary form labeled *romanza*.

[15] The description of these two sections as *cavatina* and *cabeletta* is common but not always accurate. The term cavatina is appropriate if this section is an entrance aria. In the eighteenth century a cavatina referred to an aria with no *da capo*, thus it is simpler and shorter than a da capo aria.

[16] When this form is written for an ensemble the cavatina and cabaletta are referred to as *primo tempo* and *stretta*.

Analytic Exercises

The following list gives examples of several aria forms, including da capo aria, bar form, simple binary, simple ternary, and composite forms. Use the formal diagrams (Figures 13.11–13.15) as models for your analysis.

Bach, "Mein Freund ist mein"! from Cantata 140.
*Handel, "Where'er you walk" from *Semele*.
Handel, "Cara Sposa" (Dearest Bride) from *Rinaldo*
Gounod, "Juliette's Waltz Song" from *Roméo et Juliette*
*Mozart, "Bird Catchers Song" from *The Magic Flute*
+Mozart, Duet "Bei Mannern" from *The Magic Flute*
+Mozart, "Ma tradi quell' alma ingrata" from *Don Giovanni*
Mozart, Rondò, "Non piu di fiori" from *La Clemenza di Tito*
Verdi, Aria "Celesta Aida" from *Aida*

Choral Music

To conclude this survey of vocal forms, a brief discussion of factors that influence the forms of choral movements will be given. While the various forms of vocal music discussed thus far are found in choral works, a great range of formal designs, often unique to a given piece, are encountered. The text, of course, is a strong factor in shaping the form, as are the number of voices being used and the traditions of certain genres. Of interest here is the choral writing one may encounter in its most prominent genre, the great tradition of sacred music.

Hymns or chorales are the most straightforward works written in parts for multiple singers. The textures tend to be homophonic and often homorhythmic, the setting of texts strophic, and the forms small vocal forms as described previously. Conversely, single-movement works such as anthems, or movements from larger works such as masses, cantatas or oratorios, tend to explore the possibilities of varied textures afforded by SATB settings of text. Dividing parts or scoring for two choirs increases the potential variety of vocal textures.

Unlike hymns, the vocal textures of large choral works vary according to the number of voices being used at a time. Contrast or consistency in the number of voices may shape a section. For example, phrases or sections may use a single vocal part, pairs of voices, or all voices throughout. The interactions among the vocal parts will also shape the form. The use of imitative or fugal textures is a long standing tradition in sacred music going back to the Renaissance and continuing to the present day. In *imitative textures*, the number of voices varies, and the textures gradually increase as each voice presents the principal melody with counterpoint. Other textural possibilities include:

1. *homophonic texture*, in which all voices sing in parts; *the melody, normally in the soprano, may be varied as to its voice placement*;
2. *unison texture*, with all voices on the melody;[17]

[17] By convention, the term "unison" refers to the texture and style of singing rather than the actual interval of doubling. In a choir of men's and women's voices unison singing is invariably in octaves.

3. *call and response*, in which one vocal part states a musical idea to which the other vocal parts respond;
4. *melody and descant*, in which a descant or countermelody, usually presented in the soprano voice, is sung against the melody in the other voices;
5. *contrapuntal textures*, a broad category in which two or more different lines are heard in counterpoint; the long standing tradition of cantus firmus technique is a prime example; and
6. *antiphonal textures*, in which two choruses alternate.

These represent some of the principal types of choral textures. Any imaginative choral writing may present new textures or new combinations, with the range and spacing of voices an important variable as well.

To illustrate some ways in which choral movements may be shaped, we will examine a few works briefly. As with any work, consideration of thematic, textural, and tonal design, as well as text, will guide our determination of formal design. The first work we will consider is the renowned "Hallelujah Chorus" from Handel's *Messiah*. This movement exhibits marked contrasts between homophonic and contrapuntal or imitative textures, a hallmark of Handel's style. The various phrases and sections of this movement, outlined in Figure 13.16, are articulated by strong cadences in homophonic textures and by the changes in text. Many of the phrases begin in mid-bar, phrase lengths vary, and phrases often overlap or elide. As in many choral movements, the form is sectional and seemingly through-composed, with six sections shown. The sixteenth-note rhythmic motive of the opening vocal phrase on the text "Hallelujah" serves as a refrain, however, and the repetition of text always retains the same melody.

Figure 13.16 *Handel, "Hallelujah" from Messiah, formal design.*

Measures	Text	Phrase	Texture	Tonal Motion
1–4	Orchestra Intro	2+1^{elided}	Homophonic	I-I
4–11	Hallelujah	4+4	Homophonic	I-V
12–21	For the Lord/	3+2 3+2	Homophonic/	V-I
	Hallelujah (alternate)		Unison	plagal cadence
22–33	For the Lord+Hallelujah	3+4+4+1	Contrapuntal/Imitative	I-V-I
34–41	The Kingdom	2+2+4^{elided}	Homophonic	I-I AC
41–51	And he shall reign	continuous	Fugal (B-T-A-S)	I-V PAC-V
51–60	King of Kings/	3+3+4+4+4	Call/Response	I-V-I
61–69	Forever Hallelujah	overlapping		sequence-V HC
69–74	And he shall reign	continuous	Contrapuntal/Imitative	I-V-I PAC
74–81	King of Kings	2+2+4	Call/Response	I-I PAC
	Forever Hallelujah		Homophonic	
81–94	King of Kings	2+2+4+2	Homophonic	I-I plagal cad.
	Forever Hallelujah		Orch. counterpoint	

In the "Hallelujah Chorus," the orchestra plays an accompaniment role, usually doubling the voices and providing the bass line. By contrast, in the opening choral movement of Bach's Cantata 140, an elaborate orchestral ritornello is used throughout to articulate the form and accompany the vocal parts. A basic diagram of the form of the movement is given in Figure 13.17. This movement is based on the chorale melody discussed in Chapter 11, a bar form with a repeated A section of 3 phrases, and a B section of 4 phrases. Note how the form of the chorale dictates the large-scale form of this movement. The phrase and text of the chorale are heard in order, with the chorale melody treated as a cantus firmus around which Bach writes counterpoint in the other voices. He also interpolates an exuberant fugal section on the word "Alleluia," with the cantus entering in the soprano voice after three statements of the melismatic subject. The ritornellos frame the large sections of the form. Ritornellos 2 and 4 are complete restatements of the opening sixteen-bar ritornello; the third ritornello is a slightly abbreviated form. Interjections of ritornello material link vocal phrases, and ritornello material provides counterpoint to the vocal lines. The result of the various processes is a fluid, contrapuntal texture characteristic of Bach, with the coalescing of voices generally restricted to points of cadence.

Figure 13.17 *Bach, Cantata 140, Movement 2, Choral Movement.*

R^1 A1-2-3	R^2 A1-2-3	R^3 B1-1 {alleluia} B2-3-4 A3	da capo R^4

The various textures encountered in these Bach and Handel works reflect traditions of choral writing that influence many composers to the present day, particularly in sacred writing. As new styles developed, their influence would be heard in unique and creative approaches to choral composition. An outstanding example can be heard in the *Requiem* by Fauré. The piece as a whole relies greatly on expressive, lyrical melodies characteristic of nineteenth-century styles, often presented as sectional solos. The textures are primarily melody with delicate accompaniments, though full-voice homophony is used for dramatic emphasis. The last movement, "In Paradisium," is an excellent example of Fauré's restrained, lyrical style. The movement is in two sections, each of which presents the sopranos alone in a continuously unfolding melody. The other parts are added in the closing, homophonic phrases of each section and in the last eight bars as a quiet coda to this intensely expressive movement.

More radical departures from traditional style in choral writing and writing for the solo voice are found in many works of the twentieth century, sometimes challenging the practical limitations of the voice. Other works expand upon the traditions of choral writing, using new musical languages or styles. Some of these works are discussed in the final chapter. At the same time, the tradition of choral music for use in church services continues.

SUGGESTED READING

Carolyn Abbate and Roger Parker, *Analyzing Opera: Verdi and Wagner*. Berkeley: University of California Press, 1989.

Edward Cone, *The Composer's Voice*. Berkeley: University of California Press, 1974.

Everett, Walter, *The Beatles As Musicians: "Revolver" through the "Anthology."* Oxford and New York: Oxford University Press, 1999.

Charles Rosen, *The Classical Style, 288–324*.

Deborah Stein and Robert Spillman, *Poetry into Song*, New York: Oxford University Press 1996.

Wilder, Alec, *American Popular Song: The Great Innovators, 1900–1950*. London: Oxford University Press, 1975. Reprint edition, October 1, 1990.

Analytic Exercises

1. **Bach, *Wachet Auf*, BWV 140, opening choral movement.** This movement, whose overall design was discussed earlier, will repay further study. Analyze the opening ritornello and note its phrase structure and motives. Trace the use of the ritornello within the choral sections of the movement. Is ritornello material ever used in the chorus part? Next, consider the vocal phrases and textures. Describe the different textures Bach develops and the placement of the cantus firmus within sections.

2. **Handel, "For unto us a Child is Born" from *Messiah*.** Using the diagrams for the "Hallelujah Chorus" as a model, outline the formal design and textures of this movement. Compare the style of choral writing and forms of the two choruses.

3. **Mozart, *Requiem*.** This work show Mozart's mastery and creativity in solo vocal and choral writing. The "Rex tremendae," "Confutatis," and "Domine Jesu" show a wide range of choral textures. Identify the types of textures used and consider whether the orchestra is doubling vocal lines or providing a contrasting accompaniment. How does the music convey the text? What type of fugue is heard in the Kyrie? Trace the various entrances of the vocal parts.

4. **Brahms, "Wie lieblich sind deine Wohnungen" (How Lovely is They Dwelling Place) from the *German Requiem*.** This lyrical and dramatic choral work contains a rich blend of homophonic and contrapuntal textures for chorus and orchestra, as well as some striking modulations. The form may be understood as a large ternary form reflecting principles of contrast and restatement. How has the form been expanded? What other formal interpretations can you justify? The relation of the orchestral phrases to the choral phrases bears attention. You should note instances where: 1) the orchestra provides an introduction to the choral phrase, 2) the orchestra beings the phrase melody, 3) the orchestra extends a phrase after the chorus cadences, and 4) the chorus seems to be accompanying the orchestra!

5. **John Taverner, "Little Lamb."** This short setting for chorus of a William Blake poem has rather simple textures. The relationship between the voices should be considered carefully. Sing each part and consider what compositional techniques Taverner has used to compose the piece.

6. **The choruses listed below are additional representative works.** The basic form is given for several works. The task is to determine the outline of that form in the music. For other works, the form is left for the reader to discover.

   *Handel: Chorus: "Wretched Lovers" from *Acis and Galatea*.
   Bach: Chorus, "Erschallet, ihr Lieder," Cantata 172. Da capo ternary with ritornellos.
   +Bruckner: Mass in E minor, "Kyrie."
   *Fanny Mendelssohn: Chorus: "O Herbst." Strophic.
   Vaughn Williams: "No. 5 Antiphon" from *Five Mystical Songs*.

14 Formal Innovations in Twentieth-Century Music

Introduction

The twentieth century was a time of great change in music. Composers sought new musical languages beyond the traditional tonal system of western music, resulting in diverse and often radical styles of concert music. American jazz and popular music, promulgated by new technologies and mass media, influenced the direction of musical development. The heightened interest in non-western music further fueled the diversity of musical styles and genres. A thorough survey of the many new developments in music of the past hundred years would occupy an entire text.[1] Previous chapters in this text have included twentieth-century works that drew on traditional, classical forms. The purpose of this chapter is to provide a brief introduction to some innovations in musical forms of the twentieth century, and present additional criteria for the analysis of musical form.

Despite the diversity of styles in twentieth-century music, most styles share some basic formal tendencies. First, episodic forms—forms comprised of contrasting sections—are more common. This tendency is in part an outgrowth of the interest in programmatic music such as ballet and film music, and in works that set text. The program or text provided a basis for the formal design. Works like Schoenberg's *Pierrot lunaire*, a setting of twenty-one expressionistic poems, or ballets such as Stravinsky's *Rite of Spring* or Ravel's *Daphnis et Chloé*, for example, contain episodic forms, unified motivically and stylistically. Second, many composers became interested in writing music based on thematic variation or transformation of pitch motives. In such works, motivic unity is present, but literal repetition of ideas is avoided. This tendency is particularly evident in free atonal and serial music, and is conducive to variation and developmental forms. Third, as composers after World War II sought even more radical approaches to musical sounds, forms based on contrasts in musical textures and timbres emerged. Finally, in the second half of the century, new philosophical concepts of music led to novel concepts of form such as open forms that change from one performance to the next, or forms based on slowly evolving processes. In the midst of these innovations, many works drew on traditional forms now delineated in different ways by new musical resources and techniques.

Whether drawing on traditional or unique forms and techniques, any style of music reveals form inasmuch as its contents can be segmented and grouped, and formal relations identified. In tonal music, we have repeatedly observed how progression toward cadences and tonal relations articulate musical form. In much post-tonal music, composers create pitch relations and thematic processes that articulate form in new ways. Although not an exhaustive survey, this chapter will examine several works that illustrate how new compositional resources and techniques led to new ways of shaping phrase structures and delineating formal designs.

---

[1] See Robert Morgan, *Twentieth-Century Music*, New York: W. W. Norton, 1991; Bryan R. Simms, *Music of the Twentieth Century, 2nd ed.*, New York: Schirmer Books, 1996; and Arnold Whitall, *Twentieth-Century Music*, Oxford: Oxford University Press, 1999.

New Pitch Materials, Phrase Structures, and Textures

PITCH COLLECTIONS

In the late nineteenth and early twentieth centuries, composers began to use exotic scales including whole-tone, pentatonic, and octatonic scales, as well as older modal scales and artificial (newly invented) scales. Moreover, many composers, seeking to avoid tonality, used chromatic motives. As a result, much music relied on motivic pitch collections, whose intervallic content would serve as the basis for diverse thematic ideas. The notion of pitch collections (or sets) provides a neutral term to refer to the broad array of pitch materials one may encounter. It also avoids the traditional tonal implications of the term *scales*. A *pitch collection* is a group of notes that is ordered by the composer to create motivic intervallic patterns. Any pitch collection may be identified on the basis of the number of pitches and the intervallic content. For example, a whole-tone scale is a six-note collection that is characterized by the intervals of a major second, major third, and a fourth, which are the only intervals—apart from their inversions—that can be formed using the collection. Much nontonal music is based on motivic pitch-class sets that are used in contrasting thematic ideas or in transformations of thematic ideas. A great deal of post-tonal music uses this approach, especially atonal and serial music, which is especially conducive to through-composed, developmental, and variation forms.

CENTRICITY

Another concept useful to much post-tonal music is *centricity*. This term refers to the prominence of a single pitch in a section or complete movement such that the pitch collection centers on that pitch. Pitch centers may be established by techniques such as directed linear motion, repetition, pedal points, and dynamic or timbral prominence, but will not imply the tonal hierarchy of traditional tonality. Centricity may occur in a wide range of styles and pitch languages. *Extended tonality*[2] refers to the use of tonal materials—familiar scales and chords of the tonal system, but in nontraditional progressions, extended harmonies, and linear motions. In such music, a traditional sense of key is avoided, even though pitch centers may be established.

New Pitch Materials and Form: Debussy

Claude Debussy (1862–1918) is considered one of the founders of modern music. In order to address his innovations in musical form, we must also consider important aspects of his style. A critical aspect of his music was his novel treatment of harmony and tonality. Debussy used many tertian harmonies, but avoided traditional cadences and progressions. He also used tonal centers instead of traditionally established keys, and contrasts between diatonic and chromatic textures to distinguish different sections of his forms. In the absence of traditional harmonic progressions, repetition as well as pedal points become a primary way of projecting tonal centers. Debussy's use of novel pitch material, including church modes, and whole-tone, octatonic, chromatic, and pentatonic scales, was also significant. These various scales went beyond traditional tonal resources and influenced

[2] No widely accepted term is used for nontraditional tonal music, perhaps owing to the highly individualized manner that composers developed to vary pitch and harmonic languages. Other terms one may encounter include *pan-tonality, neo-tonality*, and, more recently, *new tonality*. Each of these terms is subject to various interpretations. The term *extended tonality* is meant as a generic and broadly conceived concept.

Debussy's melodic constructions and phrase structures. In the absence of tonally directed melodies, Debussy used short, repeated motives to generate many of his phrase melodies. He described his melodies as "arabesque-like," referring to the undulating contours and free embellishments that he favored. The opening of *Prélude à "L'Après-midi d'un faune"* (Prelude to the "Afternoon of a Faun," 1894) is a good example of this type of melody.

DEVELOPING VARIATIONS

Debussy's approach to melody, harmony, rhythm, and texture resulted in new approaches to form. Although principles of repetition, contrast, variation, and restatement remained, the absence of traditional tonal syntax and Debussy's presentation of a related but *distinct* series of musical ideas generated forms unlike the standard models. Several techniques may be identified, which will be illustrated with examples from his piano Prelude *La Cathédral Engloutie** (The Engulfed Cathedral, Preludes Book I, 1910). Figure 14.1 is a diagram of the form of the prelude. The segmentation is based on similarities and contrast in 1) texture, 2) pitch collections and tonal centers, and 3) rhythmic motion and tempos. The tonal centers and linear progressions provide a sense of directed motion without traditional tonal progressions, and a basis for segmentation. However, Debussy's varied restatements, transformation of musical ideas, and contrasts in texture may obscure relations among the sections. Consequently, the type of formal design in his work is often ambiguous, even though his forms tend to be sectional. Further consideration of the manner in which the piece is generated may reveal different interpretations of the form.

Figure 14.1 *Debussy, The Engulfed Cathedral, formal design.*

A^1	B	A^2	C	A^3	D^1	trans	B′	trans	D^2	A^4
m.1	7	13	16	22	28	42	47	67	72	84

Debussy's works often begin simply, as in this Prelude, with ideas gradually emerging. His phrases tend to be generated by repetitions of short ideas that may be expanded or dissolved, or abandoned unexpectedly. The opening of the *The Engulfed Cathedral* (Example 14.1) entails repetitions of the ascending pentatonic scale pattern presented in parallel, *quartal*, or *quintal harmonies* (harmonies based on perfect fourths and perfect fifths).[3] Note how the descending, sustained bass notes G-F-E give tonal direction to the repeated chordal patterns. The opening texture and sense of meter is dissolved in measures 5–6 where the octaves on E suggest a new tonal center, and a new section begins. Measures 7–10 are based on an E lydian scale—note the pedal E and the use of A♯—in a new texture and rhythm, but the pentatonic melodic line is retained from the opening section. Measures 13–15 return to the opening pitch materials and gestures, and (notably) continue the bass line descent from G-F-E to B-C. In retrospect, the contrasting ideas of the B section are parenthetical, like an aside that interrupts a motion later resumed. This formal process, in which a series of contrasting ideas may be presented and perceived as distinct musical moments that are juxtaposed rather than integrated or connected, was a distinct departure from traditional tonal forms.

In this Prelude, some sections are clearly related by thematic content or texture, but one may observe remnants of the pentatonic melody throughout the work. The term *developing variations* is sometimes applied to formal processes in which themes and sections

[3] The use of parallel motion in all voices in a succession of chords is sometimes referred to as *planing*. Debussy would use this device with traditional chords as well to stress their harmonic color rather than their function. See mm. 62–67 of Example 14.2, which contain planing of Mm 7 chords.

are variations of one another, or are related on the basis of motivic pitch collections.[4] Contrasting sections may present the motivic collection in varied thematic or textural guise. Moreover, restatements of ideas are varied or changed in some significant way. One can hear, in the closing measures, a return to the opening theme but with a stable pedal point and fragmentary repetitions that bring the work to a quiet and rather pensive close. Many have observed that the truncated and transformed restatements give such passages the sense of an *epilogue*, a final recall and reflection on the musical ideas, rather than simply a coda that reinforces closure.

Example 14.1 *Debussy, The Engulfed Cathedral, mm. 1–15.*

Another prominent feature of Debussy's style, evident here, is the strong contrasts in harmonic rhythm. Measures 41–46 (Example 14.2) show how a static harmonic rhythm, slowly changing bass line, and persistent repetition of ideas convey a sense of suspended motion that contrasts with passages such as those in measures 62–63. Related to those features is Debussy's attenuation of traditional metric hierarchy. Pulse is often present, but the meter can be vague or ambiguous as a result of borrowed divisions, syncopation

[4] This motivic technique, also associated with Brahms, albeit in a much different style, was an important influence on a great deal of twentieth-century music.

Example 14.2 Debussy, *The Engulfed Cathedral.*

a. mm. 41–46.

b. mm. 55–71.

and irregular harmonic rhythms. This is evident in the transitional passages of measures 41–46 and 68–71, where dissonant intervals and slow surface rhythms suspend a sense of meter and contribute to a quiet tension. Finally, the extreme ranges and dynamics that Debussy exploits delineate formal units and contribute to the novel and arresting expressions he achieved.

Analytic Exercises

A. Debussy, Prelude *The Engulfed Cathedral**

1. Trace the motion of the bass line from measure 15 to the end of the prelude. Consider pedal points, noncontiguous pitches, and local interruptions of larger patterns.
2. Is this prelude in a key? Which tonal centers can you identify?
3. What type of harmonic progression shapes measures 16–22?
4. What mode is used in the D section, that is, how does the addition of the B♭ alter the scale?
5. What other interpretations of the formal design possible and convincing?
6. How might the several sections identified above be grouped into larger sections?

B. Debussy, Prelude to "The Afternoon of a Faun." Consider the following three formal interpretations of one of Debussy's most famous orchestral works, the *Prelude to "The Afternoon of a Faun."** Based on careful listening and with the aid of a score, determine the criteria for each interpretation and the relative merits of each view. What other formal divisions might one propose? The opening melody returns at several points. Analyze the harmonization of the opening C♯ each time it occurs (measures 11, 21, 26, 37, 46, 56, 79, and 94). How are the recurrences similar or different? Where is the most formally significant restatement of material in the large-scale form? In addition, what elements of Debussy's style, discussed above, may be identified? Pay particular attention to his orchestration with regard to doublings, solo designations, and the use of strings.

Figure *Debussy, Prelude to "The Afternoon of a Faun," formal interpretations*

1. TERNARY

A	**trans**	**B**	**A′**
mm.1–30	30–54	55–78	79–106
	(30–37) (parenthetical?)		

2. BINARY

A			**A′**		
1–30	30–37	37–54	55–78	79–94	94–106

3. DEVELOPING (FREE) VARIATIONS

	A	V1	V2	V3	V4	V5	V6	V7	V8
mm.	1	11	21	31	55	79	94	100	110

C. Works for Further Study The following Preludes for Piano, Book I by Debussy are recommended for analysis: *Les collines d'Anacapri+* (The Hills of Anacapri) and *Des pas sur la neige+* (Footsteps in the Snow). The first is a in ternary form while the second contains restatements of material but is formally ambiguous.

New Pitch Materials, Transposition, and Traditional Form: Bartók

Hungarian composer and pianist, Béla Bartók (1881–1945), drew on a wide range of styles in his works: dissonant chromaticism and a percussive style (prevalent in his early works), folk melodies and rhythms of his native country, which he studied and compiled, contrasts between homophonic and contrapuntal textures, and coloristic, impressionist textures derivative of Debussy. He integrated these diverse resources in works that drew on classical forms and traditional compositional techniques. One of his noteworthy works is a six-volume set of piano pieces entitled *Mikrokosmos*. Progressing from simple to complex, the six volumes provide a wealth of works for study by young pianists, and offer models for composition using a variety of pitch materials, compositional techniques, and the rhythms of Bulgarian music. We will examine one of these pieces to see how he used transpositions of nontonal pitch collections to articulate musical form.[5]

BARTÓK, *MIKROKOSMOS*, VOL. IV, NO. 101, "DIMINISHED FIFTH (1940)"

In this piece, each hand begins with the same diatonic pitch patterns a diminished fifth apart, in this case the tetrachord of a minor scale. The pitches, when put in ascending order, comprise an *octatonic scale* (Example 14.3). The octatonic (eight-note) scale is a symmetrical pattern based on alternating half steps and whole steps, starting with either interval. The scale has unique properties that may be summarized as follows:

- The ascending version that begins with a major second yields two minor-scale tetrachords (four-note collections), separated by a tritone. Note that a diminished fifth occurs between each corresponding pair of notes of the two tetrachords. These properties influenced Bartók's pitch constructs in this piece.
- The scale yields two interlocking diminished seventh chords, four dominant seventh chords, and major and minor triads on the same pitches. These recurring patterns and the symmetry of the scale allow for multiple pitch centers a minor third apart.
- Because the scale is symmetrical, the pitch collection duplicates every minor third, for example, C and E♭ octatonic scales have the same pitches.

Example 14.3 *E♭ Octatonic Scale.*

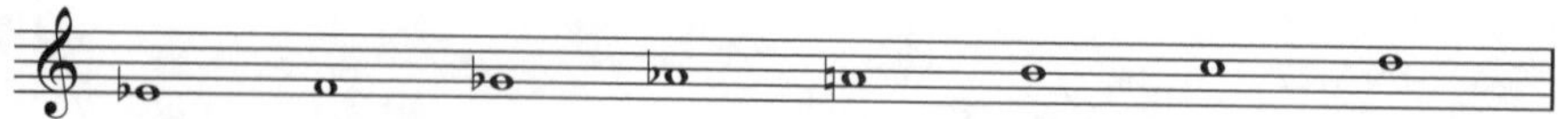

Identifying the various tetrachords in the upper and lower parts of the piece (Example 14.4) will reveal the transpositions of the initial octatonic scale. *The transposed octatonic collections differentiate phrases*. Thematic patterning and the careful placements of rests and slurs help articulate the phrases. Notice that even though measure 5 is

[5] Bartók's interest in multi-movement arch forms was discussed in Chapter 9. See Paul Wilson, *The Music of Béla Bartók* (Yale University Press, 1992), for further discussion of Bartók's music.

not cadential in a traditional sense, the similar motion between parts and a rest mark the end of the phrase. Measure 6 begins a varied repetition of the first phrase. Minor tetrachords are again used in both hands with the two parts transposed to a diminished fifth above. Comparing these two phrases, we can see that the pitch patterns in the second phrase have simply exchanged parts with those in the first phrase. This is because, as we noted, the octatonic scale is a symmetrical scale that duplicates pitch content at certain transpositions. The related pitch content groups these two phrases together.

Consider where else this version of the octatonic scale occurs. Even though there are motivic variations in measures 20–25 and 35–end, the opening tetrachords and original octatonic scale return. Thus, an element of this piece that is important to its formal shape is the periodic return of the opening pitch collection and motives. Now consider the pitch content of the intervening phrases. In measures 12–19, the tetrachords of an octatonic scale are retained, except a pitch is missing in each part: the right hand omits the pitch F♭ and the left hand omits the pitch B♭, the result of melodic skips rather than the previous stepwise motion. Measures 26–34 use yet another version of the octatonic scale by varying the melodic intervals: note here the emphasis on minor thirds. The motivic variation of contour and melodic patterns distinguishes these two short sections while the retained pitch resources—now transposed—provide unity throughout the piece.

This short piece demonstrates that, even though motivic patterning is important in shaping the form, *formal segmentation of post-tonal music normally coincides with transposition or changes in pitch content.* Further, varied repetition and contrast retain their significance as formal processes. The fact that literal repetition is avoided conveys a form based on *continuous motivic development*, characteristic of much twentieth-century music. At the same time, the alternating recurrences of pitch collections as described above suggest a traditional, sectional form, in this case a small rondo.

ANALYTIC EXERCISE: BARTÓK, *MIKROKOSMOS*, VOL. IV, NO. 101, "DIMINISHED FIFTH"

1. Certain elements of the music, notated in the score, show how a performer should convey the formal boundaries of the piece. Identify two of these elements.
2. Consider which phrase or section contains the most rapid changes in pitch content. What, if any, foreign (chromatic) pitches are used in the piece? In which phrase are they most prevalent?
3. Consider the final cadence. Which two pitches outside of the prevailing octatonic scale are introduced? How does this cadence convey closure?
4. Compare the subphrases of the first two phrases (measures 1–5, 6–11). How does Bartók expand the subphrases?
5. Use this piece to study many types of motivic variation.

Example 14.4 Bartók, *Mikrokosmos*, Vol. IV, No. 101 "Diminished Fifth."

(This excerpt continues on p. 338.)

(Example 14.4, continued.)

Diminished Fifth from Mikrokosmos (Bartók) © Copyright 1940 by Hawkes & Son (London) Ltd. Copyright Renewed. Definitive corrected edition © copyright 1987 by Hawkes & Son (London) Ltd. Reprinted by permission of Boosey & Hawkes, Inc.

Ostinati, Layers, and Irregular Phrase Structures: Stravinsky

With the three ballets *(Firebird, Petrushka*, and the *Rite of Spring)* that he composed early in the twentieth century, Igor Stravinsky (1882–1971) ushered in a new world of musical sounds and constructions. The *Rite of Spring* (1913), whose first performance invoked a riot, contains an extreme level of dissonance, complex and irregular rhythmic textures, novel orchestration, and repetitive melodic construction influenced by Russian folk melodies. The discussion here focuses on excerpts from the *Rite of Spring* that illustrate novel ways Stravinsky generated musical form. Suggestions for further study are given in subsequent exercises.

Stravinsky used ostinati extensively in his compositions. They are frequently encountered as a constructive device, providing harmonic underpinnings in the absence of traditional harmonic progressions. His ostinati are often irregular in length and his texture may superimpose several ostinati. Further, he would suddenly change and then alternate various musical ideas that are juxtaposed rather than strongly connected. These techniques delineate irregular phrases, which in turn form larger sections. Begin by listening to the Introduction to Part II, measures 1–55. See how many distinct ideas you recognize. Then, using a score, identify and label the various recurring figures that you heard. Listen in particular for these related, but distinct ideas (see Example 14.5):

- *Measure 1: undulating chords and sustained chord of the opening section.* Note the relations among the three chords of the opening. This texture may be described as polychordal, which refers to the superimposition (layering) of distinctly different harmonies that are presented in different timbres or registers. What would be a more conventional respelling of the first eighth-note chord? Speculate on Stravinsky's spellings.
- *Measure 9: a diatonic figure centered around A that is introduced in measure 9.* This figure is superimposed over the varied chromatic harmonies below it.
- *Measure 27: a repeated neighbor-note figure and falling third figure.* Note the slight expansion of the intervals in each part, from minor to major.
- *Measure 38: the repeated-note figures in the violin II and in two stands of cellos, and the irregular ostinato presented pizzicato in the rest of the cellos.* Trace the intervallic and rhythmic patterns of the ostinato. Observe the calculated irregularity of the rhythmic pattern contrasting with the repeated pitch pattern.

These various ideas show characteristics of Stravinsky's phrase structures. *First, Stravinsky varies the length of motives when he repeats them to create short, irregular phrases.* An idea may be introduced in fragments and then lengthened in a more complete form (compare measures 8–9 with 10–12), or fragmented upon repetition (compare measures 19–21 with 22–23). Some phrases or motives are simply repeated (see measures 33–34), while other times, as in bar 26, a pattern is interrupted. The irregularity of the phrase structures is evident in the metric shifts that are required to notate the changing patterns of the ostinato. *Second, the contrast between diatonic and chromatic elements in the music may delineate phrases, a characteristic we observed in Debussy's music.* In Stravinsky, however, the two elements often occur at the same time. This is most evident in measures 7–10, where the D minor melody is superimposed over the chromatic harmonies. *Third, the music is tonally very static, a result of the ostinato construction.* Various harmonic and melodic patterns are simply repeated with no sense of harmonic progression or tonal motion. While tonal centers may emerge, more than one could be evident in a passage or they might suddenly change.

JUXTAPOSITION AND SUPERIMPOSITION

Stravinsky's irregular expansion or contraction of melodic units and his kaleidoscopic textures represent a strong break from traditional thematic processes. These innovations also led to new formal processes, notably that of juxtaposition and superimposition. By definition, *juxtaposition* is the placement of two objects side by side. By implication, the objects are recognized as separate rather than connected, and contrasting in some way. In music, we hear this process when contrasting ideas alternate without apparent connections; sometimes one idea is interrupted by another and left incomplete. There is precedent for this process in tonal music, and certainly parenthetical phrases may be heard as a juxtaposition. In the music of Stravinsky, as well as many composers of the twentieth century, however, juxtaposition became a basic formal process used to generate sections.

In this particular section, we can observe this process of juxtaposition between R84 and R93 (measures 24–56).[6] Notice how the fermata in measure 26 interrupts the repetition

[6] "R84" and similar designations refer to rehearsal numbers in the score. References such as R86.2 indicate the second measure after R86.

of the melodic pattern to be followed by a contrasting motivic idea in measure 27 (the neighbor-note undulating figure). These two ideas are juxtaposed in the ensuing six bars. At R86.2 (measure 34) we hear a new idea in combination with the undulating figure. The ideas share certain pitches, but are distinctly contrasting in rhythmic and harmonic content. In this case the process is *superimposition*. This process refers to the combination of contrasting ideas in one texture simultaneously. Superimposition creates a *layered texture*,[7] in which each component has a distinct pitch content, rhythmic profile, register, timbre, and/or articulation. Though chromatic elements prevail in most of this excerpt, many other passages in the *Rite of Spring* will simply layer contrasting diatonic or modal melodies, vertically creating dissonant textures.

Example 14.5 Stravinsky, *Rite of Spring,* motives, Introduction to part II, mm. 1, 9, 27, and 38.

The forms resulting from these processes sound sectional and tonally static: sectional in that the juxtaposition of ideas results in a succession of contrasting, short passages of irregular length; static in that the pitch and rhythmic ideas remain fixed, while the patterns based on the ideas are repeated. This particular section relies more on juxtaposition of ideas than on superimposition. Other sections, discussed in the following exercises, may gradually build up to more complex textures superimposing an increasing number of

[7] The term *stratified* is also used to describe such textures. See the *Harvard Dictionary of Music*, 4th ed.

contrasting ideas. In such cases the formal process is one of *accumulation*, in which a climax is reached when the musical texture seems saturated.

ANALYTIC NOTE

While the principle of juxtaposition appears to be simple, creating formal designs with an inner logic and sense of proportion takes careful consideration when using this technique. While this is an analytically elusive aspect of the work, it was something Stravinsky considered carefully. Evidence of this is the fact that measures 27–30 (R84.4 to R86 in the score) were inserted three weeks *after* Stravinsky had signed the score as completed. This insertion introduced fragmentary anticipation of the material that enters at measure 31 (R86), and a transposed repetition of measures 24–25.

Another feature of some twentieth-century works, notably those of Debussy and Stravinsky, is the lack of a clear hierarchical form. In other words, series of small sections to do not group into larger units; instead, we hear discrete ideas that seem disconnected. The ideas may be related texturally or motivically, but often do not group into larger sections. Such works tend to be sectional, while maintaining a consistency of style and musical language that unifies the material.

Analytic Exercises

A. Stravinsky, Introduction to Part I, *Rite of Spring* (1913). This first large section of the work illustrates many of the previously described techniques. Listen to the section without a score and take note of the juxtaposition of ideas. Consider how the section as a whole reaches a climax. Note how the opening bassoon solo returns as a formal framing device to close the section. Compare the two statements of this idea. With the aid of a score you can note the number of different ideas and the contrast between diatonic and chromatic elements. Attempt to diagram the formal succession of events and textures. The second section, the *Augurs of Spring*, begins with the famous dissonant, reiterated chord that was one of Stravinsky's first ideas for the work. The blunt juxtaposition of contrasting ideas is even more evident here. You may wish to look at the many different ostinati, particularly beginning at R24 and especially R28. Throughout both sections some ostinati are persistent, some start and stop, and many change their length frequently. Which ostinati do not adhere to the notated meter, but create their own rhythmic metric patterns, resulting in cross rhythms?

B. Stravinsky, *Symphony of Psalms* (1930). The aesthetic of this work is remarkably different from the *Rite of Spring*, yet many of Stravinsky's techniques observed in the earlier work prevail. Study the last movement of the work. The formal structure may be interpreted as juxtaposition of diverse textures and themes, related by pitch elements and restatements. Tempos (slow/fast) and instrumentation (orchestra alone or chorus with orchestra) delineate sections. Three basic ideas are used: the opening, Theme A, which includes the "Laudate" refrain, Theme B (Rehearsal 3), an orchestral idea later set with chorus, and Theme C (Rehearsal 9), which combines elements of A and B using chorus and orchestra. Trace the presentation of the various ideas and diagram the formal design. How may one determine the length of the various sections? To what extent are juxtaposition and superimposition used? The coda, R22–end, takes up over 40 percent of the movement. How may it be subdivided?

Atonal and Serial Forms: Webern

Along with his teacher Arnold Schoenberg and friend Alban Berg, Anton Webern (1883–1945), was among the first important composers of atonal and serial music. Webern's interest in short concentrated musical structures based on the transformation of intervallic cells, his avoidance of clear repetition of material, and his fragmentation of material among different instruments and different registers set his music apart from his contemporaries. His novel style influenced the subsequent generation of composers who were drawn to his structural control of all elements of a composition. Below we will examine two of his works, one freely atonal and one serial, to illustrate some of his approaches to formal structure in these styles.

FIVE MOVEMENTS FOR STRING QUARTET, OP. 5, NO. 4 (1909)*

All of the movements of this relatively early composition by Webern are brief, an economy of means characteristic of his works in general. The very sparse textures and use of silence, the distinct timbres and registers for each part, the isolated, brief gestures, and the absence of clearly defined pulse are a radical departure from traditional formal processes.[8] Though clearly an atonal work, certain movements of the entire work use classical formal models. The first movement, for example, is a highly compressed sonata form with principal and secondary themes and a central development section. Our discussion will focus on the fourth movement, shown in Example 14.6.

In atonal works such as this, rhythm, texture and tempo play important roles in delineating formal segments. Several changes in tempo mark off the sections. Webern creates distinct contrasts in texture, from shimmering chords and contrapuntal passages, to solo lines and melody with accompaniment, by "coloring" his textures with many contrasts in register, dynamics, and instrumental timbre. Note the wide range of string timbres, including legato bowings, *am steg* (sul ponticello), tremolos, pizzicato, and harmonics. A first step in studying the movement would be to take note of the many detailed instructions for performance indicated in the score.

Webern tends to avoid obvious connections of material, and his use of short motivic statements results in an absence of melodic themes in any traditional sense. The discontinuity of motion and fragmented sounds are balanced with a strong sense of structural integrity and cohesion. This is achieved by the use of recurring pitch motives that are characterized by intervallic cells, ordered in various patterns. Consideration of the pitch motives is a key element in analyzing the formal structure of the movement. One may begin by careful listening, taking note of how the music might be segmented. Consider how different elements of the music might suggest different segmentation. A readily discernible element is the ascending solo line that occurs in measures 6, 10, and 12–13. This figure appears to mark off three sections. The movement may be segmented and the form may be analyzed as follows: 1–6, 7–10, 11–13, a very compressed A B A′ ternary form. This formal view, particularly the notion of a varied restatement, is not based on clear thematic restatements as much as correspondence in pitch and intervallic content. The following points may guide the analysis of this movement:

- The first two entrances of violin I and II present four-note chords. Note the intervallic content of these two chords. For purposes of indentification, these chords are labeled X and Y, respectively.

[8] These sparse, fragmented textures are referred to as *pointillistic textures*, a twentieth-century technique associated with Webern.

- Identify recurrences of the X and Y chords in measures 2–6.
- Notice the highest pitch of each chord. Where else do these two pitches occur?
- Compare the interval succession of each statement of the seven-note solo line in measures 6, 10, and 11–12. Then compare the seven-note pattern with the opening chords in violins, measures 1–2.
- Take note of the canonic imitation and intervallic patterns in measures 3–4 and 4–5.
- In measures 7–9, identify the intervallic patterns used in each part. Note: consider the violin II and cello as one combined part; the cello is sounding E^4 (E above middle C). How do these measures contrast with the rhythms, contours and registers of measures 1–5? What type of chord is the ostinato in the viola?
- Note the intervals and pitches presented in measures 11–12 in the lower three strings. What measures of the opening section are being recalled?
- Some analysts call measures 1–2 an introduction. What elements of the music support this segmentation and function?

Example 14.6 Webern, Five Movements for String Quartet, Op. 5, No. 4 (1909).*

(This excerpt continues on p. 344.)

(Example 14.6, continued.)

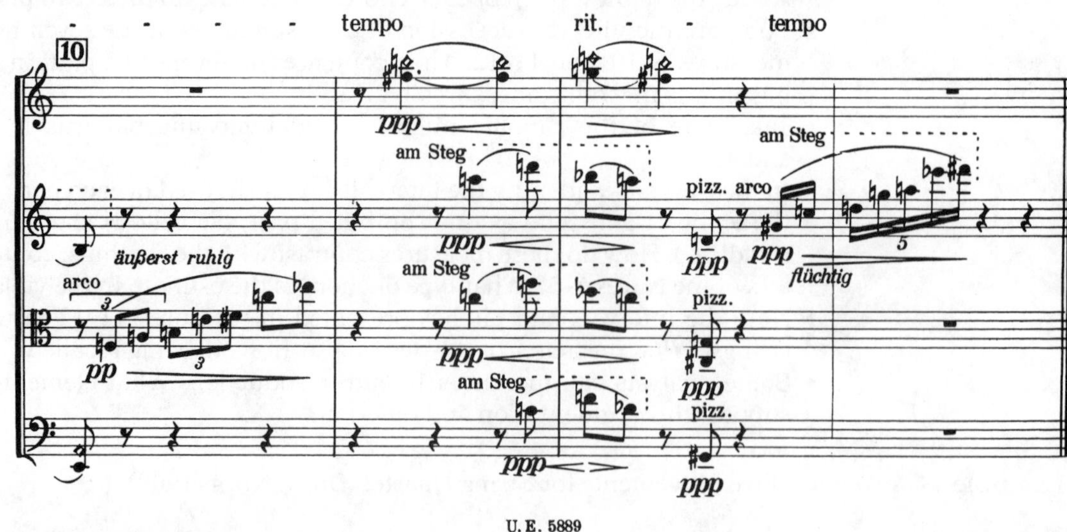

Webern, Five Movements for String Quartet, Op. 5/4. Used by permission of European American Music Distributers LLC, U.S. and Canadian agent for Universal Edition, Vienna.

Based on the identification of intervals and motives above, several analytic points can be made:

- Motivic intervallic cells (see Example 14.7) may be presented as chords (vertically) or as melodies (linearly), and may also be transposed. Chord X recurs at the end of measure 2 and then as an arpeggio in the canon of measures 3–4. The pizzicato chord in measure 12 is the Y chord.
- Motives may share common pitches and intervals. The X and Y chords share three pitches in common.
- Restatements may be transposed but retain intervallic patterns. Most noticeable here, the seven-note pattern is transposed and has different rhythms each time it is repeated, but retains the intervallic pattern.
- The viola ostinato, an augmented triad, and the first violin part in measures 7–9 are not included in other intervallic patterns; they are unique, contrasting gestures and pitch collections.

Here then we find a familiar formal design that incorporates principles of statement/contrast/restatement. At the same time transformation of intervallic patterns suggests that *continuous development or variation is vital to the form of the movement*. Recurring intervallic motives permeate the rather large variety of material in this short movement providing an underlying unity. In atonal works, such careful comparison of pitches and intervals will, as a rule, help clarify formal segmentation and underlying structure. Additional analysis, based on the concepts of pitch-class sets, will give further insight concerning such issues as transpositions and abstract connections but is beyond the scope of this introductory discussion.[9]

Example 14.7 Webern Op. 5, No. 4, pitch/interval motives.

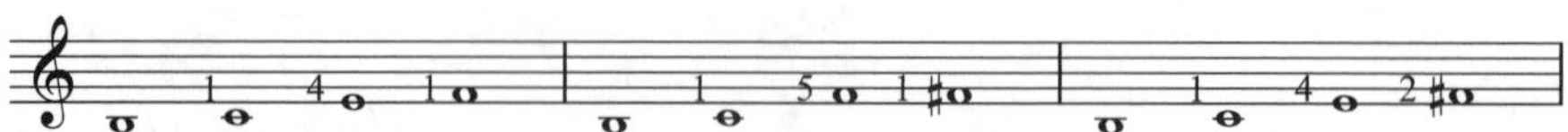

[9] There are a number of published studies of this piece. See Joseph Straus, *Introduction to Post Tonal Theory*, 3rd edition, (Upper Saddle River, NJ: Prentice Hall, 2004) 101–111, for additional analysis and bibliography of analytic studies on the work.

Motives are given in the closest order of pitches by interval. The numbers between the pitches indicate the series of intervals by the number of half steps that occur in the each motive.[10]

PIANO VARIATIONS, II (1936)*

This work was written after Webern had adopted the techniques of serial composition developed by Schoenberg. In serial works, a specific ordering of the twelve pitches of the chromatic scale, referred to as a *tone row*, forms the basis for the pitch content.[11] A row is characterized not only by a succession of pitches, but by the patterns of intervals used in the row. Generally, composers would invent rows that avoided traditional tonal patterns, such as triads and scales, to avoid tonal implications. Some serial works delineate formal sections by the grouping of rows. Other works use the row simply as a resource for pitch material, avoiding the coincidence of row beginnings and formal divisions.

Rows may be invented to exploit specific intervals, to create symmetrical patterns of intervals, and to suggest segmentation based on intervallic patterns. Figure 14.2 shows the tone row Webern used for the Piano Variations and, for comparison, another row used in his Concerto for Nine Instruments, Op. 24 (1934).

Figure 14.2 *Webern, tone rows.*

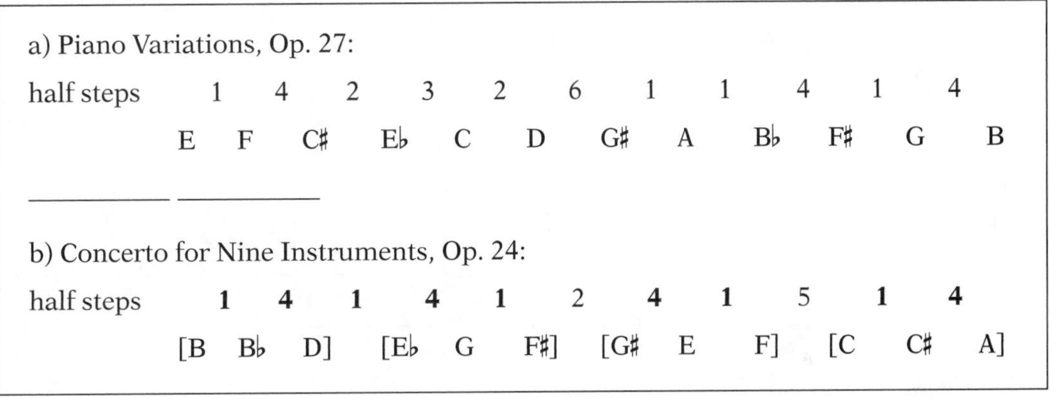

Three basic observations may be made about the series of intervals in the tone row of the Piano Variations: 1) the series is not symmetrical, 2) the tritone (ic6) is used only once and separates the two halves of the row, suggesting that the row might be segmented as two hexachords (six-note segments), and 3) minor seconds (ic1) and major thirds (ic4) are prominent. The row has some additional properties that relate to the formal structure of the work. In contrast, the tone row for the Concerto, though not symmetrical, uses a recurring pattern among the trichords (three-note segments): each of the trichords uses an ic1 and an ic4; the second and fourth trichords are a retrograde (reverse ordering) of the first and third. The limited number of intervals in the interval series and the trichord relations are properties exploited in the composition. Other rows may show symmetrical patterns while some rows use all intervals. In any case, salient properties of the row may be exploited to articulate formal divisions.

---

[10] In atonal theory, an interval, its inversion, compound forms, and enharmonic variants are considered members of the same class of interval. Therefore, when discussing atonal or serial music, there are six interval classes: ic1(m2) - ic2 (M2) - ic3(m3) - ic4(M3) - ic5(P4) - ic6 (tritone).

[11] This discussion is intended only as a brief introduction to serial composition.

The second movement of the Piano Variations uses the technique of canon as a variation on the tone row introduced in movement one.[12] As a rule, complete statements of a row must be presented before a new row begins. Four basic row forms are possible. The original version of the row is referred to as its *prime form* (P). The *inversion* (I) uses the intervals of P in the same order but in the opposite direction. The *retrograde* (R) is based on the prime form in reverse order; the *retrograde inversion* (RI) is the retrograde of the inversion (which is also an inversion of the retrograde). Because there are 12 possible transpositions of each of these row forms, 48 forms are possible. Row forms in a composition are identified by type (P, I, R, or RI) and transposition number in relation to the original row, P-O. P-4, for example, refers to the prime form transposed up four half steps (a major third).[13] Different row forms may be presented simultaneously.

In the second movement of the piano variations, two row forms are used simultaneously in a mirror canon.[14] The series of rows and pitch content used is illustrated in Figure 14.3. Each pair of row forms uses a transposition of the prime form and a transposition of an inversion. There are four pairs of rows used in this movement, with the last

Figure 14.3 *Webern, Piano Variations, Op. 27, II, row forms.*

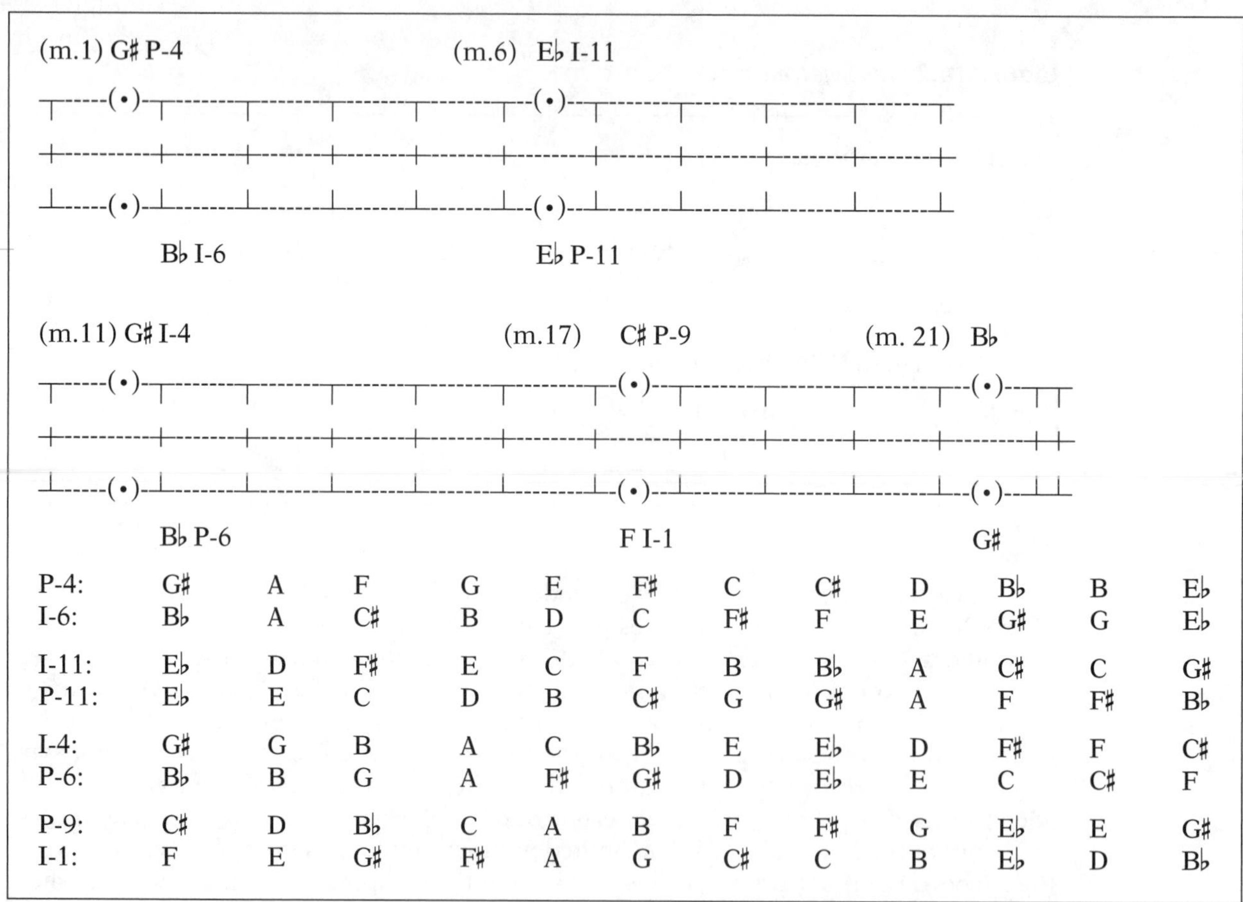

P-4:	G♯	A	F	G	E	F♯	C	C♯	D	B♭	B	E♭
I-6:	B♭	A	C♯	B	D	C	F♯	F	E	G♯	G	E♭
I-11:	E♭	D	F♯	E	C	F	B	B♭	A	C♯	C	G♯
P-11:	E♭	E	C	D	B	C♯	G	G♯	A	F	F♯	B♭
I-4:	G♯	G	B	A	C	B♭	E	E♭	D	F♯	F	C♯
P-6:	B♭	B	G	A	F♯	G♯	D	E♭	E	C	C♯	F
P-9:	C♯	D	B♭	C	A	B	F	F♯	G	E♭	E	G♯
I-1:	F	E	G♯	F♯	A	G	C♯	C	B	E♭	D	B♭

[12] Only the third of the three movements of this work is a series of variations. The first movement is in three sections, with the third section a modified restatement of the first.

[13] Two ways of labeling row forms are encountered. The method used here bases the row forms on the first statement of the row in a piece as P^0; another method is to determine P^0 as the row beginning on C, i.e. a fixed system. See Straus, 146–149.

[14] An example of a mirror canon was given previously in Example 12.2a.

note of each row serving as the first note of the next row, indicated by the pitches in brackets in the diagram.

Note: The same row is used in all three movements; the row forms of this movement are identified in relation to P-0 of the first movement.

Before considering the relation of the row to the formal structure, let us consider the movement as a whole. As notated, it appears to be a binary form with repeats. Begin the study of the movement by listening without reference to the score. Arguably, the two-part form is not readily perceivable. Of the many aspects of the movement that may be perceived, the pointillistic statements of pitches in varied articulations, the moments of punctuated chords, and the rapid changes and contrasts in register are perhaps most salient. Listen again and attempt to freely graph the form and/or the texture using any symbols that seem appropriate. You may wish to concentrate on dynamics or register. What you will find, most likely, is that whatever aspect of the piece and whichever symbols you choose to graph or draw, they change very rapidly. This exercise is meant to demonstrate how different Webern's approach is from conventional writing, with myriad contrasts in detail and constant changes in rhythmic patterns and texture.

Now let us consider some aspects of the movement with the aid of a score. Note that the same pitches begin and end the movement and the first half: B♭5 and G♯3. Since different pairs of rows are used, Webern had to calculate which row forms would continuously pair these notes together. In fact, the row structure and the row forms used result in the consistent pairings of the following pitches:

B♭	A	C♯	G	F♯	D
G♯	A	F	B	C	E

Each pitch in the top line is always paired with the pitch directly below it in the bottom line. The A, which is always paired with itself, is also in the same register each time. The doubled A is one of the most salient sounds of this movement (measures 1, 9, 13, and 19). Webern used seven pitches in fixed registers in a symmetrical intervallic pattern around the A as follows: G♯3—C♯4—F♯4—A4—C5—F5—B♭5. This use of fixed or "frozen" register is characteristic of Webern's music.[15]

In addition to the fixed elements of pitch and register, Webern uses three dynamics (*p, f, ff*) and four different articulations (slur, *staccato, tenuto*, accent). The succession of rhythmic patterns, dynamics, and articulations is asymmetrical, however, with rapid and disjunct changes in register, creating a dynamic, constantly changing texture. On the other hand, the various row forms and the "invariant dyads" articulate the phrases and sections of the composition. Thus the serial procedures, including the use of canon, create a sense of continuous development that masks the two-part form.

INTEGRAL SERIALISM

The various fixed elements of Webern's Variations are an indication of pre-compositional planning and economy of means. Webern explored the idea of pre-compositional planning of several elements in other works as well, notably the Symphony Op. 21 and the String Quartet Op. 28. The formal structure of these works is shaped by the serialization of pitch, rhythm, and timbre, and by canonic writing as well. The serialization of more than one element, often referred to as *integral serialism*, inspired many serial composers of the twentieth-century. Integral serialism was seen as a way of creating a new musical language that broke completely with music of the past. Important composers who used this technique included Oliver Messiaen, Luigi Nono, Pierre Boulez, Karlheinz Stockhausen, and Milton Babbitt.[16]

---

[15] The American composer Elliott Carter is also associated with this technique.

[16] Messiaen (1908–1992) was influential as a composer and teacher of Boulez and Stockhausen. His *Technique de mon language musical* (1944) presents his systematic and innovative treatment of pitch and rhythm.

While different systems were devised, critics of integral serialism felt that results tended to be similar regarding basic style and texture, despite the various methods of integration. Formally, the compositions were guided by principles of non-repetition that some felt created insurmountable perceptual problems.[17] Though this approach largely died out in the late 1950s, it did forge a new language and led to new idioms and techniques.

Analytic Exercises

The following compositions are recommended for study. Analysis of free atonal and serial works requires careful consideration of the elements of pitch organization. Preliminary analysis can focus on the salient details of the musical surface such as rhythm, texture, density, and timbre, which may guide segmentation and grouping of formal units. Certain works, such as Schoenberg's Op. 33a show some relation to traditional forms (i.e. sonata form), but generally these works reflect an interest in continuous development and are through-composed.

NON-SERIAL ATONAL WORKS

*Schoenberg, *Three Piano Pieces* Op. 11 (1908)

+Schoenberg, *Six Little Piano Pieces* Op. 19 (1911)

*+Berg, *Vier Lieder* Op. 2 (1910)

TWELVE-TONE WORKS

*Schoenberg: Piano Piece Op. 33a, (1928)

+Webern, Concerto Op. 24, II (1934)

Webern, Symphony Op 21, II (1928)

INTEGRAL SERIALISM

Babbitt, *Three Compositions for Piano* (1947)

Messiaen, *Quatre Etudes, No. 3* "Mode de valeurs et d'intensities" (Mode of Value and Intensity) (1948)

Boulez, *Structures Ia* for Two Pianos (1952)

Indeterminacy and Open Forms

One of the most dramatic breaks from musical traditions was the interest in using elements of chance or randomness in the composition or performance of music. This trend,

[17] See Leonard Meyer, *Music the Arts and Ideas* (Chicago: University of Chicago Press, 1967) 236–316 for a discussion of the criticisms of integral serialism. See also Reginald Smith Brindle, *The New Music, 2nd edition* New York: Oxford University Press, 1987) 52 ff.

referred to as *indeterminacy*, resulted from many factors.[18] It was seen as a reflection of indeterminacy in the real world, a desire to render each performance as a unique event, a means of exploring new sound gestures, and a way to involve performers in the creation of the piece. The number of elements subject to chance, and the degree of randomness varied from composer to composer and composition to composition. In varying degrees, the formal design results from spontaneous choice, improvisation, chance operations, or a combination of these. Two basic approaches may be distinguished, and in many compositions both approaches play an important role:

- *Compositional indeterminacy* in which compositional decisions are based on some degree of randomness or chance.
- *Performer indeterminacy* in which the performer is given choices about shaping musical ideas through indeterminate notation, or choices in the ordering of events. Composers' individual methods represent contrasting aesthetics and concepts about the use of chance in music. A brief discussion and examples of open forms will be presented to show some of the possibilities that have been explored.

COMPOSITIONAL INDETERMINACY

This type of indeterminacy was advocated primarily by the American composer John Cage (1912–1992), one of the most influential composers of the avant-garde in music. Cage developed a bold aesthetic, seeking to embrace all sound, including noises of any sort and traditional pitch, as a possible source of musical material. He also showed a strong preference for silence and developed a method of composing using a series of proportional durations for his rhythms. His aesthetic, influenced by eastern philosophy, led to the radical idea that once compositional materials are carefully chosen, they can be used in any formal structure. Each musical segment need not have any connection to what preceded or followed.

In time Cage's methods and aesthetic led him to employ chance operations in the process of composing. *Music of Changes* (1952) for solo piano was composed using the I-Ching and tosses of coins to make decisions about the ordering of material. It must be noted that materials or musical ideas were very carefully chosen by Cage in his indeterminate works so that they contained *his* preference for sounds. Charts of pitches used all twelve chromatic pitches, Western tonal harmony was avoided, rhythmic cycles or series were structured to avoid metric regularity, and dynamics and timbres tended to stress delicate sounds. Consequently the music was very stylistically consistent, which in turn allowed for the arbitrary approach to form.

PERFORMER INDETERMINACY

The concept of compositional indeterminacy led to the idea of *open* or *mobile forms*, in which a series of musical events or sections are carefully structured but may be presented in random order. Cage developed graphic notation to introduce performer decisions in the realization of the piece. Example 14.8 from Cage's *Concert for Piano and Orchestra* (1958), a work that calls for any of thirteen instrumentalists in the orchestra, shows an example of his notation of musical events that may be shaped and sequenced at the pianist's discretion. In this type of score, the performer makes choices based on the composer's instructions and the interpretation of novel notations. In this type of score, the performer makes

[18] This approach is also described as *aleatoric* (from the Latin *alea*, meaning *dice*) or "chance" music.

Example 14.8 Cage, *Concert for Piano and Orchestra (1958)*, excerpt.

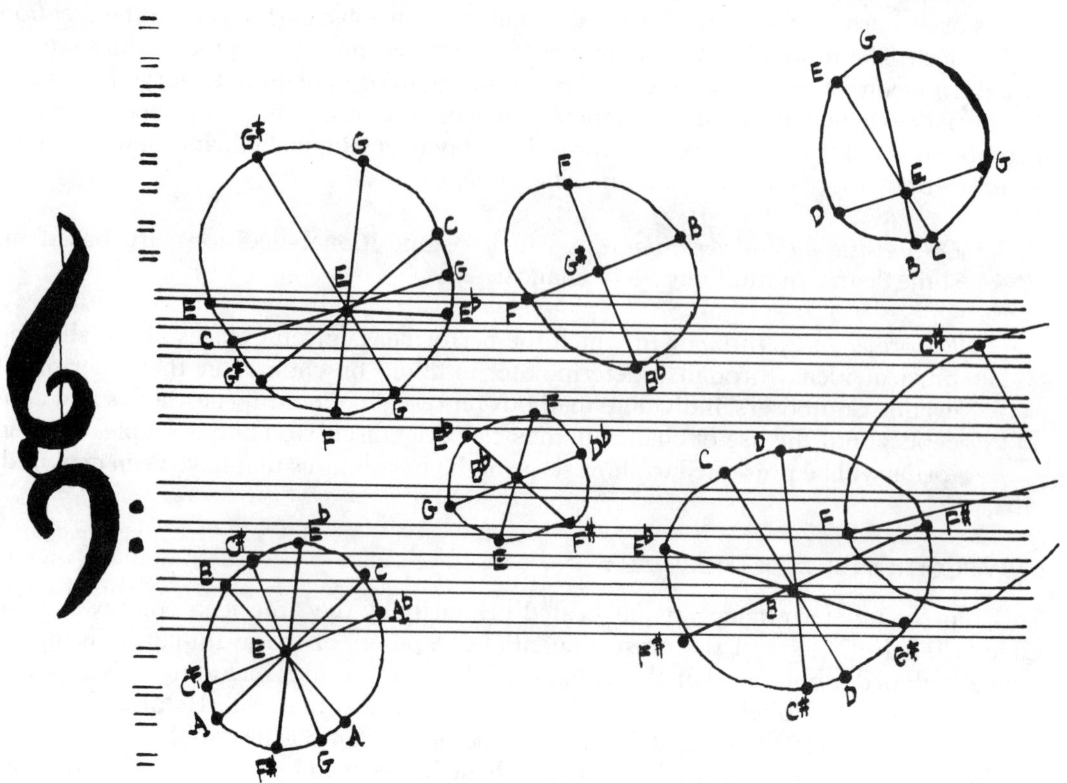

choices based on the composer's instructions and the interpretation of novel notations. In this case, Cage states in the legend of the score: "Play 'wheel' or 'axle' using ones not played as harmonic(s). Play from left to right." (See Example 14.8.) Morton Feldman (1926–1987) and Earle Brown (b. 1926), younger associates of Cage, further developed graphic notation, influenced by visual artists.

In Europe, Stockhausen and Boulez explored the concept of open forms in contrasting ways. Boulez was opposed to chance as a compositional process and to the indeterminacy of graphic notation. After retreating from integral serialism, he explored serial procedures while developing the idea of mobile forms. His Piano Sonata No. 3 (1958) uses traditional musical notation, but the segments of the work have alternate choices for continuation. Each segment may appear only once, and the form, though mobile, is limited in its number of realizations. Boulez has likened this approach to a musical labyrinth, in which the large-scale or "outer" form is rediscovered in each performance, reflecting continuous evolution of material in an open rather than closed form. The style of the work continues that of integral serialism with its absence of meter or consistent pulse, its use of complex, irregular rhythms, and its fragmentary contrapuntal textures without traditional lines or harmonies.

Stockhausen, like Boulez, was a serial composer, but he developed a concept of indeterminate form that he called "moment form." He envisioned a non-hierarchical approach in which musical ideas or "moments" are savored individually rather than heard as a continuous or hierarchic form. Each moment is actually a short section (in his terms, "a group") of a work. His groups or moments tend to have similar pitch content and are serial in nature; they are distinguished by specific tempo, dynamics, register, shape, or intervallic pattern. He explains this break from the traditional notion of forms in an article he wrote in 1960:

> **Musical forms have been composed in recent years which are far from the scheme of dramatic forms. . . . In them the customary stages of introduction, transition, tension, and relaxation are not represented. . . . In these new forms, every "now" is not simply the result of what has gone before nor an upbeat to what follows or to what is expected, but instead a personal, independent, centralized entity existing for itself.**[19]

By the time this article was written, Stockhausen had composed several works with varied approaches to moment forms. His *Klavierstücke XI* (1956) was the first European work to explore this concept. In this piece, nineteen "groups" or sections from short fragments to 15 measures (ametric in nature) can be played in any order. Six tempos, dynamics, and articulations are given for the performer to choose from once he picks a section to begin the piece. The performer is instructed to let the eyes "wander at random over the page." Using a specified dynamic, articulation, and tempo at the end of that section he randomly chooses another, and so forth. No group may be repeated immediately, but a group can be played again. The second time a group is performed, octave transpositions are designated, which naturally change the timbre. Once a third restatement of any group is performed the piece is considered over. The consistent serial style of this composition, with a wide range of very dense and very spare textures, and the focus on dissonant intervals and complex rhythms, emphasizes the contrast in timbre and motion among the groups. Stockhausen also expands his sonic and rhythmic resources with techniques such as clusters to be played with the forearm, and small notes that are to be played "as fast as possible" (Example 14.9).

Example 14.9 Stockhausen, *Klavierstucke XI,* excerpt.

While Boulez wrote only a few works using indeterminate form, Stockhausen explored its possibilities in many works. *Zyklus* (1959), a work for solo percussion, allows the performer to begin with any of the sixteen sections, but the sections must all be performed in order. The graphic score is notated with symbols for each instrument, and groups or dots in rectangles and triangles are used to indicate choices the performer may make for ordering

[19] Quoted in Simms, *Music of the Twentieth Century*, 2nd ed, 356–357.

and interpolating ("folding in") material within sections. This piece thus has a closed form that may begin at any point but allows some performer determinacy within sections.

All of the works cited here display a fundamental break from traditional concepts of form, as Stockhausen's observations quoted above aptly describe. Open forms, coupled with the serial style, resulted in music of extreme complexity that was very challenging for performers and listeners. Later musical developments were, in part, a response to these complexities.

NOTATIONAL INDETERMINACY

The graphic notations developed by Cage and Stockhausen, among others, reflected, in part, an interest in new sounds and textures as well as new ways of shaping tempo and motion in music. Many composers were drawn to the more elastic sense of rhythm and the free sound gestures that came from such experimental music, and developed new notations accordingly.[20] Two composers who created noteworthy works employing *indeterminate notation*, as they explored new forms of composition, are Luciano Berio (1925–2003) and Witold Lutoslawski (1913–1994). A work by each composer will be briefly examined to illustrate some indeterminate notations and the resulting concepts of form.

Berio was also a serial composer in his early career and studied electronic music. He was particularly interested in vocal and physical gestures, and his settings of texts by poets such as e.e. cummings and Ezra Pound explored text as meaning and text as purely vocal sonorities. In *Circles* (1960) for voice, harp, and percussion, he used different vocal styles and texts in an A B C B′ A arch form. He also wrote a series of compositions entitled *Sequenza,* each written for a different solo instrument. These compositions draw on instrumental, vocal, and sometimes visual gestures, and employ determinate and indeterminate notation. They are akin to musical essays that explore the potential range of sounds and transformations of ideas with reference to the instrument being played.

One of the most theatrical of these musical essays is the *Sequenza V* for solo trombone (1966). The piece is meant to recall his memory of a famous French clown named Grock. Though specific pitches are notated in most instances, there are no stems and the rhythmic notation is a type of temporal or "proportional notation." In this type of notation, the duration of events is determined by the space it occupies on the score with temporal duration given in seconds. (See Example 14.10.) The duration of pitches is based on the distance between them and the shape of the note heads: note heads with a slash are meant to be "as short as possible" while plain note heads are "held until the next attack." Bar lines are indicators of where breaths are to be taken, and dynamics are given by the series of numbers from 1–7. In the course of the piece, the performer modifies his sounds in several ways: he uses a metal plunger to resemble speech, produces percussive noises and vocal sounds while playing, and makes free use of the slide for varied glissando. At one point the performer speaks "why?" in a bewildered state and then sits to continue playing.

The effect of the piece is a virtuosic, theatrical exploration of the soloist as an instrumental and vocal persona. The sequence of events and sounds are precisely notated while the temporal and spatial notation insures a flexible and elastic sense of rhythmic motion. What should be observed in these new notations is that the results will be similar, even though the notation often indicates a basic gesture, shape, or sound effect rather than a precise action. *The form of the composition may be perceived in terms of varied degrees of activity and intensity, with sounds emerging very slowly, as in the opening, or presented in frenetic bursts as in the excerpt shown.*

Lutoslawski, in contrast to many composers, employed indeterminacy in a more controlled series of events. His early works were similar in style to Bartók and his works

[20] See Kurt Stone, *Music Notation in the Twentieth Century*, New York: Norton, 152–157 for discussion of new notations.

Example 14.10 *Berio, Sequenza 5 for Solo Trombone, excerpt.*

sequenza V

for trombone solo (1966)

luciano berio

Berio, Sequenza V for solo Trombone. © 1968 by Universal Edition (London) Ltd., London © renewed. All Rights Reserved. Used by permission of European American Music Distributors LLC, U.S. and Canadian agent for Universal Edition (London) Ltd., London.

in the late 1950s were highly chromatic and contrapuntal in a serial style. A change in style, according to Lutoslawski, came about when he heard Cage's *Concert for Piano and Orchestra*. The work suggested to him that one could compose music by "starting out with chaos and create order in it gradually."[21] His interest was not in indeterminate performance but in new textures and forms that involved superimposed layers of ideas in what he termed "aleatoric counterpoint." He notated pitches precisely, but allowed some improvisatory approaches to rhythm and repetition of ideas.

Example 14.11 shows an excerpt from a major work of Lutoslawski, his *Livre pour Orchestre* (1968). This passage is labeled "Íntermede" (intermezzo); in it, three clarinetists play rapid, repeated figures, starting and stopping at different times. The tempo and rests are given in temporal indications. The parts vary in length and are to be repeated until 20 seconds have elapsed (cued by the conductor), followed by a five-second pause. The effect is that of a swirling mass of sound with fluctuating density, which suddenly emerges and stops.

Example 14.11 Lutoslawski, *Livre pour Orchestre,* I, Intermede.

1er INTERMEDE
110 AD LIB.
20"
5"
Cl.
1) Prior to the commencement of this bar all keys lying between the indicated notes are to be depressed soundlessly.
2) In the ad libitum sections the notation indicates .
1) Vor dem Anfang des Taktes sind alle zwischen den angegebenen Noten liegenden Tasten klanglos zu drücken.
2) Die Notation bedeutet in den ad libitum Sektionen.

28. 915

Livre Pour Orchestre by Witold Penderecki. © Copyright 1969 Chester Music Limited for the World except Poland, Albania, Bulgaria, the territories of former Czechoslovakia, Rumania, Hungary, the whole territory of the former USSR, Cuba, China, North Vietnam and North Korea where the Copyright, 1969, is held by Polskie Wydawnictwo Muzyczne-OWM Edition, Kraków, Poland. All Rights Reserved. International Copyright Secured. Reprinted by permission of G. Schirmer, Inc. (ASCAP): 1st Intermede (bottom of page 9 of the score).

[21] Steven Stuckey, *Lutoslawski and His Music*, (Cambridge, Cambridge University Press, 1981), 84.

Lutoslawski's method of composing allows complex textures to be created precisely without the daunting complexities that traditional notation would require. Such passages would alternate or be superimposed with conventionally notated passages. His forms involve contrasts in density and timbre, often in block-like textures, but with multiple layers of different activity. This juxtapositioning and the gradual changes in texture, allows various lines to project. The spatial layout of the scores, as seen in Example 14.12, illustrates Lutoslawski's concern with careful coordination of entrances, and the importance of timbre and register for shaping the music.[22] Finally, his temporal indications require a new feeling for tempo, and for the passage of time.

ANALYTIC EXERCISE: LUTOSLAWSKI, SYMPHONY NO. 3, I

This three-movement work, composed in 1983, is one of the composer's best known and most often performed works. The first page of the score is given in Example 14.12. This work, like many post-tonal works, is episodic, consisting of a series of contrasting sections. The first movement is organized into three episodes separated by refrains, which may be outlined as follows:

I Fast Refrain II Slower Refrain-Intermezzo III Slowest

The opening eighth-note figure articulates sections. Listen to the movement and attempt to identify the number of sections you hear, and the refrain. Is there a climactic point in the movement? Contrasting rates of speed and different choirs of instruments may also be gauged to determine a formal shape. Study the lines and then attempt to conduct the work as you follow the score. What special challenges does a work such as this pose for conductors and performers?

Clusters and Textural Form

The trend toward shaping musical forms in terms of basic sound gestures—fast/slow, high/low, loud/soft, thick/thin—with an emphasis on textural and timbral processes is evident to varying degrees in the indeterminate works discussed above. An equally important influence in this regard was that of electronic music, in which the manipulation and synthesis of the constituent elements of sound—frequency, amplitude, wave shapes and so forth—explores sonic shapes and gestures.[23] These influences are heard in the works of two noteworthy composers, György Ligeti (1923–2003) and Krzysztof Penderecki (b. 1933).[24]

Ligeti, who wrote in a "neo-Bartókian" style based largely on folk music in his early works, began to work with textural compositions in the late 1950s. His first important

[22] A spatial score uses blank space to indicate rests in various parts and vertical lines to coordinate entrances.

[23] Electronic studios were developed in the 1950s in Cologne, Milan, Paris, and Princeton. Many composers worked in this medium, if only briefly, to explore new sound possibilities.

[24] Pioneers in new musical resources and sonic designs included Henry Cowell (1897–1965) and Edgard Varèse 1883–1965). See *The Banshee* (1925) for prepared piano by Cowell, and *Ionisation* (1931) for percussion ensemble by Varèse.

Example 14.12 Lutoslawski, Symphony No. 3, I, beginning.

for Sir Georg Solti and the Chicago Symphony Orchestra

SYMPHONY No.3

Witold Lutoslawski
(1983)

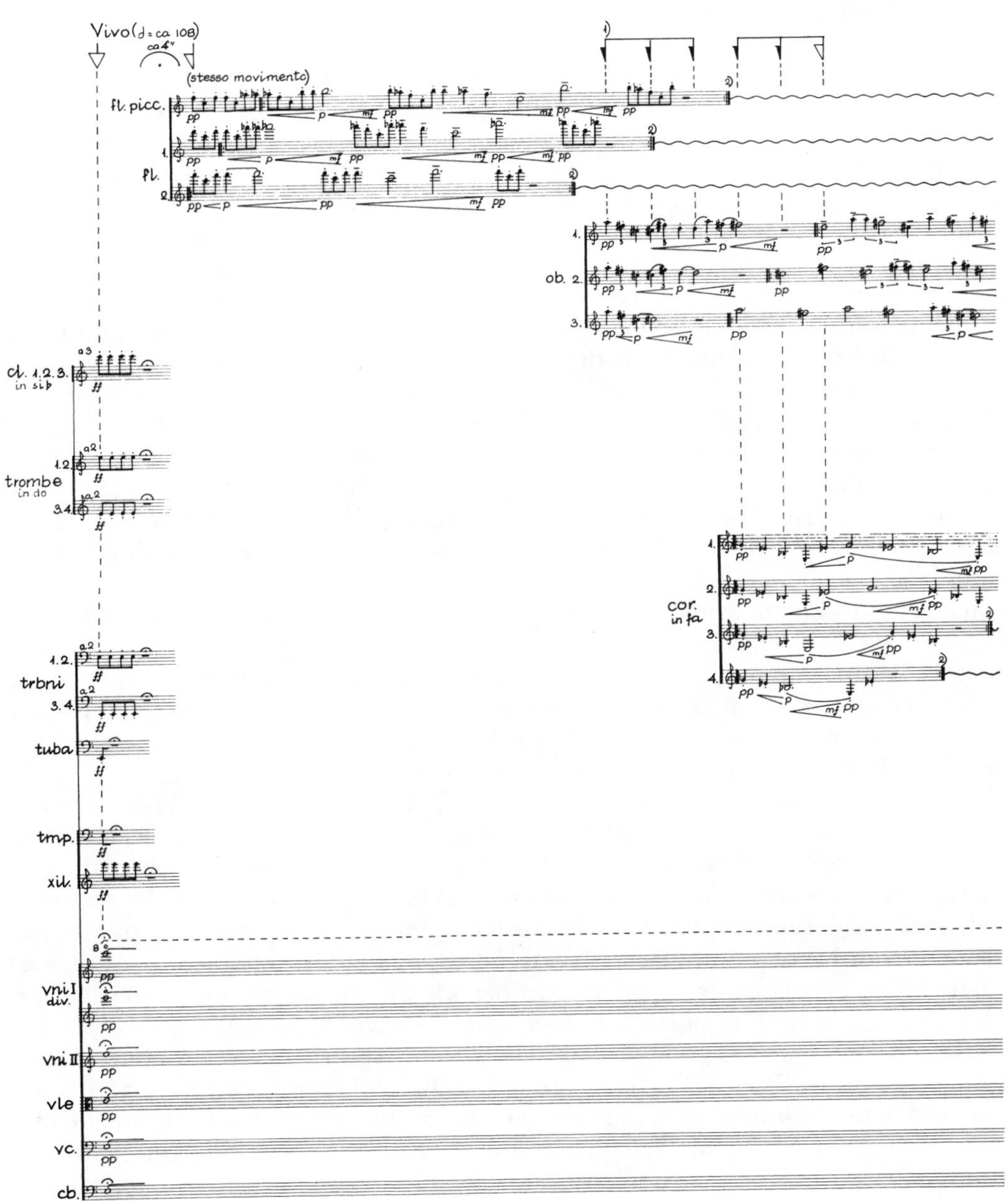

1. These six beats concern only oboes and horns.
2. The phrase with the repeat marks (‖: :‖) is to be repeated until the next single beat ( ).

1. Diese sechs Schläge betreffen nur Oboen und Hörner.
2. Die Phrase mit den Wiederholungszeichen (‖: :‖) ist nur bis zum nächsten eizelnen Schlag zu wiederholen ( ).

work in this style was *Atmosphères* (1961) for a large orchestra including two pianists. Ligeti states that in this work:

> **In *Atmosphères* I have attempted to supersede the structural approach to music, which, once, in turn, superseded the motivic-thematic approach, and to establish a new textural concept of music.[25]**

Ligeti's solution to composing in this manner was to write specific pitches in very dense, polyphonic structures, often using canonic procedures. *Atmosphères*, in fact, contains a 48-voice canon.[26] The resultant texture is a that of *clusters*—a sound mass in which individual pitches and parts are not heard. Clusters are created by having parts close together, in bands of sound based on major and minor seconds. Ligeti also called for special sound effects such as muted sounds, harmonics, *sul tasto*, and brushes on the piano strings. Though a tempo of quarter-note = 40 is given, there is no readily discernible pulse, and temporal durations of sections are given in seconds and minutes.

Atmosphères was extremely successful with audiences since its basic shape relies on contrasts in density, timbre, and sound qualities that were easier to grasp than much avant-garde music. Its form may be perceived in terms of a theme and variations, the theme being instrumental "white noise" created by the entire spectrum of orchestral colors. Rests and changes in density and timbre filter out sounds, and each rehearsal letter in the score (A through O) marks a passage with a certain sound quality. Fluctuations in density, dynamics, timbre, register, and rhythmic motion create varied transformations of these sound masses. Such textural forms and processes occupied Ligeti in other works of the 1960s, including *Continuum* for harpsichord. (See Analytic Exercise Example 14.14.)

Penderecki's textural compositions, unlike Ligeti's, rely on sound masses of undifferentiated parts. He achieves this by using clusters of pitches, including microtones (quarter step inflections), indeterminate notation such as "highest note possible," indeterminate choice of pitch from a group, and special effects, particularly when writing for strings and voices. A noteworthy example is his early work, *Threnody for the Victims of Hiroshima* (1960) for string orchestra. In addition to microtones and clusters, the score calls for a great number of special effects such as *col legno, sul ponticello*, and playing behind the tailpiece. The textures range from clusters to pointillistic sounds; its extended range of bombastic and shrill effects echoes the horror of war.

In the 1960s Penderecki wrote dramatic works for chorus, soloists and orchestra, drawing on an eclectic variety of traditional and textural resources. One of his most successful works is the *St. Luke Passion*, a setting of sections of the Passion of St. Luke, combined with passages from the Psalms and the Lamentations of Jeremiah. Its resources include psalmody, bands of twelve-tone clusters, ametric rhythms, and a passacaglia using a tone row based on the "B-A-C-H" (B♭-A-C-B) motive. The chorus is used to great dramatic effect and is called upon to whisper, shout, chant, speak in *sprechstimme (speaking voice)*, and to sing clusters. *The contrasts in different techniques of vocal production delineate the phrases*. Example 14.13 shows an excerpt from the "Stabat Mater," which he sets in part II of the "Passion." Here the chorus 1) sings clusters in antiphonal settings of the text "Christe" with each part singing a different four-note chromatic line, 2) recites text in the manner of a litany, and 3) sings chant-like patterns in chromatic, dissonant relations. Penderecki also uses a spatial layout for the score, a common convention of much music in the last fifty years.

---

[25] From liner notes by Edward Downes for *Leonard Bernstein Conducts Music of Our Time*, Columbia Records, MS 6733.

[26] The term "micropolyphony" is sometimes used to describe these extremely dense polyphonic textures.

Example 14.13 Penderecki, *St. Luke Passion,* "Stabat Mater," excerpt.

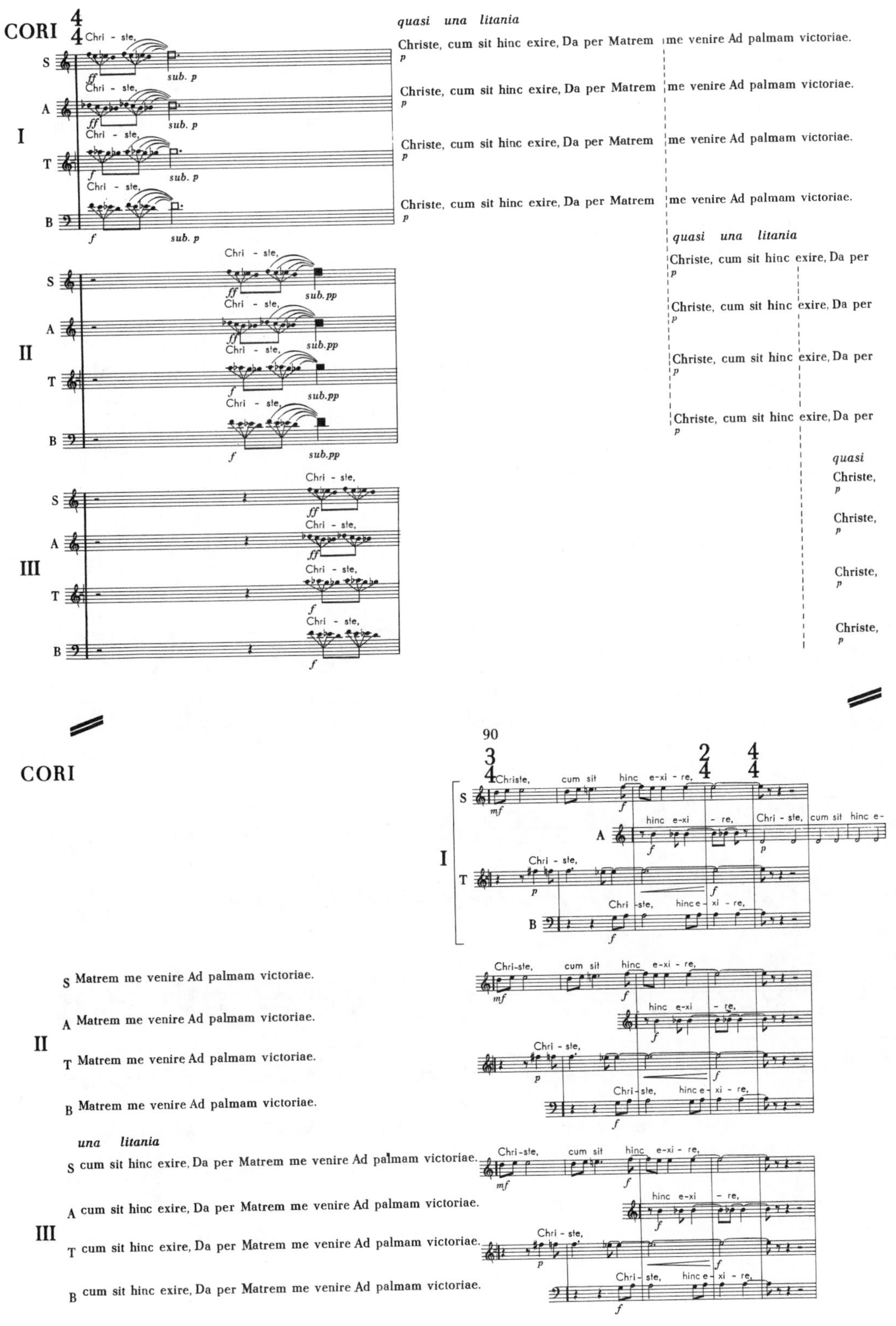

Analytic Exercises

1. **Penderecki: *Threnody for the Victims of Hiroshima.***
   Despite the unconventional nature of the sounds in this work, three large sections may be perceived. As you listen to the work, determine whether it is through-composed or ternary in nature. You may observe sudden shifts in timbre and density as well as gradual changes.

2. **Ligeti: *Continuum*, (Example 14.14).**
   This piece for harpsichord maintains a constant pulse based on tremolo and scalar patterns. Ligeti provides the following instructions: "Prestissimo—extremely fast—so that the individual tones can hardly be perceived but rather merge into a continuum." The piece progresses though a gradual expansion of individual lines related to a scheme of interval changes. As certain chromatic pitches are added, they are prominent in the texture for brief spans of time. The beginning is played in the middle registers, on two manuals. Listen to the piece and note the role of contrasts in register and pitch in delineating the form. A drawing or graph based on range and shape can be useful in gauging the form.

Example 14.14 Ligeti, *Continuum*, beginning, 1968.

Form as Process: Minimalism

In the 1950s and early 1960s certain American composers, notably La Monte Young (b. 1935), Terry Riley (b. 1935), Steve Reich (b. 1936), and Phillip Glass (b. 1937), became interested in using a limited number of simple ideas to create music in which compositional processes were audible. Their aesthetic reflected the influences of Eastern philosophy, with its interest in static motion and gradual change, the economy of means observed in Webern's music and the early works of John Cage, and a turn-away from the complexities of integral serialism. Electronic music, with its emphasis on manipulations of repeated sounds, tape loops, and synthesizer sequences, and the heterophonic textures of non-Western music were also influences. Although these composers developed varied systems of composing, their general style of music is identified under the term *minimalism*.[27]

Minimal music is characterized by 1) the use of a limited number of musical ideas, which are often simple, modal, and/or diatonic patterns, 2) tonal stasis and an extremely slow or limited harmonic rhythm, and 3) an emphasis on incessant repetition and gradual change using ostinati and additive rhythms. Consequently, the form of minimal music emerges gradually, the result of audible processes. An early work by La Monte Young, *Composition 1960 No. 7*, is an extreme example in which a perfect fifth on B–F♯ is simply sustained "for a very long time." In such a work, the form results from a single event with the only change being the dynamics or vibrations of the pitches. The most prominent composers of minimal music in the past three decades have been Glass, Reich, and John Adams (b. 1947). An early work by Glass shows his use of additive techniques, in which melodic lines are gradually lengthened while the two-voiced texture of parallel fifths remains static (see Example 14.15). *In works such as this, the form results from the additive processes being used rather than any preconceived formal design.* In later works, he expanded his harmonic content to included traditional diatonic progressions, but maintained his use of single chords for long spans of time and repetitive processes. Glass has been interested in stage works since the mid-1970s, when his opera *Einstein on the Beach* introduced new conceptual ideas about opera. The work is extremely long and presents minimal music with a series of tableaux related to Einstein, rather than a narrative.

Example 14.15 Glass, *Music In Fifths, 1969.*

Reich's interest in process music was influenced by his study of the music of Ghana. He observed that Ghanaian drumming was based on "several repeating patterns, more or less in subdivisions of twelve, but superimposed so that the downbeats aren't in the same place." These studies and his work with tape loops led to his interest in the technique of *phasing*, which he describes as follows: "Phase really has to do with canon. . . . What you have is a unison canon or round where the rhythmic interval between the first and second voices is variable and constantly changing."[28] In works using this technique, the form is

[27] The terms "system music" and "process music" have also been used to describe this style. The aesthetic of minimalism has precedent in the music of John Cage and was manifested in the fine arts as well. Cage's notorious 4′33," and is notated and monochromatic paintings such as Yves Klein's series of blue paintings (1956) exemplify a move toward minimal amounts of material.

[28] Jonathan Cott, "Interview with Steve Reich," in *Steve Reich: Works 1965–1995* (ten compact discs), Nonesuch Records, 1997.

dictated by the process of beginning in phase, working through a series of permutations that put the voices out of phase, and the eventual return to the synchronization of the parts until they are in phrase again.

Reich's *It's Gonna Rain* (1965) and *Come Out* (1966), which use tape loops based on the titles, and *Piano Phase* and *Violin Phase* (1967), are early works based on phasing. Two or more players start off in unison but gradually one player accelerates or shifts the pattern so their downbeats are out of phase. (This process is illustrated in the works discussed in the exercises.) In his work *Drumming* (1971), a one hour and 30 minute work for voices, piccolo, and percussion, he uses the process of gradually substituting beats for rests or rests for beats. He also employs gradual changing of timbres while pitch and rhythm remain constant.

In the 1970s and 1980s Reich began using larger ensembles, more contrapuntal textures, and a wider range of harmonic movement, while still using traditional chord structures and modal progressions. *Desert Music* (1982) for chorus and orchestra is one notable work from this period. Though very gradual processes of change and repetition still characterize the music, a wider range of expression and enriched musical language are embraced. Later works, such as *New York Counterpoint* (1986), use longer patterns in layers of two or three canonic voices. Large-scale patterns of change in timbre, density, mode or key create a semblance of sectional forms. The persistent pulse found in most of Reich's music, and the gradual pace of transformations, however, continues to emphasize the processive, repetitive nature of his minimal forms.

Conclusion

The new approaches to form such as those discussed here—developing variations, pitch motive variation and transformation, indeterminacy and open forms, textural compositions, and minimalist "process" forms—are some indication of the diversity of styles that emerged in the twentieth century. It interesting to note, however, that many experimental styles of the 1950s and 1960s were abandoned by the composers who initiated them. Most notable in this regard may be Penderecki and Ligeti, whose works since the mid-1970s returned to more conventional notation and less experimental approaches to composing. Graphic, non-traditional notation remains a novelty—the exception rather than the norm. Other composers have returned to a more consonant, tonal idiom with strong interest in orchestral color and novel textures that shape formal designs. Generally, approaches to formal structure are based on continuous development or variation of material, or on episodic, through-composed forms. The formal principles of repetition, variation, and contrast still shape much music that is written.

One experimental resource of the 1950s continues to evolve in this new millennium—that of electronic music. *Musique concrete*—sonic material derived from tape and recordings of real world sounds—introduced techniques of tape manipulation such as tape-delay or tape loops that are still influential. The evolution of computers and digital technology has perhaps been the most significant change in recent decades. Not only can computers store, generate and manipulate musical resources, they can facilitate real-time performance. Electro-acoustic music in which live performers of traditional "acoustic" instruments interact with their digitally manipulated sounds continues to be explored by many composers. The complex, often through-composed forms of such works is most readily studied through live performance rather than an actual score (the latter not being feasible to reproduce here). The notion of "surround sound" and the use of speakers as sources for musical sounds has introduced a new dimension to music, that of the physical space in which it occurs. Centers for the development of electro-acoustic music have been established in many universities and cultural centers, most famously in Paris at the Institute for

Research and Coordination of Acoustics and Music (IRCAM). Exploration and creation of music as sound in time *and space* may be one of the major trends of the twenty-first century. This will certainly lead to new approaches to form and structure.

The most recent decades are perhaps best characterized as eclectic. The influential and experimental works of the twentieth century have created a wealth of new techniques and resources that composers now draw on in diverse ways. No single style predominates, except as noted, and the return to more conventional notation appears to have signaled the end, for the time being, of the radical experiments of the mid-twentieth century. Some composers remain committed to the achievements and style of serial writing, while others seek to find new expressions using the tonal resources of the past. In whatever style one encounters, the ability to write a cohesive work that is stylistically consistent and formally coherent remains an important aspect of the composer's art.

SUGGESTED READING

In addition to the works cited in the reference notes, the following readings are recommended. Milton Babbitt. "Who Cares if you Listen?" in *Contemporary Composers on Contemporary Music*, ed. Elliott Schwarz and Barney Childs. New York: Norton, 1971. Pierre Boulez. "Sonate, que me veux-tu?" *Perspectives of New Music* 1, 1963: 32–44.

John. Cage, *Silence: Lectures and Writings*. Wesleyan University Press, 1961. Christopher Hasty, "Segmentation and Process in Post-Tonal Music," *Music Theory Spectrum 3* (1981): 54–73. Jonathan Kramer, *The Time of Music: New Meaning, New Temporalities, New Listening Strategies*. New York: Schirmer, 1988. See especially 20–65.

John Rahn, *Basic Atonal Theory*. New York: Longman, 1980. 1–18. Robert K. Schwarz, "Steve Reich: Music as Gradual Process." *Perspectives of New Music* 19: 373–392 and 20: 225–286. Anton Webern, *The Path to the New Music*. Ed. Willi Reich. Bryn Mawr, PA: Theodore Presser, 1963.

Analytic Exercises

A. Reich, *Clapping Music (1972).** This piece by Reich is an example of his phasing technique. The best way to examine this technique is by performing the work, which calls for two performers. It would appear that the upper (first) of the two parts is easier than lower (second). Is this necessarily the case? How is the lower part systematically changed as the piece progresses? The composer intentionally leaves out a meter marking. How would a performer play the rhythms of this music? Why are there thirteen different groups in the entire piece?

B. John Adams, *Tromba lontana* (1986) This work by John Adams is one of two fanfares for orchestra that make clear use of the principles of minimal style. The first page of the score is given in Example 14.16. Note how the various timbres differentiate the musical ideas. As you listen to this short work, identify the introduction of chromatic pitches, suggesting a modulation, and how the treatment of timbre and texture shapes the form. Examine the harmonies and progressions found in the score. In evidence, here is the use of traditional tonal materials in novel ways, which is often associated with minimalism and sometimes referred to as the "new tonality." To what extent is this work tonal? Are there modulations to other tonal centers?

Example 14.16 John Adams, *Tromba lontana for Orchestra,* opening.

HPS 1150

Printed in U.S.A. 1992

C. **George Crumb (b. 1929), *Ancient Voices of Children* (1970), IV "Each Afternoon in Granada, a Child Dies each Afternoon."** This colorful work in five movements is based on the poetry of Federico Garcia Lorca, published in 1955. The scoring is for soprano, boy soprano, oboe, mandolin, harp, electric piano, and percussion. Crumb's eclectic style incorporates several of the stylistic elements discussed in this chapter. His interest in unique timbres and sonorities is combined with fragmentary textures and sometimes indeterminate style. Movement IV is given in Example 14.17. You should begin study of the score by noting the many performance instructions. How might a formal diagram of this work be conceived? How is the score representative of the innovations noted above? Note the pitch content of the various parts. Which parts share pitch material? What types of harmonic motions are used? A quotation from Bach is used. This technique of quotation was used by many composers of eclectic, theatrical works in the 1960s and 1970s. (See for example, Berio, Sinfonia (1968) for eight singers and orchestra, III.) What may be the expressive or programmatic intent of the quotation?

D. **Additional works for study** In addition to the works given under analytic exercises, the following works are recommended for study. Initially, listening should focus on the broad outline and shape of events heard. Writing verbal descriptions, noting letter schemes of the formal design, or graphing shapes may help focus your listening. Consider which styles discussed in this chapter are represented here. Do any of the works contain traditional formal designs? What elements of the music articulate the form? Is tonality or centricity evident in any of the works?

*John Adams, "This is Prophetic" from *Nixon in China*

*Babbitt, *Play on Notes*

Boulez, *Anthemes II* for Violin and Electronics

+Bartok, *Mikrokosmos*, Vol 2, No. 61 Pentatonic Melody

+Britten, "Pastorale" from *Serenade for Tenor, Horn and Strings*

*Cage, "For Paul Taylor and Anita Dencks"

Elliott Carter, *Eight Etudes and a Fantasy for Woodwind Quartet*, No. 7 "Intensely", No. 8 "Presto"

Peter Maxwell Davies, *Eight Songs for a Mad King*

Jennifer Higdon, *Blue Cathedral* (Telarc CD 80596)

+Poulenc, *Mouvements Perpetuels*

*Bruce Saylor, *Psalm 13* for Voice and Flute

*Terry Riley, *In C*

*+Ruth Crawford Seeger, String Quartet (1931), III

+Ligeti, Sonata for Solo Viola, V

+Webern, *Five Movements for String Quartet*, Op 5, No. 3 (1909)

Example 14.17 Crumb, *Ancient Voices of Children,* IV "Each afternoon in Granada, a Child Dies Each Afternoon."

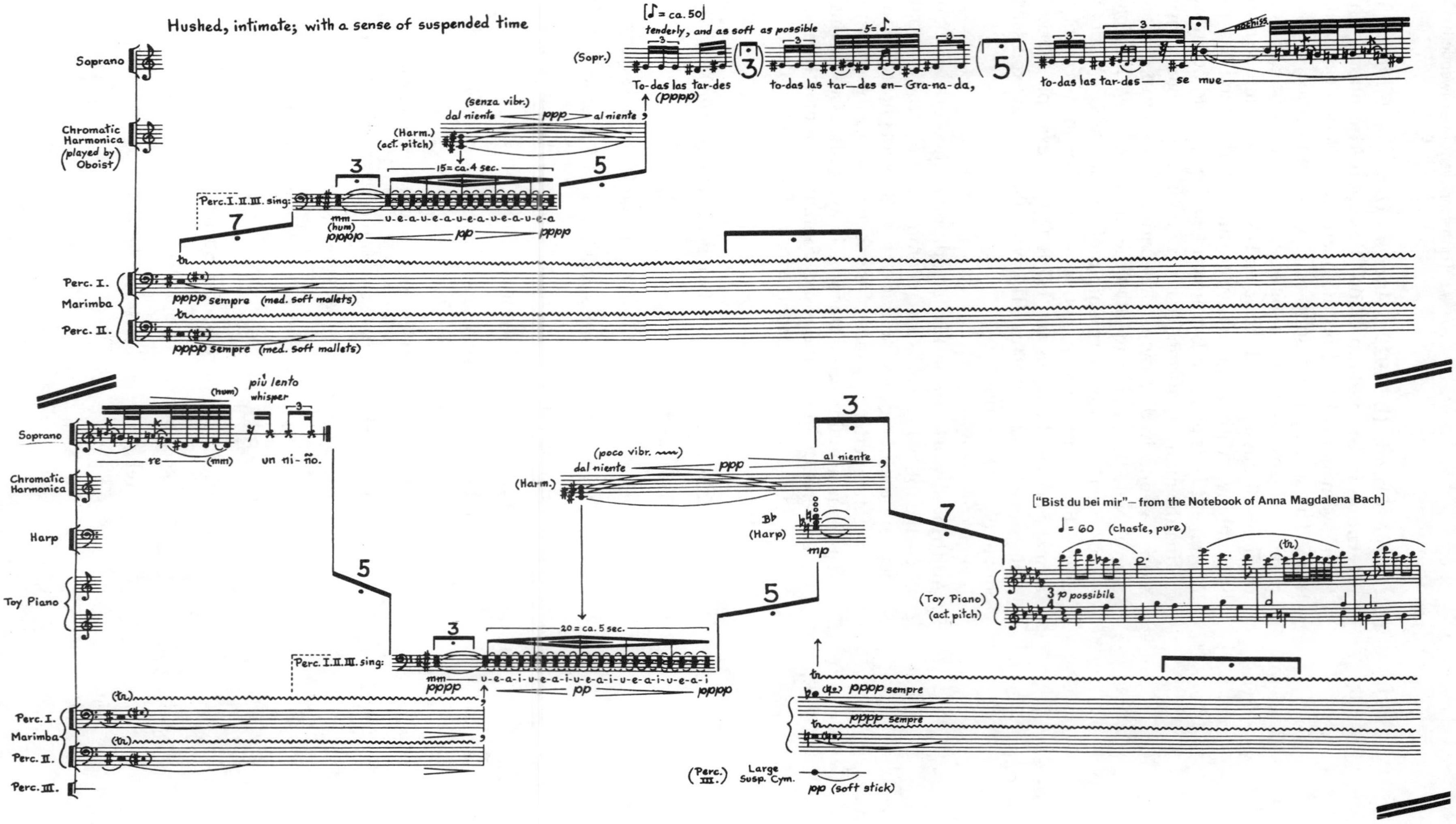

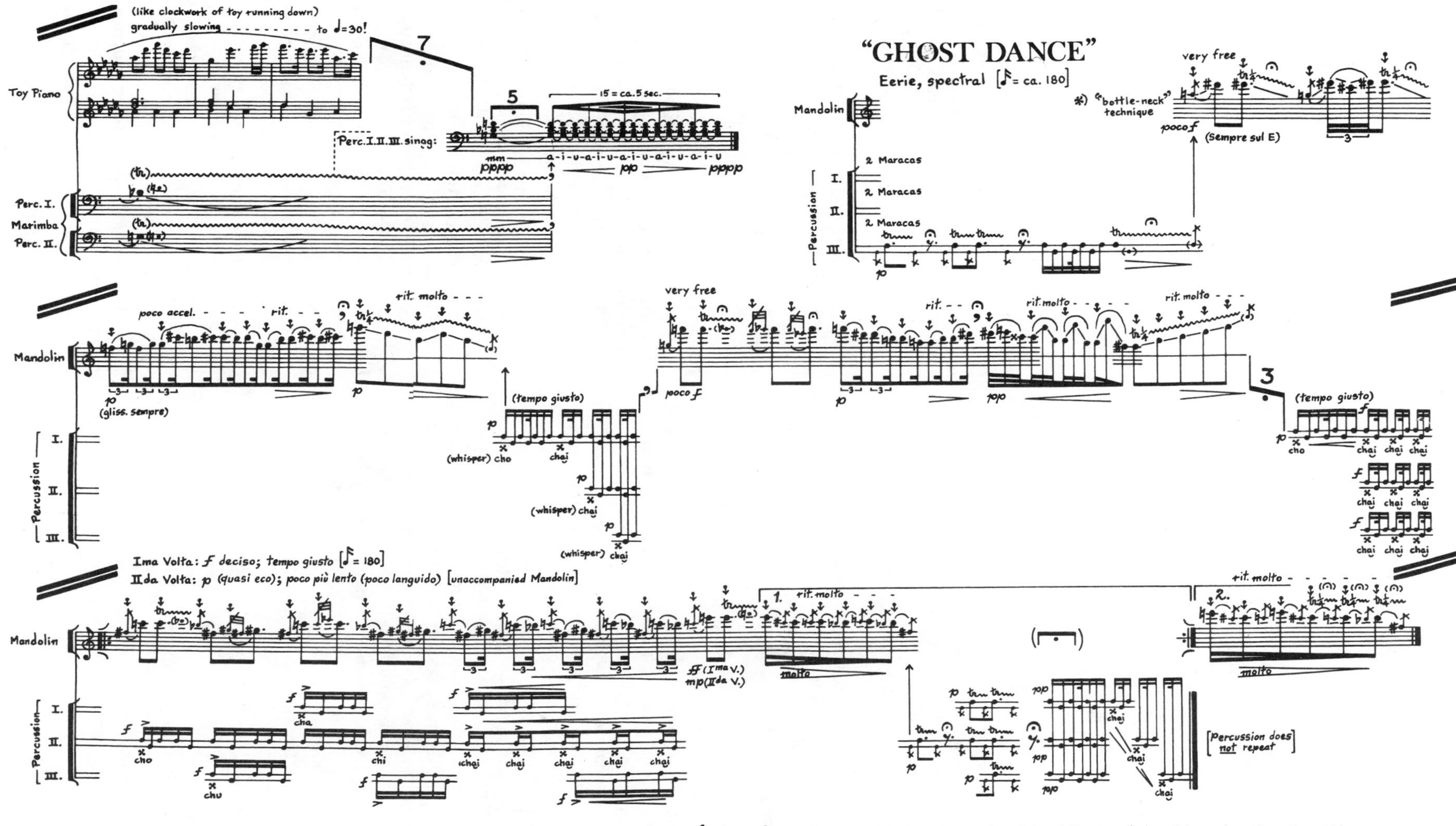
(like clockwork of toy running down)
gradually slowing - - - - - - - - - to ♩=30!
Toy Piano
7
5
Perc. I. II. III. sing:
15 = ca. 5 sec.
mm
a-i-u-a-i-u-a-i-u-a-i-u-a-i-u
pppp
pp
pppp
Perc. I.
Marimba
Perc. II.
"GHOST DANCE"
Eerie, spectral [♪= ca. 180]
Mandolin
very free
*) "bottle-neck" technique
poco f
(Sempre sul E)
Percussion
2 Maracas
2 Maracas
2 Maracas
p
poco accel.
rit.
rit. molto
(gliss. sempre)
(tempo giusto)
(whisper) cho
chai
(whisper) chai
(whisper) chai
very free
poco f
rit.
rit. molto
pp
3
(tempo giusto)
cho
chai
Ima Volta: f deciso; tempo giusto [♪= 180]
IIda Volta: p (quasi eco); poco più lento (poco languido) [unaccompanied Mandolin]
ff (Ima V.)
mp (IIda V.)
1.
rit. molto
molto
2.
rit. molto
molto
cho
cha
chu
chi
chai
[Percussion does not repeat]
*) For "bottle-neck" playing, a glass rod is held (lightly) against E string. Sliding the rod along string produces the various pitches. A metal plectrum should be used (e.g. paper clip); pluck string only at points marked ⇓. The symbol tr¼ indicates a quarter-tone trill (i.e. a wide vibrato).

Glossary

32-bar song form: A form that uses symmetrical eight-measure phrases, frequently found in the refrain of many traditional and popular songs. The formal design is most often ternary: AA (**head**) B (**bridge**) A′ (**head**).

accompanied (mixed) canon: A **canon** accompanied by a separate voice, usually the bass line that serves as counterpoint to the canonic imitation.

accompaniment lead-in: A type of phrase introduction frequently used to begin compositions or sections of a work. Its function is to establish the key and rhythmic motion of the music prior to the entrance of a melody. May also serve as a **phrase connection.**

afterbeat: A rhythmic continuation at a point of cadence that elaborates and groups with the cadential harmony.

alternating variations: Variations that incorporate two different, alternating themes, sometimes referred to as **double variations**.

anacrusis: An upbeat that begins a new phrase.

answer: The statement of a fugue **subject** at the dominant (V) or rarely, subdominant (IV). A real answer is an exact transposition of the subject; a tonal answer modifies the beginning interval of the subject—less frequently the ending— to adjust for harmonic motion.

antecedent: The first phrase of a **period**, which leads to either a HC or IAC, creating an expectation of continuation.

antiphonal texture (antiphony): The alternation of different, spatially separated ensembles, or of different timbres within an ensemble, such as strings alternating with brass, or sopranos with altos.

arch form: A multi-movement form in which motivic and formal relations exists between symmetrically corresponding pairs of movements. The patterns of movements are often either an A B A′ or an A B C B′ A′.

aria: a composition for solo voice and instrumental accompaniment, most often heard in operas, oratorios, or cantatas.

augmentation: uniform expansion of note values to lengthen a motive or theme; often associated with canonic and fugal composition.

authentic cadence (AC): A **cadence** that concludes with a dominant (V or V7) to tonic (I) progression with the I chord in root position. The AC creates the strongest sense of repose and closure. A **perfect authentic cadence (PAC)** uses root position chords and closes with the root of the tonic chord in the soprano. An **imperfect authentic cadence (IAC)** closes with the third or fifth of the I chord in the soprano and/or uses the V (or vii) chord in inversion.

balanced binary form: A two-part form that uses the same thematic material and phrase structures at the end of each section.

bar form: An AAB form frequently encountered in chorales. The repeated first section may close with a PAC in tonic or in a new key and is shorter than the B section.

bass-line link: The continuation of a bass line after a point of cadence, normally within the cadential measure, which connects the end of one phrase with the beginning of the next.

binary form: A form comprised of two sections. May be **simple**, **rounded** or **balanced** and is characterized by the repeat of each of the sections.

bridge: The contrasting section (B) of a 32-bar song in ternary form (A A B A).

cabaletta: The fast, concluding section of an operatic **rondò** occurring after the slower **cantabile**.

cadence: In tonal music the completion of a harmonic and melodic progression that serves to articulate or mark the ends of phrases by creating varying degrees of closure. Cadence types include perfect or imperfect **authentic cadences (PAC, IAC)**; **half cadences (HC), deceptive cadences (DC)**, **plagal cadences (PC),** and **evaded cadences (EC).**

cadential phrase: A phrase consisting of an expanded cadential progression characteristic of **closing function.**

cadential progression: The series of harmonies leading to and including the **point of cadence.**

A full authentic cadential progression includes I^6–IV (or ii^6)–V^{6-5}_{4-3}–I.

canon: A composition or passage based on strict imitation of a melody at a fixed time and pitch interval. Various types include **accompanied**, **mensuration**, **mirror**, **retrograde**, **canons**, and **rounds**.

Cantabile: 1) in a singing style; 2) the section of an operatic **rondó** that proceeds the **tempo di mezzo** and **cabaletta.**

cantus firmus variation: A variation in which the melody is unchanged or in slightly simplified form with variation in the accompanying parts, often in **contrapuntal textures**.

cavatina: In the eighteenth century, an aria with no **da capo**, thus usually shorter. In the nineteenth century, an entrance aria that may be used in the **cantabile** of the **rondó**.

centricity: In non-tonal music, the prominence of a single pitch in a section, or complete movement, such that the pitch content centers on that pitch.

chaconne: An instrumental work that presents a series of continuous variations over an **ostinato** bass line or harmonic progression. Typically in a slow or moderate tempo, major key, and triple meter, it begins with a full harmonic progression. Associated with the Baroque period. Closely related to the **passacaglia**.

character variation: A variation that conveys a change in character by use of a specific dance rhythm, conventional style, or genre such as a dance type. Often involves a change in meter or tempo.

chorale prelude: A composition for organ that presents a chorale melody in simple or elaborated form with varied accompaniments, which are often **contrapuntal**. A variety of approaches may be found, including cantus firmus, melodic embellishment, canonic, fugal, and variations. See also **melody chorale.**

closing function: A formal function conveyed by cadential progressions, pedal points, repetitions of thematic material, and rhythmic acceleration or deceleration in various combinations. Occurs in phrase segments or phrases that bring a phrase, section, or movement to a final cadence.

closing section: A section that brings an **exposition** and **recapitulation** to a close following a **PAC** in the **STA**. Usually characterized by introduction of new **closing themes (CT), cadential progressions,** and reiterated, short phrases.

closing themes (CT): The themes introduced in the closing section of a sonata form.

coda: (It., "tail") One or more phrases that extend a composition to emphasize final closure. Will follow a strong point of closure that could have concluded the composition, normally a marked **PAC.**

codetta: A short passage of 1-4 measures that prolongs a tonic chord or a cadential progression to close a section or movement.

comes: The traditional name for the following voice in a canon.

compound form: A form in which one or more sections are also self-contained forms, such as binary or ternary. Most common in **large ternary** and **da capo forms**.

concerto sonata form: A form that integrates sonata form with the contrast between soloist and orchestra and the use of formal **ritornellos** found in concertos. May include a **double exposition**, particularly in concertos of the Classical period.

consequent: The second phrase of a period, which completes the period by reaching a conclusive authentic cadence stronger than the cadence of the **antecedent** phrase.

continuation: Within a phrase, a function characterized by departure from tonic harmonies, a quicker harmonic rhythm, use of sequence or fragmentation of previous ideas, and a sense of motion toward cadence; the third segment of a **sentence** is a *continuation.*

continuous: A form in which the first section ends in a new key; also described as tonally open.

continuous variations: See **ostinato variations.**

contrapuntal textures: A texture of two or more lines that are rhythmically independent and equally prominent.

contrapuntal variation: A variation in which the theme is treated in contrapuntal textures, often using imitative, fugal, or canonic procedures.

contrasting period: A period in which the consequent phrase takes the form of a contrasting **continuation** rather than a **repetition** of the **antecedent** phrase.

counterstatement (CS): In sonata form, the repetition of the **principal theme,** which leads to a new continuation to initiate the transition; the opening motives or ideas are restated with a **continuation** that modulates.

countersubject: A recurring theme used as counterpoint to the subject of a fugue or invention.

couplet: The contrasting sections that occur between the refrains in a **rondeau.**

CS: See **counterstatement.**

cyclic form: The use of the same thematic material in more than one movement of a multi-movement composition. The concept can be traced back to the Renaissance period but is often associated with symphonic works of the nineteenth century.

da capo form: (It., "from the head") A three-part form in which the first section is restated in its entirety after a contrasting middle section. The restatement is indicated in the score by the designation *da capo al fine*. Common in arias and instrumental dance movements.

deceptive cadence (DC): The resolution of the dominant chord (V) in an authentic cadential progression to a chord other than the expected tonic triad. The most common resolution of V in a deceptive cadence is to a vi or VI; a V7/IV also may be perceived as a deceptive cadence. Deceptive cadences may be followed by a phrase extension that leads to a **PAC** or may initiate a new phrase.

density: The number of lines or pitches in a passage and their range and spacing; an aspect of **musical texture**. Changes in density are basic to shaping and delineating phrases.

development section: The second section in a sonata form, which elaborates thematic material and modulates through one or more keys, closing with a **retransition** that modulates to the principal key and leads to the **recapitulation**.

developmental function: **Formal function** that is conveyed by manipulation of previously heard themes and motives, modulations, harmonic instability, sequences, and fragmentation, or expansions of phrase structure. The textures will often be rhythmically more active and contrapuntal than the initial presentation.

developing variations: A formal process that emphasizes continuous variation or transformation of motives and themes. The process may be found in **through composed** or **sectional** forms in which contrasting themes are based on motivic pitch collections that unify the work. Associated initially with Brahms, and later Debussy, it was an influential approach in twentieth-century music.

diminution: 1) Systematic reduction of note values in the same increment to compress a motive or theme. 2) The elaboration of melodic patterns by the introduction of shorter note values that embellish or ornament the pattern. The first type is a specific technique of motivic manipulation, the second type a wide-ranging compositional technique.

dissolution: A reduction, whether sudden or gradual, in the number of musical components in a texture. A reduction to a single line is not uncommon in transitional phrases or introductory phrases.

dominant preparation: The expansion of dominant harmony to reinforce a modulation or cadence. The expansion may be two or more measures and often employs pedal point, characteristic of the close of transitional or re-transitional passages.

double exposition: The presentation of an orchestral exposition followed by a soloist exposition in **concerto sonata form**, particularly in the Classical concertos. The orchestral exposition will not modulate but will present contrasting themes. The solo exposition may restate orchestral themes but will modulate and introduce new themes.

double fugue: 1) A fugue with two expositions of different subjects separated by an **episode**. Normally the fugue subjects are presented together in the later stages of the fugue; 2) a fugue in which the **countersubject** and **subject** are presented simultaneously in effect presenting two subjects.

double variation: In a theme and variations, the varied repetition of phrases within a variation thus creating a variation on the initial idea for a variation.

double period: A **period** in which the **antecedent** and the **consequent** each contain two **phrases**.

dux: The traditional name for the leading voice in a **canon.**

EC: See **evaded cadence.**

EEC: See **essential expositional close.**

elision: A **phrase connection** in which the ending of one phrase is the beginning of the next phrase as one phrase leads directly to another. This type of connection normally will coincide with a strong beat, usually the downbeat of a measure.

elongated upbeat: A **phrase introduction** in which the upbeat is continued through one or more measures. It usually entails expansion of dominant harmony, continuous rhythmic motion, and repetition of a motivic figure.

embellishing variation: variation in which some segments of the melody are embellished while others are retained. The melody is readily discernible and the rhythmic motion is more varied than in a figural variation.

episodes: Contrasting or developmental sections, usually modulatory, within a larger form. In a rondo form episodes introduce new themes between **refrains;** in a **fugue** episodes are based on the themes or subjects of the fugue are thus developmental. Through-composed works based on a series of contrasting sections are episodic in form.

essential expositional close (EEC): A perfect authentic cadence that marks the strongest point of closure within the **secondary tonal area (STA)** of a sonata form exposition. The placement of the EEC varies; often it closes the secondary theme and initiates the closing section.

evaded cadence (EC): the avoidance of the final chord in an authentic cadential progression, followed by reiteration of the cadential progression. Unlike a **deceptive cadence,** which gives an unexpected resolution, the EC delays and heightens expectation of resolution, often occurring two or more times before the eventual resolution of the AC.

exposition: 1) The first large section of a **sonata form** that presents a principal theme(s), transition, secondary theme(s) and closing theme (s); the first section of a **fugue**, in which each voice enters successively with a statement of the **subject** or **answer** followed by the first **episode**. See also **redundant entry.**

expository function: A formal function conveyed by the presentation or restatement of thematic material. Characterized by the presence of distinct melodic ideas, harmonic stability, and a clear sense of closure that projects a self-contained theme.

false recapitulation: A passage in the **development** of a **sonata or sonata rondo form** in which the principal theme returns decisively but briefly in a non-tonic key, giving a momentary sense of stability before further development.

figuration prelude: An instrumental composition, often in one-part form, based on a continuous figure introduced in the beginning and used throughout.

figure: Conventional melodic and rhythmic patterns such as scales and arpeggios that are common to a particular style. Often used in accompaniment parts.

figural variation: A variation that presents the theme in **diminutions** that make use of a consistent rhythmic and/or pitch pattern.

fixed form variation: A variation that uses new melodic ideas and textures while maintaining the form and tonal structure of the theme. Phrase structure, cadences and harmonic underpinnings are retained while other elements are varied. Motivic elements of the original theme may be used, but complete theme is not presented.

formal design: The grouping of musical ideas and their arrangement into phrases and sections, as determined by tonal, thematic, and textural elements. The categories of musical form such as binary or ternary forms represent basic formal designs found in a wide range of compositions. Many formal designs are unique.

formal function: The role of segments of music at various levels of form. Formal functions such as **statement**, **repetition**, **continuation**, or **cadence** shape the internal structure of phrases. At the level of a phrase or section formal functions may be **expository**, **transitional**, **developmental**, **introductory**, and **parenthetical**.

formal process: Methods or techniques that generate and shape the themes, phrases and sections of a formal structure and design. Many of the wide number of such techniques may be categorized under the headings of **tonal, thematic, and textural processes.**

formal structure: The formal processes, and functional and proportional relations at various levels of the design determined by the specific ways in which the content of a composition is generated.

fortspinnung (Ger., "spinning out") The repetitions of motives to generate continuous lines often using **sequences.** Characteristic of Baroque style.

fragmentation: A shortening of phrase segments using motivic fragments from the original idea, presented in varied repetitions or sequence.

free imitation (modified imitation): Imitation that varies the interval succession, rhythm, or contour of a theme.

free variation (fantasy variation): A variation in which melodic or rhythmic motives of the theme may be used but are subjected to transformations and fragmentation, and the phrase structures, formal design are altered. Strongly contrasting expressive character is typical among the variations.

fugato: A developmental passage within a larger form that employs systematic imitation of a theme or motive in the manner of a fugue.

fughetta: A fugue of short to moderate length.

fugue: A composition usually in three to four voices that employs imitation and contrapuntal elaboration of the initial ideas throughout. After an **exposition** in which each voice presents the fugue theme, **episodes** alternate with restatements of the theme. See **subject** and **answer.**

fusion: The process of merging two thematic ideas and formal functions into a single unit by continuous harmonic and rhythmic motion.

grouping structure: A hierarchical segmentation of a composition into motives, phrases, and sections.

ground bass (basso ostinato): A repeated bass line of one to eight measures used throughout a composition associated with Baroque music. **Ostinato variations** are composed over a ground bass.

half cadence (HC): Cadence in which the **point of cadence** is a V chord. The half cadence makes use of progressions similar to the **PAC** but with a marked arrival on the dominant chord that separates it from the subsequent chord to which it resolves. The need for resolution of the dominant creates a strong expectation of continuation.

head: In popular music, the first section of a 32-bar song form in ternary form.

heterophony: A texture of lines that contains different elaborations of the same basic melody.

homophony: A general category of music texture in which a melody is presented in one voice with accompaniment or in homorhythmic textures such as those found in chorales.

homorhythmic: Texture in which a melody is supported by lines moving in identical or similar rhythms, characteristic of vocal compositions, notably chorales and hymns.

hypermeter (high-level meter): The organization of phrases in terms of large-scale metric patterns, with the measure or larger units as a **pulse**.

IAC: See **authentic cadence.**

imitation: The repetition of a motive or theme in a different voice or part during which the initial voice continues in counterpoint. See also **canon, free imitation**, **point of imitation**.

indeterminacy: The use of elements of chance or randomness in the composition or performance of music. The choice of materials may be random or the performer may be given choices about shaping musical ideas or ordering formal units. Also referred to as aleatoric or chance music.

invertible counterpoint: A texture of two or more melodic lines composed such that their position in the texture may be exchanged . See also **textural inversion.**

interpolation: A type of internal phrase expansion in which additional material is added upon the repetition of a phrase.

introductory function: Formal function conveyed by material that initiates a phrase, section, or movement. It is characterized by a phrase segment or phrase in which the texture or musical ideas are in some way incomplete, creating the expectation of an expository entrance.

juxtaposition: A formal process of alternating two strongly contrasting musical ideas or textures, often conveyed by the suddenness of the alternation and the absence of transitions from one phrase to the next. Timbral contrasts including instrumentation, dynamics, and articulation differentiate the ideas.

large ternary form: A **compound** three-part form in which the sections are connected and the restatement of A is written out, frequently with elaborate embellishments and sometimes expanded.

layered (stratified) texture: texture created by the process of superimposition or layering of contrasting ideas, in which each idea has a distinct rhythmic profile, register, timbre, and/or articulation.

melodic complement: Within a phrase structure the varied repetition of an initial idea that reverses the overall contour.

melodic link: The continuation of a melodic line after a **point of cadence**, normally within the cadential measure, which connects the end of one phrase with the beginning of the next.

melodic (mirror) inversion: Statement of a melody in which the direction of each interval is reversed creating a mirror of the original contour.

melodic variation: variation in which the melody is retained in its original or varied form.

mélodie: French art song of the nineteenth and twentieth century.

melody and descant texture: A choral texture in which a descant or countermelody, usually presented in the soprano voice, is sung against the melody in the other voices.

melody chorale: A **chorale prelude** in which the melody is presented continuously in the soprano part in simple or slightly elaborated form with contrapuntal accompaniment.

mensuration (proportional) canon: A canon in which the following voices perform the **canon** melody in **augmentation** or **diminution**.

middle entries: Complete statements of a fugue **subject** or **answer** that occur after the exposition and alternate with **episodes.**

minore or maggiore variation: A change in mode that inflects a variation with an obvious change in character .

mirror canon: A canon in which the follower is a **melodic inversion** of the leader.

modulating period: A period in which the consequent phrase closes on a **PAC** in a new key.

monophony: Texture of a single line.

monothematic sonata form: A sonata forms that make use of the principal theme or motives at the beginning of the **secondary tonal area.** Associated with Haydn.

motive: A short melodic idea characterized by rhythm, contour, and interval succession; often identified as the basic building block of musical phrases.

motivic anticipation: A type of phrase introduction in which motivic material begins a composition or section in an introductory gesture that anticipates the phrase melody.

musical texture: The arrangement and quality of sounds in music shaped by the **density** of lines and their functional and rhythmic relations. See also **monophony, homophony, heterophony,** and **contrapuntal textures.**

musique concrete: Compositions based on sonic material recorded on tape and derived from real world sounds.

non-modulating transition: In a sonata form , a transition that reaches a **HC** in the **PTA** followed by a direct shift to the **STA.**

one-part form: A phrase group or period that comprises a complete piece of music. Characterized by continuous harmonic and rhythmic motion, and the absence of a strong PAC in the original key until the end. Most often found in instrumental preludes and etudes, or in short songs.

open (mobile) forms: Forms in which a series of musical events or sections are carefully structured but the order of presentation is subject to varying degrees of randomness.

ostinato: A **motive, theme,** or **figure** that is continuously repeated within a phrase, section or entire composition. See also **ground bass.**

ostinato variations (continuous variations): Variations based on an ostinato bass line or harmonic progression that is repeated throughout with varied musical ideas and textures presented with each repetition. The ostinato is usually a four or eight-measure phrase or period.

PAC: See **authentic cadence.**

parallel period: A period in which the **consequent** phrase begins as a repetition of the **antecedent.**

parenthetical function: A formal function conveyed by a sudden or unexpected change in tonality, theme, or texture such that the new ideas sound as an aside or interjection.

passacaglia: An instrumental work that presents a series of continuous variations over an **ostinato** bass line or harmonic progression. It typically is in a slow or moderate tempo, triple meter, and a minor key, and begins with an unaccompanied basso ostinato. Closely related to the **chaconne.**

period: A formal unit consisting of two phrase, the first an **antecedent,** the second a **consequent**. One basic type of expository thematic presentation. May be expanded to three phrases by repetition of one phrase, most often the consequent. See also **parallel period**, **contrasting period**, and **double period.**

phasing: A technique developed by composer Steve Reich in which parts begin in **homorhythmic** textures but the rhythmic interval between parts gradually and continuously changes and thus become "out of phase." The process continues until parts are in phase.

phrase: Generally, any segment of music that is perceived as a complete or self-contained unit. Formally, a segment of music that is marked by a distinct beginning, middle and end, and completion of directed motion toward a cadence. See also **subphrase.**

phrase connection: The joining of phrases through **melodic links, bass-line links, accompaniment lead-ins,** or **elisions.**

phrase contraction: The shortening of a phrase upon repetition or restatement that alters the **hypermetric** organization and usually results in a phrase **elision.**

phrase expansion: The addition of one or more measures to a basic phrase. May be **phrase introduction**, a **phrase extension**, an **interpolation**, or an **evaded cadence.**

phrase extension: The addition of one or more measures at the end of a phrase, which also group with the phrase. Phrase extensions most often take the form of reiterated cadences or expansions of the concluding harmony.

phrase group: A series of phrases that group together on the basis of continuation and/or motivic connections without the cadential relations of a period. In a phrase group, **cadences** may vary as to strength and weight although a PAC often closes the group.

phrase introduction: A phrase expansion occurring at the beginning of a phrase. May take the form of **accompaniment lead-ins, motivic anticipations**, or **elongated upbeats.**

phrase link: A connection between the end of one phrase and the beginning of another.

phrase rhythm: A composite aspect of a phrase resulting from the length and **grouping structure**, **phrase connections**, expansions and contractions, and the hierarchy of metric accents.

pitch collection: A collection of pitches characterized by the number of pitches and the intervallic content. Much twentieth-century music is based on motivic pitch collections rather than traditional keys and scales.

plagal cadence: A cadence in which the subdominant (IV, iv), or a subdominant related harmony (vi, ♭VI, ii, or ♭II) resolves to a root position tonic triad. Most often a plagal cadence occurs in a **phrase extension** after a PAC has been reached, frequently marking the end of a section or movement.

point of cadence: The final chord of a cadence, which is the goal of a **cadential progression.**

point of imitation: The entrance of an imitating voice.

pointillistic textures: Sparse, fragmented textures in which pitches or motives are presented in different timbres. A twentieth-century technique particularly associated with Schoenberg and Webern.

postlude: 1) Music played after the conclusion of a larger work or after a church service; 2) the **coda** or instrumental closing phrase of a vocal composition.

polyphony: A texture of many different lines or melodies that are rhythmically independent and of equal importance. See also **contrapuntal textures.**

principal theme (PT): The first theme or themes presented in the exposition of a sonata form which also establish the principal tonality or key of the movement.

principal tonal area (PTA): The first section of the **exposition** and **recapitulation** of a **sonata form** in the main or home key of the movement that presents one or more principal themes (PT).

pulse: The metric level most readily perceived or projected in the music. The pulse may be consistent with the beat of the meter notated or may be above or below that level.

quatrain: A form made of four symmetrical phrases, most often eight-measure phrases.

recapitulation: The third section of a sonata form initiated by the return to the principal tonality. It presents restatements of the themes of the **exposition** with the **STA** transposed to the tonic key.

redundant entry: In a **fugue** an additional statement of the **subject** that extends the fugue **exposition.**

refrain: 1) The recurring theme of a **rondo** form ; 2) sections of songs and hymns that are repeated with the same text each time; 3) the second, main section of a popular song, usually in **32-bar song form,** and preceded by the **verse.** In many songs, the refrain is designated as a chorus.

repetition: The recurrence of a thematic idea, phrase or section immediately following its presentation. May be exact, varied, **imitative** or **sequential.**

response-repetition: Within a phrase the varied repetition of the first idea or **statement** with a change in harmony, usually to the dominant (V).

restatement: The recurrence of a thematic idea in the tonic key following a contrasting phrase or section.

retransition: The final section of a **development** or an **episode** that returns the music to the principal key. Often concludes with **dominant preparation.**

real answer: See **answer.**

retrograde (crab or cancrizan) canon: A **canon** in which the melody is played forward and backward at the same time thus there is no distinction between leader and follower.

reverse recapitulation: The presentation of the **secondary theme** in the principal key to begin the **recapitulation** in a **sonata form**.

riddle (puzzle) canon: A **canon** in which the composer gives clues in the score as to how a canon is to be performed but not explicit instructions.

ritornello: In Baroque arias and concertos the recurring thematic material played by orchestra or accompaniment alone in **tutti** textures. Soloists in a concerto may double orchestral parts in a ritornello.

ritornello form: A form used in Baroque concertos based on the alternation of ritornello (tutti) and solo sections. An opening ritornello, which confirms the initial tonic, is restated periodically to articulate formal sections and emphasize modulations. Restatements may be partial but a full restatement typically closes movements. Ritornellos thus frame the formal design. Also used in vocal genres including arias and cantatas.

ritornello phrase structure: A structure typical of a Baroque ritornello in which a statement and repetition (or imitation) is followed by sequential repetition elaboration leading to a cadential progression. The length and number of the statements and **sequences** may vary.

rondeau: A Baroque form in which a refrain alternates with couplets. Closely related to **rondo.**

rondò: An extensive operatic aria in a compound binary form. Its two parts consist of a slow section (**cantabile** or **cavatina**) and a fast section (**cabaletta**). A recitative and orchestral introduction may precede the cantabile; a transitional **tempo di mezzo** may occur between the two main sections.

rondo: A form in which a **refrain** alternates with **episodes,** typically in five or sections. The refrain is normally a **period** or a **binary** form and is always in the tonic key.

rondo variations: A rondo form in which the refrain is varied when restated, taking on the character of a set of variations with episodes.

round: A **canon** at the unison. The number of repetitions is variable thus a round is sometimes referred to as a perpetual canon.

rounded binary form: A **binary form** in which a restatement of material from part one (A) is presented to conclude the second part. The form is represented as ||:A||:BA:||. May be **sectional** or **continuous**

secondary theme (ST): The theme or themes presented in the first part of the **secondary tonal area** of a sonata form following a **transition.** The ST closes with a PAC that confirms the new key.

secondary tonal area (STA) : Section of an **exposition** of a sonata form in the second or subordinate key. Contains additional thematic material and brings the exposition to a decisive close in the new key. The **recapitulation** of the STA is in the tonic .

section: A self-contained passage of music that represents one part of a **formal design.** Marked by various degrees of closure and characterized by thematic material, tonality, rhythm, and/or texture.

sectional: In tonal music, a form in which the first section closes with an **authentic cadence** in the tonic key, also described as tonally closed. Forms comprised of two or more contrasting sections.

sectional variations: A **variation** form in which the **theme** is a **period** or short **binary** or **ternary form,** usually with pauses between the theme and each variation. See also **ostinato variations.**

sentence: A phrase comprised of a **statement,** a **repetition,** and a **continuation** that leads to a cadence. The three parts of a sentence are normally in proportions of 1: 1: 2 or multiples there of. While four and sixteen-measure sentences are found, most often they are eight measures long grouped as 2+2+4.

sequence: The repetition of a thematic idea at different pitch levels. Consists of a statement of a model pattern followed usually by two or three repetitions ascending or descending by the same interval. A melodic sequence repeats the melody only while a harmonic sequence repeats all voices of a texture. Most sequences are harmonic and melodic and are characterized by the intervallic pattern of root movements, e.g. descending fifths, and by repeated voice-leading patterns between outer voices.

simplification or skeletal variation: A variation in which the melody is presented in simplified form. Basic shape is retained but some pitches are eliminated and the rhythm is altered.

simple binary form: A two-part form in which each section is normally repeated and which is represented as |:A:||:B:|. The B section is related motivically to the A section. May be **sectional** or **continuous.**

simple ternary form: Three-part form in which each section is a sentence, period, repeated phrase, or phrase group. See also **compound ternary form** and **ternary form.**

small binary form: Short, simple two-part form that is comprised of a single phrase in each section.

sonata form: A large-scale form that presents an **exposition,** a **development,** and a **recapitulation.** Most often an instrumental form, it may also be preceded a slow introduction and expanded by a **coda.**

sonata form without development: A sonata form in which the **exposition** is followed by a direct modulation to the **recapitulation** or by a very brief **retransition**. Characteristic of slow movements in sonata form.

sonata-rondo form: A large-scale form with characteristics of a rondo and sonata form. The design is a seven-part rondo with the second **episode** being **developmental,** and the second refrain and third episode structured like a **recapitulation**. The final refrain often functions or occurs as part of a **coda.**

sonatina: A sonata or multi movement instrumental work of modest proportions and technical demands, usually for piano. The term is used by some writers to refer to **sonata form without development**.

ST: See **secondary theme.**

STA: See **secondary tonal area.**

statement: The presentation of a one or two-bar idea that initiates a phrase. May be followed by **repetition** or a contrasting idea.

stretto: A technique in which imitative entries of a **fugue subject** overlap and occur at closer time intervals than in the **exposition.**

strophic: A song or hymn in which two or more verses of text are set to the same music, each repetition of the complete song presenting a different verse.

subject: The main theme of a **fugue** or invention.

subphrase: A phrase segment, usually of two or four measures in length, that is part of a larger, complete phrase.

superimposition: The combination of contrasting ideas simultaneously in a texture. See **layered textures.**

symmetrical phrases: A musical phrase is symmetrical if its subphrases are of equal length or multiples. A phrase group or period is symmetrical if it contains an even number of phrases of the same length.

tempo di mezzo: A transitional episode occurring between the slower **cantabile** and the faster **cabaletta** of an expanded rondò. In the tempo di mezzo, the emotional situation takes a turn and harmonic instability through modulations or tonicizations are characteristic.

ternary form: A three-part form in which a contrasting middle section is followed by a restatement of the first section, usually complete and often in varied form. May be **continuous** or **sectional.** See also **simple ternary** and **compound** ternary.

textural inversion: The recurrence of passage with an exchange of registral position.

textural processes: Changes in **musical texture** such as **dissolution** and **textural inversion** that shape and articulate phrases and sections.

theme and variations (sectional variations): A genre and an additive form consisting of a short theme that is followed by any number of varied repetitions of the complete theme. The theme is usually a sentence, period, or short binary or ternary form. Slight breaks or pauses typically occur after each variation. See also **ostinato variations.**

thematic processes: The ways in which thematic ideas or motives are used to generate phrases and sections of a design. Various thematic processes include techniques such as varied **repetition, sequence, fragmentation, extension,** or introduction of a contrasting idea.

thematic transformation: Rhythmic, metric, and timbral changes in the recurrence of a **theme** that produce a marked change in the character or expressive effect of a theme.

theme: The principal melodic lines of a composition.

three-key exposition: An **exposition** found in nineteenth-century **sonata** forms in which a third tonal area and theme are presented.

through-composed form: A form in which there is an absence of distinct **restatement(s). One-part form** and **episodic forms** are described as through-composed.

timbre: The quality or tone color of sounds. Aspects of **timbre** include dynamic level, articulation, range, register, and instrumentation.

tonal answer: See **answer.**

tonal design: The order, type, and relative degree of emphasis of the **cadences** and modulations in a composition.

tonal processes: The harmonic and linear progressions, **tonicizations**, modulations, and cadences that shape **formal structure** and design.

tonicization: A passing modulation in which a reiterated secondary chord or secondary progression implies a new key but does not lead to a **cadence** in the key.

tonicized half cadence (THC): A **HC** in which the cadential dominant chord is preceded by a V/V or vii°7/V chord.

transitional function: A formal function conveyed by modulations or **tonicizations,** quicker harmonic rhythms, melodic repetitions, **sequences,** expansions of dominant harmony, or more active rhythmic textures that create instability and the expectation of resolution.

transition: A phrase or section that serves as a connection between expository statements of thematic material, or between different tonal areas and sections. See **exposition.**

tutti: (It., "all") Refers to the orchestra or ensemble in a concerto as opposed to the soloist. **Ritornello** passages are played tutti.

upbeat: A pitch or pitches on a weak beat that groups with a subsequent strong beat.

variation: A fundamental compositional technique or a formal genre. The technique of variation is a basic formal process by which musical ideas are embellished or elaborated. See also **sectional variations** and **ostinato variations.**

verse: The first part of a popular song that precedes the **refrain.** The verse is introductory with no repetitions of text although there may be repetitions of the music.

Bibliography

Adrian, Jack. "The Ternary Sonata Form." *Journal of Music Theory* 34 (1991): 57–80.

Agawu, V. Kofi. *Playing with Signs: A Semiotic Interpretation of Classic Music*. Princeton: Princeton University Press, 1991.

Aldwell, Edward, and Carl Schachter. *Harmony and Voice-Leading*. 3rd ed. New York: Harcourt Brace Jovanovich, 1994.

Beach, David. "Phrase Expansion: Three Analytical Studies." *Music Analysis* 14 (1995): 27–47.

_________. "Schubert's Experiments with Sonata Form: Formal-Tonal Design versus Underlying Structure." *Music Theory Spectrum* 15.1 (1993): 1–18.

Berry, Wallace. *Form in Music*. 2d ed. Englewood Cliffs, NJ: Prentice-Hall, 1986.

_________. *Structural Functions in Music*. Englewood Cliffs, NJ: Prentice-Hall, 1976.

Blume, Friedrich. *Classic and Romantic Music*. 1947. Reprint, New York: W. W. Norton, 1970.

Bonds, Mark Evan. *Wordless Rhetoric: Musical Form and the Metaphor of the Oration*. Cambridge, MA: Harvard University Press, 1991.

Brinkman, Alexander and Elizabeth West Marvin. "The Effect of Modulation and Formal Manipulation on Perception of Tonic Closure by Expert Listeners." *Music Perception* 16.4 (Summer 1998): 389–408.

Broyles, Michael. "Organic Form and the Binary Repeat." *Musical Quarterly* 66 (1980): 339–60.

Burkhart, Charles. "Schenker's Motivic Parallelisms." *Journal of Music Theory* 22 (1978): 145–175.

_________. *Anthology for Musical Analysis*. 6th ed. New York: Holt, Reinhart and Winston, 2003.

Cage, John. *Silence: Lectures and Writings*. Boston: Wesleyan University Press, 1961.

Cadwallader, Allen. "Form and Tonal Process." In *Trends in Schenkerian Research*, ed. Allen Cadwallader. New York: Schirmer, 1990: 1–21.

Cadwallader, Allen, and David Gagne. *Analysis of Tonal Music: A Schenkerian Approach*. New York: Oxford University Press, 1998.

Caplin, William. *Classical Form: A Theory of Formal Functions for the Instrumental Music of Haydn, Mozart, and Beethoven*. Oxford University Press, 1998.

_________. "The 'Expanded Cadential Progression': A Category for the Analysis of Classical Form." *Journal of Musicological Research* 7 (1987): 215–257.

Christensen, Thomas, ed. *The Cambridge History of Music Theory*. Cambridge: Cambridge University Press, 2002.

Cone, Edward. *Musical Form and Musical Performance*. New York: W. W. Norton, 1970.

Cook, Nicholas. *Music, Imagination, and Culture*. New York: Oxford University Press, 1990.

Dahlhaus, Carl. "Some Models of Unity in Musical Form." *Journal of Musical Theory* 19 (1975).

Davis, Shelley. "H. C. Koch, the Classic Concerto, and the Sonata-Form Retransition." *Journal of Musicology* 2 (1983): 45–61.

Dreyfus, Laurence. "J.S. Bach's Concerto Ritornellos and the Question of Invention." *Musical Quarterly* 71(1985): 327–358.

Epstein, David. *Beyond Orpheus: Studies in Musical Structure*. Cambridge, MA: MIT Press, 1979.

Everett, Walter. *The Beatles as Musicians: "Revolver" through the "Anthology."* New York: Oxford University Press, 1999.

Fischer, Stephen. "Further Thoughts on Haydn's Symphonic Rondo Finales." *Haydn Yearbook*, Vol. 17 (1995): 85–107.

Frisch, Walter. *Brahms and the Principle of Developing Variation*. Berkeley and Los Angeles: University of California Press, 1984.

Galand, Joel. "Form, Genre, and Style in the Eighteenth-Century Rondo." *Music Theory Spectrum* 17.1 (1995): 27-52.

Gauldin, Robert. *A Practical Approach to the Study of 18th-Century Counterpoint*. Upper Saddle River, N.J.: Prentice Hall, 1988.

Graybill, Roger and Stefan Kostka. *Anthology of Music for Analysis*. Upper Saddle River, N.J.: Pearson Prentice Hall, 2004.

Green, Douglass M. *Form in Tonal Music*. 2nd ed. New York: Holt, Rinehart and Winston, 1979.

Hatten, Robert S. *Musical Meaning in Beethoven: Markedness, Correlation, and Interpretation.* Bloomington: Indiana University Press, 1994.

Hepokoski, James. "Beyond the Sonata Principle." *Journal of the American Musicological Society* 55.1 (2002): 91–154.

_________ and Warren Darcy. "The Medial Caesura and its Role in the Eighteenth-Century Sonata Exposition." *Music Theory Spectrum* 19.2 (1997) 115–154.

_________ and Warren Darcy. *Elements of Sonata Theory: Norms, Types and Deformation in the Late Eighteenth-Century Sonata.* New York: Oxford University Press, 2006.

Jackson, Timothy, "The Tragic Reversed Recapitulation in the German Classical Tradition." *Journal of Music Theory* 40 (1996): 61–111.

Kerman, Joseph. *Concerto Conversations.* Cambridge, Mass.: Harvard University Press, 1999.

Kraus, Joseph. "Tonal Plan and Narrative Plot in Tchaikovsky's Symphony No. 5 in E minor." *Music Theory Spectrum* 13.1 (Spring 1991): 21–47.

Kimbell, G. Cook. "The Second Theme in Sonata Form as Insertion." *The Music Review* 52.4 (1991): 448–470.

Koch, Heinrich Christoph. *Introductory Essay on Composition: The Mechanical Rules of Melody, Sections 3 and 4*, trans. Nancy Kovaleff Baker. New Haven: Yale University Press, 1983.

Kramer, Jonathan. *The Time of Music: New Meanings, New Temporalities, New Listening Strategies.* New York: G. Schirmer, 1988.

Lake, William. "Crumb's Ancient Voices of Children: Form, Proportion, and Pitch Structure." *George Crumb & the Alchemy of Sound*, ed, Steven Bruns and Ofer Ben Omats. Colorado Springs: Colorado College Music Press, 2004.

Larsen, Jens Peter. "Sonata Form Problems." In *Handel, Haydn, and the Viennese Classical Style*, trans. Ulrich Krämer, 269–79. Ann Arbor, MI: UMI Research Press, 1988. First published as "Sonatenform-Probleme," in *Festschrift Friedrich Blume zum 70. Geburtstag*, ed. Anna Amalie Abert and Wilhelm Pfannkuch, 221–30. Kassel: Bärenreiter, 1963.

LaRue, Jan. "Bifocal Tonality in Haydn Symphonies." In *Convention in Eighteenth- and Nineteenth-Century Music: Essays in Honor of Leonard G. Ratner*, ed. Wye J. Allanbrook, Janet M. Levy, and William P. Mahrt, 59–73. Stuyvesant, NY: Pendragon, 1992.

_________. *Guidelines for Style Analysis*. 2d ed. Warren, MI: Harmonie Park Press, 1992.

Lerdahl, Fred, and Ray Jackendoff. *A Generative Theory of Tonal Music*. Cambridge. MA: MIT Press, 1983.

Levy, Janet M. "Gesture, Form, and Syntax in Haydn's Music." In *Haydn Studies*, ed. Jens Peter Larsen, Howard Serwer, and James Webster, 355–362. New York: Norton, 1981.

_________. "Texture as Sign in Classic and Early Romantic Music." *Journal of the American Musicological Society* 35 (1982): 482–531.

Lester, Joel. *The Rhythms of Tonal Music.* Carbondale: University of Illinois Press, 1992.

Lindeman, Stephan D. *Structural Novelty and Tradition in the Early Romantic Piano Concerto.* Stuyvesant, N.Y.: Pendragon Press, 1999.

Longyear, Rey M., and Kate R. Covington. "Sources of the Three-Key Exposition." *Journal of Musicology* 6 (1998): 448–470.

Marston, Nicholas. "Analyzing Variations: The Finale of Beethoven's String Quartet Op. 74." *Music Analysis* 8 (1989): 303–24.

Meyer, Leonard B. *Explaining Music: Essays and Explorations.* Berkeley: University of California Press, 1973.

_________. *Style and Music*. Philadelphia: University of Pennsylvania Press, 1989.

_________. "A Pride of Prejudices" in *Music Theory Spectrum* 13.2 (Fall 1991).

Micznik, Vera. "Music and Narrative Revisited: Degrees of Narrativity in Beethoven and Mahler." *Journal of the Royal Musical Association* 126 (2001): 193–249.

Neville, Don. "The Rondo in Mozart's Late Operas." *Mozart Yearbook,* 1994, 141–155.

Newman, William S. *The Sonata Since Beethoven*. 3rd ed. New York: W. W. Norton, 1983.

Nelson, Robert U. *The Technique of Variation*. Berkeley and Los Angeles: University of California Press, 1948.

Randel, Don Michael, editor. *The Harvard Dictionary of Music,* 4th ed. Cambridge, Mass.: Belknap Press of Harvard University Press, 2003.

Ratner, Leonard G. *Classic Music: Expression, Form, and Style*. New York: Schirmer, 1980.

Ratz, Erwin. *Einfübrung in die musikalische Formenlehre: Über Formprizipien in den Inventionen und Fugen J.S. Bachs und ihre Bedeutung fur die Kompositionstechnik Beethovens*. 3rd ed., enl. Vienna: Universal, 1973.

Roeder, John. *The History of the Concerto.* Seattle: Amadeus Press, 1994.

Rosen, Charles. *The Classical Style: Haydn, Mozart, Beethoven*. New York: Norton, 1972.

_________. *Sonata Forms,* rev. ed. New York: Norton, 1988.

_________. *The Romantic Generation*, Cambridge, Mass.: Harvard University Press, 1995.

Rothgeb, John "Thematic Content, a Schenkerian View" in *Aspects of Schenkerian Theory,* ed. David Beach. New Haven: Yale University Press, 1983.

Rothstein, William. *Phrase Rhythm in Tonal Music*. New York: Schirmer, 1989.

Schachter, Carl. "Rhythm and Linear Analysis: A Preliminary Study." In *The Music Forum, Vol. 4*, edited by Felix Salzer and Carl Schachter. New York: Columbia University Press, 1976, 281–334.

_________. "Analysis by Key: Another Look at Modulation." *Music Analysis* 6 (1987): 289–318.

Schenker, Heinrich. *Free Composition,* trans. Ernst Oster. New York: Longman Press, 1979.

Schoenberg, Arnold. *Structural Functions of Harmony,* New York: Norton, 1954.

_________. *Fundamentals of Musical Composition.* Edited by Gerald Strang. New York: St. Martin's Press, 1967.

_________. *Style and Idea.* Edited by Leonard Stein, translations by Leo Black. Berkeley: University of California Press, 1975.

Schmalfeldt, Janet. "Cadential Processes: The Evaded Cadence and the 'One More Time' Technique." *Journal of Musicological Research* 12 (1992): 1–51.

_________. "Toward a Reconciliation of Schenkerian Concepts with Traditional and Recent Theories of Form." *Music Analysis* 10:3 (1991): 233–288.

Schwarz, Robert K. "Steve Reich: Music as Gradual Process." *Perspectives of New Music* 19.1-2 (1980): 373–392 and *of New Music* 20.1-2 (1981): 225–286.

Shagmar, Ruth. "On Locating the Retransition in Classic Sonata Form." *Music Review* 42 (1981): 130–143.

Sisman, Elaine R. *Haydn and the Classical Variation.* Cambridge, MA: Harvard University Press, 1993.

Sly, Gordon. "Schubert's Innovations in Sonata Form: Compositional Logic and Structural Interpretation." *Journal of Music Theory* 45.1 (2001): 119–150.

_________, ed. "Keys to the Drama: Nine Perspectives on Sonata Form." Burlington, VT: Ashgate Press, forthcoming.

Smith, Charles J. "Musical Form and Fundamental Structure: An Investigation of Schenker's Formenlehre." *Music Analysis,* 2-3, (1996): 191–300.

Smith, Peter. "Brahms and Schenker: A Mutual Response to Sonata Form." *Music Theory Spectrum* 16.1 (1994): 77–103.

Smyth, David. "Large-Scale Rhythm and Classical Form." *Music Theory Spectrum* 12.2 (1990): 236–246).

_________. "Balanced Interruption and the Formal Repeat." *Music Theory Spectrum* 15.1 (1993): 76–88.

Spencer, Peter and Peter Temko. *A Practical Approach to the Study of Form in Music.* Upper Saddle River,. N.J.: Prentice Hall, 1988.

Stein, Deborah and Robert Spillman. *Poetry into Song: Performance and Analysis of Lieder.* New York and Oxford: Oxford University Press, 1996.

Stevens, Jane R. "Patterns of Recapitulation in the First Movements of Mozart's Piano Concertos." In *Musical Humanism and Its Legacy: Essays in Honor of Claude Palisca.* Baker and Hanning, editors. Stuyvesant, N.Y.: Pendragon Press, 1992.

Stein, Erwin. *Form and Performance.* London: Faber & Faber, 1962.

Stuckey, Steven. *Lutoslawski and His Music,* Cambridge: Cambridge University Press, 1981.

Stravinsky, Igor. *Poetics of Music.* Cambridge, MA: Harvard University Press, 1942.

Swain, Joseph. "Form and Function of the Classical Cadenza." *Journal of Musicology* 6 (1988): 27–59.

Toch, Ernst. *Shaping Forces in Music.* New York: Dover Publications, 1977, reprint of 1942 edition.

Tovey, Donald Francis. *A Companion to Beethoven's Pianoforte Sonatas.* London: Associated Board, 1935.

_________. *Essays in Musical Analysis,* 7 vols. London: Oxford University Press, 1935–39.

_________. *The Forms of Music.* New York: Meridian, 1956.

Webster, James. "Schubert's Sonata Form and Brahms's First Maturity." *Nineteenth-Century Music* 2 (1978): 18–35, and 3 (1979): 52–71.

_________. "Freedom of Form in Haydn's Early String Quartets." In *Haydn Studies,* edited by Jens Peter Larson, Howard Serwer, and James Webster. New York: Norton, (1981): 522–530.

Winter, Robert S. "The Bifocal Close and the Evolution of the Viennese Classical Style." *Journal of the American Musicological Society* 42 (1989): 275–337.

Index of Works Cited and Subjects